Rediscovering Wen Tingyun

SUNY series in

CHINESE PHILOSOPHY AND CULTURE

Roger T. Ames, *editor*

Rediscovering
Wen Tingyun

A Historical Key to a Poetic Labyrinth

Huaichuan Mou

State University of New York Press

Published by
STATE UNIVERSITY OF NEW YORK PRESS, ALBANY

Printed in the United States of America

For information, address State University of New York Press,
90 State Street, Suite 700, Albany, NY 12207

Production, Laurie Searl
Marketing, Anne M. Valentine

Library of Congress Cataloging-in-Publication Data
Mou, Huaichuan, 1946–
Rediscovering Wen Tingyun : a historical key to a poetic labyrinth / Huaichuan Mou.
p. cm.—(SUNY series in Chinese philosophy and culture)
Includes bibliographical references and index.
ISBN 0-7914-5935-7 (alk. paper)—ISBN 0-7914-5936-5 (pbk. : alk. paper)
1. Wen, Tingyun, 812–ca. 870.—Criticism and interpretation. I. Title. II. Series.
PL2677.W45Z76 2003
895.1′13—dc21 2003050525

10 9 8 7 6 5 4 3 2 1

Contents

Acknowledgments vii

Abbreviations ix

Introduction 1

The Time of Wen Tingyun: Rampant Eunuch Power

The Study of Wen Tingyun: Lasting Historical Prejudices

Is Wen Tingyun Writing Another's Dream?

Chapter One

Family Background 11

Clan Origin and Native Place

Remaining Prestige of an Aristocratic Family

Special Social Connections

Chapter Two

Wen's Birth Year 31

A Most Abstruse Allusion to the Eunuchs

The Year of Having the Way and Epistle Presented to Prime Minister Pei

Other "Circumstantial Evidence"

Chapter Three

Before the Year of "Having No Doubts" 49

Days of Diligent Studies

Far Wanderings and Wen Zao

Journey along the River and Friendship with Buddhist Monks

CHAPTER FOUR
WEN'S MARRIAGE—A CASE OF SCANDAL 69
Relationship with Wang Ya
An Initial Investigation of the Jianghuai Incident
Further Study and Clarification of the Incident

CHAPTER FIVE
SECRET ATTENDANCE UPON THE HEIR APPARENT 91
Introductory Remarks
Clues Found in Wen's Works
Evidence Elicited from a Study of Two Epistles
The Hidden Story in Hundred-Rhyme Poem

CHAPTER SIX
MYSTIFYING POETRY 123
An Enigma of the Sphinx
Theory Guiding Wen's Poetic Composition
More Examples

CHAPTER SEVEN
CHANGING NAME AND TAKING THE EXAMINATION 149
"Equivalent to Passing" Yet "Failed to Pass"
The Change of Name
Wen's Afterthought

CHAPTER EIGHT
HIGHLIGHTS DURING THE DAZHONG ERA 175
Complications in Wen's Frustrated Efforts
The Truth of the Fourteen Pusaman

CONCLUSION 215

APPENDIX 225

NOTES 239

BIBLIOGRAPHY 269

INDEX 279

ACKNOWLEDGMENTS

Upon completing this study, I must first of all express my gratitude to my professor Ma Maoyuan (1918–1990) of Shanghai Teacher's University, who initiated me into the study of Chinese classic poetry. I would also thank the professors in the Department of Asian Studies, UBC, among whom are Professor Michael Duke, Professor David Overmyer, and especially, Professor Jerry D. Schmidt, for his wise instruction, and Professor Catherine Swatex, for her generous help. I cordially appreciate the enthusiastic recommendation of Professor James M. Hargett and Professor Charles Hartman of State University of New York at Albany, without which I would not even have dreamed of its publication in English. I have also been greatly indebted to my Canadian elder sister Judy Koren, who has taken pains to polish the language. I am also grateful to my parents, who, at the age of ninety, keep encouraging me with all their might. Finally, I share my joy upon finishing this book with my wife Zhong Dai; she has extended understanding and support to me throughout the writing process. It is my responsibility, and my responsibility alone, that problems may still exist in this book.

In a time when Chinese culture is going to the world while the cultures of all the world are going to China, both in unprecedented scale, I am glad to see that Chinese classic poetry has also become a worldwide academic concern and interest. This is perhaps why this book can be published. Insignificant as it is, I would very much like to present it as a small gift to all those kind friends in whom I see the reflection of God.

Abbreviations

CS—Yao Silian (姚思廉): *Chenshu* (陳書)

DKJK—Xu Song (徐松): *Dengke Jikao* (登科記考)

HHS—Fan Ye (范曄): *Hou Hanshu* (後漢書)

HS—Ban Gu (班固): *Hanshu* (漢書)

JS—Fang Xuanling (房玄齡): *Jinshu* (晉書)

JTS—Liu Xu (劉煦) et al.: *Jiutangshu* (舊唐書)

Liji—*Liji Zhengyi* (禮記)

LS—Yao Silian: *Liangshu* (梁書)

Lunyu—*Lunyu Zhengyi* (論語正義)

Maoshi—*Maoshi Zhengyi* (毛詩正義)

Mengzi—*Mengzi Zhengyi* (孟子正義)

NQS—Xiao Zixian (蕭子顯): *Nanqishu* (南齊書)

NATW—Richard. B. Mather, trans.: *A New Account of Tales of the World*

NS—Li Yanshou (李延壽): *Nanshi* (南史)

QTS—Hu Zhenheng (胡震亨) et al.: *Quantangshi* (全唐詩)

QTW—Dong Gao (董誥): *Quantangwen* (全唐文)

SGZ—Chen Shou (陳壽): Sanguozhi (三國志)

Shangshu—*Shangshu Zhengyi* (尚書正義)

SS—Shen Yue (沈約): *Songshu* (宋書)

TFZNB—Wu Tingxie (吳廷燮): *Tang Fangzhen Nianbiao* (唐方鎮年表)

WFQ—*Wen Feiqing Shiji Jianzhu* (溫飛卿詩集箋注)

XTS—Ouyang Xiu (歐陽修): *Xintangshu* (新唐書)

Zuozhuan—*Chunqiu Zuozhuan Zhengyi* (春秋左傳正義)

YFSJ—Guo Maoqian (郭茂倩): *Yuefu Shiji* (樂府詩集)

Zhouyi—*Zhouyi Zhengyi* (周易正義)

ZZhTJ—Sima Guang (司馬光): *Zizhi Tongjian* (資治通鑒)

Introduction

The Tang Dynasty is the golden age of Chinese poetry. The Late Tang is a harvest season of the golden age, an era prolific in great poets. Wen Tingyun (798–868?) was a great master of poetry of the Late Tang and the herald of a newly emerging poetic subgenre of his time, the *ci* poetry that became prevalent in the Song Dynasty and has captivated generations of Chinese readers up to modern times.

The aim of this book is to rediscover Wen Tingyun the man, so as to reevaluate Wen Tingyun the poet. We will find out what Wen writes about in his poetry and how he writes it. To this purpose, apart from exploring Wen's intricate life with an understanding of his unique poetic style, we will also use the uncovered historical events related to his life as a key to enter and travel through his poetic labyrinth. This book is thus titled *Rediscovering Wen Tingyun: A Historical Key to a Poetic Labyrinth.*

The Time of Wen Tingyun: Rampant Eunuch Power

For all its cultural exuberance and prosperity, the Late Tang was a time filled with troubles both internal and external. The eunuch usurpation of court power was its most conspicuous and serious political problem. As an outgrowth of the highly centralized imperial supremacy, this problem arose during the An-Shi Rebellion (755–763).[1] In the decades after the rebellion the emperors seem to have taken a wrong lesson from it, by lessening their confidence in the court officials, but entrusting increasing power to the eunuchs, their "safe" household slaves. Once this transfer of power was institutionalized and became a fait accompli, the eunuchs were no longer isolated palace slaves at the emperors' mercy. Not only did they take control of religious and economic affairs, but they also played a part in military manipulations and political decision making at the top level. They even became able to enthrone and dethrone the emperors, and had the lives of emperors at their disposal.[2] This eunuch infiltration of the power structure greatly accelerated and finally precipitated the downfall of the dynasty. Controlling the emperors as an emblem of their supremacy, the eunuchs generally aggravated the dissension among the court officials and intensified factional strife. As a result of this situation, the "Southern Office" (court officials), vis-à-vis the "Northern Office" (the eunuchs), polarized into two factions, the Niu Faction and the Li Faction. Initially and essentially, the two factions stood for different political responses to the Yongzhen Reform (805), even though their later factional proclivities were often not easy to define. Faced with the factional struggles prevalent under eunuch power, any honest literary man would encounter great difficulties in establishing a successful political career for himself.

Out of a concern for their own vested interests, court officials in power from either faction often adopted a vacillating, if not ambiguous, attitude toward initiating strong measures to deal with the eunuchs. This vacillation can account in part for the failures of the "Southern Office" in both the Yongzhen Reform and the Sweet Dew Incident (836), the two events most representative of its efforts to curb the eunuchs. The Yongzhen Reform attempted to get rid of eunuch power, while the Sweet Dew Incident was aimed directly at the annihilation of the eunuchs themselves. In both cases, however, the court officials never closed ranks, but remained at odds with one another over the effectiveness of radical actions. Actually, the literati in general were willing, but not daring and firm enough, to oppose the eunuchs. As a result, the participants in the two events were politically too weak to be a match for the eunuchs, even though they succeeded in enlisting the support of the emperors. Most of the Yongzhen reformers were condemned to lifelong banishment, and all the Sweet Dew Incident plotters suffered clan extermination. It was not until toward the end of the dynasty, 901, when absolution came in form of an "Amnesty,"[3] that they were rehabilitated. Since the eunuch power existed in a kind of symbiosis with the Tang royal clan, some people preferred to join forces with them to guarantee a smoother official course of action, or a more favorable official position and career. In fact, anyone in office had to come to terms and cooperate with them in order not to invite failure. The so-called "Yuanhe Restoration" accomplished by Emperor Xianzong (r. 805–820) and Pei Du (765–839), and the Governance of Huichang effected by Li Deyu (787–850) and his followers, are two cases in point. In both cases the Tang court succeeded in recapturing territories occupied by semi-independent satraps, somewhat reanimating a body politic that was near collapse. In neither instance, however, was the eunuch problem addressed. Rather, it was because Pei and Li refrained from stirring up the "hornets' nest" of the eunuchs that they were able to enjoy a measure of success in the military campaigns they led. Their military operations were, in fact, approved by the eunuchs, because, after all, the eunuchs' parasitic benefits depended on a viable Tang state power. Actually, neither Pei nor Li could avoid the misfortunes the eunuchs inflicted. Adamant and ironhanded as Li Deyu was in rendering meritorious services to the empire, he was thrown out of the political arena as soon as the eunuchs set a successor, Emperor

Xuanzong (r. 846–859), upon the throne. Li Deyu then died in exile, a victim of factional strife, or, more accurately, of eunuch politics. Pei was luckier than Li. However, effective as he was in his official duties, he also had to suffer demotions resulting from political pressures from the opposing factions, with the connivance, or at the instigation of the eunuchs. Another striking example was Liu Fen[4] (fl. 832), who, for all his fearlessness in expressing the general indignation against the eunuchs, brought more disgrace than glory upon himself.

In the literary and ideological domain, there was a concerted effort to invigorate Confucianism, embodied by the Ancient Prose Movement and the New Music Bureau Movement, as a remedy for the maladies of the time. Many outstanding representatives of the literati, such as Han Yu (768–824),[5] Liu Zongyuan (773–819),[6] Liu Yuxi (772–842), and Li Ao (772–841),[7] contributed to the revitalization of the Confucian doctrine and blazed a trail for the Song Neo-Confucianism, which then crystallized to become the dominant ideology for the next thousand years. But this in no sense offered a miraculous cure for the political disorders of the empire, and had no effect in curbing eunuch power. Disillusioned by the grim realities, the Late Tang literati adopted a pragmatic and worldly stance and resigned themselves to uncontrollable historical forces. Apart from the Confucianism they espoused in their official or political life, they showed more interest in religious philosophies, such as Buddhism[8] and Taoism. On the other hand, in their private lives the Late Tang literati are well known for their hedonism. Even great statesmen or poets famous for their concern about the country's plight and the people's livelihoods were no exceptions. For example, Bai Juyi (772–846), the chief leader of the New Music Bureau Movement, now became a devout Buddhist layman, enjoying to the full his life of wealth and rank, having long since forgotten his dauntless remonstrance with Emperor Xianzong in his capacity as Attending Censor. One of the main participants in the Sweet Dew Incident, Wang Ya (765?–835), became notorious after his execution, when the great fortune he had amassed became known.

Living in a time with these pervasive general tendencies, Wen might have attempted to seek an official position to realize his political ideals, to look for a spiritual asylum in Buddist philosophy in his frustration, or to enjoy life as much as he could. However, he was destined to be at odds with fate.

THE STUDY OF WEN TINGYUN: LASTING HISTORICAL PREJUDICES

That Wen's reputation suffered badly before and after his death stems from the eunuch problem. The major events of his life have been distorted or at least covered up, and not even Wen himself dared record the relevant events in clear terms. Consequently, Wen's poetry and personality have been misunderstood to a very serious degree and his true features have been enveloped in a twofold veil of historical prejudice and literary obscurity. Therefore, further research concerning Wen Tingyun the man and thus the poet is a pressing academic necessity.

One of the main sources for later compilation of histories, official documents of the Late Tang, especially those closely concerned with the eunuchs' clandestine affairs, were drafted under the eunuchs' influence.[9] Moreover, the original materials surviving the chaos prior to the Song Dynasty were subjected to the biased dispositions of the Song official historiographers. Thus, the two *Tang Histories* (JTS and XTS) written by them fail to give an acceptable account of the eunuch problems that bear closely upon Wen's life. One more adverse factor is that, although containing important information, Wen's poetry and prose are too obscure and difficult for the casual historiographer-readers to fathom, and hence to utilize.

In consequence of all the above, no Chinese scholars since the Song Dynasty have made a thorough study of Wen Tingyun, and many modern scholars generally accept the view that Wen was a libertine and a dandy, a poet of aestheticist originality, capable of every mischief but incapable of any concern for his country and people. It is generally believed that there is no great artistic value to be found in his works, whatever form they might assume; hence there is a tendency to devaluate Wen's works because of his problematic personality. It follows that many of his works have been misinterpreted or simply excluded from serious studies. However, these same works often make the case in one way or another that their author was a poet engagé. Readers of them can sense to some degree that there is a unique and profound beauty in his poetry that must have at its root some foundation in reality, compelling a serious reading. Recognition of this has given rise to another approach, by critics who sense the artistic beauty in many of Wen's poems and disregard former criticisms of all shades. They do not hesitate to praise Wen in the highest terms, likening him to Qu Yuan and Li Bai,[10] poets of everlasting popularity in Chinese literary history. In the eyes of the orthodox critics, however, such a view overestimates Wen's poetic attainments. To mediate between the two extreme tendencies, there is a third approach that eschews the efforts to seek conformity between the personality of the poet and his poetry, and is interested only in passing judgment on Wen's individual works. This approach, however, while seeming justifiable, may lead to another kind of falsehood.

To judge which of these three tendencies is the more reasonable, a comprehensive study of Wen Tingyun is requisite, for which an exhaustive research of *Wen's Collected Poems* is indispensable. The *Annotations and Explanations of Wen Feiqing's Collected Poems* (WFQ), the only effort heretofore aimed at understanding all of Wen's extant poems, unfortunately fails to make any logical and chronological arrangement of Wen's poems and thus is unable to point out what each poem it annotates is about, leaving the reader in darkness to find his own way. In consequence, very few modern scholars in last century have bothered to take up this study, and few significant breakthroughs have appeared. Scholars have attached more importance to his *ci* than to *shi* poetry, but have not yet reached a just and sound reevaluation of Wen Tingyun as a whole, thus conforming to the general tendency of studying his works without adequate knowledge of his life.

Since Wen was capable of writing with both simple and complex artistic expression, it is only logical that he adopted an ambiguous style when dealing with subtle political taboos, especially the eunuch problems. By exposing the eunuchs' ulterior activities, Wen's poetry fills in this historical gap, providing very precious pieces of information, which can enable us to view his time from a fresh perspective. Wen's ambiguity serves to keep his enigmas from being unraveled and to prevent him from being understood. But ambiguity was Wen's only option. He employed it to ensure that the concerns in the inmost recesses of his heart would not die with him and could wait for future understanding. It has been regrettable that some of his literary creations have misled the vast majority of his readers, exceeding and going counter to his expectation. To give him a relatively pertinent reappraisal, we must first try to clarify the major events of his life.

The key to clarifying Wen's life lies in maximum utilization of the limited sources available. To do this, we must make a painstaking study of his most ambiguous poems, those that are bound up with the most sensitive parts of history, and through this study break through to actual events in his life. For this breakthrough, we will depend on Wen's epistles for the underlying messages, and weave together all the narrative threads into a biography that can stand close scrutiny. To base our rewrite of the poet's life on solid arguments, we will use the information derived from the following poem as a foundation for our framework. The lengthy title of this poem reads:

> "In the Autumn of the Fifth Year of Kaicheng, Because of Contracting a Kind of Disease Lying in Bed in the Suburban Wilds of the Capital, I Could not Go to the Princely Establishment in the Company of the Local Representative. I Was About to Betake Myself to a Far Place. Amidst Feelings of Self-pity in the Depths of the Winter, I Unbosomed Myself in One Hundred Rhymes and Sent Them to Palace Censor Xu [Shang], Investigating Censors Chen [Gu] and Li [Yuan], Attending Censor Su of Huizhong, and Defender of Hu County, Wei; And Also I Presented the Poem to Three Friends of Mine: Yuan Jiao, Miao Shen And Li Yi"[11]

This autobiographical poem ("Hundred-Rhyme Poem" henceforward) includes important information concerning all the events of Wen's life up to the fifth year of Kaicheng (840) when Wen composed it; it even hints at many consequences Wen had to face after that year. With a view to adumbrating Wen's life, we use it as a time coordinate when we study the relevant events. Thus, many of its couplets, designated by the number of the rhymes in it, appear and reappear in the chapters to follow.

We will not agree with some old-type Chinese scholars who fill their annotations with specious statements quoted out of context, and seldom bother to give a line-to-line paraphrase of the poem itself. Nor will we follow some new-style critics who apply their general theory to a poem even before they really understand each of its lines. We will concentrate our efforts on finding out the major events reflected in the poem, which relate to Wen's life and affect his poetry. To do this, we will encounter difficulties, because, sardonically, it is not always safe to unlock the Sphinx imprisoned in Wen's poems.

Since it is a reflection of his life, it is only reasonable that Wen's poetry should be complex; to regard him either as one who played with words or as one who was unable to express himself clearly is equally wrong. Few other Chinese poets had as many ups and downs and twists and turns in their lives. In Wen's case, these were closely linked to the concurrent political situation and left imprints in his personality. Some of Wen's poems, regarded as inexplicable by tradition, are undoubtedly explicable, as we have to stress repeatedly. In writing about his life, Wen only followed the traditional path of belles lettres. Traveling farther along that path, however, he reached the summit—a summit that is at the same time a dead end. In Chinese poetic history, few poets have produced poetry as beautiful and elegant as his, which explains why we say that Wen has reached the summit of poetic beauty. On the other hand, few poets have resorted so heavily to erudition and literary artifice as he did, to the bewilderment of later readers, and thus the summit Wen reached is also a dead end.

I find it very interesting that Wen was, in one way or another, linked with many important figures of the time mentioned earlier. It is even more interesting that many favorable or unfavorable turns of his life and his poetry are so closely related to the major political events of his day. Wen did, after all, leave in his works all the key information that enables us to really know his life and feelings, and he did this quite deliberately. Facts can really be stranger than fiction. After long deliberation, I have discovered and wish to add to the life of a misunderstood Wen Tingyun the following details:[12]

1. Born in 798 into a family of imperial relatives, since his very childhood, Wen had carried on an inherited feud against the power-entrenched eunuchs.
2. Wen's marriage in Jianghuai region with a singer-prostitute (836) typifies the "misconduct" that was exploited by his enemies to block any political advance on his part.
3. Wen's professional teacher Li Cheng (768?–841) recommended him (837) to Emperor Wenzong as literary attendant to Li Yong (827–838), the Heir Apparent; thus Wen found an opportunity to directly serve his country and lord, even though deeply involved in a series of inner palace political conflicts.

4. In 839, after the Heir Apparent's tragic death, and with the aid of powerful recommendations, Wen changed his name to participate in the Metropolitan Prefecture Examination, on the first try achieving "Equivalent to Passing"; however, when the change of his name came to light, he "failed to pass" and was forced to run for his life (840).
5. During the Dazhong era (847–860), as a result of persistent attempts over many years, Wen *passed* the Presented Scholar Examination, and *passed* with a meaningful demotion (859).

Equipped with these clarified details concerning his life, we also come to a new understanding of Wen's poetic style, especially of his magnum opus, the series of the Fourteen Pusaman *ci* poems, whose explanation has long been a matter of vehement academic controversy in Chinese literary history. By taking into consideration the background against which the Pusaman series was composed, I have attempted to use Wen's own poetic techniques to fathom his poetry and conclude that this series is much more than merely a group of palace-style poems, as traditional critique represents them. For throughout the series we find messages that convey all of Wen's relevant experiences, although not explicitly and chronologically. Wen is not merely describing love, but is writing about political affairs under the guise of love. This series evidently has hidden motifs that require further exploration, and which will challenge any pedestrian reading.

IS WEN TINGYUN WRITING ANOTHER'S DREAM?

I will take a published book, Paul Rouzer's *Writing Another's Dream—The Poetry of Wen Tingyun*, as an example, to illustrate how Wen is understood and misunderstood and why we must know about Wen's life before we can appreciate his poetry.

Rouzer quotes Wang Fuzhi's (1619–1692) *Jiangzhai Shihua*:

> "A monk knocks on a gate under the moon" is only a random guess or a false speculation, as though speaking of another's dream. Even if you make the description vivid, how could it ever affect the heart? Those who know this will know that brooding over the choices of "push" or "knock" is only speculating on the behalf of some other person.

Then he comments:

> Wang's criticism here, though negative, summarizes precisely a major characteristic of Wen Tingyun's verse: an ability to stand outside of the self and to "speculate on the behalf of some other person."

> For a later imperial reader, then, Wen's poetic vices could be summarized as twofold. First, when he wrote of morally dubious experiences, he brought into question the important role poetry was meant to play in society. Second, and more important, as a historical actor he was often "unreadable" for later generations. Frequently he left behind only the poem (a morally ambiguous aesthetic artifact) or, at most, an image of a sophisticated versifier manipulating language for pure entertainment.

Rouzer takes Wang's comment on one of Jia Dao's (779–843) couplets "as though speaking another's dream" as "a major characteristic of Wen Tingyun's verse." Thus, he uses it in the title of his book. Most learned readers would frown at this title, because it is based on a biased summary of Wen's poetry. The approach Rouzer assumes seems problematic, although there are many insightful points in his book.

Jia was pondering his couplet, hesitating as to whether he should use the verb "push" or "knock," when he came across the retinue of Han Yu, who expressed his preference for "knock." As any reader will know at first glance, the couplet, "The birds roost in trees by the pool / A monk knocks on a gate under the moon" (鳥棲池邊樹，僧敲月下門), in Jia's poem serves only as scenic description. It is common sense that any scenic couplet in a lyric poem does not necessarily reflect objective reality. Rather, it reflects the writer's subjective reality. It presents an empathic objective world, by combining fragmentary images of a poet's vision into meaningful pictures. Therefore, Wang's criticism that Jia's choice of terms is "only a random guess or a false speculation, as though speaking of another's dream" is not to the point. As to whether the whole poem "could ever affect the heart" or not, that is quite another matter. It is unreasonable to demand that Jia be faithful to what was really there, when writing a scenic description. Taking this comment as "a major characteristic of Wen's poetry" is too far from both Wang's criticisms and Wen's actual poetics alike, and also too far from the general response of Chinese scholars to Wen's poetry. In Wen's works, contrary to Rouzer's judgment, Wen's central concern is always his own affairs rather another's dream. The precision and vividness of his descriptions demonstrate his penetrating observation and subtle representation, indispensable in any major poet.

According to Rouzer, for the imperial reader, Wen's poetry never accomplishes "the important role poetry was meant to play in society"; moreover, as it is "unreadable" and was composed by "a sophisticated versifier manipulating language for pure entertainment," "it actually conceals the immoral mind that frames it. It is deceptive and fraudulent" (10). Fully aware that "this is judging Wen's works not by his own personal standards but by the calcified laws of composition that grew up after his death," Rouzer chooses to "look at Wen's work on its own terms" (10), a tendency I have pointed out. However, in his reevaluation of Wen's works, we can hardly see "a new appreciation of a neglected Tang master" as he promises. Rather, in more than one case, Rouzer seems to identify himself with "the calcified laws" he disagrees with and joins in "the frequent choruses of disapproval" of Wen's poetry and person, despite his intention to pass favorable comment on this poet.

Rouzer declares, "In spite of our difficulty in bridging language and cultural distances, we are comfortable with two concepts that might still seem strange to late classical Chinese: (1) that a poem can be read as a product of an age and a personality without relating it explicitly to events in the poet's life; and (2) that a writer may still produce fine work despite his moral failings" (10). These plausible concepts may be applicable when there is no special difficulty—semantic, syntactic, or otherwise—in understanding the poetry, and when dealing with lyric poetry that may seem irrelevant to a specially designated event in the poet's life. But when the poem is essentially narrative, and the reader does not even grasp the outline of the narration, as in so many cases in Wen's work, how is the reader able to make any pertinent reevaluations or pass any valid judgments concerning it? As a result of knowing too little about Wen's life, neither praise nor censure of him can be convincing. How can we say that Wen is "writing another's dream" even though Wen has "an ability to stand outside of the self" (10)?

Rouzer might have grounded himself "in the few facts known about the poet's life," that is, unfortunately and naturally, "a few minor details in both *Tang Histories*" (11) and other unofficial histories. However, the unreliable information about Wen's life provided in the two *Tang Histories* is not help, but hindrance for reevaluating him.

To illustrate how Wen's poetry is deceptive and fraudulent, Rouzer cites Wen's "Carefree Wandering" (j. 4, WFQ, 21–2 in his book). His reading of this poem leads him to comment that "We can see how Wen's tendencies toward objectivity and lush descriptive language naturally move him toward a sort of voyeuristic eroticism, in which a woman is described in fetishistic detail from a seemingly dispassionate distance." Our reading of this poem testifies to the contrary, that the woman described is none other than the singer-prostitute whom Wen fell in love with and married.

Since in the last couplet the poet declares, "You and I are just like mandarin ducks / So don't [or I won't] seek any other companion in the human world" (與君便是鴛鴦侶，休向人間覓往還), there is not much sense in Rouzer's assertion that "Wen describes the woman from a seemingly dispassionate distance." Here Rouzer's translation is "With you I'm surely paired just like mandarin ducks / So don't seek to go back and forth out there in the human world." Even if he suggests that it was not the poet but the woman who speaks these remarks, where is the dispassionate distance he finds here?

To sum up, in the final analysis Wen Tingyun is understandable. To understand him, however, we have to overcome the historical obstacles, which create misunderstandings, the literary barriers, which frequently baffle, and longstanding misconstructions, which frustrate better understanding. It is time that our poet no longer be misunderstood and that we discover what led to the making of a unique Wen Tingyun.

Finally, a few remarks of apology for my translations and approaches. For many recondite and subtle poems, my translations fail to conjure up the beauty of the originals. Unfortunately, in translating poems, I can avail myself of little help from any polisher, but am obliged to cudgel my brains in my awkward English. I would be gratified if, with the help of the paraphrases and notes, these translations could retain generally the intrinsic meanings of, and would not add numerous detrimental elements to, their Chinese originals. As to my approaches, although only reasoning and inference can help in finding more about Wen's life, these approaches are not always rewarding. While blundering upon some hitherto unexposed events in Wen's life, I may have exposed faults or flaws that I have been unable to detect or overcome.

To conclude, allow me to use Chinese classic metaphors. Just like the legendary priceless pearl *Lizhu* under the neck of a ferocious dragon, the information concealed in Wen's works cannot be reached without some danger (of misconstruction). Or like the Jade of *Heshi* wrapped in hard stone, Wen's value as a poet can be exposed only at the price of the man who presents the jade. Wen has already paid the price for it. My greatest wish is that this study can help to pave the way to a comprehensive reevaluation of Wen Tingyun. I look forward thankfully to any comments and criticisms.

Chapter One

Family Background

During Wen Tingyun's lifetime, the Tang Empire was steadily on the wane, while the aristocratic clans, a mainstay of its rule, were also in decline. Coming to the fore in the political arena were instead some forces in the ascendant: first, the eunuchs, who had in the main usurped state power and sapped it at its core; next, the military satraps, who maintained a semi-independent position, defying the imperial authority in the capital Chang'an; and then the factions with their incessant contention, rendering the decision-making process all the more inefficient. It was against the backdrop of this situation that the Wen clan experienced its own vicissitudes of life. A study of Wen's family background, therefore, will serve not only to initiate our efforts to uncover hitherto unnoticed events concerning his life, but will also present a particular case for understanding the Late Tang problem of the politically entrenched eunuchs.

The texts of "Biographies of Wen Tingyun" in the two *Tang Histories*[1] are too inadequate and misleading to be used to draw a clear picture of Wen's life. Hence, we will consult various sources, especially his own works, for more reliable information.

CLAN ORIGIN AND NATIVE PLACE

To begin with, we will study Wen Tingyun's clan origin and his native place, as a convenient start to unraveling his poetic puzzles and probing into his life.

As indicated in Wen's biography in XTS, Wen Yanbo (573–636), the great-grandfather of his grandfather, was a native of Qi County of Taiyuan. This corresponds fairly well with one of Wen's notes to the fifth rhyme in "Hundred-Rhyme Poem":

> My forefathers were dukes and ministers of our state dynasty, and after having helped effect the Heavenly Mandate in Jinyang, they were enfeoffed in the commanderies of Bing and Fen (余先祖國朝公相，晉陽佐命，食采于并汾也).

Jinyang was the locale of the administration of Taiyuan Commandery (太原府), where the first emperor of the Tang, Li Yuan (李淵, 566–625, r. 618–625), rose up in arms against the Sui Dynasty (589–618), and Wen's forefathers rose to power and position by dint of their meritorious services to the Tang. The Wen clansmen had lived in the Taiyuan area, especially in the so-called Qi County (祁縣), up to Wen's lifetime. Qi is an older name for the county called Qingyuan (清源) during the Tang times.[2]

Since the aristocratic clans still had influence at this time, a Tang literatus would not take the locale of his immediate family as his native place unless the family had lived there since the time of his preeminent ancestors. Instead, he would identify his origins with the place where the family's famous forefathers lived, however distant they might be. The Song historiographers, when dealing with Tang biographies, followed the same practice. Therefore, we ought to take Taiyuan or Qingyuan as nothing more than the place of Wen's clan origin. Indeed, an eminent clan with the surname Wen had lived in Qi County since the Han (206 B.C.–220 A.D.).[3] During the Tang Dynasty, some of the Wens, including the branch to which Wen Tingyun belonged, had moved to the south, perhaps because of the An-Shi Rebellion. From Wen's extant works we can infer that Wen was a native of Wu or Yue, the present-day south of the Jiangsu or the Zhejiang province. To pinpoint Wen's "native place," we shall have to cite more of his works.

In his first of the two "Epistles Presented to Vice Minister Jiang" (上蔣侍郎啓二首之一), Wen mentions Qingyuan in a meaningful manner: "Therefore I left the 'Qingyuan' of the mainthreads in the southern country,[4] and had a commoner's audience from the eastern plain" (遂揚南紀之清源，因效東皋之素謁). "Qingyuan," beside referring to the county under Taiyuan in the north, literally means "pure source" or pure origin (of the family), thus denotes here Wen's native place in the south, which became Wen's second homeland after his progenitors emigrated to the south.

In "Fifty-Rhyme Poem Inspired by the Bygone, for Pouring My Heart, Presented to Chancellor Li of Huainan" (感舊陳情五十韻獻淮南李僕射, j. 6, WFQ, henceforward "Fifty-Rhyme Poem"), a poem presented to Li Shen (李紳),[5] Wen writes at the beginning:

When Ji Shao was a lad with hair streaming down his forehead,	嵇紹垂髫日，
It was the year Shan Tao began his official service.[6]	山濤筮仕年。
Your lute and wine-pot were placed between the seats.	琴尊陳座上。
I, in silk and brocade, prostrated myself in front of your couch.	紈綺拜床前。

Li Shen was a Presented Scholar of the first year of Yuanhe (806) when he began his official career as lecturer at the State Son's University; but in the same year he returned to Jinling and became secretary for Li Qi (李錡),

the Surveillance Commissioner of Zhexi Circuit (浙西道) at the time.[7] In his childhood Wen may have lived somewhere close to Jinling, where he would have had easy access to Li Shen. Wen's "Sent to Scholar Lu" (寄盧生, j. 9, WFQ) supports this inference, with its mention of a nearby estate that Wen had inherited:

Close to the ancient capital, my inherited estate laid waste.	遺業荒涼近故都，
In front of the gate, the dike road stretched across the lake.	門前堤路枕平湖。

The so-called ancient capital described here can only be Jinling, where Wen's late father had once lived and where Wen was born, but it is not the place to which Wen frequently refers with nostalgia. Related to this place, in his "Epistle Presented to Prime Minister Pei"(上裴相公啓)[8] Wen says:

> Since the days when my ancestors were bestowed imperial favor and conferred fiefs, our family had enjoyed everlasting glory, which was inscribed on the imperial tripod. Then I took my registered residence in Liaoxi, before I studied the classics in Jixia (自頃爰田錫寵，鏤鼎傳芳。占數遼西，橫經稷下).[9]

Wen mentions briefly the Wen clan's ancestral glory, the emigration of the clan branch to which he belonged, and his experience of being a student at a state-managed university. Since the last two sentences give information about his native place and early career by recourse to elegant historical allusions, we cannot take seriously that he lived in Liaoxi, the modern region covering a part of Hebei and Liaoning in the north; even less can we take for granted that he studied in Jixia, a state school in the capital of the Qi Kingdom of the Warring States (475–221 B.C.) in Shandong. "Taking up registered residence in Liaoxi" alludes verbatim to "Biography of Zhao Zhi"[10] (趙至, fl. 310):

> [Zhao] went to Luoyang at fourteen. . . . After the death of Zhang Sizong, he went to Liaoxi to take registered residence (年十四，詣洛陽……嗣宗卒，乃向遼西而占戶焉).

We do not know the exact reason why Wen uses the allusion to Zhao Zhi to speak of his own residence, but there might be similarities in their early experiences. Anyway, the so-called "Liaoxi" should be somewhere close to Yuezhou, where Wen lived for most of his early years, as can be inferred from the following evidence:

1. Throughout Wen's literary works we have some twenty poems and essays showing that Wen cherished a special feeling toward the Yuezhou district.[11]

For example, lines such as "Filling your room is the moonlight of my home mountain" (一室故山月) and "A former lecturer in Lanting" (蘭亭舊都講) in "Presented to the Yue Monk Yue Yun" (贈越僧岳雲, j. 7, WFQ), must imply something. The place "Lanting," which Wen considered as his "home mountain" was in Yuezhou, the present Shaoxing.

2. In Wen's "Epistle Presented to Grand Master Cui" (上崔大夫啓)[12] we read:

> I, your humble servant, feel like I am seeing the spirited and charming Mount Ji, and the lucid and bright Lake Mirror, when looking upward to its [your] august loftiness, which stands firm and awe-inspiring. Secluded in my poor abode, I stay home while listening to stringed and wind instruments played; as a transferred immortal, you travel about, having banners and flags flying (伏想嵇山靈爽，鏡水澄明，仰止尊高，居然勝絕，隱貧居而坐聞絲管，謫仙家而行有旌旗).

Mount Ji and Lake Mirror are in Shaoxing; therefore without a further investigation of the epistle, we know that Tingyun's place of reclusion was not far from Yuezhou.

3. In his poem "Li Yu the Recluse Sends Me His Newly Brewed Wine, I Playfully Thank Him with an Impromptu Verse" (李羽處士寄新醞，走筆戲酬, j. 4, WFQ), Wen likened himself to "Xie the Guest" (謝客)—an appellation for Xie Lingyun (謝靈運, 385–433), who, an orphan since infancy, had been entrusted to a relative in the Yue district. This further suggests that Wen might have taken his registered residence in Yue by relying on a certain relative, as had Xie Lingyun.[13]

4. In *Yanlingji* (嚴陵集)[14] by the Southern Song Dynasty writer Dong Fen (董棻) we have one lost poem written by Wen Tingyun:

"YEARNING FOR MY OLD ABODE IN TONGLU, I SEE OFF THE NOBLE MONK JIAN "思桐廬舊居便送鑒上人

Don't you say the southeast is not far away,	莫道東南路不賒，
A mere step is a great distance in my nostalgia.	思歸一步是天涯。
The forest of night, the two terraces, in the moonlight,	林中夜來雙臺月，[15]
Spring in its prime, the blossoms on the Nine Li Isle.	池上春深九里花。[16]
Soaked in a fine drizzle, round the village are the green trees,	綠樹繞村含細雨，

Rolling the level sand, against the city wall is a cold tide. 寒潮背郭卷平沙。
Knowing that you, my master, are going into the hills, 聞師卻到山中去，
For me and to the tavern owner, please earnestly apologize. 為我殷勤謝酒家。

This poem, one of Wen's representative works, presents the transparent aspect of his poetic personae. Its third couplet was also taken as an exquisite sample for its "picturesqueness" (入畫).[17] *Yanlingji* contains only the compositions of poets from the vicinity of Mount Yanling and Torrent Yanling, both named in memory of the famous recluse of the Eastern Han, Yan Guang (嚴光, 37 B.C.–43 A.D.). This strengthens the authentication of this poem as written by Wen.[18] Since Wen had an old residence in Tonglu to which he was eager to return, he must have lived there long enough to call the place his homeland. Hence, "Liaoxi" in his allusion probably means Tonglu County of Mu Zhou (睦州), which was adjacent to Yuezhou.

REMAINING PRESTIGE OF AN ARISTOCRATIC FAMILY

Wen was descended from Wen Yanbo, Prime Minister of Emperor Taizong (r. 627–649). During the next two hundred years, the Wen clan's social position had been downgraded considerably. It inescapably shared in the general disintegration of all aristocratic clans. Contrasting finely with this, the following statement in "Biography of Wen Yanbo" gives a clear idea of the role the Wen clan played in its glorious days:[19]

> The Yans and the Wens were once the most illustrious surnames during the Sui Dynasty. Now Yan Silu and Wen Daya both served in the Eastern Palace, while Yan Minchu and Wen Yanbo both served in the Secretariat, and Yan Youqin and Wen Dayou served in the Palace Library as proofreader. In the Tang Dynasty the Yan clan distinguished itself by its academic achievements, and the Wen clan by its official rank (初，顏氏溫氏在隋最盛。思魯與大雅俱事東宮，愍楚彥博同直內書省，游秦大有典校秘閣。顏以學業優，而溫以職位顯于唐云).

Apart from its ancestral glory in early seventh century, the clan had produced other famous figures. From *Yuanhe Xingcuan* by the Tang genealogist Lin Bao (fl. 812–840) and "Genealogical List of the Prime Ministers,"[20] we find reference from the time of Wen Yanbo's father, Wen Junyou of the Sui Dynasty, to the seventh year of Yuanhe (812), to the following seven generations of preeminent Wen clansmen:

WEN JUNYOU'S (溫君攸) SEVEN-GENERATION DESCENDANTS

1	Wen Daya	溫大雅	*Wen Yanbo	溫彥博
2	Wen Wuyin	溫無隱	*Wen Ting	溫挺
3	Wen Kerang	溫克讓	Wen Weng'gui	溫翁歸
4	Wen Jingqian	溫景倩	Wen Mian	溫緬
5	Wen Jie	溫佶	*WenXi	溫曦
6	Wen Zao	溫造	*Wen Xihua	溫西華
7	Wen Zhang	溫璋	Wen Yang	溫暘

In this table we list the name of only one clansman for each generation, representing each of the two main branches of the Wen clan, one of which Wen Tingyun claimed as his own. Many of these names bear high official titles, though not as exalted as those of Wen Yanbo. By Wen Tingyun's time, the Wens seem to have produced very few distinguished clansmen, especially in Wen Yanbo's line. No wonder that Wen spoke of his ancestral glory in "Hundred-Rhyme Poem" not without dismay:

The [ancestral] enfeoffment in the forlorn wild is left waste, 采地荒遺野，
And our fief by the old capital has long been divested. 爰田失故都。

From Wen's already quoted note to this couplet, it is evident that the later Wens failed to equal the distinction of their forefathers. Though we know little about the Wen clan's history before Wen's day, we have in our possession important information that helps to identify Wen's genealogical status: the Wen clan had for generations made marriages with the imperial family. There are three Wen clansmen who married imperial princesses and became imperial sons-in-law, with the special official title Commander of the Reserved Horses (駙馬都尉).[21] All three were descendants of Wen Yanbo, as was Wen Tingyun: Wen Ting (Wen Yanbo's son) married Princess Anding (安定公主), daughter of Emperor Gaozu (r. 618–626); Wen Xi (a great-grandson of Wen Yanbo) married Princess Liang'guo (梁國公主), daughter of Emperor Ruizong (r. 711–712), and Wen Xihua (Wen Xi's son) married Princess Song'guo (宋國公主),[22] daughter of Emperor Xuanzong (r. 712–756). These marriages indicate that Wen Yanbo's descendants had kept the imperial favor to a remarkable degree. In addition, we have some internal evidence in Wen's poems proving that Wen was an imperial relative. In "Western Pool of the Heir Apparent" (太子西池二首, j. 3, WFQ), we have the following allusion, referring to Wen himself:

Do not believe that Prince Zhang, 莫信張公子，
Will cancel his secret rendez-vous in front of the window. 窗間斷暗期。

And in "Ode to a Night Feast" (夜宴謠, j. 1, WFQ), we find the same allusion:

The Prince of Zhang family at night heard the rain fall,	張家公子夜聞雨，
And at night, thought of the Chu dance in the Orchid Hall.	夜向蘭堂思楚舞。[23]

"Prince Zhang" alludes to the Fuping Marquis, Zhang Fang (富平侯張放),[24] a well-known imperial relative of Emperor Yuan of Han (漢元帝, r. 48–33 B.C.). Another example, from "Sent to Chuwang on the Cold Food Festival" (寒食節寄楚望, j. 9, WFQ), reads:

Only the Marquis of Royal Blessing,	獨有恩澤侯。
Returns to watch the Chu dance.	歸來看楚舞，

Wen calls himself "the Marquis of Royal Blessing," which was an appellation used exclusively for imperial relatives.[25] Considering that Wen Xi and Wen Xihua had been imperial sons-in-law, if Wen were not a near kinsman of Wen Xi or Wen Xihua, how else would it be possible for him to call himself an imperial relative?

Although little is known about Wen's father, we can attempt to find out Wen's genealogical position by tracing his relations with Wen Zao[26] (温造, 765–835), Tingyun's clan uncle and foster father. Wen's "Epistle Presented to the Prime-Minister-Duke of the Honor Seat" (上首座相公啓),[27] as I shall prove, was addressed to Wen Zao. Since Wen Zao once told Emperor Dezong, "Your subject's fifth generation ancestor is Wen Daya,"[28] we can say with certainty that Tingyun, as Wen Zao's nephew, was the sixth generation offspring of Wen Daya's brother, Wen Yanbo. Thus, Tingyun was probably a nephew of Wen Xihua, if not his son, and there is no doubt that he was the grandson of Wen Xi. In our later discussions, I will present more evidence supporting this.

The Wens played an important role in helping the first two Tang emperors found and consolidate the dynasty's state power, by rendering both civil and military service to them. As can be seen from "Biography of Wen Daya," the three Wen brothers all reached very high official rank, in one case the position of Prime Minister, and were enfeoffed as dukes. Wen Yanbo on his death was even honored with burial in the imperial tomb, Zhaoling. In acknowledgment of the meritorious service of the Wen clan, Emperor Gaozu once said to Wen Daya: "It was by the support of all your clan that I could rise up in arms in Jinyang " (吾起兵晉陽，為卿一門耳).[29] This is no overstatement. It was because of this blood connection that Wen Tingyun took the prosperity and decline of the Tang Empire as his own affair and made every endeavor to bring about a restoration of the dynasty's past grandeur.

In addition to being important ministers, both Wen Daya and Wen Yanbo were well-known writers, as can be seen from "Records of Literary Works" (藝文志) of XTS (j. 58). Wen Daya's works are *A Record of the Present Emperor's Imperial Enterprise* (今上王業記, 1467), *The Imperial Diary of the Great Tang in Its*

Founding (大唐創業起居錄, 1471), and *The Subordinate Officials of the Grand Prime Minister, The Prince of Tang* (大唐丞相唐王官屬記, 1477); Wen Yanbo's works are *Anthology of Imperial Edicts of All Times, Thirty Juan* (古今詔令集三十卷, 1473).

Wen Tingyun often refers to his family with a feeling of mingled pride and anxiety: he is proud of his ancestors' past glory, and he is anxious to restore his family's position by distinguishing himself. In "Hundred-Rhyme Poem," the following lines extol the Wen clan's distinguished stock:

7 For generations the Wens partook of the Zhou emoluments, 奕世參周祿，
As family tradition, we used to emulate the Lu Confucians. 承家學魯儒。
8 Witness of our family feats: the remaining swords and court boots, 功庸留劍舄，
Inscribed on imperial plates and basins: our ancestors' admonitions. 銘誡在盤盂。

Here we see that the Wens rendered remarkable services to the Empire for generations by adhering to the Confucian principles. In Wen's grandiloquent language, Wen's forefathers won the highest imperial favor: they were privileged to attend the court with a special sword and courtly boots and their admonitions of the emperors were inscribed on the vessels the emperor used. Tingyun himself, however, was born too late. The family past, of which he often boasted, obliged him to *restore* its glory, by reanimating the Confucian tradition. In other words, he desired to devote himself to the restoration of the country and to the simultaneous reglorification of his family, which, at this time, was somehow in a state of political disgrace. In his "Epistle Presented to Prime Minister Pei,"[30] Wen tells us: "I was thinking of sewing up the broken drapery[31] of the Confucian House, and restoring the magnificence and grandeur of the Constant Norm," that is, reviving declining Confucianism and restoring imperial supremacy. What happened to Wen's forefathers that caused them to lose their hereditary honors and titles? In "Hundred-Rhyme Poem" we find the following hint:

6 Having lost the sheep, I still toss the dice, 亡羊猶博塞，
Letting go the horse, I weary of shouting for stakes. 放馬倦呼盧。

This couplet has rather complex implications and requires explanation. The first line alludes to the following fable:[32] "Zang and Gu fed the sheep together, but they both lost their sheep," because "Zang had brought a book to study; Gu had been idling away the time tossing dice." So it implies that even though Wen's ancestors had somehow lost their official positions, Wen refused to change, adhering to the old way of his forefathers (the so-called" tossing the dice"). In the second line, "Letting loose the horse,"[33] in antithesis to "having lost the sheep," might be a reference to a political behavior; it might be an extended use of its source in *Shangshu*: "[The King] hushed all the movements of war and proceeded to cultivate the arts of peace. He sent back his horses to the south of Mount Hua and let loose the oxen in the open country of the Peach Woods."[34] Thus, it suggests retreat from politics. The reason for the retreat is that Wen "wearied of shouting for stake,"[35] which conveys that Wen, at the time, was no longer inclined to "play" the political game. This metaphorical usage can be found in another of Wen's poems.[36] Briefly put, because of his adherence to family tradition, Wen was frustrated and showed a tendency to give up his political efforts. Now we must ask: what is the family tradition to which Wen always adhered, despite repeated rebuffs?

After a thorough reading of Wen's works, we infer that it must be *the straight way* (直道), that is, straightforwardness, a dauntless spirit daring to speak against any social injustice, as Confucian doctrine advocates. It was *because of* this moral principle that Wen's forefathers had lost their official positions, and it was *with* this principle that Wen confronted his troubled life filled with twists and setbacks. Another example that underscores this point is found in Wen's "Epistle Presented to Bureau Director Han of the Ministry of Personnel" (上吏部韓郎中啓):

> My wisdom is different from comprehensive mastery; my ability lacks a proficiency in any particular line. Fortunately I took over the august instruction [of my forefathers], so as not to lose the pure fragrance [of our clan]
> (某識異旁通，才無上技。幸傳丕訓，免墮清芬).

"Comprehensive mastery" alludes to a remark in Ji Kang's "Letter for Breaking Off Relations with Shan Juyuan"(與山巨源絕交書):[37] "Your Excellency is a talent of comprehensive mastery, hence in most cases you say 'yes' and seldom show discontent" (足下旁通，多可而少怪). Since the Bureau Director Han was one of Wen's father's friends whom Wen compared to Shan Tao, Wen's father was very possibly not a man of "comprehensive mastery," but he must, instead, have been a man of strict principles and strong eccentricity, like Ji Kang. It was from his father that Wen inherited a character that made himself a worthy scion of the Wens. Such is the family tradition and reputation. As he says in "Hundred-Rhyme Poem":

7 Among my compeers I was honored as a good friend, 時輩推良友，
Of my pedigree, I have carried on an honest fame. 家聲繼令圖。

Judging from the extant writings of Wen's contemporaries such as Li Shangyin, Zhang Hu (張祜, 805–860?), Ji Tangfu (紀唐夫, fl. 860), Duan Chengshi (段成式, 805–864), and Pei Tingyu (裴庭裕, fl. 820–860),[38] all famous poets or writers of the Late Tang times, the self-evaluation in this couplet is no exaggeration.

Here, Wen's allusions to Ji Kang merit particular study. We can find nothing about Wen' s father in all Tang and Song Dynasty sources. But Wen mentions his father in a way that is suggestive enough to enable us to infer what kind of person he was, or at least how he died. Wen seldom mentioned his father explicitly, but when he did refer to him elusively in his writings, he alluded to Wang Zun (王尊, fl.20 B.C.), Lu Ji (陸績, 187–219), and Xie Lingyun, all of whom were, perhaps by unhappy accident, orphans in their childhood,[39] as was Wen himself, "a distant scion and orphan of Wen Yanbo"(彥博裔孤).[40] Most noteworthy is that he repeatedly alludes to the trio of Ji Kang-Shan Tao-Ji Shao in such a way that, by likening himself to Ji Shao, who sought help from Shan Tao, he metaphorically likens his late father to Ji Kang. Ji Kang entrusted his son Ji Shao to Shan Tao before he was executed by the Jin Dynasty ruler. Wen's repeated use of the allusion no doubt tells us something about his father. Therefore, this allusion should not be allowed to slip by carelessly but must be rechecked. In addition to the couplet I have quoted: "When Ji Shao was a lad with hairs streaming down his forehead / It was the year Shan Tao began his official service"; which suggests that when Wen was a mere child like Ji Shao, his late father's friend Chancellor Li of Huainan had just begun his official service, like Shan Tao. We have the following four examples, all referring to different aspects of the same allusion, and all likening his late father to Ji Kang. I will examine each of them.

1. In "Epistle Presented to Prime Minister Linghu" (上令狐相公啓) Wen writes: "The boy of the Ji clan, eight years of age, is under the protection of an old friend" (嵇氏則男兒八歲，保在故人), alluding to Ji Kang's remark in his "Letter for Breaking Off Relations with Shan Juyuan": "My daughter is thirteen and my son is eight years of age" (女年十三，男年八歲). If Ji Kang entrusted his orphans to Shan Tao, here "the boy of the Ji clan, eight years of age" must refer to Wen, and the "old friend" to a friend of his late father, expected to fill the role of Shan Tao in his relation with Wen Tingyun.
2. In Wen's "Fifty-Rhyme Poem" we find the following lines:

Whom shall I, a helpless man, seek asylum from?	有客將誰托？
Without a mediator, I inwardly have pity on myself.	無媒竊自憐。
Falling and rising is the melody of the Palace Leisure,	抑揚中散曲，
Drifting and wandering is the ship of Filialty and Incorruption.	飄泊孝廉船。

In the first couplet Wen is unburdening himself to Chancellor Li of his grievances, saying that in his frustration, what he needs most is the recommendation of a powerful mediator; and, to his dismay, no such recommendation is forthcoming. But to what does the second couplet refer? It must have something to do with Wen's personal situation. "Filialty and Incorruption" refers to Zhang Ping (張憑, fl. 370), who led an unsteady life in a ship before his talent was appreciated by Liu Shan[41] (劉惔, fl. 370). So the line expresses a disappointment that, unlike Zhang Ping, Wen had as yet met no one who could appreciate his talent, and thus the line before it is a poetic description of the root cause of all his misfortunes. According to Ji Kang's biography, Ji, the Grand Master of Palace Leisure (中散大夫), was taught the exquisite tune *Guanglingsan* (廣陵散) by a superman (奇人 [*sic*]). Immediately before his execution, Ji asked for a lute on which to play the music for the last time; then he heaved a sigh and said: "*Guanglingsan* from now on is extinct." The "Melody of the Palace Leisure" thus allusively refers to something almost extinct—a particular principle that scarcely anyone of the day still adhered to. Set against the background of the Late Tang political ambiance, the term is used as metaphor for the "straight way" Wen's father had upheld, a political fearlessness in resisting the eunuchs, regardless of personal safety. The "falling (and rising)"[42] of the "melody" is thus a reflection of the historical reality, in the face of which people could only sporadically raise their voices against the eunuchs. We can further infer that, after Wen's father's death as a consequence of his open criticism of the eunuchs, political protest, except in a few instances, became almost inaudible. One of these instances was the Sweet Dew Incident of 835 (which met complete failure).

3. "Epistle Presented to Prime Minister" (上宰相啓): "The former dependent of Shanyang will not be heartbroken alone" (山陽舊曲，不獨傷心). As "Biography of Xiang Xiu" (向秀) relates, Ji Kang for a time irrigated a vegetable garden with Lü An (呂安) in Shanyang. After Ji was executed, Xiang Xiu once passed by Ji's old residence and heard Ji's neighbor playing the flute, thereupon he wrote his "Rhapsody on Yearning for Old Days" (思舊賦).[43] "The former dependent of Shanyang" refers to Wen himself, and here again Wen likens his late father to Ji Kang, without mentioning him directly.
4. "Epistle Presented to Bureau Director Han of the Ministry of the Personnel": "Then a wretched orphan will find something with which to shelter himself, by always relying on the friendship of Shan Tao" (然後幽獨有歸，永托山濤之分). This line shows clearly that Wen assumed the role of Ji Shao, hoping Han would be like Shan Tao and help him. The allusion once more places his late father in the role of Ji Kang.

In all the above cases, Wen's implication is the same: his father was a man like Ji Kang. Because of his reluctance to cooperate with them, Ji Kang was executed by the Sima clansmen when they usurped the power of the Wei state. According to "Biography of Shan Tao" in JS, prior to his execution Ji Kang said to his son Ji Shao: "So long as Juyuan [Shan Tao] survives, you are not an orphan" (巨源在，汝不孤矣). Thus, Ji Kang entrusted his orphans to Shan Tao; and it was in this sense that Wen used the allusion.

Normally one cannot derive substantial information from one casual use of an allusion. However, the frequency with which Wen used this allusion to the same person forces us to probe more deeply the factual basis for its repeated use. Even the fact that Ji Kang was the son-in-law of the Cao-Wei royal family suggests an analogy to Wen's case: that Wen's father or uncle might have been son-in-law of the Li-Tang royal family. The frequency with which Wen likens his late father to Ji Kang amounts to a confession that his late father was put to death for political reasons. Had the father not been similar to Ji Kang, how could Wen Tingyun have so insistently adhered to this peculiarly humiliating and ominous way of mentioning him? This unusual choice of allusion must be closely linked to Wen's personal experience. It is unlikely that he used the comparison repeatedly without careful consideration of its connotations. On the contrary, we can speculate that this was a deliberate choice intended to convey the very idea he wanted to express.

Such is our premise for further research with the limited materials available. By analogy, Wen was comparing the Sima usurpers at the end of the Wei Dynasty to the eunuchs who had usurped almost all court power during his time. This, then, is the basic assumption: Wen's father died as a result of persecution by the eunuchs for his straightforwardness. As to how he died, though it seems to have been death by execution, it was, more probably, death by exile. That would explain why Wen never speaks of his father explicitly, and why in his childhood, after being orphaned, he still enjoyed some degree of inherited privilege. We will draw more inferences to corroborate this explanation.

When did Wen's father die? Inferred from "When Ji Shao [himself] was a lad with hairs streaming down his forehead / It was the year Shan Tao [Li Shen] began his official service" (in 806), it seems that in about the year 806 Wen was orphaned, or that at that time something happened that precipitated his father's death.

History tells us that immediately preceding 806 was the year of the Yongzhen Reform (805). This was an effort on the part of the court officials to restore the Empire's normal functioning by seizing back imperial prerogatives from the eunuchs.[44] The organizers and the main participants of the Yongzhen Reform—"the two Wangs and the eight Prefectural Assistants" (二王八司馬)—should be more positively evaluated than they were by the Song Dynasty's prejudiced historiographers, as is now increasingly emphasized by modern scholars. What interests us here is Wen's connection with the Yongzhen Reform participants. Eunuch persecution caused Wen's father's death at the time, connecting both the father and the son to the same event. Based on the few traces that time has fortunately not yet effaced, we can indeed verify this point. Although Wen was a mere child at the time the Yongzhen Reform occurred, it precipitated the death of his father and had a far-reaching effect on his life.

Wen passed his early childhood in a wealthy and influential family. His "Epistle Presented to the Prime Minister" compares his past luxurious life to his present poverty:

> An abider of a mansion with adorned pillars and towering lintels now dwells alone in a hut like a snail shell; and a man of brocade jacket and silk trousers has to sleep on a cattle's grass coat (梓柱云楣，獨居蝸舍；綺襦紈絝，已臥牛衣).

While we cannot imagine precisely how rich his family used to be, we can, more readily, paint a picture of Wen's "poverty." In his "Epistle Presented to Bureau Director Han of the Ministry of Personnel," he says of himself: "Like Ji Shao, I had an old mansion in Xingyang." In "Sent to Scholar Lu" (寄盧生, j. 9, WFQ), he tells us: "Close to the ancient capital, my inherited estate is laid waste." The title of another poem, "Sent to an Intimate Friend from My Villa of the Hu County Suburbs" (鄠郊別墅寄所知, j. 8, WFQ), tellingly offers information that Wen had some estates in Hu county (of the Metropolitan Prefecture). All these references indicate that, as the scion of a declining aristocratic family with estates in several places, Wen was not quite as poverty-stricken as his frequent complaints suggest. He still enjoyed considerable privilege inherited from his ancestors, despite his father's untimely death. An aristocratic family in decline could still afford him a comfortable life, a life that Wen called "poverty" because it was different from that of the rising powerful families and degraded from that of Wen clan's past wealth and rank. To give an exact description of the financial status of Wen's early life in Wen's own terms, there is the following couplet from his "Hundred-Rhyme Poem":

> My loom shuttle is unlike that of *the mulberry lady*, 機杼非桑女，
> And my grove and garden differ from *the Wood Slaves*. 林園異木奴。

"*Mulberry lady*"[45] suggests a life of an ordinary farmer, while "*Wood Slaves*,"[46] meaning orange trees, indicates a well-to-do economic situation. Wen does not need to work in the field like a mulberry lady to earn his daily bread, though he considers that his inheritance is less than that of "*the Wood Slaves*." The family's economic situation was neither bad enough to force him to engage in field labor nor good enough to separate him completely from husbandry. With such social status, it would not be difficult for Wen to live the life of an ordinary country gentleman. However, his problem was that he could not rest content with what his seniors had left him and wanted to restore his family's glory by advancing himself as a successful court official. He was proud and confident of his family glory and literary talent, but the character he inherited from his forebears involved him in numerous troubles.

From Wen's poems and prose works, we can see that he still enjoyed relations with a wide circle of people of rank and fashion, including many noble lords and even members of the imperial family. Unlike Li Shangyin, who had no more than two or three patrons, Wen was closely connected with many of the influential and powerful court officials of the time. Indeed, we find that it was through surviving family influence that he was introduced into the circle of the *élites societées.* In his own terms, in "Epistle Presented to Prime Minister Linghu," he asserts that his family was such:

> I have extensively sought help from my family's former favored subordinates, and it has taken me extremely long years [to be conferred an office] (某旁征義故，最歷星霜).

Aided by such social relations, as well as his own reputation, he made every effort to open the way for a successful official career when the situation was favorable to him, and sought protection and refuge when he was in adversity.

SPECIAL SOCIAL CONNECTIONS

Of the dirges on Liu Yuxi's (772–842) death, only those of Bai Juyi and of Wen are extant. Wen's poems give a clear account of the friendship between the two men.

"TWO ELEGIES FOR THE LATE MINISTER LIU, DIRECTOR OF THE PALACE LIBRARY"[47] (秘書劉尚書挽歌詞二首, j. 3 WFQ)

Like Wang's calligraphy, yours is as vivid as live phoenixes,	王筆活鸞鳳，
And like Xie's poetry, yours is as charming as blooming lotuses.	謝詩生芙蓉。[48]
When crimson curtain opened, you presided over academic lectures,	學筵開絳帳，[49]
Your eloquent discourses were [as amazing as] striking a huge bell.	談柄發洪鐘，
But when in the whitewashed office appeared a flying owl,	粉署見飛鵩。[50]
Of the jade mountain was slandered a sleeping dragon.	玉山猜臥龍。[51]
You left to us a shining image with spotless integrity,	遺風灑清韻，
As the pines in the Nine-Plain stand in towering seclusion.	蕭散九原松。[52]

After praising Liu's calligraphy, comparing him to the great Jin calligrapher Wang Xizhi (王羲之, 321–379), this poem extols Liu's poetry, matching him to Xie Lingyun. Next, by alluding to Ma Rong, it recalls with admiration the occasions on which Liu gave insightful and eloquent lectures. Then the poem alludes to Jia Yi and Ji Kang, both talented and honest men frustrated by their lot, to represent how the antireform slanderous talks at court led to the failure of Yongzhen Reform and the dismissal of Liu from his "whitewashed office."[53] The allusion to Ji Kang evidences that Wen regarded Liu with the same respect he would show his father. In the end, Wen pays high tribute to both Liu's career and personality, mourning Liu's decease with a deep-felt grief. (Poem Two)

A deer-tail duster in hand, you were a priceless jade, 麈尾近良玉，
When, the white crane-down of your robe waves in the breeze. 鶴氅吹素絲。
Like a Yin Hao banished, for failing to renovate the imperial tombs, 壞陵殷浩謫，[54]
With a Xie An playing chess, in a spring villa, at ease, 春墅謝安棋。
And what a noble prince of Jingkou you were, 京口貴公子，[55]
Also many a girl of Xiangyang you praised. 襄陽諸女兒。
[Even now], picking flowers or dancing in the moonlight, 折花兼蹋月，
[For your blessed memory] most people are singing Mr. Liu's lyrics. 多唱柳郎詞。

The second poem starts with more depiction of Liu's impressive personality. Then it turns to a representation of Liu's life from a fresh perspective. The allusion to Yin Hao (?–356), who failed "to renovate the imperial tombs," seems at first glance strange in this context. But if we notice that in the year of Yongzhen (805), apart from holding the post Investigating Censor (監察御史), Liu Yuxi was concurrently Assistant to Commissioner of Venerating the Imperial Tombs (崇陵使判官),[56] its connotation becomes clear. It is an analogy to Liu's political reform in 805 whose failure was partly due to Emperor Shunzong's (r. &. d. 805) forced abdication and untimely death. Liu was even good at playing chess.[57] The allusion to Xie An[58] thus is also a reflection of Liu's friendship with Prime Minister Pei Du, by way of compliment to Liu's insight and wisdom in his late years. During his lengthy banishment in Langzhou and Kuizhou, Liu wrote a number of verses in the style of folk songs, such as the "Ballads of Bamboo Branches" (竹枝詞), by drawing from and revising the popular ballads. This fact, in Wen's mind's eye, is alluded to by "Many girls of Xiangyang,"[59] written by an eminent man. In conclusion, Wen declares affectionately that Liu's poems enjoyed great popularity and would be forever remembered, by alluding to Liu Yun.[60]

After a careful paraphrase, we find that almost all of Liu's accomplishments are reflected in Wen's dirges, and that even from our vantage point,

Wen's evaluation of both Liu's political role and his literary attainments is comprehensive and fair. The Qing Dynasty commentator Wang Mingsheng found in the above poems an indication of the profound friendship between Wen and Liu,[61] a point with which I fully agree. In fact, Liu was Wen's senior and superior. With respect to political standpoint, literary career, and poetic style, they had much in common, and in particular, it was their shared political orientation that caused Wen to hold Liu in great esteem.

Even from a purely literary perspective, Liu and Wen are very closely related to each other, as can be seen from the similar comments on their poems, whether in positive or negative terms. For an example of the former: "The eight pieces of 'Nanxiangzi' by Feiqing, with their refined language and classic exquisiteness, are no less masterful than Mengde's [Yuxi] 'Ballads of Bamboo Branches'" (飛卿"南鄉子"八闕，高古不減夢得"竹枝詞").[62] Here we see how the two poets both excelled in drawing from the folk literature and how Wen inherited and carried forward Liu's typical poetic expressions. For an example of the latter: "From the masters of the Qi and the Liang dynasties down to the Tang writers such as Liu Mengde and Wen Feiqing, poets often spoiled their pure style with dazzling descriptions of wind and flowers; their failure lies in that their poetry lacks principle and is excessive of diction" (上自齊梁諸公，下至唐劉夢得温飛卿輩，往往以綺麗風花，累其正氣。其過在于理不勝而詞有餘也).[63] Despite the apparent misevaluation, this statement at least notes some identical features and puts both poets in one category. Bai Juyi called Liu a "poetic hero" (詩豪) for Liu's indomitable spirit in the grip of misfortunes and for the undying vigor in his late-year poetry. This poetic individuality Liu evidences also occurs in Wen's poetry. The following is an example revealing Wen's indebtedness to Liu:

"Passing the Residence of the Late Hanlin Academician Yuan" (經故翰林袁學士居, j. 5, WFQ)

The jade's left in the dust, the sword gone with the surging waves,	劍逐驚波[64]玉委塵，
Now under Xie An's patronage, what soul could still stay?	謝安門下更何人？
Outside Western Prefecture (Xizhou) city, the blossoms of a thousand trees,	西州城外花千樹，
Are all spring splendors, after Yang Tan has been inebriated.	盡是羊曇醉後春。

Both "jade in the dust" and "sword gone with the surging waves" are metaphors for the death of a talented and worthy man. To begin with, Wen laments his deceased friends the late Hanlin Academician Yuan and a Prime Minister. The late Hanlin Academician Yuan would have been under the Prime

Minister's patronage for a time. How did the two die? The poem implies that they died in some violent political incident (the surging waves); otherwise he need not vainly have shed his tears. "Outside Xizhou city, the blossoms of a thousand trees" is a reference to the political upstarts in the capital after the incident, which resulted in the death of both the Prime Minister and, later, Yuan. Yang Tan[65] was Xie An's sister's son, who did not walk in the lanes near Xizhou (the locale of administration of Yangzhou), where Xie An died; once when he was heavily drunk, when arriving unexpectedly in Xizhou, he burst into tears. By using Yang's story, Wen unbosomed himself of his sorrow for the incident that bereaved him of his beloved friends, and he castigated those who rose to power by taking advantage of the incident. Wen seems to have every reason to compare himself to Yang Tan, and he might even be a relative of the dead minister. Who this Prime Minister was will become clearer. For now let us compare this poem to the following one by Liu Yuxi:

"In the Tenth Year of Yuanhe, I Was Called Back from Langzhou to the Capital, and I Jokingly Presented This Poem to Several Noble Men Who Were Enjoying the Blooming Flowers"
(元和十年自朗州承詔至京，戲贈看花諸君子, *Liu Yuxi Ji*, 24: 218)

The red dust in the purple alleys caresses travelers' faces,	紫陌紅塵拂面來，
"Back from admiring the flowers," they all say.	無人不道看花回。
In Xuandu Monastery, a thousand peach trees,	玄都觀里花千樹，
All are transplanted after Sir Liu's leave.	盡是劉郎去後栽。

When he was called back to the capital, after ten years' banishment, Liu did not show deference to the hostile forces at court. For this poem, a satire on the ruling clique, he was banished to an even more remote region. It is clear that this poem was the prototype for Wen's, whose second couplet models itself on Liu's.

Since there is a close relation between the two, we will try to unravel an allusion in Wen's works by recourse to Liu's use of the same allusion. In his "Epistle Presented to the Censor-in-Chief" (投憲丞啓), Wen once called himself "*the junior party of Ganling*" (甘陵下黨).[66] In attempting to explain this, we can consult Liu's use of a similar term:

"The Drafter Bai Condescended to Answer My Clumsy Poem, And I Sent This Poem to Express My Gratitude"
(白舍人見酬拙詩，因以致謝, *Liu Yuxi Ji*, 1034)

For all my presence in the company of the third rank sinecures,	雖陪三品散官中，

I had, from the very beginning, different records
and qualifications. 資歷從來事不同。
My name, once for a while, was carved on
the stone pillar. 名姓也曾鐫石柱，
My poetry, a failure, cannot be written on the
imperial screen. 詩篇未得上屏風。
The former party of Ganling is all withered
and decayed, 甘陵舊黨凋零盡，
While my new friend at court shows to me
high courtesy. 廟堂新知禮數崇。
If ever I could find a partner in the
misty-water of the Five Lakes, 煙水五湖如有伴，
To be an old fishing man, I think, could yet
suit my taste. 猶應堪作釣魚翁。

Sixteen years after Liu Yuxi's banishment as magistrate of Hezhou, he was appointed Guest of the Heir Apparent (太子賓客), a third rank position. As a man who had survived his long political distress, Liu wrote this poem to Bai to express his feelings.[67] To understand its implication, we have to ask: what is "the former party of Ganling"? Ganling alludes to Filial Prince of Qinghe, Liu Qing (清河孝王劉慶, 78–106) of the Han Dynasty,[68] who was for a time appointed Heir Apparent. However, Empress Dowager Dou substituted his brother Liu Zhao for him. When Liu Zhao succeeded to the throne as Emperor He (r. 89–105), he treated Liu Qing very amiably. After Emperor He's death, it was Liu Qing's son, Liu You, who came to the throne as Emperor An (r. 107–125). Subsequently, Emperor An honored Liu Qing's tomb as Ganling, where Ganling County was established. Another account of this term is the following: Du Mi (杜密, fl. 150–160), a native of Ganling, had a large number of followers. Du's fellow townsman Fang Zhi (房植, fl. 150–160), the magistrate of He'nan, also enjoyed great fame at the time. The retainers of the two households took each other as objects of mockery and jealousy, and developed a mutual hostility. The two men from Ganling and their followers were known as the Southern and the Northern Party of Ganling.[69]

In the historical context in which the poem was composed, Liu Yuxi evidently referred to all those participating in Yongzhen Reform as "the former party of Ganling." He did this because, during the short period when the reforming party headed by Wang Shuwen (王叔文, 752–806) was in power, the reigning Emperor was Shunzong, who supported the new policies of the reforming party and was forced by the eunuchs to abdicate in his son's favor, dying soon after. Shunzong's role in the royal succession bore a strong resemblance to Liu Qing's. Hence, Liu Yuxi ingeniously chose this historical allusion to express his idea. He used Liu Qing to point to Shunzong; and with "the former party of Ganling," he referred to those who had taken part in

Yongzhen Reform—by the time Liu wrote his poem (821), almost all of them had died, with the exception of Liu himself. In the same way, the Southern and the Northern parties of Ganling in the late Han resembled the Niu and the Li Factions of the Late Tang, being opposed to each other in regard to almost all important decisions at court, especially those involving the eunuch problem. Briefly, Liu's allusion indicates, in a way, that the Late Tang factional strife had its origin in Yongzhen Reform.

If Liu was one member of the "former party of Ganling," while Wen called himself the "junior party of Ganling," they must have belonged to the same political faction. If Liu's self-label came from his involvement with the Yongzhen Reform, Wen's must also have to do with this same political event. Junior by a generation, Wen was too young to be a member of the "former party of Ganling," so when identifying himself with the Yongzhen Reform participants, he called himself the "junior." If he is one of the "junior party," a senior member of the "former party" is implied, that is, his late father. As a result of eunuch interference in all document drafting, few materials revealing the hidden truth of the Reform and the subsequent Niu-Li factional strife have survived. The names of many who had a role in the events are not recorded. Taking all these together, it is not far-fetched to regard Wen's father as a participant in, or at the least a supporter of, the Reform. Only from such a perspective can Wen's life long bitter hatred of the eunuchs be understood.

Liu Yuxi played a considerable role in the formation of Wen's personality. In Liu's works, there are more than ten poems and prose works addressed to or written for Li Cheng,[70] the man who, as Wen's professional teacher, had exercised an immense influence on Wen's personality and political orientation. The friendship between Li Cheng and Liu Yuxi may in a way reveal Li's attitude toward the Yongzhen Reform, and suggest influences that Wen received from his teacher.

Though they did not have much chance to be together, Liu Yuxi and Li Cheng maintained a friendship for more than forty years, throughout the difficult time of Liu's exile, when many of his friends kept their distance from him for fear of being implicated in political trouble. The two friends became acquainted in Chang'an in the eleventh year of the Zhenyuan era (795). Liu passed the Presented Scholar Examination in 795 and Li was the Principal Graduate (狀元) of 796. During the time of the Yongzhen Reform, Li was promoted from the position of Investigating Censor to that of Vice Director of the Bureau of Waterways and Irrigation (水部員外郎).[71] Liu's poems reveal that, in the tenth and fifteenth years of Yuanhe (814 and 819), the first year of Changqing (820), and the fifth and eighth years of Dahe (831 and 834), Liu and Li exchanged poems. Li Cheng at least sympathized with the Yongzhen policies, as can be seen from his attitude toward Liu Yuxi and Liu Zongyuan. In the year following Liu Zongyuan's death in 814, Liu Yuxi wrote on Li Cheng's behalf a "Condolence Essay Written for the Grand Master Li of Ezhou as an Offering for the Supernumerary Gentleman Liu" (為鄂州李大夫祭柳員外文),[72] which includes a full account of the friendship between Liu Zongyuan and Li Cheng. The two men had passed the Erudition and Eloquence Examination (博學宏詞科) together in the twelfth year of Zhenyuan (796), and became Proofreaders of the Academy of Scholarly Worthies (集賢院校書) at the same time. Then they worked together as Defenders of Lantian County (藍田尉) before both were promoted to the post of Investigating Censor. Above all, both men shared the same political ideals. That is why the essay, although written by Liu Yuxi, praises Liu Zongyuan for his political attainments as well as for his literary achievements, and even expresses a determination to raise Liu Zongyuan's orphan as his own son. Since Li was the good friend of the two Lius, the two most talented participants in Yongzhen Reform, his political stance regarding the event can be deduced. As a royal scion and minister of great importance who served the Tang Empire for about half a century, Li Cheng certainly saw fully the problems of the Li-Tang Dynasty, especially the disasters brought about by the eunuchs. Like Bai Juyi, Li in his later career had adopted a self-protecting philosophy when confronted with turmoil of the age, but this political pose never prevented him from having a decisive say at crucial moments. Wen's choice of Li Cheng as his teacher surely had to do with Li's political orientation and personality.

In summation, Wen Tingyun was born into an aristocratic family, which was connected by marriage to the imperial clan and enjoyed great privilege and renown for several generations, continuing until the time of his infancy. However, the family had gradually lost its distinction. And after Wen's father's death as a victim of the eunuchs' power, the family fell into disgrace. This alteration left a deep impression on the boy Wen Tingyun, and from a very early age he felt impelled to restore his family's glory and to contribute significantly to effect the revitalization of the empire. Confronted with the reality that the eunuchs monopolized all state power and blocked his way to success, and that even the emperors were under the eunuchs' yoke, Wen faced enormous difficulties in achieving his ambitious goal. If Wen was to succeed in doing anything, he would have to pay a much higher price, and follow a much more tortuous path, than anyone else, in spite his seeming advantages of talent and social connection. With this in mind, let us explore his early life.

Chapter Two

Wen's Birth Year

A MOST ABSTRUSE ALLUSION TO THE EUNUCHS

As we have seen in chapter 1, eunuchs played an extremely important role in shaping the family's fate from the beginning of Wen's life. Throughout Wen's life, eunuchs did remain an obstacle precluding him from attaining any political success. Although Wen often responded with animosity and anxiety to the eunuchs' acts of sabotage, we can never find the word *eunuch* in his works. If he needed to mention them, he did so with rarely used abstruse and misleading historical allusions or subtle metaphors. To clear the way for further research and avoid digressions, I shall first unravel one of his most difficult allusions and clarify why Wen had to refer to the eunuchs in such an ambiguous manner. However, before proceeding to this task, let us first examine a couplet in "Angling by the Pond of the Xue Family" (薛氏池垂釣, WFQ, j. 9), to see how he alludes to the eunuchs using "outspoken" terms.

> Zhu Yu vainly stole the water of the Imperial Ditch, 朱瑀空偷御溝水，
> "Brocade scales" with red tail belong to Yan Guang. 錦鱗紅尾屬嚴光。

Of all examples where Wen refers to the eunuchs this is the clearest. Zhu Yu was a eunuch of the Eastern Han (25–220) who, like the Late Tang eunuchs, amassed great wealth and even channeled water from the Imperial Ditch into his own pond, in defiance of the royal authority.[1] Yan Guang, a famous recluse, had been a classmate and friend of Emperor Guangwu (r. 25–57). When the emperor asked him to serve in the court, he refused with the excuse that he preferred a life as a recluse. Here the poem seems to say that Wen was only commenting on the Han eunuch Zhu and the recluse Yan, with no evident interest in the affairs of his own time, although he is actually strongly condemning the eunuchs who forced him to into reclusion. Thus, we see why and how Wen availed himself of historical allusions to refer to something he would not express in clear terms. He wanted to make indirect some of his most pointed castigations of the eunuchs. The allusion, often possessing more than one explanation, can serve just this purpose. This peculiar trope of Chinese classic versification, though in ordinary cases highly effective, does a disservice to some of Wen's poems, when the allusions he uses are too uncommon for ordinary readers to follow. That Wen's most important autobiographical poems have remained, by and large, ignored or misunderstood by scholars illustrates his "failure" in this respect, since few readers possess both the knowledge and patience to make sense of them.

Now we turn to a very obscure allusion to the eunuchs, an allusion to Du Zhi (杜摯), in the following couplet from Wen's "Hundred-Rhyme Poem." It intends to say that (from the outset of his office-seeking life) Wen was faced with such a predicament:

52 In my loves and hates I took precautions against Du Zhi, 愛憎防杜摯，
In my laments and sighs I felt melancholy, as did Yang Zhu. 悲嘆似楊朱。

Even before we know to what the name alludes, we know that Du Zhi must refer to Wen's enemies (most probably the eunuchs), even though it is an insinuating reference to them. We must determine what kind of a figure this Du Zhi is, since this will enable us to identify the precise connotation of Wen's poems as well as some prose passages. Among all pre-Tang historical characters, we find only two men bearing this name, both mentioned in someone else's biography and referred to very briefly.[2] In both cases, the Du Zhis must be excluded as a referent, as neither of them seems to have anything to do with the context. Thus, two possibilities suggest themselves: some other Du Zhi (related to the eunuchs) alluded to by Wen was recorded in a historical text that is no longer extant; or there may be a textual corruption, and the name Du Zhi was originally something else. Further investigation verifies the latter possibility.

In Wen's "Epistle Presented to Prime Minister Pei" (we will study all its texts), we find another mention of the same Du Zhi:

> Later on, I spent many years at one or another Marquis' before I traveled to the valley of the Huai River, where I presented myself by writing letters, and sought recognition holding a calling card. But I had not expected that Du Zhi was to make a false charge and Zang Cang to harbor a bitter hatred against me.

In this context, Du Zhi is clearly the same kind of person as was Zang Cang, who, fortunately, is easier to identify. It alludes to a story of Duke Ping of Lu[3] (魯平公): The duke was about to give audience to Mencius (孟子, 390–305 B.C.) when his favorite, Zang Cang (臧倉) by name, stopped him from doing so by speaking evil of Mencius. Here Zang Cang was a favorite (嬖人) of the duke, analogous to the eunuchs who were habitually regarded as playthings or house-slaves of the monarch. So, we come nearer to our expected conclusion: besides representing Wen's enemy, the Du Zhi in question must have been a figure similar to the eunuchs.

In "Hundred-Rhyme Poem," the twenty-eighth rhyme provides decisive evidence for the identification of Du Zhi. Since Wen directs his castigation mainly at the eunuchs all through this poem, his manner of using historical and literary allusions should, very naturally, be consistent from beginning to end. Between the couplet cited above and the one we are going to discuss next there is just such conformity, as they both allude to the eunuchs by making use of the same historical episode. The difference is that the former alludes to the name Du Zhi, while the following one alludes to what the man Du Zhi did:

28 Letting drop my bow case, I was ashamed of finishing the cup, 垂櫜羞盡爵，
Raising the goblet, they insulted me for curving the bow. 揚觶辱彎弧。

Both lines in this couplet consist of two verb-object units, with a verb inserted in between. The couplet is unusual in that the four verb-object units designate men who act, instead of only an action, as would be more common.

"Letting drop the bow case" has its origin in the following classic text: "Wu Ju, knowing that they had taken precautions against him, asked to enter by letting drop his bow case" (伍舉知其有備也，請垂櫜而入), and Du Yu's annotation to this is: "To let the bow case drop shows that he had no bow with him" (垂櫜示無弓也).[4] As a term related to archery, a metaphor in common use for literary competition in Tang poetry, this reference is used here ironically for Wen himself, the subject of the line, to show that he had no ambition or energy to declare himself against the injustice he suffered upon being rejected as a Presented Scholar. "Finishing the cup" may refer to himself as one who drank a cup as a forfeit (because of failure), as expressed in my translation, or more preferably, to those successful Presented Scholar who drank their full. The first line thus gives a meaningful account of how he was too perplexed and ashamed to face those who had passed, despite his achieving an "Equivalent to Passing" (等第) in 839.

"Raising the goblet" alludes to the following story:[5] Viscount Zhi Dao (知悼子) died, and was not buried yet. Duke Ping of Jin (晉平公) had one of his drinking parties with his musician Shi Kuang (師曠) and favorite sycophant Li Diao (李調) attending, and enjoyed striking the bell. Now, the royal cook (膳宰) Du Kui (杜蕢) entered from outside. After some arguments, the cook succeeded in proving that both Shi and Li were to blame for their dereliction of duty; because, on a day when an important minister had just died, they failed to dissuade the duke from drinking. In consequence, both were given a forfeit of wine. Then the cook proceeded to give himself a forfeit since he had overstepped his official responsibility by speaking out in this way. Upon hearing and seeing all this, the duke said: "I, too, am to blame. Pour the wine and drink me the forfeit;" upon which, "Du Kui, after washing it, raised the goblet [to the duke for a forfeit]." Wen's teacher Li Cheng once also used this allusion:

"As to a case where *The Rites* failed to scorn what it should, I think about Du Kui's raising up the goblet" (禮失所譏，想杜蕢之揚觶).[6] Like his teacher, and unlike most orthodox commentators of the classics,[7] Wen took Du Kui as a negative figure, representing the usurping eunuchs of his time, because Du Kui's post, royal cook, was always taken by eunuchs throughout the imperial times. It was not by sheer coincidence that on another occasion Wen used "royal cook" to speak of the eunuchs: in "Epistle Presented to the Academician-Drafter" (上學士舍人啓), Wen says, "I was downcast and haggard, at the bottommost of retainers; humiliated and distressed, in the presence of the royal cook" (委悴館人之末，摧殘膳宰之前). Therefore, "raising the goblet" alludes to the royal cook Du Kui, a disguised appellation for the eunuchs.

"Curving the bow" also points to the doer (Wen himself) through an allusion to Guan Zhong (管仲, ?–645 B.C.). To annotate this line, the Qing annotator Gu Sili correctly quoted Ban Gu's (32–92) "Rhapsody on Communion with the Mystical" (幽通賦): "Guan, curving his bow, was to shoot his foe, and the foe, after ascending the throne, became his own fulfillment" (管彎弧欲斃仇兮，仇作后而成己).[8] Ban's remark again contains an allusion.[9] Before Guan Zhong served Duke Huan of Qi (齊桓公, ?–643 B.C.), he had been the Mentor of Prince Jiu, Duke Huan's brother. When the two brothers were vying for the throne, Guan Zhong in a battle shot an arrow straight at Huan, and almost took his life. Later Prince Jiu was defeated and killed by Huan. At the recommendation of his bosom friend, Bao Shuya, Huan's Mentor, Guan Zhong was spared and promoted as chief minister. Wen had reasons to use this allusion to Guan Zhong to mean himself, for, as a loyal attendant of Emperor Wenzong's (r. 827–836) Heir Li Yong, he could have never suspected that it would be Emperor Wuzong (r. 840–846), one of Wenzong's inconspicuous younger brothers, who would succeed to the throne, placed there with the evil-intentioned support of the eunuchs. In his speeches or in the previous year's (839) examination paper, he may have expressed his hostility toward the eunuchs' monopolization of the imperial succession, a hostility that could easily have been interpreted by the eunuchs as blaspheming the succeeding monarch. At a time when the throne was shifting, the eunuchs used Wen's devotion to the former emperor as a weapon to thwart his possible promotion in the new court. By alluding to "curving the bow," Wen likened himself to Guan Zhong, declaring his allegiance to the new emperor as a means of justifying himself.

Now it is clear that the Du Zhi (杜摯) so baffling us should be Du Kui (杜蕢). It is likely that the Chinese ideograph *kui* (蕢) was corrupted and mistakenly discerned as *zhi* (摯), as Du Zhi (杜摯) is a better-known name. The corrupted form appeared as early as in the Song Dynasty encyclopedia *Wenyuan Yinghua*, which includes most of Wen's extant epistles. In every instance, the name Du Zhi must refer to the eunuchs in the context.

Through this example we come to realize how, under the terrifying pressure of the eunuch rule, Wen made use of his erudition to impart the truth while avoiding adverse consequences. Because the way in which Wen composed his poetry and prose works is peculiarly logical, once we succeed in discovering the origins of his diction and allusions, the factual threads are laid bare, enabling us to unravel the enigmas of these works with more confidence. I determine Wen's birth year in much a similar manner.

THE YEAR OF HAVING THE WAY AND EPISTLE PRESENTED TO PRIME MINSTER PEI

The accepted birth year of Wen Tingyun, 812, was worked out by Xia Chengtao in his "Chronicle of Wen Feiqing" published in the 1930s and reaffirmed by Gu Xuejie's "Revision and Supplement to 'Biographies of Wen Tingyun' in the two *Tang Histories*"[10] published in 1940s. However, Xia meant it as no more than a guess[11] and it would have been overthrown long ago but for the fact that it is the earliest study of this difficult and seemingly unrewarding topic, and that thereafter not many adequate studies have been focused on it. However, establishing Wen's true birth year is of crucial importance in gaining a correct starting point for research on his life and poetry. Without an accurate time reference we will be unable to understand many of Wen's works, and it will become all the more difficult to reevaluate Wen properly.

Gu reached his conclusion mainly on account of the following couplet in "Fifty-Rhyme Poem": "When Ji Shao was a lad with hairs streaming down his forehead / It was the year Shan Tao began his official service." Taking this couplet at face value, we can be certain only that by the time Wen had audience with the so-called Chancellor Li (李僕射, referred to by the allusion to Shan Tao), he was a boy aged about eight years.[12] Wen's birth year cannot be determined unless we can pinpoint who Li was, in which year Wen had his audience with him, and finally what age Wen had in mind by the year "when Ji Shao was a lad with hairs streaming down his forehead."

Unfortunately, "Fifty-Rhyme Poem," with its archaic allusions, does not present an easy account for such identifications. One must first decode the poem's difficult language and work out a picture of Li's life. Then one must compare this with various biographies of men bearing the surname Li who had an official position of chancellor and was in charge of Huainan Circuit, in order to find the one that is identical with the picture. Such a task can be fruitless, because there was more than one "Chancellor Li" roughly fitting the inexact definition of the "Ji Shao-Shan Tao" allusion. Each of these will elicit a different conclusion. Moreover, in ancient China, only when a young man arrived at the age of twenty (弱冠) did he have to put his hair up. Aged either above or under twenty, boys could always have "hairs streaming down his forehead." Thus, the phrase indicates no exact age, only that the subject is still a child. We have no reason to suppose the age it denotes is eight, even though it has to do with Ji Shao's childhood. Thus, we cannot be sure that Wen had such a number in mind when he availed himself of the image. Simply put, all academic efforts, including Gu's, to use this phrase to calculate Wen's birth year come to little fruition.[13]

In order to ascertain Wen's birth year, Xia and most Chinese scholars touching on the topic strain at this same poetic hint. It is only natural that their conclusions vary considerably.[14] With respect to this issue, we will finally arrive at the conclusion that the Li here referred to is Li Shen, that Wen saw him in 806, and that therefore Wen was born sometime around the turn of the century. Since using only this poem to determine who the chancellor was will lead to unnecessary digressions and prove fruitless, we must turn to other extant sources to find more solid evidence on which to build our conclusion. By happy coincidence, we do have another important hint, "the Year of Having the Way," in the following epistle.

Wen's epistles, in a manner characteristic of the Late Tang parallel prose style, are dense and full of literary and historical allusions. Most of them are saturated with important information about the major events of his life, which any study of Wen's life and poetry cannot afford to ignore. Therefore, in dealing with this epistle, we have no choice but to decipher the whole text. The exposed information not only will contribute toward a clarification of his birth year and an understanding of Wen's situation in 839, but also will provide an outline for further exploration of Wen's life in the chapters to follow.

"THE EPISTLE PRESENTED TO PRIME MINISTER PEI" (上裴相公啓)

Your humble servant wishes to say: I hear that he who wants to offer a precious treasure must first go to Marquis Sui and Bian He, and he who hopes to cure his disease must ask instructions from Lord Cang and Doctor Bianque.[15] Without an unusually powerful potion, it is hard to expect a miraculous cure. I have now come to the Year of Having the Way,[16] while still harboring the remorse of a wronged innocent. Hence even though I perish, I will become a miasmal cloud, to disturb your most impartial Excellency [by my indignation], and I will make the voice of a wronged man, to resound forever in the history of unjust verdicts. For such matters the princes, dukes and ministers have raised their righteous indignation, while men of rectitude and ambition can only sigh and shed tears (某啓: 聞效珍者先詣隋和，蠲養者必求倉扁。苟無懸解，難語奇功。至于有道之年，猶抱無辜之恨。斯則沒為瘴氣，來撓至平；敷作冤聲，將垂不極。此亦王公大人之所慷慨，義夫志士之所噓欷).

My nature, truly, is that of an idiot, and my personality one of stubbornness. With regard to succeeding to my ancestor's undertakings, I am ashamed of comparing myself to Kong Lin, distant in the past; and in taking up the family tradition, I am not the equal of Zhang Dai nearer to the present.[17] Since the days when my ancestors were bestowed imperial favor and conferred fiefs, our family had enjoyed everlasting glory, which was inscribed on the imperial tripod. Then I took my registered residence in Liaoxi, before I studied the classics in Jixia.[18] Thereupon I looked up to and exhausted the lore my teacher handed down to me,[19] and engaged in the composition of poetry and prose. I was hoping to sew up the broken drapery of the Confucian House, and to restore the magnificence and grandeur of the Constant Norm (某性實顓蒙，器惟頑固。纂修祖業，遠愧孔琳；承襲門風，近慚張岱。自頃爰田錫寵，鏤鼎傳芳。占數遼西，横經稷下。因得仰窮師法，竊弄篇題。思欲紐儒門之絕帷，恢常典之休烈).

Soon after, it happened that I was reduced to a grief-stricken traveling orphan, hardly able to manage my daily coarse food.[20] Like Chumo, having no comforter, I hopelessly sighed at night, and like Xiuling, running out of rice, with what was I to make my breakfast?[21] Later on, I spent many years at one or another Marquis' before I traveled to the valley of the Huai River, where I presented myself [to them] by writing letters, and sought recognition holding a calling card. But I had not expected that Du Zhi was to make a false charge and Zang Cang to harbor a bitter hatred against me. In consequence, the local magistrates became increasingly hostile toward me, regardless of their past friendship, and, in response, those in power at court added slanders to my distress, yielding to the "decree." A forsaken orphan with an insecure life, I was crudely bullied and mistreated. My route of flying and galloping [political advance] was blocked, and my means for drinking and pecking [daily life] was impeded. It is an unjust charge that I ever shot [blaspheming] blood, and there is no way for me to call [the attention of] Heaven.[22] Such being the case, the sagacious ministers have shown their commiseration for me, and many an official has heard of it. Nevertheless, all have vainly sighed over the case, and none could exonerate me of the wrong charge (俄屬羈孤牽軫，藜藿難虞。處默無衾，徒然夜嘆；修齡絕米，安事晨炊！既而羈齒侯門，旅游淮上。投書自達，懷刺求知。豈期杜摯相傾，臧倉見嫉。守土者以忘情積惡，當權者以承意中傷。直視孤危，横相陵阻。絕飛馳之路，塞飲啄之途。射血有冤，叫天無路。此乃通人見憫，多士具聞。徒共興嗟，靡能昭雪).

In my humble opinion, in the first years when Emperor Xuanzong ascended the heavenly throne, His Majesty's royal heart immediately came to be filled with compassion for the people. Thereupon, he took to correcting drawbacks and mistakes and redressing the wronged when Prime Minister Liu helped bring forth the imperial edicts, and the Duke Xu Su added radiance to the royal plan.[23] In the five decades [of his reign], customs and mores among the people could not be more honest and pure. Nowadays, however, when neither the flying nor the swimming [various officials] could have their peaceful settlement, and both the rainfall and the sunlight cannot follow each other in harmony; every man and woman in the country heaves grievous sighs, and each community and each village is in melancholy dejection. To look forward to a prosperous time of restored order, all must depend upon a great statesman with statecraft like you (竊見玄宗皇帝初融景命，遽惻宸襟。收拭瑕疵，申明枉結。劉丞相導揚優詔，蘇許公潤色昌謨。五十年間，風俗敦厚。逮及翔泳未安其所，雨陽不得其和。匹夫匹婦之吁嗟，一聚一鄉之幽郁。欲期昭泰，必仰洪鈞).

Now if I advance in my official career, I harbor fear for my life; if I retreat, I will have nothing to fall back upon. With my name secretly listed for arrest, I could hardly benefit from imperial favor. Together with the embers I am to be thrown away [like a burned zither], and compared with insects [that also have their share of imperial favor], I am more hopeless.[24] There are parallel highways and thoroughfares, but I am weeping at a dead end; there are the sun and the moon hanging high in the sky, and it is only I that am trapped in the darkness (某進抱疑危，退無依據。暗處囚拘之列，不沾渙汗之私。與煨燼而俱捐，比昆蟲而絕望。則是康莊並軌，偏哭於窮途；日月懸空，獨障於豐蔀).

I know your Excellency Prime Minister did meritorious service to Yao and set up valuable feats in assisting Yu. All people have benefited from your kindness, and none was forced to go against its nature. If you were to heave a compassionate sigh when meeting me on the road, you would then cast loose the horse yoked at the right; or should you have heard my song from tapping on my sword, you would move me away from the second class room.[25] I divine for myself by looking on the wind, and am convinced that you will follow the example of antiquity. Since this Way of Confucianism is not false, pure and bright governance will not be far away. I respectfully hold in my arms my prose, poetry and rhapsody works, each in one *juan*, all presented to Your Excellency. My scrolls and papers are in poor condition, and my calligraphy and handwriting are dense and in a mess, therewith I venture to beg your condescending attention, while my anxiety and yearning are beyond expression (伏以相公致堯業裕，佐禹功高。百姓咸被其仁，一物不違于性。倘或在途興嘆，解彼右驂；彈劍有聞，遷于代舍。瞻風自卜，與古為徒。此道不誣，貞明未遠。謹以文賦詩各一卷率以抱獻。縑緗儉陋，造寫繁蕪。干冒尊高，無任惶灼).

This epistle offers a brief, if not clear, description of what had happened to Wen's family and to himself up to the time he presented it to Pei. It concentrates on telling the story of how Wen found himself in a dilemma, to the degree that his name was secretly listed by the eunuchs for arrest and even execution, as a result of the role he had played in the political arena. After introducing the reasons why he, in his desperation, had come to Prime Minister Pei for help, Wen recapitulates what had happened to him by enumerating his experiences in the following order:

1. He attended the National University of Luoyang coming from Liaoxi, so-called.
2. A misfortune befell his family, and he found himself reduced to a traveling orphan, no longer with the means to support his life, much less his studies.

   On the occasion of presenting an epistle to a senior guardian, Wen made his point concisely. It was inappropriate to give a full-length account of what had happened to him, and Prime Minister Pei was presumed to have known what was left unsaid. Suggestively, after mentioning his Luoyang University days, in "Hundred-Rhyme Poem" Wen describes the situation that forced him to embark on a precarious office-seeking career, in the following couplet, which can be compared to the account above.

   The noisy swallows were shrieking on the short eaves, 短檐喧語燕，
   While a hungry squirrel fell from a tall tree. 高木落飢鼯。

   Though the metaphor is intricate, its implication is easy to see: in addition to describing a scene, it indicates that Wen experienced a fall in his family's social status. The shrieking swallows in the short eaves remind us of those who vied for wealth and fame on an unsteady and crowded stage, where our poet Wen had to begin his political career. The hungry squirrel is the natural counterpart for himself, because he had "fallen" from a relatively high position to lead his precarious life. In any event, Wen was forced to give up his studies, presumably because of some fall in his family's fortunes. Considering that his father died long before Wen quit the University, we can infer that at this time the remaining family prerogatives he still enjoyed were stripped away, although we cannot infer further.
3. The result was that Wen Tingyun began a life of wandering all over the country, "spent many years at one or another Marquis'."[26] From the very beginning of his vagrant life, he had to be on guard against the tyranny of the eunuchs, referred to as Du Zhi (Kui).
4. Next, he "traveled the valley of the Huai River."[27]

   Fate decreed a face-to-face meeting between Wen and the eunuchs on a narrow path. The result was miserable suffering for the poet. This is the first time Wen was personally involved in some incident with the eunuchs, the cause of a series of subsequent setbacks and adversities.
5. It was some time after this confrontation with the eunuchs that something more complex and serious put Wen into greater straits.[28] The injustice he

suffered forced him to turn to the powerful and friendly Prime Minister Pei for support, to enable him to survive his crisis and allow him to pass the year's civil recruitment examination.[29]

In this study we will follow the order of topics contained in this epistle. Now we will commence with a determination of Wen's birth year.

Since Wen clearly says his age is forty-two by alluding to "Having the Way [Guo]," the key to identifying his birth year is to date this epistle, and while doing so, we will also identify Prime Minister Pei. From Wen's own accounts, we know it was while traveling in the Huai River valley that Wen encountered the eunuchs' attack. What Wen refers to here is the Jianghuai Incident that occurred in the first year of Kaicheng (836). Therefore, it was a certain length of time after the Jianghuai Incident (836) that Wen presented this epistle to Prime Minister Pei.

Wen gained access to the Heir Apparent through the recommendation of his minister teacher Li Cheng, in the autumn of second year of Kaicheng (837), and served the Heir until the boy's sudden death in the tenth month of the following year (838). This experience is also subtly implied in this epistle. It must have been after his attendance upon the Heir Apparent that Wen presented this epistle to Pei; otherwise, he would not have stated that "If I advance in my official career, I harbor fear for my life; if I retreat, I will have nothing to fall back upon." To be offered the opportunity to attend the Heir, thus being within possible direct access of the emperor, was for Wen an unusual advance and unexpected imperial favor, even though it led to a tragedy. Moreover, in the face of such a highly confidential appointment, Wen's sense of honor called forth his courage to "advance" without hesitation. After the Heir's death, however, Wen could not escape from his political entanglements, but had to brave all the dangers the eunuchs presented to him. The situation he describes here is thus a reflection of the reality he faced after the Heir's death in the tenth month of 838.

Although in this epistle Wen made no explicit mention of his attendance upon the Heir, this information is implied in the context. Prime Minister Pei, who was especially concerned with the issue of the imperial heir [as we will see immediately after we identify him],[30] would understand this and not need a precise reference to it. Wen praised the governance of Emperor Xuanzong and attributed his own misfortune to the situation in which "neither the flying nor the swimming could have their peaceful settlement, and both the rainfall and the sunlight cannot follow each other in harmony." This is a circuitous castigation of the eunuchs who had been in the ascendant ever since Xuanzong's reign, and hence a mild criticism of Xuanzong himself.[31] After that time the eunuchs usurped more and more power, until they seized control of the Divine Strategy Army (神策軍), during Emperor Dezong's reign (785–805). Eunuch command of the imperial army finally precipitated the disaster of the Sweet Dew Incident of 835. Both the Heir Apparent's death

(838) and Wen's sorry plight represented in this epistle were, in a sense, an aftermath of the Sweet Dew Incident.

Adding to our argument, at the end of this epistle, Wen says: "I respectfully hold in my arms my prose, poetry and rhapsody works, each in one *juan*, all presented to Your Excellency." This is termed "warming the scroll" (溫卷), by means of which Late Tang literati sought to impress those who were politically powerful and influence them to speak on their behalf to the examination administrators. In fact, in the autumn of the fourth year of Kaicheng (839), for the first time in his life, Wen sat for the examination held by the Metropolitan Prefecture and succeeded in obtaining an "Equivalent to Passing." Unless this epistle had succeeded in enlisting the help of Prime Minister Pei, any gain in the examination would have been impossible for Wen. Therefore, this epistle must have been presented to Pei no later than the tenth month of the fourth year of Kaicheng when the examination of the Metropolitan Prefecture was held.[32] Thus, we can date it to a time between the tenth month of 838 and the autumn of 839.

The only Prime Minister bearing the surname Pei who meets such specific criteria was Pei Du (765–839).[33] Pei Du was one of the most outstanding prime ministers in the Late Tang period, famous for his service to the Tang court beginning in the time of Emperor Xianzong (r. 805-820), during which he led the victorious military campaign that crushed the recalcitrant warlord Wu Yuanji (吳元濟, 783–817) and laid the groundwork for the Yuanhe Restoration.[34] In the succeeding reigns of emperors Muzong (r. 821–824), Jingzong (r. 825–827), and Wenzong (r. 827–840), Pei distinguished himself by most effective local governance and fierce allegiance to the court. Wen's remark in the epistle—"I know Your Excellency the Prime Minister did meritorious service to Yao and set up ample feats in assisting Yu"—is nearer to hard truth than to conventional flattery. As the most influential veteran court official at the time, Pei was the only man who had the power to assist Wen in some way, by offering "an unusually powerful potion."[35]

According to his biographies, Pei was sent out to be Military Commissioner of Taiyuan in the fifth month of the second year of Kaicheng. "You just sleep there and guard well the north gate for me" (為朕臥鎮北門可矣), Emperor Wenzong bade him when Pei begged for retirement. In the twelfth month of the following year, Pei was called back to the capital to be Director of the Secretariat; and in the fourth year of Kaicheng, "In the first month, Du came [from Taiyuan] for a court audience." In the third month of the same year, he died, three months after his last audience[36] (the first month of that year, 839, was an intercalary month). If we reconsider Wen's statement that "I now come to the year of Having the Way (42)," we believe more firmly that it was in the first month of 839 that Wen took the occasion to present this epistle to Pei. According to the Chinese method of calculating age, therefore, Wen was born in the year 798. This conclusion is identical with the one inferred from the "Ji Shao-Shan Tao-Ji Kang" allusion, and we have more evidence to support it.

Taken separately, the individual statements may seem confusing and ambiguous, but considered together, they are instrumental in bringing to light the major events in Wen's life. This determination is applicable in explaining any of Wen's experiences and can thus withstand any challenge.

OTHER "CIRCUMSTANTIAL EVIDENCE"

"Biography of Pei Du" in JTS also relates that, in his late years, because of the literati-officials' failure to curb the eunuchs' power, "after dealing with his official routines, often he spent all his time carousing with the poets Bai Juyi and Liu Yuxi, chanting vehemently and chatting unreservedly, and indulged in writing poems, drinking wine, enjoying music and reading books. Most of the renowned men of letters of the time came to join him" (視事之餘，與詩人白居易劉禹錫酣醉終日，高歌放言，以詩酒琴書自樂。當時名士，皆從之游). For a time Wen was among Pei's retainers, although we are uncertain whether this was effected through Liu Yuxi. We are able to derive a substantial message from the following poems:

"TWO ELEGIES FOR THE DIRECTOR OF THE SECRETARIAT, LORD PEI"[37]
(中書令裴公挽歌詞二首, j. 3, WFQ)

You were a Wang Jian, a model of virtue and style,	王儉風華首，
You were a Xiao He, a leading subject of the Empire.	蕭何社稷臣。
As a cloth-robe commoner from Danyang,	丹陽布衣客，
You spent your life in the Lotus-isle till white-haired.	蓮渚白頭人。[38]
Inscriptions engraved when Mount Yanran was in dusk,	銘勒燕山暮，
And a stele sunk into River Han in its spring tide.	碑沉漢水春。
From now on I vainly drink and eat my fill,	從今虛醉飽，
But will no longer defile your carriage-mat.	無復污車茵。

In identifying "the Director of the Secretariat" as Pei Du, we must emphasize the fact that in Wen's time Du was the only man bearing the surname Pei and this official title that we can take into consideration.

In the first two couplets Wen compares Pei with famous Prime Ministers such as Wang Jian (452–489) of the Southern Qi, Xiao He of the Han (?–193 B.C.), and Tao Hongjing (陶弘景, 452–536) of the Liang Dynasty, in order to praise his personality and political achievements. Then Wen stresses Pei's unquestionable role in crushing Wu Yuanji, the treasonous Military Commissioner, by alluding to Dou Xian (?–92) and Du Yu:[39] Dou, after defeating the Huns, inscribed his military merits on Mount Yanran, and Du made two steles to assure his reputation for posterity, one sunk in River Han, and the other set up on the summit of Mount Xian. Despite the fact that the "Monument for Quelling Huaixi" (平淮西碑) written by Han Yu had to be rewritten by Duan Wenchang[40] (段文昌, 773–835) as a consequence of factional strife, Wen's poetry asserts that Pei's contribution in winning the war is indelible. In the last couplet, by mourning Pei's death with deep grief, Wen obviously revealed himself to be a retainer under Pei's patronage.[41]

(Poem Two)

With your arrow flying, the evil star fell,	箭下妖星落，
In the blast, the killing air turned back.	風前殺氣回。
When the State's Redolence, Director Xun, departs,	國香荀令去，
For the Tower's moonlight, Lord Yu will never return.	樓月庾公來。[42]
The jade seal will eventually be in no danger,	玉璽終無慮，
But your golden case will not be opened, forever.	金縢竟不開。
I vainly sigh over the avenue for recommending worthy men,	空嗟薦賢路，
As fragrant herbs are laying waste on the Yan Terrace.	芳草滿燕臺。

The second poem begins by restating the military feats Pei had performed for his country. Wen also recalls Pei's elegant manners when he was with his subordinates and retainers. In Wen's terms, by means of Pei's efforts and influences, the royal jade seal, that is, the imperial power, was kept from danger. But Pei died at a time when the Tang court needed him badly. The allusion "golden case"[43] functions here as a metaphor for Pei's stature, which matched that of Duke Zhou. According to Pei's biographies, Emperor Wenzong in his last years increasingly appreciated Pei's loyalty and consulted Pei about everything important. He even wrote a poem expressing his admiration for and confidence in Pei—an extraordinary honor—just before Pei's death. As with the last couplet in Poem One, the last couplet in this poem tells of Wen's own relation to Pei. From it we can infer that Wen once had won Pei's promise of recommendation,[44] but now had grievously lost it.

In the two elegies, Wen does not limit himself to praising Pei's contributions (especially the feat of crushing Wu Yuanji). He also expresses his sorrow at losing a good guardian who knew him well and would, but for an untimely death, probably have helped him advance in officialdom and contribute to the revival of the country.

Comparing the "Epistle," in which Wen requested Pei to help him through his crisis, with the two poems, in which Wen admired and bemoaned the dead Pei, we conclude that "Prime Minister Pei" of the "Epistle" was certainly Pei Du. Since Wen managed to obtain an "Equivalent to Passing" in the autumn of that very year of Pei's death, we are all the more convinced that this must have been effected at Pei's recommendation. Without such a recommendation, Wen would not even have had the chance to take the examination, and "the avenue for recommending worthy men" would have been totally blocked.

Clarifying the time when Wen was married can yield further evidence to confirm the birth year we have determined. In Wen's extant works, we have three apparent statements regarding his marriage. The first one is in "Hundred-Rhyme Poem":

82 Coming as guest, the green-ants I poured, 客來斟綠蟻，
Trying to ransom a wife, on the blue-beetles I trod 妻試踏青蚨。

Even before we deal with the exact connotation of this couplet, we can say with safety that it is about his marriage, which occurred before the fifth year of Kaicheng, when he wrote the poem. Further evidence concerning Wen's marriage is in "Fifty-Rhyme Poem," written in the second year of Huichang (842):

To seek an official post, I had no appointment as that of Mao Yi, 宦無毛義檄，
In dealing with marriage, I had no money like that of Ruan Xiu, 婚乏阮修錢。

Wen reveals here that he did not have the luck of Mao Yi in getting an official post. Nor did he have the fortune of Ruan Xiu in collecting donated money for his marriage.[45] Because of poverty Ruan Xiu did not marry until he was in his forties. Wen's marriage, too, occurred very late, nearly as late as that of Ruan Xiu.

A third proof is found in his "Epistle Presented to Bureau Director Han of the Ministry of Personnel": "Like Zhongxuan, I am a traveler constantly moving; and like Zhuge, I am afraid of taking a wife too early" (仲宣之為客不休，諸葛之娶妻怕早). The comparisons of himself with Wang Can and Zhuge Liang[46] once more emphasize that his marriage took place rather late in life, when he was in his forties.

Now we turn to another important piece of evidence found in "Fifty-Rhyme Poem." The topic of the poem tells us that Chancellor Li[47] was a former senior acquaintance and friend of Wen's, and held the post of Military Commissioner of the Huainan Circuit at the time Wen presented it to him. Since its poetic account of Chancellor Li's life is in highly sophisticated language characteristic of the Late Tang literati's virtuosity, I will not bother the reader by paraphrasing the whole poem. Rather, I will pick out and study a few key lines, testifying to the accuracy of my conclusion about Wen's birth year.

First, in "Hundred-Rhyme Poem" (composed 840), after the eighteenth rhyme:

18 My answer could be "a rare playing of the lute," 對雖希鼓瑟，
So my name was passed off among those who blew the flute. 名亦濫吹竽。

We find a footnote by Wen himself: "Last autumn I sat for the Metropolitan Prefecture Examination, and got my name recommended on the supplementary list" (原注：去秋試京兆，薦名，居其副).

The couplet means that because of his excellent performance in the examination, Wen gained a passing degree, the so-called "Equivalent to Passing."[48] The footnote shows that Wen took the examination one year prior to the composition of the poem, that is, in the year 839. Thus, it tallies completely with the following record in *Tangzhiyan*, under the title "Equivalent to Passing but Failed to Pass": "In the fourth year of Kaicheng, Wen Qi" (溫岐).[49] "Fifty-Rhyme Poem," when relating the same experience of being recommended by the Metropolitan Prefecture, employs the following remarks:

Not knowing where the carp should jump,	未知魚躍地，
I was vainly ashamed to hear Deer Singing played.	空愧鹿鳴篇。
Now again it's approaching the Jixia date,	稷下期方至，
But my Zhang-Riverbank disease is not yet healed.	漳濱病未痊。

Between the two couplets, Wen inserts a footnote: "I was once recommended by the Metropolitan Prefecture, and had my name on the supplementary list" (余嘗忝京兆薦，名居其副). Then, at the end of the second couplet, Wen puts down another footnote: "For two years I have contracted a disease, hence did not respond to the local recommendation, to be examined by the office concerned" (二年抱疾，不赴鄉薦試有司).

Here the first couplet means that Wen vainly became an "Equivalent to Passing," having no chance to be really passed as a Presented Scholar. "Not knowing where the carp should jump [over the Dragon Gate]"[50] is a metaphor for Wen himself being unable to become a Presented Scholar. "Deer Singing" is the title of a poem in the *Book of Songs*, which was sung when "feasting the court officials as distinguished guests."[51] In the civil service recruitment system of the Tang, the music was used in the ceremony for accepting new Presented Scholars.[52] The so-called Jixia date should be understood as the examination date, because, every year, the universities of the state as well as of the prefectures sent their graduates as candidates for the upcoming state-managed examination. "Zhang Riverbank disease" alludes to the following lines by Liu Zhen:

I contracted a disease chronic and incurable,	余嬰沈痼疾，
And fled to the bank of the clear Zhang River.	竄身清漳濱。[53]

If Liu were only physically ill, he would not have had to flee to the bank of the Zhang River. The couplet thus shows that Liu's, and hence Wen's, disease was a political one. Therefore, the second couplet says that as the date of the year's examination again approached, certain political reasons still barred Wen from participating in it.

Establishing such context makes possible a precise understanding of the two footnotes. The first footnote merely recalls Wen's experience of being recommended in the fourth year of Kaicheng (839). The second footnote reveals that, because Wen had to flee to the south in the winter of the fifth year of Kaicheng (840), the year 840 was the first year in which he "did not respond to the local recommendation, to be examined by the office concerned." The following year, the first year of Huichang (841) is then the second year. Although the focus in each case is different, both "Hundred-Rhyme Poem" and "Fifty-Rhyme Poem" mention Wen's experience of being recommended by the Metropolitan Prefecture, while his political "disease" remained unchanged. Therefore, the "two years" must be 840 and 841, when Wen remained unable to "respond to the local recommendation." "Fifty-Rhyme Poem" also states:

In my vagrant life, I meet again the end of spring,	旅食逢春盡，
When something forces me to travel without end.	羈游為事牽。

The so-called "end of spring" could not be that of the first year of Huichang, for, at that time, he "did not respond to the local recommendation" only in the previous winter. Instead, it should be the spring of the second year of Huichang (842).

Additionally, in "Fifty-Rhyme Poem," among many laudatory descriptions of Chancellor Li's personal experiences, there are two couplets, referring to Li's official prospects, that deserve our special attention:

After having raised your wings made for soaring on high,	既矯排虛翅，
You are to hold the power of Heaven's creation.	將持造化權。
The myriad beings will look forward to your molding,	萬靈思鼓鑄，
And various talents will be subject to your cultivation.	群品待陶甄。

We can infer that Chancellor Li of Huainan was about to assume the post of Prime Minister. Li Deyu did become Prime Minister, after he left the post of Military Commissioner of Huainan Circuit with the title of the Honorary Right Chancellor (檢校右僕射), but it happened in the ninth month of the fifth year of Kaicheng, when Wen had not yet composed "Fifty-Rhyme Poem." Another Military Commissioner of Huainan, Li Shen, who replaced Li Deyu, was also a chancellor. According to Kong Wenye's "Edict for Appointing Li Shen Prime Minister" (李紳拜相制),[54] Li was appointed Prime Minister on the twelfth day of the second month, the second year of Huichang. Therefore, it was just before Li Shen was appointed Prime Minister that Wen presented "Fifty-Rhyme Poem" to him in Huainan, in the hope that Li would be able to assist him to resolve his political impasse.

As we have seen from the Ji Shao-Shan Tao-Ji Kang allusion, the study of Li Shen's relationship with Wen definitely serves to strengthen our conclusion concerning Wen's birth year, especially since Li's identity as the subject of the poem is corroborated.

Finally, evidence is found in Wen's "Epistle Presented to Drafter Du" (上杜舍人啓): "I used to have great ambition in my juvenile years, but I suffered many calamities in my middle age" (某弱齡有志，中歲多虞). This epistle was composed toward the end of the Dazhong era (847–860) and presented to Du Shenquan (杜審權, fl. 830–860). Even without taking into consideration when it was composed and to whom it was addressed, we can easily determine what Wen's "middle age" refers to. Wen was seriously injured and insulted by the eunuchs and was involved in a scandal because of his marriage with a singer-prostitute. After he gained access to the Heir Apparent, he also became the target of the eunuchs' persecution, and had to change his name to take the examination held by the Metropolitan Prefecture, even though he was rejected once his name change was divulged. All these disastrous incidents occurred in the Kaicheng era when Wen was in his forties: "Middle age" can only logically refer to the years of the "forties." Wen's experiences in the Kaicheng era should be highlighted because no other period in his life was filled with so many misfortunes.

In conclusion, it is possible to ascertain Wen Tingyun's birth year, because Wen left behind some particular works bearing concrete information. Following the clues Wen arranged in them, we are able to work out a reliable date, which provides a correct starting point for the study of his life.

Chapter Three

Before the Year of "Having No Doubts"

Very few experiences of Wen Tingyun's early years appear as clear and plain facts. Basing our arguments upon dozens of Wen's extant poems and essays, which contain important information, and upon other available sources, we can merely construct, by inference and reasoning, a broad outline of Wen's experiences before he came to be embroiled in the political events of the time. Simply put, before Wen was forty, the "year of having no doubts" (不惑之年) as Confucius called it, he studied for some length of time at the National University of Luoyang, lived a reclusive life in Tonglu, and then wandered all over the country. For each of these experiences, we can at best determine only an approximate date, even though each experience is significant in forming a complete picture of Wen's life.

In the last two chapters, I touched upon Wen's experience of having been a student at the National University of Luoyang. Now I will supply more evidence for this and clarify some of the details surrounding it.

Days of Diligent Studies

In all of Wen's extant works, we find a total of three pieces of evidence pointing to his attendance at the National University of Luoyang. Each example, in addition to corroborating the others, presents a new aspect of the same experience. The following comparison of the three evidential statements enables us to identify the school where Wen studied as National University of Luoyang.

First, in Wen's "Epistle Presented to Prime Minister Pei" we read: "Then I took my registered residence in Liaoxi, before *I studied the classics in Jixia*. Thereupon I looked up to and exhausted the lore my teacher handed down to me, and engaged myself in the composition of poetry and prose." "*Jixia*," the state school where King Xuan of the Qi (齊宣王) gathered the so-called Jixia Academicians (稷下學士) to comment on and discuss the affairs of the country, here signifies a state-managed university where Wen studied the classics under the instruction of his teacher. This same experience is once more referred to in Wen's "Epistle Presented to the Censor-In-Chief":

> I, *one of the students from the Luo River* and a member of the junior party of Ganling, *once attended National University*, failing to know Cheng Gong; but I happened to go to the frontier and luckily met with Zhong Hao (某洛水諸生，甘陵下黨，曾游太學，不識承宮；偶到離庭，適逢种暠).[1]

Since "Luo River" refers to the city of Luoyang, through which the Luo River flows and where the university was located; it follows that the National University of Luoyang is the very "Jixia" where Wen studied. Throughout the Tang Dynasty, being accepted as a student at National Universities in the capital(s) remained an extraordinary honor, guaranteeing a successful official career. It is no wonder that Wen always mentioned this with a sense of pride. Finally, the following couplet in "Hundred-Rhyme Poem" tells how Wen brought his literary talents into full play when studying at the university:

47 I yearned for the taste of watercress at *the Semi-circular Pool*, 泮水思芹味，
I found the source of ricefield rent in Langye Commandery. 瑯琊得稻租。

"Semi-circular pool" is an official school of the Lu Kingdom, the Semi-circular Palace, where, it was said, people plucked watercresses and observed the good order of the school and thus of the country.[2] Here it can only refer to the National University of Luoyang. "To yearn for the taste of watercress" may imply Wen's aspiration to employ his extraordinary talents in helping his country attain ideal governance. "*Ricefield rent in Langye Commandery*," which is an allusion in itself, alludes to Li Baiyao[3] and has the implication that Wen in his university days was as talented as Li had been. This couplet thus lends credibility to Wen's fame as a prodigy,[4] which had been well known ever since Wen attended the National University of Luoyang.

According to "Records of Selections and Recommendations" (選舉志) of XTS (44: 1159), students of the imperial universities in Chang'an and Luoyang had to be sons of officials not inferior to the fifth rank, and admission was granted only to those who were between thirteen and nineteen years of age. Since Wen was born in 798, his student days in Luoyang would likely have fallen between the years 810 and 816. The above source also records that, beginning the year 807, the total number of students in the Eastern Capital State Son's University had been stipulated as one hundred, and student enrollment in Luoyang National University was limited to only fifteen (44: 1164). However, Wen only "once attended" this university and could not have remained there long, perhaps at most one year, before he was forced to quit.

Of course it was Wen's family status that had provided him the opportunity to attend the National University of Luoyang. In like manner, it was the changes in his family fortunes that forced him to quit. His time at the University was extremely important for our poet because it was there he met his teacher Li Cheng, whose erudition and personality elicited Wen's lifelong admiration. Thinking himself second to none in literary talent, Wen seldom yielded to anyone, with the exception of his beloved and respected teacher. Most probably it was at the university that they first formally became teacher and student, although it is difficult to say in exactly which year the two met each other for the first time.

What did Wen do after quitting the National University of Luoyang? Hints can be found both in his "Epistle Presented to Prime Minister Pei" and in "Hundred-Rhyme Poem." According to the former, something disastrous befell Wen's family and turned Wen into "a traveling orphan." In the latter source, besides a metaphor containing an identical message, we find a lengthy pastoral description,[5] which may be based on Wen's long-year reclusive life in Tonglu. The following is a summary recollection of that life:

48	The light rattan cane was gnarled and bumpy,	杖輕藜臃腫，
	My lotus attire was disheveled and shabby.	衣破芰披敷。[6]
49	I was sad for the shrike with his fragrant spirit,	芳意憂鶗鴂，
	And empathized with the cicadas in their mournful chirps.	愁聲覺蟪蛄。[7]
50	The noisy swallows were shrieking on the short eaves,	短檐喧語燕，
	While a hungry squirrel fell from a tall tree.	高木落飢鼯。
51	Urged by pressure, I had to leave my calm solitude,	事迫離幽墅，
	And driven by destitution I ventured upon the fearful way.	貧牽犯畏途。
52	In my loves and hates I took precautions against Du Kui,	愛憎防杜蕢，
	In my laments and sighs I felt melancholy, as did Yang Zhu.	悲嘆似楊朱。[8]

Despite the dazzling diction and allusions, we can discern the pressure underlying Wen's difficult decision to begin his official career. "The gnarled and bumpy" "light rattan cane" is an epithet depicting Wen's talent, which was out of keeping with the time; "the disheveled and shabby" "lotus attire" gives expression to the poverty and disgrace in the last days of Wen's reclusion. Wen's sadness on hearing the cry of the shrike and the summer cicadas voices his yearning to be able to serve his country before it is too late. The "hungry squirrel" is, as we already discussed, Wen's self-image after his family's social position had fallen, when he had been driven to leave his hermitage and exert himself in the crowded and chaotic political arena. However, from the very beginning of his political life, Wen found himself in immense difficulties as he faced the eunuchs' threatening power. In brief, after quitting his studies in Luoyang and then continuing a life of study in bucolic reclusion in Tonglu, he eventually adopted a vagrant and precarious office-seeking existence.

Tonglu acted as the breeding ground for Wen's personality and poetic style. Here, while constantly studying hard and enjoying all that a quiet seclusion could offer him, Wen cultivated two lifelong tendencies. On the one hand he developed an eagerness to achieve his political ideal to aid his country and his people. On the other hand, his enjoyment of nature and valuation of individual freedom also increased. In a sense, Wen was content and would remain in his reclusion, unless the urge of his ambition and the pressure of life forced him to give it up. In his reclusion, he had acquired all the qualifications requisite for an official career, but was innately endowed with an unfettered spirit that was diametrically opposed to any official hypocrisy. Thus, all his life Wen was torn between the predilection to be a recluse and the aspiration to realize his political ambition. This inner conflict may partly account for the retardation of his office-seeking journey.

"Formerly for long you lived in oblivion and isolation" (當年久索居).[9] This is what a good friend of Wen's, Li Shangyin, said about Wen's reclusion, most probably the reclusion in Tonglu. Having returned to Tonglu, Wen lived there for about ten years, from some time between 810 and 816 to about 822. After that, he returned to the Guanzhong region once more and remained there for five years until about 827 when he set out for the Shu region. Even after beginning his office-seeking career, he found himself unable, despite his literary talent, to follow the common course of entering into officialdom by passing the Presented Scholar Examination. He chose instead to travel all over the country in search of an opportunity. Evidently, there were political reasons underlying this decision: his family background subjected him to persecution from the eunuchs, forcing him to go to the provinces instead of the capital.

During his Tonglu years, as a scion of an eminent clan and a prodigious talent, he associated with the local literati-officials and became famous for his literary brilliance. "The landscape of Kuaiji has been surpassing and unique from time immemorial"(會稽山水，自古勝絕),[10] and during the Tang Dynasty, the region of Wu and Yue was also one of the centers where the provincial poets gathered and prepared themselves for their future political careers in the capital. As can be seen from his "Epistle Presented to the Grand Master Cui" quoted in chapter 1, young recluse that he was, Wen already enjoyed the friendship of the local élites including Cui, the Grand Master, Wen's "twenty-third elder brother," who, very possibly, was the magistrate of Yuezhou Prefecture for a time.

Another point we must make is that it was in Tonglu, a resort for reclusion since the Eastern Han, that Wen Tingyun's poetic style took shape. This style, which has been labeled as a style of "license and luxury" (淫靡), has caused him to be frequently criticized and misunderstood in Chinese literary history. Considering that Yuan Zhen held the position of Surveillant Commissioner of Zhedong Circuit for a period (823–829) including Wen's Tonglu days, and that during his tenure, he "promoted many men of letters to serve in his secretariat,"[11] Wen may very possibly have had a connection with poets centered around Yuan and earned poetic fame by doing so. At the same time that Yuan made a considerable contribution to the formation of the so-called Yuanhe Style, this poetic style characteristic of the Yuezhou provincial poets and of Yuan Zhen must also have had an impact on Wen's early poetic practices. Wen must have been affected by this influence from the beginning of his career as a poet. This is evident, because critics have also labeled Yuan's poetry "license and abandon."

> Since the era of Yuanhe, in composing prose writings, people have tried to follow Han Yu's strangeness and abruptness, and Fan Zongshi's awkwardness and obscurity; in composing Music Bureau verses, people followed Zhang Ji's fluency and smoothness; in creating poetry, people followed Meng Jiao's sophistication and fondness of extremes, Bai Juyi's simplicity and vividness and Yuan Zhen's license and abandon. All labeled their writings "Yuanhe style" (元和已後，為文筆則學奇詭于韓愈，學苦澀于樊宗師；歌行學流蕩于張籍，詩章則學矯激于孟郊，學淺切于白居易，學淫蕩于元稹，皆名曰元和體). (Li Zhao, 57)

By all accounts, when Wen entered society, he was already well known as a remarkable poet at the forefront of his time. He was full of self-confidence and ambitious goals, but he knew the way before him would not be smooth.

FAR WANDERINGS AND WEN ZAO

After Wen was forced to give up his reclusive life, he spent many years wandering around the country. It was a common practice for Tang literati to make long journeys, in order to see the world and search for opportunities for entering official service, as a preparatory step for their future political careers. Among the important places Wen visited were first, the Metropolitan Prefecture, where he lived for about five years (during which period he once went to the western frontier); Sichuan, where he lived for several years; many scenic spots downstream along the Yangtze River; and again, Luoyang, where he had an audience with Wen Zao. Then he returned to the Jianghuai region—the place where he first became involved in a political scandal. What follows is a tentative attempt to illustrate each of the preceding experiences.

As we see in Wen's "Epistle Presented to Prime Minister Pei":

> Later on, I *spent many years at one or another Marquis'* before I traveled to the valley of the Huai River, where I presented myself by writing letters and sought recognition holding a calling card.

The "many years" Wen spent "at one or another marquis'" in fact spanned nearly twenty years. This state of affairs would have continued indefinitely, were it not for the scandal in the Jianghuai region, the most conspicuous event of Wen's life and one of the important points made in this epistle. Studying this period of the "many years" amounts to rearranging all Wen's travels, as reflected in his works, in a chronological order. To this purpose, we will examine several couplets in "Hundred-Rhyme Poem," covering Wen's experiences from the beginning of his wandering years to his Huainan misadventure.

53 Traveling for a living, I often passed by the country of Wei. 旅食常過衛，
And tarrying in my journey, I almost crossed the River Lu. 羈游欲渡瀘。[12]
54 On the frontier I lamented the "Song of the Protector-General," 塞歌傷都護，
By the border I meditated on the horn "Tune of Chanyu." 邊角思單于。[13]
55 At the military fords lances and spears were clashing, 堡戍摽槍槊，
In the River Pass boats and ships were blockaded. 關河鎖舳艫。

The narrative clues in these lines are easy to follow: Wen might have spent some time on the frontier, and he certainly stayed in Sichuan for some years. At any rate, he could only make a living under some local patrons, this he called his "many years at one or another marquis'." Dealing these experiences of "many years," we shall first discuss his stay in the capital region, and then single out his journey to Shu for closer study.

In his "Epistle Presented to the Prime-Minister-Duke at the Honor Seat" (Wen Zao, see below) Wen told how, before his journey to the Shu region, he spent "five years" "in the fertile land":

> Before this [coming to see you], I spent five years in *the fertile land*, and went ten thousand *li* from Sichuan along the Riverbank (昨者膏壤五秋，川途萬里).

"*The fertile land*" here must be a reference for a specific place, otherwise Wen would not have used it in this manner. We find two literary uses of the term prior to Wen's time. The first is, "There are thousands of *li* of *fertile land* in the Guanzhong region" (關中膏壤千里).[14] The second is "There are beautiful trees of Penglai, planted in the *fertile land* of the Divine Prefecture"

(有蓬萊之嘉樹，植神州之膏壤).[15] Since even in the Tang, Chang'an, or the Metropolitan Prefecture, was called the "Divine Prefecture" (神州), both sources agree with each other that *the fertile land* must refer to the Metropolitan Prefecture, or more broadly, the Guanzhong region around Chang'an.

Wen's statement thus indicates that before he presented the epistle to Wen Zao, he had first spent five years in Guanzhong, and then had gone to Shu, from whence he had just come to the place where Wen Zao held his official post, in order to present to him this epistle. Wen traveled to the Shu region in about the year 827; thus, the time he spent in Guanzhong would roughly cover the period from 822 to 827. This was the second time Wen had come to and stayed in the capital region seeking an official career. Although we know very little about his whereabouts during this period, we can infer from the following poems that he once traveled to the western frontier, and had resided somewhere near to the capital.

"WRITING MY FEELINGS ON MY JOURNEY TO THE WEST"
(西游書懷, j. 7, WFQ)

The Wei River is connected to a deserted pass,	渭川通野戍，
Where I find my way to the frontier of Sanggan.	有路上桑乾。[16]
A lonely bird hovers in the blue, darkening sky,	獨鳥青天暮，
A startled deer strays before a worn-out wildfire.	驚麞赤燒殘。
In high autumn, I bid farewell to my native city,	高秋辭故國，
Since yestereve I've cherished a dream about Chang'an.	昨日夢長安。
Such is a traveler's mood of itself,	客意自如此，
That has nothing to do with "The Road Is Hard."	非關行路難。

This is almost the only poem in Wen's extant works expressive of a confident young mind filled with ambition to serve his country, and untainted by the gloomy political frustration that permeates most of his later poems. This kind of mood is rare even in his early years, but we can only date it to this early period.

"Luoyang" (洛陽, j. 8, WFQ) may have been written during the same period.

The Gong trees first see spring, twigs laden with "snow,"	鞏樹先春雪滿枝，
On the Shangyang Palace willows are warbling the orioles.	上陽宮柳囀黃鸝。
How could Huan Tan so easily forget smiling westward,	桓譚未便忘西笑，
Just because there is in Chang'an a phoenix pool?	豈為長安有鳳池?[17]

Wen hints that something other than political concern attracts him to Chang'an, the capital. Since he is reticent about the exact reason for "smiling westward" from Luoyang, we may venture a guess: apart from his ambitions, what drew him to Chang'an, the symbol of imperial power and glory, was that he was an imperial relative. As we have noted, he had some houses in Hu County (鄠縣) of the Metropolitan Prefecture, which permitted him to live near the two capitals as frequently as he chose to.

In an attempt to fix the approximate year in which Wen began his Shu journey, we will study a group of poems bearing relevant messages.

"MAILED TO ASSISTANT DU OF HE'NAN PREFECTURE"
(寄河南杜少府, j. 4, WFQ)

After ten years I'm back, my temple hairs not yet gray,	十年歸來鬢未凋，
Hawksbill hairpins and pearled boots—face an ordinary clerk.	玳瑁珠履見常僚。
Not that fame and wealth separate us on the glorious way,	豈關名利分榮路，
Though talent and gift must omen auspicious career.	自有才華作慶霄。
Now shadows of the birds linger over the Shanglin Garden,	鳥影不飛經上苑，
And din of hooves clatter along the Middle Bridge.[18]	騎聲相續過中橋。
Below the Setting-Sun Pavilion is a picturesque mountain,[19]	夕陽亭下山如畫，
You must know how lonely I am with my rural song.	應念田歌正寂寥。

Evidently this poem was written near the capital after a ten-year separation from it. At the time, although a mere "ordinary clerk," Wen seems to have had a hopeful perspective on his official career, and his hair was not yet gray. All the descriptive details bespeak the uniqueness of the occasion. It can only refer to one specified time in Wen's life, the second year of Kaicheng (837), when he had come all the way from Huainan to the capital, where he would live for the following three years. In other words, it has been ten years since about 827 or so. In actuality his tour to Sichuan fits broadly within these ten years, as is indicated more clearly in the following poem.

Presented to a Shu General (贈蜀將, j. 4, WFQ)

Poet's note: He had considerable success fighting the Nanman [the southern barbarians], when the latter entered the city of Chengdu (蠻入成都，頗著功勞).

Since the autumn we parted company on Sword Pass ten years ago,	十年分散劍關秋，
Myriad happenings have all followed the Brocade River's flow.	萬事皆從錦水流。
Your ambition and spirit were proved to merit a Staff of Han,	志氣已曾明漢節，
Yet distinction and renown went amiss, despite your dagger of Wu.	功名猶自滯吳鉤。[20]
By the [fallen] hawk I recognized your arrow, as cold clouds thickened,	雕邊認箭寒雲重，
On horseback we heard a reed-horn, amid border grasses depressing.	馬上聽笳塞草愁。
Today's meeting with you renders me doubly disheartened:	今日逢君倍惆悵，
Han Xin and Guan Ying [not we] are all offered rank of Marquis.	灌嬰韓信盡封侯。[21]

Historical records indicate that, before the Xiantong era (860–873), an event, which could be described as "southern barbarians entered Chengdu," happened only once: "On the *Bing-shen* day of the eleventh month of the third year of Dahe (829), the *Nanman* reached Chengdu. . . . They stayed in the western city of Chengdu for ten days."[22] It was some years before Kaicheng, and during Wen's stay in Sichuan, that he made the acquaintance of the Shu general. Therefore, it must be around the year 829 that the Shu general rendered remarkable military services to the Tang court by warding off the *Nanman* assault on Chengdu.

It can be inferred from this poem that some time before 829 Wen had already arrived in Shu and made the general's acquaintance. When the two men enjoyed each other's company in the army barracks before Wen bid farewell to the Shu general, the latter may not yet have accomplished his military feats. Comparing the first line of "Mailed to Assistant Du of He'nan Circuit" (dated 837) with the first line in this poem, it is therefore inferential that the "ten years" in the two cases differ only slightly, covering virtually the same period. Adding this to the information that Wen had last left the capital in around 827 or so, we can infer that soon after Wen had left Chang'an, he arrived in Shu. In other words, he left Chang'an for Shu.

In "Respectfully Mailed to a Few Intimate Friends When Lodging in Xinjin" (旅泊新津卻寄一二知己, j. 8, WFQ), after describing the landscape and his feelings during his stay in Xinjin County of the Shu region, Wen ends the poem with this couplet: "As sentimental as was Wang Can in a troubled life / My heart is being broken when I ascend the tower" (王粲平生感，登臨幾斷魂). Here Wen likens himself to Wang Can, who also led a wandering life for almost twenty years. Wen's age when traveling to the Shu region is quite similar to that of Wang Can in his wandering, another example of how Wen uses historical allusions with multiple implications.

Wen's residence in Shu was at least two or three years in duration. He could not have made such a long journey into the center of the Shu region without a purpose; he must have had several motives: to go sightseeing, to make a living, to find a way to establish himself, and even to seek political refuge under the patronage of some local officials. Serving at the frontiers was a commonly accepted avenue for Tang literati to gain recognition and distinction. Together with the Shu general, Wen might have served for some length of time on the frontier, as the subaltern of a Military Commissioner. He says in "Hundred-Rhyme Poem": "And tarrying in my journey, I almost crossed the River Lu"—that is, he almost decided to go to the southernmost border. Although we cannot say exactly when he left Shu, we know that in the sixth year of Dahe (832), he was continuing his journey eastward along the Yangtze River Valley.

The following poem is the most representative work Wen wrote while in Shu, a poem that reflects the complex mentality of the young traveler, the orphan of a persecuted loyal court official and the scion of a traditional aristocratic family.

"ODE OF THE BROCADE CITY" (錦城曲, j. 1, WFQ)

Shu mountains in the sun, a mass of dark eyebrow
are capped with unmelted snow, 蜀山攢黛留晴雪，
Like bamboo shoots and bracken sprouts
Winding themselves around the Nine-Turn
Slope. 簝筍蕨牙縈九折。
To cut the brocade of colored clouds
the River breeze sends forth a nimble blow, 江風吹巧剪霞綃，
When the flowers ascend a thousand boughs
as red as the cuckoo's tears of blood 花上千枝杜鵑血。[23]
The Cuckoo (*Dujuan*) hovers and flies
into the groves at the foot of the cliff, 杜鵑飛入巖下叢，
It sends forth a homesick cry at night
amid the mountains in the moonlight. 夜叫思歸山月中。

The Ba River is flowing with this feeling,
And this feeling will be everlasting. 巴水漾情情不盡，
While Wenjun is weaving her yearning
into the red brocade on a loom of spring. 文君織得春機紅。[24]
Since the soul of the wronged one has not
returned and the fragrant herbs all decease, 怨魄未歸芳草死，
At the River's head I can only learn
to sow seeds of the lovelorn tree. 江頭學種相思子。[25]
When the tree grows up to bear peas,
I will send one to the home-yearning man. 樹成寄與望鄉人，[26]
But the forlorn city of the White Emperor
is five thousand *li* away. 白帝荒城五千里。

The information implied in this poem can help us trace what motivated Wen to tour the inland Shu region. There is some profound emotion, linked possibly to the poet's lamentation for his father or to his father's friends, underlying the heartbroken tone. The deep feeling and powerful appeal of the poem are too thought-provoking for the reader to misunderstand it as a poem on a trivial subject.

The opening scenic depiction is startling and ingenious as against the background of the threatening Sichuan hills, the glaring red flowers are suddenly thrown into bold relief, with the colored cloud as their natural counterpart. Through the red flowers the legendary tragic *Dujuan* is introduced and subsequently plays the leading role in the poem. Why is he unable to go home, and why is he called a "wronged soul"? Beyond evoking the *Dujuan* image itself, the poet has some deeper reason for relating the *Dujuan* story to himself. Since *Dujuan* is a symbol for a wronged emperor (such as Emperors Shunzong, Xianzong, or Jingzong, all of whom died at the hands of the eunuchs), and "the fragrant herbs" is a symbol for worthy and honest court officials, the line "the soul of the wronged one has not returned and the fragrant herbs all decease" must have some relevance to a situation in which both the emperor and the ministers loyal to him have been subjected to a great injustice. Wen, when referring to himself, declares that he followed someone's (perhaps Liu Yuxi's) example of sowing the seeds of red peas in memory of the dead, with the earnest hope of consoling those who were exiled and yearning for home. Thus, it is only logical to infer that the killing or banishment of the wronged soul(s)—the wronged ministers—ensued from the death of the emperor(s). These tragic elements commingle in this poem, making its subject matter difficult for the readers to fathom. For all its gorgeous diction, this is not a poem expressing lovesickness. It is, rather, a political poem with covert personal feelings hidden behind the lines. An attractive clue is provided by the manner in which Wen mourns the death of "the fragrant herbs." This reference could be linked with his late father, who, very possibly, died in exile to the Shu region. In brief, only an understanding Wen's early life can enable us probe into the deeply hidden motif. In turn, this poem enriches our knowledge of that early life.

To find out more about Wen's earlier life, we shall peruse the following epistle.

AN ANNOTATED TRANSLATION OF "THE EPISTLE PRESENTED TO THE PRIME-MINISTER-DUKE AT THE HONOR SEAT" (上首座相公啓)

I hear that Wang Ji's recommendation avoids none of his own clansmen; I also hear that Xie Xuan's advancement is because of his being a near kinsman [of Xie An].[27] Such is the norm by which a man of wisdom shows his kindness, and also the way the former worthies lived in amity, with their clansmen (某聞舉不違宗，得于王濟；近因其族，聞自謝玄。雖通人與善之規，亦前哲睦親之道).

I fortunately partake of your eminent genealogical line, and was able to shelter myself under our ancestral protection. Consequently I was favored by your fatherly benefaction, just as Kong Li passed the court; and I received your promise of tacit approval, like a Ruan Xian who lived in the southern alley.[28] Thereupon I had my flesh and bones grafted [to this branch of ours], so as to uphold the trunk and make the blossoms [of our family tree] flourish. Hence, like a hard-pressed bird flying into your arms, I should not look elsewhere; and, as a migrating bird circling a tree, what other twig but this one shall it perch upon (某謬參華緒，得庇餘蔭，固已鯉庭蒙翼長之恩，阮巷辱心期之許。遂得遷肌改骨，擁本揚英。則窮鳥入懷，靡求他所；羈禽繞樹，更托何枝)?

Before this I spent five years in the fertile land, and went ten thousand *li* from Sichuan along the River bank. Far away from your fatherly instruction, I found myself this poor shelter. I will divine a good date [to sit for the examination], when the end of the year is approaching.[29] This adds to my sighs and sorrow, while I stay in the hostel of the metropolitan port[30] (昨者膏壤五秋，川途萬里。遠違慈訓，就此窮棲。將卜良期，行當杪歲。通津加嘆，旅舍傷懷).

Minister-Duke Your Excellency, your river-like nourishment has provided more than generous benefaction; and your cloud-like movement has distributed widespread kindness. The taste in the soup you season,[31] however, has not benefited a clansman; the surplus benevolence in your care for the people will, I hope, favor the young and weak. If I could avail myself of one word of your recommendation, I would be able to follow the awakening to life of the hundred hibernating creatures. Then, the shade of the twining creeper could offer equal safekeeping to all beneath them; and the seeds of the pepper-plant would thus be enabled to flourish. I could then follow the example of Zhong Yi, in performing the Southern music, and relieve myself of the anxiety of Gu Ti, kneeling before the letter from his father. My humble feelings are beyond expression (相公河潤餘津，雲行廣施。調羹之味，未及宗親；育物之餘，希沾幼弱。倘或假一言之甄發，隨百蟄之昭蘇。庶令葛藟之陰，均其煦育；椒聊之實，遂彼扶疎。[32]成鍾儀操樂之規，寬顧悌拜書之戀。[33]下情無任).

After a careful perusal of this epistle, we find out that the so-called "Prime-Minister-Duke at the Honor Seat" was one of Wen's clansmen, although only a distant uncle. Wen Tingyun lived for a time under the fatherly patronage of this man, and was appreciated by him. Thus, the uncle adopted Wen as a foster son by moving his name to the genealogy of his own branch of the clan.

As is revealed by the title as well as in the contents of this epistle, "the Prime-Minister at the Honor Seat" was at the time a figure of such renown that the histories could not afford to ignore him. Among those who bore the surname Wen, the most famous person in the ninth century with a biography in the standard histories is Wen Zao. Referring to Zao's biographical records and other sources, we find the following reasons to identify him with the subject addressed here.

The position "Honorary Minister of Finance, Imperial Deputy of the Eastern Capital, in Charge of the Chancellery in the Eastern Capital" (檢校戶部尚書東都留守判東都尚書省事), held by Wen Zao in the fifth year of Dahe (831), in its own right entitled him to be styled Prime-Minister-Duke (相公) [34] After his promotion in 833 to Censor-in-Chief, he occupied a position in which, in most cases during the Tang period, he was all the more qualified to be thus addressed. The Censor-in-Chief (御史大夫), Councilor-in-Chief (丞相), and Defender-in-Chief (太尉), were referred as the Three Dukes (三公) during the Qin and Han dynasties. During the Tang Dynasty the case was similar, as can be proved by *Fengshi Wenjianlu:*[35] "Ever since the founding of the Tang, most of the Prime Ministers ascended to power from the censorship, thus Censor-in-Chief is called Prime-Minister too."

Because Wen was a junior clansman, he did not use the surname when addressing Zao in his epistle.

"The Honor Seat" originally refers to the seat at the head of the table, which the most senior or respected man took in a feast or assembly. The term is also a proper name for the head monk in a monastery, who, as chief preacher, was responsible for giving lectures on Buddhist doctrine. According to *Sengshilue* (僧史略) and *Shishi Yaolan* (釋氏要覽),[36] Xuanzong (r. 847–859) once appointed the monk Bianzhang (辨章) as the Honor-Seat [Preacher] for the Three Religions (三教首座). This epistle provides the only example in any

Chinese historical sources where "the Honor Seat" (a Buddhist title) and "the Prime-Minister-Duke" are combined to form a title. We know that Wen Zao once discussed the Buddhist doctrine with Zongmi (宗密, 779–840),[37] the well-known Buddhist master of the time. Zao, referred to as Minister Wen of Shannan (山南溫尚書) in the discussion, raised a question that Zongmi answered at great length; Zongmi then also summed up the main points of his argument with a Buddhist verse that he later chanted for Wen Zao. It is apparent that Zao in his late years became devoted to the Buddhist faith and, after completing his official routine, might on some occasions preach the Buddhist doctrines to his subordinates or retainers. Thus, imaginably, he may have received the appellation "the Prime-Minister-Duke at the Honor Seat" from his auditors.

In the course of his official career, Wen Zao more than once organized the people to dig canals to irrigate their fields, both when he was the magistrate of Langzhou and when he held the post of Military Commissioner of Heyanghuai Circuit (河陽懷節度使). It was for this that Wen praised him for his "river-like nourishment." Moreover, Wen Zao was well known for his courageous action, when he held the post of the Military Commissioner of the Western Circuit of Shannan (garrisoning in Xingyuan), of executing without hesitation those who had murdered Li Jiang (李絳, 764–830), the former Military Commissioner. Liu Yuxi praised Wen Zao's heroic deeds on that account: "Henceforth all people of the country will open their eyes / To know that an outstanding general rose up from among men of letters" (從此世人開耳目，始知名將出書生).[38] From this, as well as from other details in Wen Zao's biographies, we become aware of his political tendencies and actual influences, both of which could have enabled his clansman Wen to enter into the officialdom without the necessity of sitting for the civil examination. Such an avenue is illustrated in the case of Wen Zhang (溫璋, ?–869), Wen Zao's son, who began his official service by dint of family privilege. Herein lies the possible reason why Wen begged for a chance "to follow the example of Zhong Yi, in performing the southern music." This implies that, Wen wished, by dint of the family privilege, to directly take up a position to succeed the official career of his late father, bypassing the ordinary examination. That position, most probably, refers to one in the Palace Library, because Wen's father Wen Xihua (?) once was Director of the Palace Library (秘書監).[39]

Therefore, the "Prime Minister at the Honor Seat" is Wen Zao, Wen's clan uncle.

From this epistle, we can deduce that, after a long vagrant life, spent for five years around the Guanzhong region (the so-called fertile land), and then "ten thousand *li* from Sichuan along the River bank," Wen came to the place he called the Metropolitan Port, Luoyang, where Wen Zao held his post. He hoped that, with the coming of spring and with the help of this uncle and foster father, he could benefit from the family's prerogative and advance in the political world. Wen Zao was Military Commissioner of the Eastern

Circuit of Shannan (山南東道節度使) from the fourth (830) to the fifth year of Dahe, but only after he was promoted to be in charge of the Chancellery in the Eastern Capital (831) could he have been called Prime Minister (as he remained, as Censor-in-Chief [833], until his death [835]). Therefore, this epistle must have been presented between 831 and 835. As it was within the time of Zao's tenure as Military Commissioner of the Heyanghuai Circuit (from the eighth month of 831 to the eleventh month of 834) that he organized the people to dig canals (in 833), this epistle probably was written some time at the end of either 833 or 834.

JOURNEY ALONG THE RIVER AND FRIENDSHIP WITH BUDDHIST MONKS

Bearing his special relationship to Wen Zao in mind, we know that toward the end of the Dahe era, Wen traveled back to Luoyang. Prior to this, between his audience with Wen Zao (833?) and his sojourn in Shu (827–), there were years of constant wandering, termed the "ten thousand *li* from Sichuan along the River bank." Changing patrons from time to time, he sailed down from Sichuan along the Yangtze River.

First, Wen sailed through the Three Gorges, passing Qian (黔) and Kui Prefectures (夔州) in the east of Sichuan, as can be elicited from the following lines from "Sending Off Bureau Director Cui to Military Service" (送崔郎中赴幕, j. 4, WFQ):

> Having parted company in Qian and Wu, we were like broken strings, 一別黔巫似斷弦，
> My old friend now is going eastward, and I am all in tears. 故交東去更潸然。
> My mind distracted, my gaze blurred, a distance of three thousand *li*, 心遊目想三千里，
> The rain scattered, the clouds flown, a separation of twenty years . . . 雨散雲飛二十年…

Although this is a poem written at a later time, it tells clearly that Wen and Bureau Director Cui once were together in Qian and Wu (Kui) Prefectures and then parted company with each other. The title of another of his poems, "The Temple of the Goddess of Mount Wu" (巫山神女廟, j. 7, WFQ), reaffirms the inference, since Mount Wu is situated on the eastern border of Sichuan at the entrance to the Three Gorges.

After a voyage along the Yangtze River from Sichuan, Wen arrived in the Eastern Shannan Circuit (Yangtze-Han River Plain), and left to posterity nearly twenty poems,[40] written in prefectures such as Xiangyang, Jiangling, and Wuchang. From these poems, however, we deduce that he traveled to these places more than once. The last time he came to the Yangtze-Han region was in his late years, and the poems he wrote in these years are easily discernible as those of an old man who has survived the hardships of a lifetime. The poems that reflect his early-year travel to this region, therefore, are not difficult to identify, although we cannot determine any exact date for them.

Basing himself in the area of the Yangtze-Han Valley, Wen may have made many side trips. We know, for example, that he once went to the south of Dongting Lake, far into modern Hu'nan. However, since this is an acknowledged fact, we will concentrate on his stay at Mount Lu, because this is something that has not yet been much studied.

In "Two Poems Written in the Courtyard of the Monk Taigong" (題僧泰恭院二首, j. 7, WFQ), we find a couplet "In the former year, under the Eastern Woods, Senior Shen knew my surname and name" (昔歲東林下，深公識姓名), which indicates that Wen once followed the Buddhist monks at Mount Lu.[41] In actuality, enchanted by the landscape, he did tour Mount Lu and study there for a considerable length of time. "Why do the scholars of Mount Sumen / Hand in hand, roam atop the South-Eastern Peak?" (何意蘇門生，攜手東南峰) [42] (Sent to Someone in the Mountains, 寄山中人, j. 8, WFQ) implies similar information. Furthermore, the remark in "Gatherings and Feasting on Mount Lu" (廬山宴游集) of Li Zhenggu (李徵古, fl. 930) reaffirms this judgment:[43]

> In the Ji-chou year of Qianzhen [929], I wandered to this spot, and found the relic of the reading hall of Wen Tingyun, the Four Gate Erudite of our state dynasty (乾貞己丑歲，余旅游及此，得國朝四門學士庭筠書堂舊基).

Having ascertained that Wen studied at Mount Lu we can fully understand the narration in Wen's "Epistle Presented to Minister Feng" (上封尚書啓):

> I am in a muddy quagmire, and have none to act as my mediator. I always try to impel myself, so as to rid myself of disgrace and humiliation. Although endowed with a dull mind, I have long had a predilection for poetry. *Consequently I built my cottage on the summit* and weeded the grasses in the wild (某跡在泥途，居無紹介。常思激勵，以發湮沉。素稟顓蒙，夙耽比興。因得誅茅絕頂，薙草荒田).

If Wen had not had the personal experience of studying on Mount Lu, he would not have talked of his "cottage on the summit [of Mount Lu, evidently]." According to Wen's own account, it seems that he had resided there for some time. The footnote of Wen's poem "Presented to Appointed Scholar Zheng" (贈鄭徵君, j. 5, WFQ) gives the approximate time of Wen's stay in the vicinity around Mount Lu: "[Zheng] abided in Mount Kuang [Lu] and exchanged visits with Prime Minister Duke of Zanhuang, in the beginning of spring" (家匡山，首春與丞相贊皇公游止).[44] Therefore, Wen had access to Li Deyu when the latter was demoted to Jiangxi, in about 832 or so. This supports the assertion that Wen had traveled Mount Lu.

Now we have come to the appropriate time to study Wen's friendship with Zongmi,[45] the fifth patriarch of the Hua Yan Sect and the seventh patriarch of the Chan School. As a Buddhist master, he had played a political role of considerable importance and exhibited anti-eunuch tendencies. In the Dahe era (827–835), he "was called to the court. The emperor more than once asked him about the essentials of the law. . . . Only Pei Xiu [Prime Minister during 852–856] understood and gained a deep insight into his lore, so he received the precepts as an outside patron of the Buddhist religion." In spite of being a Buddhist monk, Zongmi once tried to save Li Xun (李訓, ?–835), the leading figure of the abortive coup d'état against the eunuchs in the Sweet Dew Incident, and was almost put to death by Qiu Shiliang (仇士良, 779–841). However, after some hesitation, Qiu, a Buddhist disciple himself, spared Zong Mi's life.

Wen maintained a constant connection with Wen Zao, Liu Yuxi, and Pei Xiu (?–864), all of whom were among Zongmi's best friends among laymen.[46] This is only one fact bespeaking Wen's intimate relationship with Zongmi. In Wen's works we can find more evidence revealing the nature of Wen's contact with the Buddhist master.

"Revisiting the Aranya of the Chan Master Zongmi on the Eastern Peak" (重游東峰宗密禪師精廬,[47] j. 4, WFQ)

Atop a hundred-foot black cliff, a three-foot grave,	百尺青厓三尺墳，
Your subtle words are gone, never to be heard again.	幺言巳絕杳難聞，
A Dai Yong of this day became a Buddhist layman,	戴顒今日稱處士，
The Zhi Dun of old year knew the Army Commander.	支盾他年識領軍。[48]
Firs, pines and I unite, as if forming an association,	暫對杉松如結社，
Occasionally joining the deer we are of the same herd.	偶因麋鹿自成群。
Your disciple of the old mountain looks back in vain,	故山弟子空回首，
On Onion Ridge perhaps have you met with Song Yun?	蔥嶺還應見宋雲。[49]

First we must point out that in this poem, Wen calls himself Zongmi's "disciple of the old mountain." Other examples of the relationship include "Lodging in the Yunji Temple" (宿雲際寺, j. 8. WFQ), where he more clearly refers to himself as "the disciple of the Eastern Peak," and "Visiting the Senior Zhixuan" (訪知玄上人, j. 9, WFQ), where he calls himself "a disciple of Mount Zhong." Thus, Wen confesses that he was a Buddhist lay disciple and had once followed Zongmi, studying Buddhism on Mount Zhongnan and Mount Zhong.

In actuality, Wen possessed some estates in Hu County, as can be seen from his poems "Living in the Suburbs of Hu Du" (鄠杜郊居, j. 4, WFQ) and "Sent to An Intimate Friend from My Villa of Hu Suburbs" (鄠郊別墅寄所知, j. 8, WFQ). Zongmi's Biography in *Jingde Chuandenglu* (13:12) says: "[Zong] traveled north to the Pure and Cold Mountain, then returned to live in the Cottage Temple of Hu County, and soon afterwards, he entered the Gui Peak Aranya, to the south of the Cottage Temple." Comparing Zongmi's biography with Wen's travels enables us to infer that for a considerable length of time Wen had access to Zongmi and remained the latter's disciple.

Secondly, we must pay special attention to the fifth line of the above poem: "Firs, pines and I unite, as if forming an association." We find that there was a certain kind of association gathered around the group of monks headed by Zongmi, and formed by some half dozen literati, including Wen himself. The association was more than merely a religious one, having to do with literary and even political matters. More examples having similar implications are the line from "Sent to the Monks in the Pure and Cool Temple" (寄清涼寺僧, j. 4, WFQ): "If people in the White-Lotus Association[50] asked me"(白蓮社里如相問) and the couplet from "Presented to the Yue Monk Yue Yun" "I will accompany the White-Lotus Association members / To wait for one another among the pines and osmanthus" (應共白蓮客，相期松桂前).

Thirdly, the second couplet of the poem also contains noteworthy information. The allusions used in this couplet can also be found elsewhere, for example, from "Lodging in the Mount Study of a Monk of Qin" (宿秦僧山齊, j. 9 WFQ):

From Wu or from Heng, my way can be different 衡巫路不同，
But you have your cottage on the Eastern Peak. 結室在東峰。
When the year approaches its end, I come upon a
  Zhi Dun, 歲晚得支盾，
And as the night turns cold you meet a Dai Yong. 夜寒逢戴顒。

And from "Sent to the Monk in the Pure Cold Temple":

A bamboo path, with no dust, opens on the stony
  road, 石路無塵竹徑開，
Where in old days, you came in the company of
  Dai Yong. 昔年曾伴戴顒來。

The allusion to Dai Yong is meant to refer to Wen himself as a pious lay Buddhist and a native of Tonglu, just as Dai Yong was. In any event, Wen's frequent identification with Dai Yong poses a question for us to study. Since

"Dai Yong" refers to Wen himself, then it follows that Zhi Dun refers to Zongmi, but to whom does the "Army Commander" that "the Zhi Dun of old year knew" refer? By analogy, it should be somebody other than Wen himself, a special figure selected from among Zongmi's friends. Considering Zongmi's particular political capacity as a Buddhist master, I venture the suggestion that it must refer to Li Xun, the architect of the Sweet Dew Incident! That is to say, Wen must have had, in addition to the consolation of his frustrated self, one political purpose in following Zongmi to learn Buddhism. Even when he chose to be a follower of the Buddhist religion, discussing dharma and emptiness with the Buddhist masters, he did not abandon his worldly concerns, that is, how to deal with the eunuchs. However, we cannot be certain whether he ever realized any political aims in connection with this.

CHAPTER FOUR

WEN'S MARRIAGE—A CASE OF SCANDAL

Since he was Tingyun's uncle and foster father, and also an official of considerable political influence, Wen Zao had been kind to Tingyun. But he could at most recommend him to other influential ministers for a local subordinate post, and was not able to introduce him directly into officialdom within the central bureaucracy, as Tingyun had hoped. There are no clear records of what resulted from his audience with his uncle. Soon afterward, Wen Zao died (835), and by that time, Tingyun had traveled back to Huainan. There he began his more troubled years, and the most notorious affair in Wen's life, the Jianghuai Incident, took place.

RELATIONSHIP WITH WANG YA

One of the victims of the tragic "Sweet Dew Incident"(835), Wang Ya,[1] had been Wen's guardian. Within the general situation of the time, the Jianghuai Incident, which involved the person of Wen Tingyun in a scandal, is only a small aftermath of the Sweet Dew Incident, which precipitated the clan extermination of more than ten court ministers, including Wang Ya, who plotted the annihilation of the eunuchs. Most probably, it was immediately before the Jianghuai Incident and the Sweet Dew Incident that Wen had served under Wang's jurisdiction. Since the two men were on friendly terms, when we examine Wen's tribulations in the Jianghuai Incident, we have every reason to set them against the background of the Sweet Dew Incident. We must also consider both the overwhelming power of the eunuchs and Wen's hostility toward them. We will first study Wen's relation with Wang using the following poems:

"TWO POEMS WRITTEN IN THE FOREST PAVILION OF PRIME MINISTER WANG IN FENG'AN ALLEY" (題豐安里王相林亭, j. 7, WFQ)

Poet's note: His Excellency is conversant with the *Taixuan* Scripture. (原注：公明太玄經)

In the filmy dust of flowers and bamboo, 花竹有薄埃。
At exquisite parties once gathered talented men. 嘉游集上才。
Either on Anshi's Isle amidst the white duckweeds, 白蘋安石渚，
Or at Ziyun's Terrace with the red leaves. 紅葉子雲臺。
By the vermilion door, one sets sparrow-nets, 朱戶雀羅設，
While the Yellow Gates come along in their carriages. 黃門馭騎來。
Alas you did not know the Huai River grew turbid, 不知淮水濁，
Now for whom does the pink lotus flourish? 丹藕為誰開?

In the "Records of Art and Literature" of XTS (59: 1512) are recorded "Six *juan* of the *Taixuan* Scripture annotated by Wang Ya." In Wang Dang's *Tangyulin* (1: 18) are similar records: "Prime Minister Wang Ya annotated the *Taixuan* Scripture, and often used it to augur, saying it worked better than the divination in the *Book of Changes*." Thus, from the title and Wen's note, we know the Prime Minster in question must be Wang Ya, who was an expert in Yang Xiong's *Taixuan* Scripture. The following key points in this poem deserve our special attention.

First, the second couplet implies important information. It is composed after the fashion of Liu Yuxi's aphorism in his "Inscriptions to My Humble Study"(陋室銘):[2] "[It is like] either Zhuge [Liang]'s cottage in Nanyang, or [Yang] Ziyun's Study in Xishu" (南陽諸葛盧，西蜀子雲亭). Liu compares his own residence with those of Zhuge Liang and Yang Xiong[3] (揚雄, 53–18, B.C., style Ziyun), exhibiting a sense of self-pride. Wen's replication of Liu's couplet, in a way more refined than Liu's and meant to pay his homage to Wang, likens Wang to Xie An (style Anshi) and Yang Xiong, with the implication that Wen had access to Wang both in the Shu region and in Huainan. "Anshi's Isle," believed to be Xie An's hermitage, was close to Yangzhou,[4] where Wang Ya performed his official duty as Salt and Iron Commissioner from 830 to 835.[5] "Ziyun's Terrace" was in Yang Xiong's homeland, Chengdu of the Shu region, a place where Wang Ya also had held office for several years.[6] Next, the third couplet tells us that, after Wang Ya's clan extermination during the Sweet Dew Incident, few dared to visit his old residence,[7] and only those eunuchs, referred to as the "Yellow Gates" (see what follows), exerted power there. Then the last couplet alludes to Wang Dao's (王導, 267–330) divination [8] and Guan Fu's (灌夫, ?–131 B.C.) clan extermination,[9] lamenting that Wang Ya was unaware of the impending disaster. "For whom does the pink lotus flourish," besides being an empathic scenic depiction, indicates that, as Wang's retainer, Wen was overcome with affliction at the late Prime Minster's death.

Poem Two

By chance I betook myself to Raven Robe Alley, 偶到烏衣巷，
With emotion unexpressed, I feel all the more
dismal. 含情更惘然。
Finding the Western Prefecture: willows at the
curved bank, 西州曲堤柳，

Pondering over the Eastern Mansion: lotus in the old pond.	東府舊池蓮。
The star crashes down to lament the senior statesman,	星坼悲元老，
Clouds gather to see off the "ink immortal."	雲歸送墨仙。[10]
Who would have thought the river-crossing boat,	誰知濟川楫，
Today becomes a rustic's skiff?	今作野人船？

Because of the information provided in Poem One, Poem Two needs only a brief explanation. At the "Raven Robe Alley,"[11] where Wang Ya lived, Wen ponders the incident in which Wang lost his life. In the "Western Prefecture," the "willow along the curve-bank" could serve as a reminder of the appalling way in which Wang Ya died—he was cut in half under the Isolated Willow (獨柳). Thus, it is a heartrending object for Wen Tingyun—the "lotus in the old pond" of the "Eastern Mansion" (conventionally, the Prime Minister's mansion)—an old retainer of the murdered Prime Minster. In his sad recollection of Wang's person and his tragic death, Wen mournfully asks: who would have known that an important minister of the state dynasty, a "river-crossing boat,"[12] would become a "rustic's skiff," a wronged and wretched man?

The two poems contribute much to our understanding of Wen's relations with Wang Ya. Wang Ya was Wen's Taiyuan fellow townsman and was enfeoffed as Viscount of Qingyuan County, place of the Wen clan's origin. Very possibly, Wen may have been Wang Ya's kinsman and Wang Ya may be the very Prime Minister hinted by the poem "Passing the Residence of the Late Hanlin Academician Yuan" (discussed in chapter 1). Their connection probably began early in Wen's life, continued in the Shu region, and was sustained up to the time of Wang's death. It was probable that Wang's support enabled Wen to maintain his living in Huainan. For a time, Wen might have been counted among the "talented men" gathered at the "exquisite parties." Wen held Wang's political statecraft, literary attainments, and fortune-telling lore in high esteem, hence his comparison of Wang to Yang Xiong and Xie An. When Wen revisited the remains of Wang's residence in Huainan, he could not hold back his deep sorrow for and fond memory of the deceased man. Against the dark backdrop of the political upheavals of the time, scarcely anyone dared speak on Wang Ya's behalf after the extermination of his clan. However, Wen's poems boldly protest the injustice Wang suffered. Each of his two poems ends with a rhetorical question, by means of which Wen appears to grieve over Wang's inability to foresee and avoid disaster, despite his familiarity with the fortune-telling skills of the *Taixuan* Scripture. He expresses poignantly a profound insight into his age, a time when even the life of a veteran minister such as Wang Ya might hang in the balance at any moment. Very naturally, along with Wen's somber reflections on Wang's death, his bitter hatred of the eunuchs manifests itself between and behind the lines.

In "Hundred-Rhyme Poem," we can pick out some narrative threads that may shed light upon Wen's relationship with Wang Ya; there is, for example, the following couplet:

56 I venerated the august bearing of General Big Tree, 威名尊大樹，
And tried to shun Autumn-Tu, the law and penalty. 刑法避秋荼。[13]

In Wen's wanderings over the country, it was after having taken shelter under the protection of a "Big Tree" (serving in the secretariat of a patron) that he committed some "misconduct" and evaded the penalty by fleeing to the capital (by 837). Evidently, the "Big Tree" must have fallen. In view of Wen's long friendship with him, "General Big Tree" very possibly refers to Wang. If so, "*Autumn-Tu*, the law and penalty" indirectly satirizes the eunuchs' brutal abuses of the law in order to purge their opponents after the Sweet Dew Incident.

Wen's subsequent return to the capital is related in "Hundred-Rhyme Poem" directly after the couplet we have just quoted:

57 From afar I gazed back beyond a thousand leagues, 遠目窮千里，
And my returning heart flew to the Nine Highways. 歸心寄九衢。[14]

Since, at the latest, the year of Wen's return to the capital was the second year of Kaicheng (837), Wen's stay in Huainan must have ended prior to that year, possibly in 836. But what happened in Huainan that forced him to flee to the capital? Of all the events in Wen's life, this is one of the most noteworthy and complicated; without its clarification, no lucid account of his life is possible.

AN INITIAL INVESTIGATION OF THE JIANGHUAI INCIDENT

The Jianghuai Incident occurred while Wen was in Huainan. On one occasion he was whipped and seriously injured. The incident itself is rather confusing, and fraudulent accounts of it in various sources have been frequently cited to disparage Wen's personality. Since even the early records in the Tang and the Song anecdotal literature are contradictory and misleading, we shall examine them carefully one by one, and using comparison and contrast to distinguish truth from fallacy, we will establish the time, the place, the cause and the result, and the interested parties—all the particulars of the event.

In *Tongxin* (桐薪, quoted in WFQ, 257) by an unknown Tang author, we read:

> Wen Qi in his young days was whipped in the Jianghuai river valleys by a senior relative, hence he changed his name to Tingyun (雲), with

> the style name Feiqing. But some other books refer to him as Tingyun (筠). I really cannot understand what sense there is in referring to him like this (溫岐少曾于江淮為親表櫝楚，故改名庭雲，字飛卿，而他書或作庭筠，不曉所謂).

While Sun Guangxian's *Beimeng Suoyan* (4: 29) says the following about the same event: "Shen Hui of Wuxing said: My maternal uncle Wen once was whipped in the Jianghuai valleys by one of his senior relatives, and thereafter changed his name" (吳興沈徽曰：溫舅曾于江淮為親表櫝楚，由是改名焉).

The *Tongxin* and the *Beimeng Suoyan* records indicate:

1. that the event happened perhaps when Wen was as yet "young";
2. that it happened in the Yangtze-Huai river valleys, that is, the Jianghuai region;
3. that Wen was whipped;
4. that his senior relative whipped him;
5. that no reason was given for the whipping;
6. and that the incident might have had something to do with Wen's change of his name to Tingyun (庭筠) or Tingyun (庭雲).

In *Yuquanzi* (11) by another unknown writer of the Late Tang period, the story becomes longer and more details are provided:

> Wen Tingyun had great renown for composing poems and rhapsodies. At an earlier time, when he was about to follow the local recommendation, he went traveling between the valleys of the Yangzi and the Huai Rivers. Yao Xu (姚勖, fl. 830–850), the Imperial Deputy of Yangzi Court [of the Salt and Iron Monopoly Commission], offered him a handsome sum of money. Tingyun, still a young man at the time, however, squandered the money in the brothels. Yao, enraged with Tingyun for this, gave him a good whipping and drove him away. Subsequently, Wen could not pass the Presented Scholar Examination, in spite all his efforts. His elder sister, who was the wife of Zhao Zhuan, often gnashed her teeth and blamed Yao for this. One day there was a guest at the district office, and she happened to ask who it was. When the servants told her it was Yao Xu, Madame Wen burst into the office, took hold of Yao's sleeve, and cried loudly. Yao was more startled than confused. What is more, she grasped his sleeve so tightly that he could not get free, and was at a loss for what to do. It was some while before Madame Wen found her tongue: "My younger brother was young, and it is a common human desire to indulge in pleasure-seeking. How could you, just for that reason, flog him? Is it not you who caused him to have been unsuccessful up to now?" Then, she wept loudly again. Only after a long time did Yao manage to free himself. Yao went home enraged and bewildered; he fell ill on account of this and died

(溫庭筠有詞賦盛名。初，將從鄉里舉，客游江淮間。揚子留後姚勖厚遺之。庭筠年少，所得錢帛多為狹邪所費。勖大怒，笞且逐之，以故庭筠卒不中第。其姊，趙顓之妻也。每以庭筠下第，輒切齒于勖。一日，庭有客，溫氏偶問客姓名。左右以勖對。溫氏遂出廳事前，執勖袖大哭。勖殊驚異；且持袖牢固不可脱，不知所為。移時，溫氏方曰：我弟年少宴游，人之常情，奈何笞之？迄今無有所成，得不由汝致之？復大哭。久之，方得解。勖歸憤訝，竟以此得疾而卒).

The *Yuquanzi* record includes the following points:

1. The event happened right before Wen was about to follow the local recommendation, when he was "young";
2. It took place in the Jianghuai region;
3. Wen was given a good whipping and driven from the Yangzi County Salt and Iron Monopoly Commissioner's Office;
4. It was Yao Xu, the Imperial Deputy of Yangzi, who punished Wen;
5. The reason Yao punished Wen is that Wen squandered in the pleasure quarters the money Yao bestowed on him, money that was likely bestowed to facilitate Wen's studies for a Presented Scholar degree;
6. According to the author, the resulting scandal also accounts for Wen's lifelong failure to attain a Presented Scholar degree, although the account of Madame Wen's performance could be distorted by Late Tang factional prejudices and fabrications.

The above-cited works certainly have their merit as historical data, if we read them with a historical perspective. Similar statements can also be found in most of the later "poetry talks (*shihua*)" or other anecdotal literature. Particulars concerning Wen's flogging contained in them both differ from and agree with what we already know. As an echo of the early accounts, these works often epitomize the political fallacies of Wen's lifetime, although they may suggest the truth in one way or another. Wang Dingbao's *Tangzhiyan* (11: 121), Ji Yougong's *Tangshi Jishi* (54: 822), and You Mao's *Quantang Shihua* (4: 36) are just such later examples. Comparison of the contradictory pictures of the Jianghuai Incident, which they provide, will enable us to discover some grains of truth. A thorough study of all this anecdotal literature will bear fruit. As we will point out later, gossip about Wen's scandal in Jianghuai finds its most absurd expression in Wen's biographies in the standard histories, the two *Tang Histories*.

The assertion that Wen was whipped by Yao Xu (*Yuquanzi*) refers to the same whipping by one of his senior relatives (*Beimeng Suoyan*)—even though we have no evidence that Yao was one of his senior relatives. Wen could not have undergone such a notorious scandal a second time, even though for the time being we must accept "the first time" as our starting point for further research. We can, however, employ our sources to elicit further basic points.

We are given to understand that Wen involved himself in a scandal of the pleasure quarters, most probably brought about by his relationship with a singer, or courtesan, and that he was harshly lashed as a result. But the facts relevant to the fictions are of greater intricacy than the fictions suggest, and require further investigation before we can arrive at any conclusion. We must regard many details of the narratives as questionable; we must also ask: did Wen spend his money in the pleasure quarters just to satisfy his sexual desire? Using Tang moral standards as a basis for our judgment, what was wrong with Wen's consuming his money in this way? Why did Yao Xu first give Wen money and then chastise him so seriously? How much credibility can we expect of *Yuquanzi* and like sources?

The above sources state that as a result of the whipping, Wen was forced to change his name—this, too, sounds extremely doubtful, and we need to gather more evidence to clarify what is meant here. What would a change of his name do for him—would it salvage his reputation or indicate a determination on his part to change his ways? Neither alternative seems plausible. The statement that attributes all of Wen's failures in the Presented Scholar Examination to this whipping also needs explanation. As for the story's minor plots—both that Shen Hui called Wen (maternal) uncle, and that Wen's elder sister held Yao Xu to blame—they need not concern us. In fact, since Wen for a time became the target of much vilification, it was only natural that he was subjected to all kind of hearsay. Although we have no reason to question the relationship between Shen and Wen, it is difficult to give full credence to Madame Wen's performance, which is too theatrical to be credited as fact.

Notwithstanding the uncertain nature of the materials at hand, we are able to believe that the Jianghuai Incident took place just before Wen first "followed the local recommendation", that is, before his first participation in the Presented Scholar Examination. To judge by his extant works and other sources, Wen's first participation in the Metropolitan Prefecture Examination took place in the fourth year of Kaicheng (839). The incidents we are concerned with, therefore, could have happened no later than 839.

Information concerning Yao Xu's official career in the corresponding period compels the same conclusion. Yao "was repeatedly recommended by the local commissioners or magistrates and promoted to Investigating Censor before he took to assisting in the affairs of the Salt and Iron Commissioner";[15] "In the fifth month of the fourth year of Kaicheng, Yao Xu, the Assistant Commissioner in the Salt and Iron Monopoly, thanks to his capability in dealing with difficult lawsuits, was promoted to the position of Honorary Bureau Director of the Ministry of Ritual, Concurrent with the Previously-held Title of Assistant Commissioner in the Salt and Iron Monopoly" (檢校禮部郎中依前鹽鐵推官);[16] "The Assistant Commissioner in the Salt and Iron Monopoly, Yao Xu, as the director of the Heyin Salt and Iron Monopoly Bureau, excelled in rehabilitating wronged cases; the Salt and Iron Commissioner Cui Gong (崔珙) reported this to the throne, to reward and encourage him for his merits."[17] We thus know that up to the fifth month of the fourth year of Kaicheng (839), Yao Xu was continuing to assist in the affairs of the Salt and Iron Commissioner, and as director of the Heyin Salt and Iron Bureau, he had been advancing well in his official career. Subsequently, in the Huichang era (840–846) and after, Yao Xu "assumed the posts of magistrate of Hu and Chang Prefectures," and according to Tan Yao's *Jiatai Wuxingzhi*, "Yao Xu was appointed magistrate [of Wuxing Commandery—Hu Prefecture in Tang Dynasty] in the third year of Huichang (843) from his former post, Left Bureau Director of the Department of State Affairs (尚書左司郎中); later he was promoted to Bureau Director of the Ministry of Personnel" (吏部郎中). These records help reaffirm that it must have been during Yao's tenure as assistant in the Yangzi Salt and Iron Monopoly Bureau (揚子鹽鐵院)—several years before the fourth year of Kaicheng—that he bestowed money on Wen. Once again we come to the conclusion that the Jianghuai Incident happened some time before 839.

We shall expose the truth of a matter that has been obscured in various confusing records composed after (though in a sense, *before*) Wen's death—all of which reflect the gossip and rumors fabricated either by eunuchs or by pro-eunuch literati. In fact, the Jianghuai Incident presents itself as political persecution entangled with a private affair, a tangled skein of eunuch interference during a time when Wen's affections were set on a singer from the pleasure quarters. As for the political background, we should remember Wen's words in his "Epistle Presented to Prime Minister Pei": when he "traveled to the valley of the Huai River," he "had not expected that Du Zhi was to make a false charge and Zang Cang to harbor a bitter hatred against" him. As we have demonstrated, "Zang Cang" and "Du Zhi" were Wen's lifelong enemies—the eunuchs who had played a leading role in spreading rumors and fomenting trouble for him. Owing to the fact that the histories have recorded few substantial details concerning the behind-the-scenes activities of the eunuchs during the Kaicheng era, the case at hand is made all the more difficult to resolve. Moreover, researching Wen's private life can never be a simple and straightforward task. However, an exhaustive examination of all the exact details concerning the Jianghuai Incident is called for. Without such an examination, Wen's subsequent behavior recorded in the standard histories, together with his posthumous reputation, will not do him justice.

In order to find the solution to these difficulties, we must provide a thorough explanation of the following epistle, which will not only support our inference that Wen Tingyun traveled to the Huai River valley several years previous to 839, but will also provide a complete solution to the whole puzzle.

"EPISTLE PRESENTED TO BUREAU DIRECTOR HAN OF THE MINISTRY OF PERSONNEL" (上吏部韓郎中啓)

My wisdom is different from comprehensive mastery, and my ability lacks proficiency in any particular line. Fortunately I took over the great instruction [of my forefathers], so as not to lose the pure fragrance [of our ancestral glory]. But when the beam of the wagon is closer to the yoke,[18] I am sadly on the downslope and if I cannot take a look at the string and the bow, is my case different from what happened in the former era of our dynasty?[19] Like Guo Fan, I have not inherited land in "Jianye,"[20] and like Ji Shao, I have an old mansion in "Xingyang." A burden to friends of old, I am offered barely a piece of pig liver; my poor skill survives, to become the rib of a chicken[21] (某識異旁通，才無上技，幸傳丕訓，免墮清芬，衡軛相逢，方悲下路；弦弧未審，可異前朝？郭翻無建業先疇，嵇紹有滎陽舊宅，故人為累，僅得豬肝；薄技斯存，殆成雞肋).

When the wheels of time constantly revolve, my tears of sorrow can hardly be held back. I am a Zhongxuan, a traveler constantly moving; I am a Zhuge, fearful of marrying a wife early. What I live on is but several acres of land that can hardly support my life of leisure; and my wisdom is adequate to fill one office, but I can never obtain such a favor [I resemble] a desolate oak tree standing by the village shrine,[22] lagging along at the dead end of my way. No longer high halls, now even a vat room is hard to sustain; poverty-stricken in the lower marsh, where I can barely maintain a life (分陰屢轉，尺涕難收。仲宣之為客不休，諸葛之娶妻怕早。居惟數畝，不足棲遲；智效一官，靡能沾沃。荒涼散社，流寓窮途。高堂之甕社難充，下澤之津蹊可見).

I humbly think that a "forsaken mat" reminiscent of the past can inspire profound charity;[23] and that "to angle together while pouring out one's heart" can lead to a promising friendship.[24] That is why I venture to unfold my confidential feeling for your wise consideration. To have a recommendation letter from a Prime Minister of a time of peace would be an honor.[25] But the kerchief box forever conceals the secret [of his recommendation].[26] His condescension in commending and recommending me, however, will hopefully give me a chance (竊以棄茵懷舊，尚動深仁；投釣言情，猶牽末契。敢將幽懇，來問平衡。升平相公，簡翰為榮，巾箱永秘。頗垂敦獎，未至陵夷).

Were Your Excellency to speak my name and show consideration for me, so as to allocate me a position among the [Salt and] Iron Bureau's minor clerks, and let me rank myself among the ordinary officials of salt and sauce, then you will not be obliged to offer me food and clothes, and I need not conceal my ability and quality. A hard-pressed monkey who finds a tree, or a fish in a dry rut, who flings itself into a stream, could not be more fortunate than this![27] Thereafter, the poor orphan will find his shelter, by always

> depending on the friendship of Shan Tao and never begs brazenly at the door of Cheng Xiao.[28] My humble feelings are beyond expression (倘蒙一話姓名，試令區處。分鐵官之瑣吏，厠鹽醬之常僚。則亦不犯脂膏，免藏縑素。豈惟窮猿得木，涸鮒投泉。然後幽獨有歸，永托山濤之分；赫曦無恥，免干程曉之門。下情無任).

Like most of Wen's epistles, this one is replete with allusions and hidden references, and contains textual corruptions besides. It has never received the scholarly attention it deserves, because of its archaisms and obscurity. However, we must try to understand the basic gist of the text. In it, Wen first boasts of his family's glory and complains about his poverty, hinting at the fact that it was the constant persecution of the eunuchs that led to his disgrace. Wen's purpose in presenting this epistle was to induce Han to recommend him as a subordinate clerk in the Salt and Iron Monopoly. In seeking to achieve his purpose, he emphasizes the hardships and misfortune of his life. Wen stresses that, once he was granted that position, he would be able to earn himself a decent living and would not be forced to curry favor with the eunuchs, a path followed by many of his contemporaries. We find in this epistle the following vitally important points:

First of all, we find from this epistle that its time and place of presentation coincide exactly with that of the Jianghuai Incident: "I am a Zhongxuan, a traveler constantly moving; and I am a Zhuge, fearful of marrying a wife early." As cited in chapters 2 and 3, this sentence indicates that, after many years of wandering and until he was about forty years of age, Wen remained unmarried, but perhaps was about to marry soon (thus he was prompted to ask Han for a post). Since Wen married several years prior to the fourth year of Kaicheng (838), and in this epistle seems to be preparing to get married, it should also be datable a few years prior to the year 838. In other words, this epistle was composed during the period of Wen's Jianghuai stay, the time of the Jianghuai Incident.

In this epistle, Wen asks Han for a minor post in the Iron and Salt Monopoly Bureau, and there is no possibility that he could have been involved with more than one Iron and Salt Monopoly Bureau at same time. Therefore the Monopoly Bureau in question must have been the Yangzi Court located in Yangzi County of the Huainan Circuit. Yao Xu was said to have been Imperial Deputy there, although it is more likely that Bureau Director Han held the post. In fact, Wen's request of a favor from Han is a clear indication that Han must have been in charge of the Salt and Iron Monopoly in Yangzhou. This epistle must be regarded as a very important document reflecting the true character of the Jianghuai Incident. As we scrutinize it intently, we uncover more and more substantial information.

In this situation, Wen's declaration that "I cannot take a look at the string and the bow" implies that he did not have even the chance to sit for the civil service examinations, not to mention pass them. Indeed, Wen's experience presents a striking contrast to what happened in "the former era" of the Tang

Dynasty, the Dahe era, when Liu Fen, candidate of "Straightforward Criticism and Daring Remonstrance" (直言敢諫), leveled a drastic attack at the evil rule of the eunuchs. At the time, Liu's memorial to the throne was widely circulated and admired, but "the Examination Administrator dared not accept him for fear of the eunuchs' revenge." Wen Tingyun's case, similar to that of Liu Fen of "the former era," was emblematic of the struggle between the southern and northern offices, and must also have been well known. As a result, he would not need to have spoken more plainly, since the rhetorical question "is it different from what happened in the former era of our dynasty?" is indication enough of the unspoken allusion to Liu Fen. Therefore, we can conclude that this epistle was presented in the Kaicheng era (836–840), because only then could Wen have referred to Liu Fen's event as having taken place in "the former era of our dynasty." From 837 on, Wen was in Chang'an attending the Heir Apparent, and so the Jianghuai Incident under discussion most probably took place in the first year of Kaicheng (836), immediately after the Sweet Dew Incident, when every aspect of political life was completely dominated by the eunuchs.

Who was this Bureau Director? We find him to be Han Yi (韓益, fl. 820–840).

We cannot be sure that Yao Xu was the man who whipped Wen, because it is doubtful that he ever was an Imperial Deputy of the Yangzi Court. We know that when Yao was assisting in the affairs of the Salt and Iron Commissioner, he was steadily promoted; but a move from the post of Imperial Deputy (留後) of the Yangzi Court to that of Director of the Heyin Court was in many ways a demotion. The Salt and Iron Monopoly Bureau located in Yangzi County was the national headquarters of all branch offices of the Salt and Iron Monopoly Bureau.[29] After the An-Shi Rebellion, Yangzhou became the center for the transportation of grain and other products from south of the Yangtze River, and the Salt and Iron Commissioners themselves often had to reside in Yangzhou for considerable periods of time. Yao very possibly held a post in the Yangzi Court, for instance, that of Assistant Commissioner, which the author of *Yuquanzi* mistook for the post of Imperial Deputy of the Yangzi Court. On the other hand, the so-called Bureau Director (upper fifth rank) Han, whose official rank was much higher than that of Yao, must have been in charge of the Yangzi Court. One reason for this inference is that it was as late as the year 839 that Yao was promoted to the post of Honorary Bureau Director of the Ministry of Ritual, a position still lower than Han's. However, it does not seem likely that either Yao or Han would have given Wen a beating merely for squandering his money in the pleasure quarters. The inference from Wen's own account is that it must have been the eunuchs who framed him by taking advantage of his liaison with a singer-prostitute.

According to Wang Pu's *Tanghuiyao*, after Wang Ya was killed in the Sweet Dew Incident, his position of Salt and Iron Commissioner was filled first by Linghu Chu (令狐楚, 765–836), and then, in the first year of Kaicheng, by

Li Shi (李石). During Li Shi's tenure as Salt and Iron Commissioner (836), he promoted Han Yi, the then Supernumerary of the Treasury Bureau (金部員外郎), to the post of Supervisor of Affairs for the Ministry of Revenue (判度支) in charge of financial affairs. We can thus judge that the Han addressed in this epistle is in all likelihood Han Yi.

This epistle yields more evidence of Wen's animosity for the eunuchs. Wen likened the Bureau Director Han to Shan Tao, with the implication that his late father was like Ji Kang and he himself like Ji Shao. This hidden analogy runs through the whole epistle. When, at the very beginning, Wen says "My wisdom is different from comprehensive mastery," he is quoting Ji Kang's letter to Shan Tao, thus hinting that he adhered to his dead father's political stance against the eunuchs. When referring to his financial status, Wen also expresses his idea by alluding to Ji Shao. At the end of the epistle, when voicing his purpose in presenting this epistle, he addresses Han as Shan Tao and adds one more allusion: "never brazenly begging at the door of Cheng Xiao." As we have pointed out, the fact that for a time "Cheng Xiao assumed the official position of Minister of the Yellow Gate Ministry" is the only possible reason why Wen would make use of this name as an insinuation about the eunuchs. In Ji Kang's "Letter for Breaking Off Relations with Shan Juyuan," we find the following remarks: "Since I have so many diseases and ailments, I really want to get rid of [political] affairs in order to protect myself. What I lack is just this purity. How can I call myself pure after seeing the Yellow Gate?" (若吾多病困，欲離事自全，以保餘年，此真所乏耳，豈可見黃門而稱貞哉). Having excused himself from seeing the "Yellow Gate," Ji Kang finds a pretext for his reluctance to serve the usurping Sima clan, the Jin Dynasty royal family, and hope to keep his "purity." "Yellow Gate" originally referred only to the palace gate, but the term derived from its original meaning a range of connotations: from inner palace official institutions and positions such as the Yellow Gate Ministry and Minister of the Yellow Gate, to professional positions such as Yellow Gate Director of Attendance and Palace Yellow Gate of Attendance, positions which were assumed exclusively by the eunuchs. Here "yellow gate" refers quite clearly to the eunuchs. Wen covertly employed this meaning simply because, under the despotism of the eunuchs, he could not attack the eunuchs openly. Faced the eunuchs' rampant actions in the political arena, Wen wanted to speak out but was not able to voice his opinions freely; this is the psychogenic complexity that underlies most of his political poems. When dealing with Wen's accounts of the eunuchs, we must pay particular attention to this point.

From "Hundred-Rhyme Poem" we know that Wen, from the very beginning of his vagrant life, was in such a predicament that "In my loves and in my hates I took precautions against Du Kui / In my laments and sighs, I felt melancholy as did Yang Zhu." In his "Epistle Presented to Prime Minister Pei," he says concerning his experiences in Jianghuai: "I had not expected that Du Zhi (Kui) was to make a false charge and Zang Cang to harbor a bitter hatred against me." When Wen presented this epistle to Han, he had not yet married or entered officialdom, or received the chance to attend upon the Heir Apparent. At this time he also had never taken the civil service examination. However, he still requested help from his late father's friend, disdaining to seek the favor of the eunuchs. This fact adds to the persuasiveness of the argument that the eunuchs, who had caused the death of his father, were his deadly foes. Therefore, the rancor that he bore against the eunuchs began early, and was not based merely on his own experiences. Had it not been for the eunuchs, there would not have been a Jianghuai Incident. It was the eunuchs who fabricated the story and publicized it, seeking to block Wen's possible advancement.

FURTHER STUDY AND CLARIFICATION OF THE INCIDENT

Now let us return to the Jianghuai Incident itself and try to discern what Wen did in the pleasure quarters, and who plotted his persecution. Because the whole event has much relevance both to his marriage and to his struggles with the eunuchs, we will proceed our search by scrutinizing the particulars of the two aspects from various angles.

In "Hundred-Rhyme Poem," Wen confesses reluctantly that something he had done, like a flaw that obscures the whole jade, had occasioned him endless distress from slanders. He attributed the slanders he suffered—

83 By incessant aspersions, even bones are destroyed, 積毀方銷骨，
I fear that a slight blemish would spoil the whole gem. 微瑕懼掩瑜。

—to the following behavior on his part, stating the fundamental reason of his failures in the examinations, and bringing the causality of the poem into a strict logical whole:

82 Coming as a guest, the green-ant, I poured, 客來斟綠蟻，
Trying to ransom a wife, on the blue-beetles, I trod. 妻試踏青蚨。

It was the eunuchs who blocked his way from the beginning to the end. Here Wen lays out the details of the event that caused him so many troubles: he was drinking in a brothel, and, squandering his money, he redeemed a singer to be his wife. Comparing this with the tale of *Yuquanzi* brings the whole truth to light and breaks through the many layers of misapprehensions and misconstructions. A reading of *Yuquanzi* has already caused us to wonder why Wen wasted his money in this manner, and to doubt that he could really be a poor but generous patron of the brothels. Now we know that what Wen did was to spend the money he acquired from the Salt and Iron Monopoly Bureau on the purchase of a wife from among the singers in the brothel. This "indiscreet behavior" became the handle of a spear that Wen gave the eunuchs to be wielded against himself. The eunuchs wielded it, first to inflict a humiliating attack on Wen and then to rain all kinds of abuse upon him, both excluding him from any success in his official career.

That Wen had purchased a singer to be his wife can also be discerned in his "Epistle Presented to the Vice-Minister, Salt and Iron Commissioner," where he articulates the idea in the following unusual manner:

> I tried to tame my nature of moose and deer, to emulate the character of mandarin-ducks. As a result, the solitary orchid in the nine acres [himself] had to suffer anguish for rumors and slander; and the avenue to picking one twig of the crimson osmanthus [passing the Presented Scholar Examination] was unexpectedly blocked (強將麇鹿之情，欲學鴛鴦之性，遂使幽蘭九畹，傷謠諑之情多；丹桂一枝，竟攀折之路斷).

"Nature of moose and deer" connotes a spontaneous and wild disposition; specifically, it hints at a licentious and sensual character.[30] "Mandarin-ducks" in Chinese tradition is the symbol of love between husband and wife. In other words, Wen stubbornly transformed his merrymaking and dalliance with the singer into a serious conjugal affection. Defying the prejudices of the Tang social estate system under which men of aristocratic or gentle family never married beneath them, he took the liberty of taking for his wife a singer-prostitute, a creature who ordinarily serves merely to satisfy the sexual desire of any patron of the brothel. As a result, a "solitary orchid" in "the nine acres" suffers from "rumors and slander."[31] This was the fundamental cause of the endless rumor mongering to which Wen was subjected, which, in turn, led to his numerous failures to "pick one twig of the crimson osmanthus," that is, to pass the Presented Scholar Examination.

Among the Late Tang literati, frequenting the pleasure quarters was quite common. Tang literati, in general, lacked a sense of morality in their behavior toward the opposite sex. To take a singer as a playmate, or to desert a girl after robbing her of her chastity, was regarded as something quite usual. Even serious poets such as Bai Juyi and Li Shen kept singers for private service. Du Mu, representative of his time, went so far as to boast of his sexual conquests in the well-known line: "After ten years, I awake from my dream of Yangzhou / Only to win renown for heartlessness in the brothels" (十年一覺揚州夢，贏得青樓薄倖名).[32] However, taking a prostitute as wife, as Wen did, is virtually without parallel. Comparing Wen's case with the prevailing attitude expressed in *The Story of Yingying* (鶯鶯傳),[33] by Yuan Zhen, we cannot but regard him as a man who bravely challenged the accepted absurdities of his time. In the story, Yingying, daughter of a distinguished lineage and a second cousin of Scholar Zhang (張生), having been lured by Zhang into a secret rendezvous and having lost her chastity, believes herself to be unqualified to be Zhang's wife. At the same time, Zhang, once so intent upon his importunate infatuation with Yingying, readily finds an excuse to abandon her, even though she has offered him all she has and is waiting longingly for him. Many of Zhang's contemporaries applaud "the skill with which Zhang extricates himself from this entanglement." Seen in the historical context, the personalities of Scholar Zhang and Wen Tingyun stand in bold contrast to each other. For Wen, the problem was merely that he took his love affair too seriously. A son of a declined aristocratic clan, he decided to marry a singer at the expense of his reputation and in defiance of the prevailing bias in favor of family power and influence. It was precisely this unconventional behavior that brought a whole succession of troubles upon him later in his life. It is ironic that it should have been the eunuchs, those most contemptible to convention, who took the lead in brandishing the traditional Confucian weapon against Wen.

The following is one of Wen's poems referring to his marriage with the singer:

"A CASUAL ENCOUNTER" (偶游, j. 4, WFQ)

In a curved lane slanting over a stretch of the river,	曲巷斜臨一水間，
The small gate all day long remained unopened.	小門終日不開關。
Like a red pearl canopy—the cherries are ripe,	紅珠斗帳櫻桃熟，
With his golden-tail screen—the peacock is at leisure.	金尾屏風孔雀閑。
Butterfly on your cloud coiffure almost captivates fragrant herb,	雲髻幾迷芳草蝶，
Hill of your forehead-yellow will not limit the setting sun,	額黃無限夕陽山，
You and I are just mates like mandarin ducks,	與君便是鴛鴦侶，
So don't seek any other companion in the human world.	休向人間覓往還。

This is one of a few of Wen's poems expressing his true feelings for his prostitute-lover. Here Wen describes what he experienced in a brothel. The second last line reveals that Wen indeed demonstrates "the character of a mandarin-duck," that is, a conjugal love, toward the heroine addressed in the poem. We suggest the lady addressed in this poem is Wen's lover involved in the Jianghuai Incident, although we must explore the poem at greater length to identify her as the singer-prostitute whom he later married. Wen has been portrayed as a libertine who gave free rein to his passions and destroyed his career prospects through his unrestrained conduct, but there is no evidence that he went any farther than many of his famous contemporaries, such as Yuan Zhen and Du Mu, in this respect. Quite contrary to the conventional censure of him, Wen was more faithful in his love and more extreme in his affection than many of the figures in the contemporary romances. In the matter of love he was really an exception to his times.

The following poem is his love song written for that singer.

"HEARTBROKEN LOVESICKNESS" (懊惱曲, j. 2, WFQ)

With silk of lotus root to make thread, it is hard to apply a needle,
With pollen of pistils as dye, how can the yellow become deep?
藕絲作線難勝鍼，蕊粉染黃那得深？

Employing a pair of subtle metaphors, the first couplet ushers the reader into an agonizing and captivating world of love. The fine silk drawn from the lotus root is too fragile to be used with a needle, and pollen of pistils, unsuitable for use as a yellow dye, augments the sense of impossibility. Understood literally, these images are already redolent with the depression and persistence of love. If we realize that the term "silk of lotus root" (*ousi*, 藕絲) and "needle" (*zhen*, 針) are homophonic puns for "yearning for the lover" (*si'ou*, 思偶) and "true [affection]" (*zhen*, 真), the first line means "the yearning for love is hard to bear when emotion is strong and honest," while the dainty image of pollen in the second implies that such love is unacceptable to the conventions of the society.

If the "white jade" and the "fragrant orchid" cannot love each other,
For the charming smile in the green tower I squander a thousand taels of gold.
白玉蘭芳不相顧，青樓一笑輕千金。

Our poet and the singer fell into love with each other, but there were obstacles to overcome before they could be united in wedlock. To that end, he spent all the money (said to have been bestowed on him) for the sake of the woman's favor, "a smile in the green tower." The "thousand taels of gold [spent] for a mere smile" is an old epithet meaning that in order to win the favor of a beauty, one is willing to pay whatever price. In Wen Tingyun's eyes, only this is true love.

Don't say that since time immemorial, things were always like this,
A sharp sword that strikes a bell can coil round a finger like a piece of lead.
莫言自古皆如此，健劍刜鐘鉛繞指。

Such love has been praised since antiquity, but very few dare really to put it into practice. Yet even a man of iron can be softened in the face of true affection.

At the end of autumn, all the courtyard green yields to the frost,
But the lotus flower keeps its red, until death.
三秋庭綠盡迎霜，唯有荷花守紅死。

This love will yield to no pressure, not even to death. The image of the lotus flower that keeps its red color even when withered is a symbol of such devoted feeling.

The minor clerk of Lujiang drove out his [carriage with] ruby wheels,
When the willow twigs sent forth their sprouts the fragrant jade were in spring.
盧江小吏朱斑輪，柳縷吐牙香玉春。

To protest against the injustice of an arranged marriage by their mother, both Jiao Zhongqing (焦仲卿) and his wife died as martyrs to their love.[34] Wen alludes to the story to voice his determinaton to marry the singer, despite the consequent pressures he would have to confront. The two lovers, "the fragrant orchid" and "the white jade," are enjoying the blessing of their union to the fullest.

Since the two halves of a golden hairpin were the token of mutual affection,
How could the one bear to let the other turn to dust alone and in vain?
兩股金釵已相許，不令獨作空成塵。

This is not merely a declaration of devotion; it is Wen's pledge of action to sustain their conjugal felicity until death. Neither will let the other die alone.

On and on goes the Chu river flowing like a galloping horse,
Grieving purples and distressed reds are spread all over the level plain.
悠悠楚水流如馬，恨紫愁紅滿平野。

How many lovers could not marry each other, and how many tragedies constantly occurred throughout the country, to which the Chu River [Yangtze] is witness and of which the flowers on the vast plains retain sad memories!

The soil of the fields, for thousands of years bears a grudge against the injustice,
And up to now, is fired into mandarin-duck tiles.
野土千年怨不平，至今燒作鴛鴦瓦。

Generation after generation, the affection of love and its protest against injustice are undying, and the mandarin-duck tiles, its everlasting substantiation.

Reading this poem convinces us that Wen Tingyun can, at least, be regarded as a devoted lover. There are more poems attesting to this.[35] The profound sorrow and resolution given expression here have their basis in the reality of his antitraditional behavior in marrying a singer with whom he had fallen deeply in love. As far as we can determine from the extant materials, Wen also ransomed another singer-prostitute. This is shown by his best friend Duan Chengshi's three poems "On the Occasion that Rouqing Annulled Her Registration of Prostitute, I Playfully Presented This to Feiqing" (柔卿解籍戲贈飛卿).[36]

Wen's marriage with a singer-prostitute and his love for her, although not equivalent to modern conjugal affection, form a striking contrast to the prevailing norms. What Wen did was also in defiance of the Tang Dynasty penal law, which, although never forbidding a literary man from patronizing brothels, did lay down strict regulations prohibiting marriages between individuals from different social classes. Marriages between members of aristocratic families and those of the low classes of society were definitely proscribed.[37] Wen's family status, although already in decline, was at least that of the "scholar class," while a singer (courtesan) at most belonged to the category of "official household." In a sense, Wen's marriage to a singer can be taken as a sign of his betrayal of the privileged social stratum to which his family belonged. It must have elicited strong distaste from many powerful ministers of aristocratic origin and been one more factor in his conspicuous failure to pursue an official career. It also led some traditional Chinese critics to condemn his failure to behave as a decent man.

Nevertheless, Wen Tingyun's love story was not completely forgotten by later Chinese, especially by discriminating scholars. It is no wonder that the great author of *A Dream of the Red Chamber*, Cao Xueqin, once ranked Wen as one of the most antitraditional figures in Chinese history. Cao puts forward the following theory:[38]

> All men, apart from the very good and the very bad, are much alike. The very good are born at a propitious time when the world is well governed, the very bad in times of calamity when danger threatens. Examples of the first are Yao, Shun, Yu and Tang, King Wen and King Wu [the sage kings], Duke Zhou and Duke Shao, Confucius and Mencius [the sages]. . . . Examples of the second are Kong Kong, Chieh, Chou, Chin Shihuang [the evil kings], Wang Mang, Tsao Tsao, Huan Wen, An Lushan and Chin Kuai [conspirators or evil ministers]. But there is another kind of human being that are gifted with an ambivalent spirit of both the good and the evil. The pure intelligence with which they are endowed sets them above their myriad fellow creatures, but their perversity and unnatural behavior sink them lower than other men too. Born into rich and noble families, such people will become romantic eccentric; born into poor but cultured families, they will become high-minded scholars or recluses. Even if born into luckless and humble homes, they will never grow up into yamen runners or servants at the beck and call of the vulgar—they'll turn out celebrated actors or courtesans. People of this type in the past were Xu [Ling], Yu [Xin], Tao Qian, Ruan Ji, Ji Kang, Liu Ling, the two families of Wang and Xie, Gu Hutou [Gu Kaizhi, the painter], Chen Shubao [Later Monarch of the Chen], the Tang Emperor Minghuang, the Song Emperor Huizong, *Wen Feiqing*,

> Mi Fei, Shi Yannian, Liu Yong and Qin Guan [high minded scholars]. . . . All of these, in their different fields, were essentially the same.

Cao places Jia Baoyu, the protagonist in his novel, into this category and gives the highest praise to those figures who are characteristic of Baoyu, including Wen Tingyun.

However the basic details mentioned above concerning Wen's romance have disappeared from view after a thousand years; consequently, in this regard as in many other respects, Wen has been continually misunderstood.

Now that we are informed about Tingyun's marriage with a singer-prostitute and his subsequent endless troubles thereafter, we have the ability to scrutinize the Jianghuai Incident in a clearer way. In Yangzhou, the biggest commercial center of the Late Tang times, the eunuchs, political representatives of the rising merchants and of miscellaneous urban residents, wielded influence and power that should on no account be underestimated. As seen from the "Epistle Presented to the Bureau Director Han," Wen begged Han, who was in charge of the Yangzi Court over which the eunuchs also exercised a considerable influence, for a minor post. Han, and Yao Xu as well, seemed friendly toward Wen, at least at the beginning, and they may have helped him in some way. But the eunuchs were not willing to allow Wen to procure the lucrative post so easily. At the same time that Wen was purchasing his future wife's freedom, the eunuchs, ever alert to any opportunity, sent their agents to give Wen a warning: do not dream of laying your hand on this. Consequently, Wen suffered a beating and certainly failed to take the post.

Wen gave an account of the eunuchs' persecution of him in the Jianghuai region, as already noted, in his "Epistle Presented to Prime Minister Pei." Not only was Wen's advance by means of the civil service examination utterly blocked, but his chances of obtaining a post in the Yangzi Court were also destroyed. Thus wronged, he could not be rehabilitated, and even many powerful and sympathetic ministers to whom he appealed were not able to do anything for him. It was the eunuchs who were responsible for all Wen's sufferings. In regard to Wen's disastrous encounter in Jianghuai, we have no choice but to believe his own accounts; with Wen's family background and political orientation, it is only natural that he would have been regarded by the eunuchs as an implacable enemy and have encountered their constant retaliation.

Concerning the Jianghuai Incident, we have so far succeeded in discovering the following details: Wen importuned the Yangzi Court for a post, he received money and spent it on the purchase of a singer-prostitute to be his wife, he suffered subsequent humiliation and whipping, and throughout the whole affair the eunuchs were maneuvering in the background. The event took place in the year 836. Wen suffered from the eunuchs' vindictiveness, which was implemented by a certain official (not necessarily Yao Xu). The event was precipitated when Wen recklessly tried to obtain a lucrative post in the eunuch-controlled Yangzi Court. The result was a scandal. Many writers between the Tang and the Song dynasties believed that the scandal forced Wen to change his name and ruined his future official career.

A series of questions remain to be answered: Did Wen really change his name merely because he was whipped in Jianghuai? Did the event prevent him from passing the Presented Scholar Examination? If so, how? If not, what happened next, after he went to the capital? These questions will occupy our subsequent discussions.

Throughout the affair, there were men who sympathized with Wen. There would also have been those who were forced to act at the eunuchs' behest and attack Wen. There may even have been a scapegoat who had to bear the charge of unfairly insulting him. However, the eunuchs, the true culprits, always remained in the background. The true story has never been completely revealed. On the contrary, during Wen's lifetime, the nature of the event was obscured by all kinds of rumors and gossip; after Wen's death, it was distorted by various records based on the rumors spread while he was alive. We have already attained some understanding of Wen's complex net of social relations, which were woven through the multiple oppositions of the Southern-Northern Offices and the Niu-Li Factions. More often than not, these complicated alliances make it difficult for us to identify many of those with whom Wen was linked. In treating Wen's biographical materials, we must above all bear in mind the disparaging tone of the Song Dynasty historiographers. They never deigned to attempt a full and accurate record of the eunuchs' deeds, but wantonly criticized such unorthodox figures as Wen Tingyun, and simply ignored the anti-eunuch import of many events in Wen's life.

In order to clarify what role this event played in Wen's life as a whole, and what its role has been in shaping Wen's posthumous reputation, we must deal with Wen's biographies in JTS and in XTS. Only after refutation of these seemingly veritable records can Wen's true face be revealed. Records in these "standard histories" strongly influence the thinking of traditional Chinese chroniclers, and with respect to Wen's biographical studies, these untrustworthy records have proved extremely detrimental to any reevaluation of his life. With this in mind, let us take a look at the picture of the Jianghuai Incident given by the standard histories. In actual fact, both histories depart so far from the truth that not even the fictions composed in the Tang and Song dynasties can surpass them in absurdity. JTS says (190: 5082):

> In the middle of Xiantong, frustrated and disappointed, he returned to Jiangdong by way of Guangling.[39] As Wen still harbored complaints that Linhu Tao had not helped him to become a Presented Scholar during his long tenure as Prime Minister,[40] after arrival, and in company with young parvenus, he reveled crazily in the brothels, and for rather a long while did not have audience with Linghu.[41] What was worse, he begged and importuned for money in the Yangzi

> Court,[42] and violated the curfew law by going out intoxicated at night. He was attacked by the police patrol, having several of his teeth knocked out and his face disfigured. Thereupon he returned to Yangzhou to appeal his case. Linghu Tao put the police patrol on trial, but the police patrol spared no effort in speaking about Tingyun's scandals in the brothels, and Linghu Tao had to set both sides free.[43] Henceforth gossip about Tingyun's immoral behavior spread even to the capital.[44] Tingyun now personally went to Chang'an, presenting letters to various ministers in the hope of clearing himself of the false charges laid against him.[45]

While XTS records (91: 3792):

> He left to return to the Jiangdong region. At this time, Linghu Tao was in charge of the garrison of Huainan Circuit. Tingyun, harboring the complaint that Linghu during his tenure as Prime Minister did not help him to become a Presented Scholar, passed by the gate of Linghu's mansion without paying a visit. Moreover, he begged for money at the Salt and Iron Monopoly Bureau in Yangzi County, and became so drunk at night that he was beaten by the patrol soldier, and his teeth were broken before he went back to Yangzhou to appeal to Tao. For Wen's sake, Tao accused a clerk, who in turn laid all the blame on Wen's debauched manners. Tao had to set both of them free. The incident was heard about even in the capital, where Tingyun tried to have audience with almost all the high-ranking officials in an effort to unburden himself of the clerk's vilification and slander.

From these narratives, other than discovering that the details in XTS are but a copy of those in JTS, we can elicit the following main points:

1. that the event happened in the middle of Xiantong (860–873), that is, almost thirty years after the "first" Jianghuai Incident (836), and a short time before Wen's death;
2. that Wen returned to Huainan once more;
3. that Wen was attacked and beaten, his face disfigured, and his teeth broken;
4. that it was a police patrol (虞侯) or a patrol soldier (邏卒) who inflicted such rude and humiliating blows on him;
5. that Wen, old as he was, "reveled crazily in the brothels" with young parvenus and "importuned for money in the Yangzi Court, and violated the curfew";
6. and that, having failed in his appeal to Linghu Tao in Huainan, Wen "personally went to Chang'an, presenting letters to various ministers in the hope of clearing himself of the wrongful charge laid against him."

Comparing the time, place, interested parties, and the causes and results of the event with those recorded in *Tongxin*, *Beimeng Suoyan*, and *Yuquanzi*, we find:

The event happened in the same place, Huainan, and once more Wen was subjected to personal attack and injury, though this time it is a police patrol or a patrol soldier that dealt the blows to him instead of Yao Xu or a senior relative. In both versions the beating was connected with Wen's indiscreet behavior in the pleasure quarters, as well as some matter in the Yangzi Court, where Wen was said to have brought troubles on himself. In addition to causing a name change and lifelong failures in his political career, the whole affair now becomes entangled with Linghu Tao. Finally, it was after having been attacked in Huainan that Wen went to Chang'an to clear himself of the charges laid against him. Except for the statement that the incident happened in the middle of Xiantong, we can observe that the contour of the event completely conforms to that of the "first" or "earlier" account, and that there are additional concrete details supporting our conclusion that the narratives in *Tongxin*, *Beimeng Suoyan*, and *Yuquanzi* all refer to the same event.[46] Now we must add this one further record to the chain of extant sources.

It is inconceivable that such a scandalous event should have happened to Wen twice. Judging from the internal evidence in Wen's works and external evidence in various sources, in particular the exactly identical details recorded in them, we must point out that the two *Tang Histories* commit a serious mistake in their handling of the Jianghuai Incident. Misdating an event of 836 to the 860s is by no means an accidental phenomenon. Rather, it is the necessary product of the combined function of rumors spread by the eunuchs, of anecdotes recording these rumors, and of prejudices cherished by undiscriminating historiographers. In other words, the Song historiographers encountered the miscellaneous anecdotes, disbelieved them, but were unable to surpass them in truthfulness, within the limitation of their own time. Only by exposing the mistakes in the standard histories, can we view the Jianghuai Incident in its true light.

How and to what a degree Linghu Tao could be involved in the Jianghuai Incident will be taken up in chapter 8, an account of Wen's later life. That the aftermath of the Jianghuai Incident could extend over thirty years is sufficient to show what a far-reaching role it played in Wen's life and how necessary it is for us to clarify this matter on his behalf, penetrating the dual obscurities of the histories and of literature.

All accounts agree that, after the Jianghuai Incident, Wen went to the capital, where more evils and further misadventures befell him, a misunderstood poet engagé in the turmoil of his times.

Chapter Five

Secret Attendance upon the Heir Apparent

INTRODUCTORY REMARKS

Despite the anachronisms found in the two *Tang Histories* concerning the Jianghuai Incident, their account of Wen's return to the capital after the Incident is faithful to what really happened. This can be seen clearly in the following couplet of "Hundred-Rhyme Poem," as already cited earlier:

57 From afar I gazed back beyond a thousand leagues, 遠目窮千里，
And my returning heart flew to the Nine Highways. 歸心寄九衢。

This provides the information that after Wen reached Jianghuai, thus ending his long journey, he returned to the capital. What motivated Wen to go to the capital once more? In the black and white terms of the two *Tang Histories*, he did so "to unburden himself of the clerk's vilification and slander," "in the hope of clearing himself of the false charges laid against him." In other words, he was seeking to escape the eunuchs' persecution and extricate himself from his predicament. As we know, it was precisely because of his unfavorable family background that Wen purposely avoided a career in the capital, the political center, preferring instead a vagrant life under various local patrons. Now in desperation, he found himself in such straits that he was forced to give up his life in the provinces and travel to the capital for support, disregarding the dangers he had to face in the capital, "at the feet of the emperor." The following lines give a vivid description of what Wen faced before he was successful in finding a position in capital society.

58 To enjoy sound sleep the price is to suffer long depression, 寢甘誠繫滯，
To be served free soup, I have to act with caution and attention. 漿饋貴睢盱。

59 I kept a calling card in my pocket, even though
I'm far famed, 懷刺名先遠，
To help the time, very few appreciated my Way. 干時道自孤。
60 By molars and incisors I was repeatedly
recommended and praised, 齒牙頻激發，
With umbrella and bookcase my road was yet
rugged and rocky. 簦笈尚崎嶇。

"To be served free soup," a metaphor for being offered any favor, alludes to *Zhuangzi*: "I went into ten soup-shops to get a meal, and in five of them the soup was served before I had paid for it."[1] "Pocketing calling cards" alludes to Ni Heng (禰衡, 173–198), who went to the capital but, because of his pride, found it hard to visit anybody until the characters on his cards were worn illegible.[2] "By molar and by teeth" means to be commented upon by many people. "Umbrella and bookcase" make up the outfit of a traveling literary man, and are hence here a synecdoche for Wen's own official career.

It was unlikely that Wen would be able to find any position in aristocratic circles in the capital, acting completely on his own; therefore, in order to gain an access into fashionable society he had to look attentively about for an opportunity. Wen reminds us that, endowed with a nature similar to that of Ni Heng, and numbering the eunuchs among his mortal enemies, it was difficult for him to progress. Few officials in the capital were willing or courageous enough to accept him, given both his fame and infamy. Because of his unyielding loyalty and rectitude to the Tang Empire, his Way with respect to state policy asserted itself as an ambition to curb and even to eliminate the eunuchs. This was the dream of many honest literati during this time. However, after many disastrous failures, it proved to be unfeasible, and was "appreciated by few."

Subsequently, Wen tells us about his fruitless attempt to progress in the central bureaucracy of the capital. Nevertheless, he was in high favor with several important statesmen, including his teacher, Li Cheng, who at one time was Prime Minister, and Pei Du, the most influential and meritorious minister of the Late Tang period. But as a result of the eunuch politics, he was treated as an alien pariah by his snobbish contemporaries, and was denied any opportunity for promotion through normal channels. For this reason the way before him remained "rugged and rocky."

Following the couplets cited above from "Hundred-Rhyme Poem" is an extremely obscure account of Wen's attendance upon the Heir Apparent, the central topic of this chapter. This obscurity necessitates an examination of all the details contained in every relevant record, despite the baffling difficulties such inquiry entails. Initially, we will give a brief introduction.

Professor Zhan Antai[3] first suggested that there may have been a close relationship between Wen and the Heir Apparent, but because of lack of evidence, his argument is not convincing. An examination of this episode, from the point of view of Wen's private experience, commits us to numerous investigations into the complexities of both the historical and literary sources. In the Late Tang period, poetic artistry had fully matured; simultaneously, eunuch politics impelled Wen to make maximum use of his scholastic ability, in order to express his political view without incurring persecution. "Hundred-Rhyme Poem" is a unique composition created against this background. The true circumstances of Wen's attendance upon the Heir are lost in the perplexing labyrinth of Wen's poetic contrivances and in the maze of the histories. In particular they are deeply obscured behind the camouflage of the abstruse artistic expressions found in this long poem.

Before we go into the details of our study, we must first of all reach a basic understanding of the general situation in which the Heir Apparent Incident took place, so as to get a better look at Wen's particular role in this historical event. By the "Heir Apparent Incident," we mean the incident in which the Heir Apparent, Li Yong (827–838) or *Zhuangke* (莊恪), as he was posthumously honored, became a victim of eunuch power. What Wen did and said during this incident, once clarified, will provide evidence sufficient to refute most, if not all, of the traditional prejudices toward him. In order to reverse the verdict, however, we must exercise great caution and consult as many historical sources as possible.[4]

After the Sweet Dew Incident of 835, as the eunuchs revenged themselves upon Emperor Wenzong (808–840, r. 827–840) for his participation in the machinations against them, the emperor became increasingly subject to their control. Having relinquished almost all his power and hopes, Wenzong now attempted in every way possible to set up his Heir Apparent, Li Yong, in a desperate effort to save his dynasty. He chose famous Confucian scholars to be his son's mentors[5] in the vain hope that training him to be a worthy successor would release his empire from the prevailing impasse. Unfortunately, conflicts arose between two imperial consorts: Worthy Consort Yang (楊賢妃, d. 840) and Virtuous Consort Wang (王德妃, d. 838), Li Yong's mother. Taking advantage of these conflicts, the eunuchs clandestinely took the Heir's life. Before discussing the details of this aftershock of the Sweet Dew Incident at greater length, we will first introduce the relevant records in the official histories, revealing how the incident developed, step by step, to its inevitable end.

Li Yong, the eldest son of Emperor Wenzong, was designated Heir Apparent in the sixth year of Dahe (832). His mother, Wang, was given the title Virtuous Consort in the eighth month of the second year of Kaicheng (837), and Worthy Consort Yang accepted her title at the same time. Yang was successful in monopolizing the emperor's favor, perhaps because she was younger and possessed of more ingratiating glamour. As a result, Virtuous Consort Wang fell prey to Yang's slander and jealousy, and in the eighth month of the third year of Kaicheng (838), was ordered by the emperor to commit suicide. Consort Yang, fearing that the Heir would subsequently do her harm, spared no efforts to slander him and to effect his deposal. She spread gossip that the

Heir "knew nothing but immoderate entertainment while disregarding proper etiquette and decency."

Li Yong was too young to answer these charges. Emperor Wenzong, having been totally misled by his favorite consort, decided to depose the Heir for his faults. He convened a conference to discuss the matter, giving audience to all his court officials of the fifth rank or higher. This meeting took place in the Yanying Palace (the royal meeting hall for great occasions), on the Renxu day of the ninth month of the third year of Kaicheng (Oct. 25, 838). At the meeting, many important and influential ministers, including perhaps Pei Du and prime ministers belonging to the Li Faction, tried their utmost to consolidate the young Heir's position. Consequently, several ministers and all of the attending officials agreed unanimously that the Heir Apparent was still very young and could be expected to mend his ways. Most impressive was the Censor-in-Chief, Di Jianmo's (狄兼謨, fl. 810–840) vehement and tearful remonstration against Wenzong's intended course of action, which brought the emperor to his senses. On the following day the Heir was ordered to return to his normal residence, the *Shaoyangyuan* (少陽院), and the trouble seemed for the moment to have come to an end. However, the Heir unexpectedly died on the Gengzi day of the tenth month of that year (Dec. 5), about forty days after the Yanying conference. In the following year, Wenzong put to death a musical officer and a palace lady, saying, "It is your like that entrapped my heir." Concerning this event, the Song Dynasty historiographers remark only that "the Heir after all did not mend his ways, but his death was not a normal one," and "affairs in the inner palace remained a secret, to which none of the outsiders could know the details."[6]

Regarding the details surrounding the Heir Apparent's death, including both its cause and its result, the following aspects of the incident merit our attention.

First, the opposing factions, Niu and Li, originally held clearly different attitudes toward the two imperial consorts. Worthy Consort Yang was a clan aunt of Yang Sifu, one of the chiefs of the Niu Faction, who, it was said, had tried to persuade his aunt to follow the example of Empress Wu (武后, 624–705, r. 684–701), and "administer the state's affairs from behind the curtain" (i.e., to become the second female ruler of the empire). At the Yanying Palace conference, however, the court officials had spoken with one voice against the deposition of the Heir. This is an indication that events had developed to such a point that the eunuchs would flagrantly intervene, so that the two factions, despite their different political attitudes toward the event, were forced for the moment to join forces against the eunuchs.

Secondly, "Since the Heir Apparent's death, the emperor felt deep regret" (for his own mistake). His regret was not that he had adopted the suggestion of his ministers (that "the Heir, as the most important basis of the empire, should never be removed without serious consideration"), but that he had recklessly brought about the destruction of his own son, having presented an opportunity to the eunuchs, who were always seeking to revenge themselves upon him and to achieve their ulterior purposes. In the tenth month of the fourth year of Kaicheng (839), the emperor remarked to one of his ministers: "I, honored as the Son of Heaven, could not even protect my own son" and "I am under the sway of my house-slaves, in a much worse status than King Nan of the Zhou [周赧王, r. 268–256, B.C.] and Emperor Xian of the Han Dynasty [漢獻帝, r. 190–219]." From such recorded remarks we can infer that the eunuchs were those who dared murder his Heir, and not the musical officer or palace lady, put to death as scapegoats.

Thirdly, the Li Faction had supported the Heir more effectively than had the Niu Faction, but after the Heir's death, Emperor Wenzong placed more confidence in Yang Sifu and Li Jue, prime ministers from the Niu Faction, which had the upper hand at the time. Thus, factional strife was renewed in a different situation. In the historical context, however, vying for power as they were, the two factions were able to be vying for power only by vying for more imperial favor. Since both factions subjected themselves to mutual supervision in the face of their common enemies—the eunuchs—they remained in constant allegiance to the state dynasty and seldom exhibited the slightest disobedience to the emperor. It is out of the question to suspect either faction of a crime such as murdering the Heir.

Fourthly, the eunuchs had been displeased with Wenzong for a long time, and following the Sweet Dew Incident, they had conspired to replace him with another royal clansman. Two days before Wenzong died an untimely and wretched death,[7] the eunuchs advanced the timing of the coup d'état. Despite the fact that another crown heir had been named, they positioned Li Chan, one of Wenzong's inconspicuous younger brothers, to assume the throne, bearing the bizarre title Imperial Fraternal Heir (皇太弟), who was known as Wuzong (r. 840–846). Immediately following Wenzong's death, the eunuchs incited the newly enthroned Wuzong to slaughter Worthy Consort Yang, Prince An, and Prince Chen. In close succession, the Niu Faction prime ministers Li Jue and Yang Sifu were dismissed from office, allowing the Li Faction to rise to full power.

Even after Wuzong's ascension to the throne, the eunuchs still "bore grudges against" the dead Wenzong because he had never resigned himself to their control and desired to eliminate them once and for all. They chose and set up Wuzong in the expectation that doing so would earn his gratitude and result in his becoming their puppet emperor. They instigated him to kill Consort Yang, not merely because of the charge of "plotting to administer the state's affairs from behind the curtain," but also because they desired to deceive the public by placing the blame for the Heir's murder solely on Yang. They killed Prince An and Prince Chen as part of their conspiracy to eliminate any witnesses to their secret crime, as well as to aggravate the contradictions between the Niu and Li factions, making it easier to take control of the new emperor and to monopolize all court power. Therefore, though Worthy Consort Yang must bear much of the responsibility for the death of the Heir Apparent, the true culprits were the eunuchs. The eunuchs, however, did not murder the Heir to aid Consort Yang. They also did not want to effect the murder openly, because this would not serve their political goal. Instead, their aim was to tighten their control on court power by exploiting the conflicts between the imperial consorts and the attending factional strife. In this sense, the Heir Apparent Incident was an extension of the Sweet Dew Incident, and a concentrated expression of the various contradictions within the ruling clique. Obviously it was enmeshed in backstage maneuvering in the inner court, the struggles between the Southern and the Northern offices, and in the factional strife. If Wen did indeed become entangled in any of these intricacies, his experiences must have been closely linked with the political taboos of his day, and any works he wrote that reflected the relevant truth concerning these taboos must needs be obscure, otherwise their circulation would have been prohibited and they would never have been handed down for our study. However, this analysis of the secret history of the inner court must remain more inference than proven conclusion, unless we can discover concrete references in Wen's works to substantiate it.

CLUES FOUND IN WEN'S WORKS

The following are the only poems in Wen's works directly bearing the title of the late Heir.

"TWO DIRGES FOR THE LATE HEIR APPARENT ZHUANGKE" (莊恪太子輓歌詞二首, WFQ, J. 3)

Amidst the fast drumbeats your soul is leaving the palaces,	迭鼓辭宮殿，
While grief-laden reed-notes descend from the gloomy firmament.	悲笳降杳冥。
The shadow is detached from the sun behind the clouds,	影離雲外日，
And the light is extinguished on the Star in Front of the Fire.	光滅火前星。
The retainers of Ye looked up to the Qin Garden,	鄴客瞻秦苑，
Then the Seniors of Shang came down to the Han court.	商公下漢庭。
Heartbreaking is the color of the trees on your tomb,	依依陵樹色，
Which vainly remains green surrounding the Nine Plains.	空繞九原青。

In this dirge saturated with profound sorrow, the poet not only laments Li Yong, but he meditates on the contributory causes of the young prince's untimely death. The second and the third couplets are more than mere scenic descriptions.

In traditional usage, "The sun behind the clouds" is a metaphor for a deluded emperor, hence it hints that Wenzong was controlled by his "house-slaves" and duped by his favorite consort. In the same fashion, "shadows are detached" refers to the young heir's helpless alienation from his emperor-father. "The light is extinguished" plainly refers to the death of Li Yong: apart from referring to the sparks in front of a fire of burned paper (as an offering to the dead), "the Star in Front of the Fire" (火前星), or "the Front Star of the Heart Constellation" (心宿前星, the Mars) of the Twenty-Eight Constellations (二十八宿), is the heavenly counterpart of the Heir Apparent[8] in Chinese traditional astrology.

The third couplet recalls the situation before Zhuangke died: how many court officials, especially those serving him, supported the Heir as much as they could. "The retainers of Ye" (鄴客), here used in antithesis to "the Seniors of Shang" (an allusion), must allude to something. As Ye City was one of the five capitals of the Wei Dynasty (220–265), the allusion must concern the literati of Ye City (鄴下文人), that is, the famous Seven Masters of the Jian'an Era (196–219), here used to refer to the assistants of the Heir, including Wen. Logically, the line has no implication that Wen was traveling in Ye;[9] rather, it means that as an assistant of the Heir, Wen looked to Emperor Wenzong for an act of grace to his young lord. Reasons why Wen likened the assistants of the Heir to the literati of Ye City will be brought to light in what follows.

In Wang Qi's (王起, 760–847) "Imperial Memorial Essay for the Late Heir Apparent Zhuangke" (莊恪太子哀冊文),[10] we read:

> Now the waves of *Shaohai* have vanished, and the canopy of the Western Garden no longer flies.[11] The assistants and aides from Mount Shang have dispersed, and the guests of Bowang Park have all gone[12] (有少海之波逝，無西園之蓋飛。商山之羽翼已散，望苑之賓客咸歸).

The "Western Garden" is a famous garden where the Wei princes, Cao Pi (曹丕, 187–226) and Cao Zhi (曹植, 192–232), once amused themselves with their retainers. In Wang's essay, undoubtedly, the term refers exclusively to the Heir's residence, even though in ordinary cases, it indicates imperial gardens without particular designation. In Wen's dirges, the term is used in like manner. The "assistants and aides from Mount Shang" in Wang's essay, like the "Seniors of Shang" in Wen's dirge, alludes to the well-known Four White-haired Seniors of Mount Shang (商山四皓), who came down from their seclusion to dissuade Emperor Gaozu from deposing his Crowned Heir.[13] In this context, the term refers to the veteran ministers who were against Wenzong's move to depose his Heir. Thus, the connotation of the "retainers of Ye" is further defined. It does not allude to the retainers of other Cao-Wei princes. Rather, it alludes exclusively to Cao Zhi, who met a miserable end after Cao

Pi took the throne. Thus, this allusion fits Wen's purpose of alluding obliquely to the Heir's tragedy.
Poem Two

At the Eastern Mansion there are honor guards in vain,	東府虛容衛，[14]
To the Western Garden I send my yearning dream.	西園寄夢思。
When a phoenix was hung, 'twas the night to play tunes,	鳳懸吹曲夜，
As the cockcrow interrupted, the time to salute your parents.	雞斷問安時。
On the dusty road the capital people feel resentful,	塵陌都人恨，
In the frosty suburbs the mourning horses neigh sadly.	霜郊賵馬悲。
What is left is only the land where the jade was buried,	惟餘埋璧地，[15]
Where misty grasses encroach upon the crimson steps.	煙草近丹墀。

Now that the "Eastern Palace" is bereft of its master, the "Western Garden" is bereft its parties. If Wen had no memory of frequenting the "Western Garden," it would make no sense for him to mention "sending his yearning dream" there.

What often haunted his dreams were former days when he was in company of the Heir, as revealed in the second couplet. "Phoenix" is the short form for "phoenix pipe," that is, *xiao* (簫). It was said that the *xiao* resembles in shape the wing of the legendary phoenix.[16] "To salute your parents" refers to set etiquette observed by royal heirs and alludes to King Wen's story: when he was Heir, he went to inquire about his parents' health three times a day, early in the morning, at noon, and at night.[17] It is certainly not the Heir alone playing (the pipe) at the time, to the exclusion of "the retainers of Ye." Playing the *xiao* or *sheng* (笙) at night at the Heir's palace is exactly what Wen was capable of, because he "could play all stringed and wind instruments that come to his hands" (有弦即彈，有孔即吹).[18] A synecdochic description of the etiquette the Heir followed serves to reaffirm the legality and sanctity of his capacity as imperial heir, witnessed most certainly.

A careful reexamination of Wen's choice of words in the second couplet will disclose some more subtle implications. "Interrupted" (斷) also means "broken" or "cut off," that is, the formality the Heir followed came to an end. Even the verb "hung" (懸) has a melancholy overtone: the former happy meetings, now suspended, had vanished like mist and fog, never to return.

These two dirges, besides expressing the poet's deep emotions toward the imperial heir and forming a mournful reflection upon his death, hint to the readers that Wen might have had a special and familiar relationship with this young person. There is a unique quality of feeling to these poems that far surpasses in depth the ordinary "resentment" harbored by the "capital people." These two poems voice the profound grief of a close attendant to the Heir, the focus of many hopes, whose tragic death had spelled the ruin of the poet's prospects. The information they contain must not be ignored. But even if we for the time being set aside the indications found here, we can still find ample clues, which, once correctly analyzed, fully support our inferences here. After all, Wen was impelled to vent his feelings and opinions on this issue, although he did so in very obscure terms. Consider the following example (Ancient Idea, 古意, WFQ, j. 3):

> I do not worry that it takes me long to meet my "spring," 不慮見春遲，
> I vainly grieve for having presented myself in the wrong way. 空傷致身錯。

That is to say, what has disheartened Wen is not that he had his opportunity too late in his political career, but that he had followed the "wrong" way to begin with, dooming himself to lifelong misfortune. If it were not his attendance upon the Heir that once briefly opened and then forever blocked his way to any promotion, what could it be?

Another example is from "Hundred-Rhyme Poem":

> 11 I was indeed seeking fish by climbing a tree, 定為魚緣木，
> And for a second rabbit, by the stump I'd vainly waited. 曾因兔守株。

"Climbing a tree to seek for fish" and "to wait by a stump for a second rabbit to come" are both common metaphors for expecting the impossible to occur by ridiculous means. Here Wen hints at the fruitless efforts he once made in a bid for official advancement. Again we are compelled to connect the "impossible" to the Heir Apparent Incident, which excluded Wen from political success once and for all. Oblique references such as these are found throughout Wen's existing works and are too numerous to ignore. The following couplet from "Fifty-Rhyme Poem" also deserves attention:

> I had taken the wrong way to present myself, 投足乖蹊徑，
> And then I absorbed myself in the classics and scriptures. 冥心向簡編。

It is plain that this unseen event happened immediately before Wen decided to take the civil service examination in the fourth year of Kaicheng (839). Taking into consideration the information offered in his two dirges, we can reasonably infer that the political experience he wishes to keep from being publicized very probably had something to do with his connection to the Heir, although we are uncertain at the moment about the exact nature of the relationship.

EVIDENCE ELICITED FROM A STUDY OF TWO EPISTLES

The following epistles serve to enlighten us on this special question.

"Epistle Thanking Minister Li of Xiangzhou" (謝襄州李尚書啟)

Your humble student wishes to say: endowed with the trite material of an altar oak-tree and the useless qualities of Void-space Village,[19] I had really no merits to serve your wise and beneficent Excellency. Would that I could pull [His Majesty's] sleeve in the Purple Polar [palace], and carry the writing brush on the crimson steps. Thinking about my shallow and futile person, I know it certainly goes too far to wish so. How could I know that while following you in the decorated boat I was all of a sudden promoted to the Cassia Garden[20] and without betaking myself to the Orchid Gate, I already took hold of the iris ink-paste[21] (某啟：某櫟社凡材，蕪鄉散質。殊無績效，堪奉恩明。曷當紫極牽袂，丹墀載筆！顧循虛淺，實過津涯。豈知畫舸方游，俄升于桂苑。蘭扃未染，已捧于芝泥).

All this is because of the favor of ascending your hall and the honor of being recorded and registered.[22] The tiny being of a swan's down was revitalized by riding on a whirlwind of sheep-horn.[23] The daily blessing I got from you is boundless, and I will forever look up to your loving kindness of rebirth; and the coming of this chance follows its own course, how could I know the way to go forward? In my awe and fear and hesitation, I know not what to say. And until I find an opportunity to express my gratitude in your presence, my yearning and reverence for you are vainly deep and everlasting (此皆寵自升堂，榮因著錄。勵鴻毛之眇質，托羊角之高風。日用無窮，常仰生成之德；時來有自，寧知進取之規？兢惕彷徨，攀戀空深).

In studying this epistle, we must pay particular attention to the fact that this epistle appeared in the Song Dynasty encyclopedia *Wenyuan Yinghua* (653: 3357), under the subtitle *Xieguan* (謝官), "Thanks for Having Obtained an Official Position." That is, Wen was appointed to a position that we cannot ignore. From this text we do see that he is extending his deepest gratitude to Minister Li for providing a recommendation, which resulted in Wen, despite his "useless qualities," being unexpectedly put into an important position. Moreover, Wen also demonstrates his determination to devote himself to that position, in spite of its precarious nature and to live up to Li's expectation despite facing a very menacing situation.

The first question we must ask is: what kind of relationship could there be between Minister Li and Wen, which would prompt Li to sponsor him? Minister Li must have been Wen's teacher. This can be understood from the phrase "the favor of *ascending your hall* and the honor of *being recorded and registered*." Because Wen was Li's student, and, we might add, an excellent student, Li recommended Wen for the position mentioned, offering him an opportunity for rapid and direct advancement. "Teacher" here must be understood to imply a relationship much more meaningful than its modern counterpart. In the Late Tang period a teacher was somebody who chose and instructed his disciples in all the learning necessary for passing the civil recruitment examination; he was more important than an Examination Administrator (座主) in that, from beginning to end, the students and teacher shared a common political orientation. In other words, the teacher usually exerted immense influence on his students. This was particularly so when he was at once the student's patron and official superior, as was the case with Wen and this Li. As our later studies will bear out, Minister Li and Wen were truly an extraordinary teacher-student pair.

Our second question is: what exactly was this position, eliciting both ecstasy and scruples on the part of our poet? This might be more baffling than our first question. In an attempt to discover an answer, we will follow Wen's own train of thought as manifested in the epistle.

Because of his "trite material" and "useless qualities," Wen really had not expected that he would be offered such a position as the one for which Li recommended him. That is to say, never before had he dreamt of becoming an official directly serving His Majesty, with the possibility to "pull the sleeve [as Remonstrator, say, an Attending Censor]" or "carry the writing-brush [as an Imperial Diarist]." Nevertheless, it is not likely that Wen would have hinted at these two official titles without substantiation or purpose. The implication is that the position to which he was appointed resembled the ones alluded to here. He tells us that while he was accompanying his teacher and waiting for a chance, he was, to his surprise, promoted to "the Cassia Garden"; and, without troubling himself to go to the "Orchid Gate," was directly raised to such a status that he could "take hold of the iris ink-paste."

We must endeavor to find out the answer of the following question: what did Wen mean by "the Cassia Garden" and "Orchid Gate"?

"Cassia Garden" can refer to nothing else but "the Cassia Area," the Editorial Service under the Left Secretariat in the Household of the Heir Apparent (太子左春坊司經局). The reasons for this inference are as follows:

1. "Promoted to the Cassia Garden" is a phrase which strongly suggests that "the Cassia Garden" is an official institution.
2. According to the "Records of the Hundred Officials" (XTS, 49:1294), "In the third year of Longshuo (663), the Editorial Service was changed to Academy of Cassia Fragrance" (桂芳館), which was also called "the Cassia Area" (桂坊). Apparently, in these terms, the Chinese characters Fang (坊, area), Yuan (苑, garden), and Guan (館, academy) are terms that were used interchangeably in the context to refer to the same official institute. The Cassia Garden is none other than the Editorial Service.

3. The official institutes of the Heir Apparent are related to "Cassia," as can be traced as far back as the Han. According to "Annals of Emperor Cheng":[24] "Emperor Xiaocheng, the Heir Apparent of Emperor Yuan, originally lived in the Cassia Palace." This Cassia Palace is identical to the Cassia Garden, which was the conventional abode of the Heir Apparent. "Cassia Garden" used in place of "the Cassia Palace," besides alluding to history, is an exact reference to fact.
4. There are precedents showing that poets prior to the Tang substituted "Cassia Garden" for the palace where the Heir Apparent lived. Yu Xin's (庾信, 513–581) "Poems about the Painted Screen" (詠畫屏風詩) has the lines: "Easygoing and carefree we are playing in the Cassia Garden/ Single and alone I come to the Peach Spring" (逍遙游桂苑，寂寞到桃源). Zong Guai's (宗夬, 456–504) poem "Bidding Farewell to Consular Xiao" (別蕭諮議) states how: "Dismally and glumly I come over to the Cassia Garden/Pityingly and Calmly I look on the beautiful pond" (悵焉臨桂苑，憫默瞻華池).[25] Yu Xin's poem was written when he served in the Eastern Palace whereas Zong Guai's was the product of his service as the Western Mansion Academician under the Jingling Prince of Qi (齊竟陵王),[26] both readily analogous to the Heir Apparent.

Taken together, this becomes strong evidence that Wen once served in the Editorial Service under the Left Secretariat in the Household of the Heir Apparent. This will be further clarified and doubly confirmed by establishing the exact meaning of "Orchid Gate," which, in this context, should also refer to an official institution closely connected with and similar to that of "the Cassia Garden." As the Censorate was also called "the Orchid Terrace" (蘭臺), it is logical that we take "Orchid Gate" as a variant for "Orchid Terrace" and thus for the Censorate. But what did the Censorate have to do with the Editorial Service under the Left Secretariat in the Household of the Heir Apparent? According to the "Records of the Hundred Officials" (XTS, 49:1295), "In the third year of Longshuo (663), the Editorial Service was changed to the Cassia Area, no longer subordinate to the Left Secretariat of the Heir Apparent, having under it the Academy for the Veneration of Worthies" (崇賢館); and as a governmental institution in the service of the Heir Apparent, compared with the official apparatus in the entire official system of the emperor, it 'resembled the Censorate' (比御史臺); one of the two Supervisors of the Household of the Heir Apparent (太子詹事) was made its director and resembled the Censor-In-Chief (比御史大夫); it had two Rectifiers, who resembled the Attending Censors (比侍御史), and four Literary Assistants (文學). . . . In the second year of Xianheng (671), the Cassia Garden again was made subordinate to the Left Secretariat of the Heir Apparent."

Hence, the Editorial Service could also be called the "Orchid Gate," although Wen's descriptive term is somewhat exaggerated. However, this institution was analogous to the Censorate, even though it was not the

Censorate. That is why Wen, while serving in the Editorial Service, claims that, "without betaking myself to the Orchid Gate, I already took hold of the iris ink-paste" (芝泥). The implication is that, originally, one did need go to the "Orchid Gate" "to take hold of the iris ink-paste"; thus what Wen had now attained was not the "Orchid Gate." Since nonetheless he managed to "reach hold of the iris ink-paste," he is telling us he had obtained an appointment in the Editorial Service. A governmental institution pertaining to the Heir Apparent, the Editorial Service was the counterpart of the Censorate in the complete official system under the emperor.

Since Wen "took hold of the iris ink-paste" in the Editorial Service under the Left Secretariat of the Heir Apparent, he is telling us that he served in that institution as a literary attendant. "Iris ink-paste" is a laudatory reference to the sealing ink-paste of more recent times, which was originally something so rare and precious that it related directly to the emperor,[27] or at least to the confidential attendants of the emperor. On the other hand, censors and iris (芝) have been mentioned together since earlier time, for example: "For the immortal officials, those who take doses made of ordinary iris are censors" (仙官食眾芝為御史).[28] Tang literati thus used the iris as a synecdoche for the Censorate or Censors, such as "From among the censer-perfuming censors comes the immortal, with cloudy saddle and feather canopy going down from the iris field" (薰爐御史出神仙，雲鞍羽蓋下芝田).[29] In brief, Wen Tingyun did attend on the Heir Apparent at one time, holding a post similar to that of an Attending Censor.

Next, we will proceed to establish the identity of Minister Li of Xiangzhou.

Since no standard history has ever touched on this question, we must guard against unwarranted assumptions in our effort to substantiate our conclusion about this man's identity. Who was the Li with enough power to raise Wen to such a height?

Because Wen came to the capital Chang'an after the Jianghuai Incident, which took place no later than the first year of Kaicheng (836), and because the Heir Apparent Li Yong died on December 5 of the third year of Kaicheng (838), in dating this epistle, we must confine our search to the years 836–838, during which period Wen gained access to the Heir by means of Li's recommendation.

As indicated in the title of the epistle, Minister Li must have been one of the Military Commissioners in the garrison of Xiangzhou, the administrative headquarters for the Eastern Circuit of Shannan. Those who held the position of Military Commissioner of the Eastern Circuit of Shannan from 836 to 838 are Li Ao (from the eighth month of 835 to some time before the seventh month of 836), Yin You (殷侑, from the seventh month of 836 to the third month of 837), and Li Cheng (from the third month of 837 to sometime before the eighth month of 839).[30] Careful deliberation between Li Ao and Li Cheng must result in the exclusion of Li Ao. Our arguments that Minister Li of Xiangzhou must be Li Cheng are as follows:

1. Li Cheng was a person powerful enough to recommend Wen for the important and confidential position of attendant to the Heir Apparent. In the Tang Dynasty Li was one of the few Prime Ministers issued from the imperial clan[31] who enjoyed the full confidence of the emperors. Furthermore, after obtaining the Presented Scholar degree as the first candidate in 796, Li held many important official positions in an official career spanning almost fifty years, both in the central bureaucracy and in various circuits. During the Kaicheng era, he became one of the most influential and respected veteran officials of his time.
2. Prior to being appointed Military Commissioner of the Eastern Shannan Circuit, Li had held the position of the Honorary Minister of the Ministry of Military Affairs. That is why Wen addressed him as "Minister." Actually Li Cheng, as a veteran court official, enjoyed a prestige even greater than that of a Prime Minister after his tenure in that position (825–827). We further note that Li had once held the position of Examination Administrator, which means his political influence over the contemporary officialdom was also wide and deep, since there were many who had gained their Presented Scholar degree through Li, subsequently becoming important officials.
3. During the Late Tang period, it gradually became the fashion for erudite scholars to set up schools of their own and accept students as a means of disseminating the teacher's academic and political thought. Li Cheng was a teacher of great reputation. According to his Biography in JTS (167:4372), he

   > Was a man of excellent and profound scholarly insight. However, he had an unconventional and unrestrained character, and paid little attention to trivial formalities. Moreover, as a teacher and senior court official, he was humorous and fond of making jokes, thus he incurred censure from some people (藝學優深，然性放蕩，不修儀檢，滑稽好戲，而居師長之地。物議輕之).

   Like teacher like student. And what great similarities existed, in the criticisms to which both teacher and student were subjected, if not in their personalities!
4. According to Li's Biography in XTS (131:4511), Li

   > Was a man of quick witticisms and eloquence. He had a simple and unpretentious style, and lacked an impressive and dignified manner. Moreover, despite the many confidential and distinguished appointments he had won, he was not well renowned. However, he was greatly appreciated by Emperor Wenzong, who once remarked: "The birds flying on high have their senior take the lead, and you are the senior one in my court" (為人辯給多智，然簡兑無儀檢。雖在華密，而無重望，最為文宗所遇，曰：高飛之翮，長者在前。卿朝廷羽翮也).

It is not by sheer accident that, when referring to his manner of composing poetry, Wen says in one of his two "Epistles Presented to Vice-Minister Jiang" (上蔣侍郎啟):

> I have acquired a thorough mastery of the fair designs of the former worthies, because I heard the discriminating remark of the *senior one* (頗識前修之懿圖，蓋聞長者之餘論).

Obviously "the *senior one*" indicates an individual person. I suggest that it refers to Wen's teacher Li Cheng, employing Emperor Wenzong's commendatory remark.

5. We have an additional reason supporting our identification of Li Cheng as Wen's teacher. Among his contemporaries, Li was regarded as an exemplar in literary writing, as a Late Tang author Zhao Lin says of him (3: 16):

> From the era of Yuanhe onwards, among those who excelled in both literary and applied writings are Magistrate of Liu Prefect Liu Zongyuan, Minister Liu Yuxi and Lord Yang; the latter two, in addition, were conversant with poetry. Beside these, Course Director Zhang Ji was good at composing songs and ballads, while Li He was adept in making new Music Bureau verses; all those having a fondness for songs and poems modeled themselves on these two. However, *Prime Minister Li Cheng*, Joint Director Wang Qi, Junior Mentor Bai Juyi and his brother, and Drafter of the Secretariat Zhang Zhongsu excelled in writing poems and prose works for examinations, those speaking about literary form and style followed the example of these five men (元和以來，詞翰兼奇者，有柳柳州宗元、劉尚書禹錫及楊公。劉楊二人，詞翰之外，別精篇什。有張司業籍，善歌行；李賀能為新樂府。當時言歌篇者，宗此二人。李相國程、王仆射起、白少傅兄弟、張舍人仲素為場中詞賦之最，言程式者宗此五人).

In conclusion, taking everything into account, Minister Li must be Li Cheng. Nobody but Li Cheng would have been willing and able enough to be Wen's teacher. In our later discussion concerning Wen's change of name, we will find more details illustrating the immense influence Li exerted upon his disciple Wen.

Since this connection has remained totally undiscovered, readers of later generations have been ignorant of it. Not a single one of Wen's contemporaries has passed down any reference to Li Cheng as Wen's teacher. Therefore, our discovery concerning the role played by Li Cheng becomes more meaningful than it appears to be at first sight. It broadens the scope of inquiry into the details of Wen's hidden relationship with the Tang imperial clan in general, and with Wenzong and his son Li Yong in particular.

Emperor Wenzong in his later years became a puppet in the hands of the eunuchs and the Tang imperial clan lost most of its power. This, however, does not imply that gaining access to the imperial heir would be a simple matter. Wen's success in obtaining the opportunity to attend the Heir was the result of a long and cautious process. Even though he was an imperial relative with an imperial-clan Prime Minister as his teacher and mediator, Wen still had to pass a special examination, and his appointment had to be authorized by the emperor in person. All these details are revealed in Wen's poetic or prose works, but never in clear and unequivocal terms. They constitute our story—history—of Wen's attendance upon the Heir Apparent. The following epistle would appear more confusing, were it not for the above study of Li Cheng, but it does serve to uncover more hidden aspects of the same event.

"Epistle Thanking Minister-Duke Hegan" (謝紇干相公啟)

Your humble servant wishes to say: My talent [timber] cannot compare with trees such as teak and oak, and my literary compositions are neither brocade nor embroidery. Having roamed about thousands of *li*, I was appointed as no more than Aide to the Man-barbarian headquarters; having frittered away my time within a hundred years, I rested content with the rank of Clerk of Jingzhou Prefecture.[32] I never dreamt that I would get wings and soar up with wind and cloud (某啟：某材謝楩柟，文非綺組。間關千里，僅為蠻國參軍；荏苒百齡，甘作荊州從事。寧思羽翼，可勵風雲).

How could I have expected that, with my trite and indolent person, I would find myself posted among the most confidential and privy [royal office]?[33] Looking backward, I am going further and further from dirt and dinginess; going up on high, I am approaching the zenith of the blue heavens. The glory far exceeds my original expectation, and the position surpasses my initial wish (豈知持彼庸疎，棲于宥密。回顧而漸離緇垢，冥升而欲近煙霄。榮非始圖，事過初愿).

All this is a consequence of promoting the fragrance [value] of literary worthies, allowing me to rise up from within our teacher's door and wall. Now in the year when the School of Kong Qiu is making use of the rhapsody, Xiangru will enter the chamber; and on the day when the Kingdom of Chu is appointing its officials, Song Yu will ascend the platform.[34] The glory of a single day will brighten my life within a hundred years. Before I manage to extend my gratitude to you, I prostrate myself here at your feet, in reverence and awe (此皆揚芳甄藻，發跡門墻。丘門用賦之年，相如入室；楚國命官之日，宋玉登臺。一日光陰，百生輝映。未由陳謝，伏用兢惶).

This epistle can be understood as another revelation of Wen's liaison with the Heir. First, We notice that it was put together with the "Epistle Thanking Minister Li of Xiangzhou" under the subtitle of "Thanks for Having Obtained an Official Position" in *Wenyuan Yinghua*. It must therefore also be connected with Wen's appointment as the Heir Apparent's attendant, expressing Wen's thankfulness to Hegan who helped him gain the position. The obvious reason is that, in Wen's distress-filled life, another rapid advancement is inconceivable.

Having resigned himself to his destiny, Wen found himself "approaching the zenith of the blue heavens," an extremely surprising occurrence. What can this mean but gaining direct access to the emperor? To be "posted in the most confidential and privy [royal office]" does mean to serve in an office under the Editorial Service in the Household of the Left Secretariat of the Heir Apparent. To further confirm this inference we must explain why we use "the most confidential and privy" to translate the original term 宥密 from its origin "High Heaven Had a Firm Charge." This is an ode singing praise of how King Cheng, as the successor of King Wen and King Wu, carried on his forefathers' enterprise. According to Zheng Xuan's annotation and Kong Yingda's sub-annotation, the term 宥密 should mean [that King Cheng would put into practice a policy of] *leniency and peacefulness* (寬寧). To be used to describe a man, 宥密 can mean generous and serene. To be used to describe an office, it takes on the meanings from its original: closely related to the (succeeding) monarch, important and confidential. Following this usage, later literati used the term to refer to a confidential and privy office related to the monarch in general, while Wen used it to refer to the official institution of the Heir Apparent in particular.

Another reason, furthering our argument, is found in Wen's statement that "all this is a consequence of promoting the fragrance [value] of literary worthies, allowing me to rise up from within my teacher's door and wall." This suggests that Wen's promotion through Hegan was closely linked to his teacher Li Cheng's recommendation. Here we can infer that Li Cheng, as a senior minister, recommended Wen to Hegan, who happened to share part of the responsibility for the selection of the Ministry of Personnel. We are also justified in saying that becoming a member in the Heir Apparent's retinue was an involved matter. The consent of the emperor himself was necessary in order to secure an important appointment such as aide to the Heir Apparent; if it were not given, the appointment would not be possible.

In this epistle, we find other important references, such as the allusion to Sima Xiangru and the Kingdom of Chu, through which we will discover more than we expect. When Wen says, "Now in the year when the School of Kong Qiu is making use of rhapsody, Xiangru will enter the chamber," he is likening himself to Sima Xiangru, the Han Dynasty eminent literatus, and declaring that when the opportunity presents itself, he will gain employment by displaying his outstanding literary talent. Wen's pride in his own literary talent would be one of his reasons for referring himself as Xiangru incarnate.

An additional reason for this self-styled epithet is that throughout the Heir Apparent Incident, Wen played a role somewhat similar to that of Xiangru—he composed poems sympathetic to Virtuous Consort Wang, in an effort to dissuade the fickle emperor from abandoning her. These poems were also designed to help her to regain His Majesty's favor, a point that our later discussions of this topic will make apparent.

Wen's remark that "on the day when the Kingdom of Chu is appointing its officials, Song Yu will ascend the platform" is also noteworthy. Wen compares himself to Song Yu of Chu, thus intimating that the official institution of the Heir is analogous to the Chu Kingdom. Since in Wen's works, we find frequent references to "Chu," we can draw out an important clue for unraveling other enigmas in his works: "Chu" stands for the Heir, and through the Heir, the whole empire. This knowledge is instrumental in clarifying many textual ambiguities in Wen's works, such as the passage from "Epistle Presented to Minister Feng":

> Although I was unable to accompany Your Excellency wherever you went when the Kingdom of Chu was in search of talented men, as a student entrusted to you from inside the Confucian house, I had lived up to the expectation of my teachers. . . . Silly orphan that I am, I frequently found shelter or refuge (雖楚國求才，難陪足跡；而丘門托質，不負心期，……顧惟孤拙，頻有依投).

Based on the rewarding study of the "Epistle Presented to Minister-Duke Hegan," we immediately understand what Wen is saying here: he was chosen to be an attendant of the Heir Apparent, thus he could not have followed Feng to the place where the latter held his official position. Recommended as an honest and competent attendant for "the Kingdom of Chu"—service to the Heir Apparent—Wen had fulfilled the hopes of his teacher. This is the reason why many officials, including this Minister Feng, appreciated Wen's person and were willing to lend him the shelter of their name and position, and is another consequence of his attendance on the Heir Apparent.

In our later discussion we will find more items, which substantiates the analogy between Wen and Xiangru. But what interests us most now is identifying this Hegan and firmly establishing the relevant inferences we have drawn up to this point.

In the first half of the ninth century, there was a man of considerable reputation by the name of Hegan Qi (紇干臮, fl. 820–850), who, though he has no biography in the two *Tang Histories*, is mentioned in various Tang historical sources. Concerning this Hegan Qi, there is an interesting anecdote recorded in Zhao Lin's *Yinhualu* (3: 18):

> In the third year of Kaicheng, I, to make up the number, was accepted as a Presented Scholar. The Examination Supervisor, Sir Hegan the Vice-Director under the Ministry of Justice, used to be a student of

> Prime Minister Cui Qun (772–832). When Hegan acquired the Presented Scholar degree, he joined others gathering in the small hall in the Prime Minister's Xinchang mansion, to have audience with the Examination Administrator Cui. Now that he was appointed to be examining official, he borrowed Prime Minister Cui's old mansion to accept his own student. . . . The first candidate, Sun Jue of He'nan, later became Assistant to Councilor prior to the Duke of Yanmen. Hegan was transferred as Inspection Commissioner of the Jiangxi Circuit, then returned [to the capital] to be Vice-Minister of the Ministry of Works, and was appointed Military Commissioner of Nanhai. He ended up being enfeoffed as the Duke of Yanmen (開成三年，余忝列第。考官刑部員外郎紇干公，崔相群門生也。公及第日，于相國新昌宅小廳中，集見座主。及為考官之前，假舍于相國故第，亦于此廳見門生焉。敕頭孫河南穀先于雁門公為丞。公後自中書舍人觀察江西，又歷工部侍郎，節制南海，贈雁門公).

We are given to understand that in the third year of Kaicheng Hegan Qi was the Examination Supervisor, concurrently holding the post Vice Director of the Ministry of Justice. The identical detail is also seen in Wang Dang's *Tangyulin* (4: 135):

> In the third year of Kaicheng (838), the Examination Supervisor of Calligraphy and Judgment, Sir Hegan, the Vice Director under the Ministry of Justice, was a student of the Prime Minister Cui. . . . (開成三年，書判考官刑部員外郎紇干公，崔相國門生也).

From the position Hegan Qi held in the year 838, we can roughly assume what kind of position he held in the previous year. Although we cannot pinpoint it exactly, we can safely say that it must have had something to do with the selection of civil officials, conducted by the Ministry of Personnel, the so-called "promoting the fragrance [value] of literary worthies." Otherwise Wen would not have thanked Hegan upon attaining the position as mentioned in the epistle. The civil-official selection presided over by the Ministry of Personnel had as its purpose the selection of eligible officials, rather than Presented Scholars. The latter were chosen by Presented Scholar examinations presided over by the Ministry of Ritual. In the Late Tang period, the Presented Scholar Examination was the only option, and thus the most popular avenue, through which men of the common gentry entered into official services. However, because there were always too many candidates vying for the limited degree offered, many would bypass the examination and go directly into official employment, if they could claim the so-called "hereditary privilege" (蔭). Although Wen's family was in disgrace, theoretically Wen was still in a position to enjoy his "ancestral privilege," and for this reason, among others, many were willing to allow Wen the opportunity to advance without sitting for the examination.

According to "Biography of Gao Yuanyu" (高元裕) in XTS (177: 5283), Gao in his tenure as Left Assistant Chancellor (尚書左丞) in the second year of Kaicheng, was in charge of the selection for the Ministry of Personnel. About that time, Hegan Qi held the post of Vice Director of the Left Chancellery (左司員外郎), and Feng Ao was the director of the same office (左司郎中). Both might have played a part in the selection.[35] But we may logically raise the question: if we cannot find a Hegan Qi in the "List of Prime Ministers," why is he addressed as "Minister Duke" (*Xianggong*, 相公) in Wen's epistle? To answer this question, we will examine his official career and any possible relationship that might have existed between him and Wen.

Although no biographies of Hegan Qi are found in the two *Tang Histories*, we find many references concerning him in extant sources. His style-name was Xianyi (咸一),[36] and he was a Presented Scholar of the tenth year of Yuanhe (815).[37] In the third year of Dahe (829), when the Southern Barbarians entered the city of Chengdu, Hegan, then Assistant Commissioner of Jian'nan and Xichuan Circuit, was demoted to Chief Executive Official (長史) of Yingzhou Prefecture, for his dereliction of duty. During the Kaicheng period, he held the posts of Director of the Treasury Bureau (金部郎中) and Director of the Left Office (左司郎中).[38] At the beginning of Huichang, he was shifted to the post of Director of the Granary Bureau (庫部郎中). Later, in the middle of Huichang, he became Drafter in the Secretariat (中書舍人).[39] At the beginning of Dazhong, as Palace Aide to the Censor-In-Chief (御史中丞), he was sent out as the Inspection Commissioner of the Jiangxi Circuit.[40] Next, he reentered the court as Vice-Minister of the Ministry of Works,[41] and then he became a minister in the central bureaucracy at court.[42] Finally, he went out to be the Military Commissioner of the Lingnan Circuit.

Judging from the records available, two possibilities present themselves, either of which might have qualified Hegan Qi to be addressed as *Xianggong*. First, in Zhao Lin's account of *Yinhualu*, Sun Jue "became Assistant Councilor prior to the 'Duke of Yanmen'" [Hegan Qi]; that is to say, Hegan Qi once was Left or Right Assistant to the Councilor, which qualified him to be addressed as "*Xianggong*" which we translate as "Minister-Duke" in most cases. Second, Hegan was Examination Supervisor, in charge of the civil official selection for the Ministry of Personnel, and Wen Tingyun, as a result of Li Cheng's recommendation, was chosen through Hegan. Their relationship, therefore, now resembled a relationship between the Examination Administrator and candidate student. A common practice since the Tang was for students to call their Examination Administrator *Xianggong*, causing the term, in this case, to lose its original meaning of "Minister-Duke." Therefore, "Minister-Duke Hegan" is Hegan Qi.

Granted that Li Cheng was appointed Examination Administrator in the twelfth year of Yuanhe (817), while Hegan Qi, Feng Ao, and Pei Yizhi (裴夷直, to whom Wen also presented an epistle appealing for support),[43] were all Presented Scholars of the tenth year of Yuanhe (815), we can understand why Li Cheng was considered a veteran minister in the eyes of his junior contemporaries such as Hegan Qi, Pei Yizhi, and Feng Ao, even though they had gained remarkable distinction themselves.

THE HIDDEN STORY IN HUNDRED-RHYME POEM

Being involved in such an unusual experience would make it impossible for Wen to remain silent about it in his insightful and powerful autobiographical representation found in "Hundred-Rhyme Poem," written in the winter of 840. Now we turn to the central concern of this chapter, attempting to offer a relatively satisfying annotation of this poem. Among the very few critics who have mentioned this poem in their researches, no one as yet has succeeded in determining its basic purport, much less its precise implications. However, this is a poem that a modern scholar, wishing to explore any topic connected to Wen Tingyun, cannot afford to leave misunderstood and unexamined.

In paraphrasing "Hundred-Rhyme Poem," we must be cognizant of two facts. First, in this poem, we find an abundance of erudite allusion and archaic diction, and numerous terms used exclusively only in certain circles of the Late Tang literati society. The connotations of these terms are not completely accessible through modern reference works. Consequently, painstaking effort must be exerted in order to coax out the rich implications of each line. Once those obstacles are overcome, solutions become available, placing us in a position to grasp the poet's meaning more exactly. Second, "Hundred-Rhyme Poem" is in the full sense an autobiographical account, with every line having a direct bearing on the author himself. We know that the syntax of Chinese prosody, especially that of regulated poetry, requires that personal pronouns, particularly first person pronouns, be avoided in most cases. This practice finds its unique expression in "Hundred-Rhyme Poem" in that, no matter how complicated the connotations of each line are, the grammatical role played by narrator, either as subject or as object or as anything else, is always implied but not stated, to be understood and filled in by the discriminating reader. In the meanwhile, the poem as a whole maintains an intrinsic logical consistency of its own. In a sense, the poem becomes an artifice in which its author tells his story without the use of first person pronouns to refer to himself. In paraphrasing "Hundred-Rhyme Poem," we must carefully insert these pronouns wherever desirable, discerning how the poet constantly shifts his roles: sometimes placing himself either in the front of the stage or behind the scenes, sometimes appearing with others or all alone, and sometimes voicing himself in asides or monologues or as part of a chorus with other voices.

What follows is our explanation of the passage extending from the sixty-first to the seventy-fourth rhyme of "Hundred-Rhyme Poem." This explanation supplements and complements, in many respects, our story of Wen's secret attendance upon the Heir.

First of all, the poem reiterates Li Cheng's recommendation of Wen for the appointment with the consent of Emperor Wenzong.

61 The lotus mansion and the Marquis' gates valued my talents, 蓮府侯門貴，
Thus, to the Frost Terrace came the consent of the royal mandate. 霜臺帝命俞。

The first line of this couplet tells very clearly that Wen was valued by "the lotus mansion" and "the Marquis' gates," that is, he has the support of a distinguished Prime Minister. In view of our findings, we can say without hesitation that the Prime Minister referred to here was Li Cheng. As a result of Li's recommendation, the emperor's consent was issued to the Frost Terrace (the Censorate), prompting it to grant Wen a position there. As we know, in the Tang official system the Editorial Service of the Left Secretariat in the Household of the Heir Apparent resembled the Censorate, since as a component part of the miniature empire of the Heir, it functioned as the Censorate did in the state apparatus of the Empire. Therefore, it was to the appointment of Wen Tingyun as one of his son's assistants in the Editorial Service that Emperor Wenzong gave his consent. Remembering that Wen came from a family of imperial relatives who had participated intimately in the changing fortunes of the royal clan, we are not surprised that he could conceivably serve Li Yong with Wenzong's personal approval.

62 Now the steed's hooves began to run swifter than gale, 驥蹄初躡景，
And the roc's wings were about to spiral up to the zenith. 鵬翅欲摶扶。

A detailed account of what Wen witnessed as an attendant to the Heir begins with this couplet. Here both "steed's hooves" and "the roc's wings" are metaphors for Wen himself, who was a man of great talent and expectation, as he himself boasted. The first thing to impress the reader here is Wen's reaction to his sudden promotion, giving him direct access to the Heir and connecting him directly to His Majesty himself. Now the poet envisages his tremendous opportunity to serve his young lord and his country, and resolves to do everything within his power to serve His Majesty's heir. Here is an opportunity that normally leads directly to great distinction and high office.

Then we are first shown how the Heir gave audience to his palace subjects:

63 Having stayed on duty, I returned on my dapple horse, 寓直回驄馬，
Sitting in different sections, we faced the dusky crows. 分曹對冥烏。

This is a description of the official routines Wen witnessed and participated in. On the surface, these routines resemble those of the Censorate, especially of the Attending Censors. "Dapple horse" is an allusion to an Attending Censor, Huan Dian, who often rode such a horse; "Dusky crows" alludes to a Censor-In-Chief, Zhu Bo. It was said that near Zhu's mansion, thousands of wild crows perched on the cypress trees every day in the dusk.[44] However, since the Editorial Service in the Household of the Heir Apparent "resembled the Censorate" and "the two Rectifiers" of the Editorial Service "resembled the Attending Censors," Wen is actually referring to officials of the Editorial Service, such as the Rectifiers (including himself), rather than the Attending Censor under the Censorate. The unusual frequency with which the "Attending Censors" or similar officials appear in this poetic passage adds more conviction to our argument: Wen would not have mentioned it so frequently, unless the title referred to his own official position in the Editorial Service, where he spent his most memorable days.

64 The Hundred Spirits attended, as it were, enjoying offerings, 百神歆髣髴，
Isolated Bamboo was sending notes, dim and lost. 孤竹韻含胡。

Now we are invited into the Editorial Service where, as the first line of the couplet demonstrates, a solemn and imposing atmosphere reigned when "the Heir Apparent gave audience to his palace subjects." If we remember that the Heir was once enfeoffed as Prince of Lu, it is likely that Wen is intentionally reminding his reader of the topic at hand, by alluding to the "Rhapsody on Ling'guang Palace of Lu."[45] The "Isolated Bamboo" is a flute made from a kind of bamboo that grows in isolation, which, yielding a sound peculiarly pleasant to the ear, was used in the sacrificial rites venerating the spirits.[46] Here, antithetical to the "Hundred Spirits," it suggests the pomp with which affairs were conducted in the Editorial Service. The "dim and lost notes" seem to betoken the Heir's impending death.

65 In the Phoenix Hall we stood in lines to each side, 鳳闕分班立，
From the egret rows with sword erect we paced forward. 鴛行竦劍趨。[47]

Here the poet depicts the scene of the Heir giving audience to his palace subjects, demonstrating all the majesty of the occasion. Wen must also be present in the "Phoenix Hall" and "egret rows." During the court audience, the military and civil officials stood in separate groups paying reverence to their monarch; some of the Rectifiers on duty solemnly held (wooden) swords erect, in the performance of their official duty.

66 At confidential behest we butted against evil, 觸邪承密勿，
On behalf of the royal plan we maintained the law. 持法奉訏謨。

67 With jades clanging we strutted up and down, 鳴玉鏘登降，
And the pendants' soundings lingered faintly on. 衡牙響曳婁。[48]

"Butting against Evil" was the name of the official cap worn by Censors. It was said that the King of Chu captured a legendary divine sheep, *Xiezhi* (獬豸), which could differentiate right from wrong and butt against evil people; thus the king ordered that the Censor's cap be modeled from it. The Censor's cap, the shaft of which was made of iron, symbolizes the holder's irresistible and incorruptible power.[49]

These two couplets represent how the Attending Censors, that is, the Rectifiers, including Wen, carried out their official duties. In Wen's account, they were honest officials who held firmly to justice and to the imperial law without yielding to any unorthodox force. In Wen's representation, all the officials serving the Heir assume a demeanor even more imposing and important than those ministers and dukes in the emperor's court. Such rhetorical touches, we must point out, indicate Wen's intention to commemorate the late Heir in a grand and spectacular way, especially since his miniature court had such a fleeting existence, in spite of all Wen's own exertions to support it.

The following is a direct description of the Heir employing the most deceptive camouflage.

68 His Worship showed intimacy with Heshi's Jade, 祀親和氏璧，
The Fragrance was attached to Boshan Censer. 香近博山爐。

An analysis of its connotation is of paramount importance to an understanding of the poem as a whole, and to the confirmation of our conclusion. We must reemphasize that this passage is exclusively a narration of the story of Wen's attendance upon the Heir. In the verses leading up to it, we encounter vivid depictions of the working of the court etiquette in the palace where the Heir Apparent gave audience. In the verses following it, we will encounter more detailed representations of the imperial pomp and grandeur witnessed by Wen at meetings between the Heir Apparent and his subjects. Logically speaking, it would be very unusual if this passage were not to contain reference to the Heir himself, the key figure in these scenes. And, indeed, this couplet itself is designed precisely for the purpose of referring directly but subtly to the late Heir, concerning whose death at the hands of the eunuchs it had become taboo to speak openly. By "taboo" I mean not only that the eunuchs, as murderers of the Heir, would never allow their conspiracy to be exposed, but also that the succeeding Emperor Wuzong's political sensitivity was acute concerning this ignominy, the crucial event leading to his enthronement. The court officials, in no position to interfere in "the family affairs" of the emperors and unable to contend with the eunuchs, were forced to remain silent and to feign ignorance of this event. Whoever uttered the truth brought trouble upon himself. Therefore, Wen was forced to resort to roundabout language and to contrive a most sophisticated artistic expression of the whole story—especially because he had been the Heir's personal attendant and knew full details of the matter. Fortunately, Wen's many subterfuges enabled him to escape the eunuchs' censorship. Unfortunately, the truth of the matter has remained undiscovered by later generations, to whom Wen wished to relate the full story.

A first step toward a solution of this enigmatic couplet is to suspect that the unusual usage of the verbs "shows intimacy with" (親) and "be attached to" (近), which are ordinarily applied to human subjects or personifications, implies some deeper meaning. The Chinese character *si* (祀), which we translate as worship, means offering sacrifices or paying worship to the spirits and grammatically serves as the subject of the first line. Such a subject should have as its predicate the verb-object structure "showed intimacy with Heshi's Jade." It is apparent that both "Worship" and "Heshi's Jade" are substitutes for unnamed human figures. In all probability, they are the Heir Apparent and his subjects. In like manner, the "Fragrance" (香) and the "Boshan Censer" in the second line must also imply a hidden metaphor. We must, however explain these metaphors clearly, offering not guesswork but proofs.

A tentative suggestion is that this couplet represents a ceremony of worship performed during a court audience: in the palace where the audience was held, joss-sticks (香) were burned in an exquisite Boshan Censer, from which fragrant smoke curled upward; to burn joss-sticks was to pay homage to "Heshi's Jade," which was the hereditary imperial seal made of precious jade and handed down as the symbol of royal power. This is a ceremony that may have actually taken place in the palace. But a paraphrase of this kind does not throw new light on the hidden meaning of "show intimacy with" and "be attached to," which are both verbs metaphorically representing some sort of human actions. A more careful scrutiny of the complex picture found in this couplet focuses our interest on the two pairs of nouns. Let us examine them one by one.

"Heshi's Jade" is richly charged with metaphorical meanings. The primary meaning is derived from the original story in *Hanfeizi*: as the precious jade carved from the jade-enfolding stone, it is often used as a symbol for worthy and virtuous men. Judging from historical records, it may even have had some connection with the assistants of an Heir Apparent.[50] In the text under discussion, even if limited to serving as a metaphor for worthy and virtuous officials, it takes on a personified meaning referring to the attendants of the Heir including Wen himself. To further illuminate this reading, we ought to refer back to the tenth rhyme in "Hundred-Rhyme Poem":

10	Not in a position to sound the Jade of Chu,	未能鳴楚玉，
	In vain I desired to hold the Pearl of [Marquis] Sui.	空欲握隋珠。

The "Jade of Chu," as we know, refers to Heshi's jade. "To sound the Jade of Chu" involves another allusion: "Zhao Jianzi (趙簡子), sounding his jade, became the Prime Minister,"[51] with the connotation of distinguishing himself as an honorable and important court official attending a court audience. As we have pointed out earlier, Wen often refers to himself using language relevant to Chu in order to suggest his connection with the Heir. This couplet is thus more than a confession of Wen's failure to serve the court with his brilliant talent, by means of the hint "the Jade of Chu," it also is connected with his private experiences of attending the Heir. By the same token, Heshi's Jade is a metaphor for himself as the attendant of the Heir.

Since that which "Worship" "showed intimacy with" is metaphorically the Heir's competent and honest attendants, the term *Worship* should be a term equivalent to "Heir Apparent" using a pun, a homonym, or an insinuation. Is it really interchangeable with some term referring to the Heir? The answer is yes. We know that the Chinese character *si*, "Worship," refers to the etiquette of offering sacrifices to the spirits. In Chinese imperial times, such sacrifice was looked upon as one of "the Eight Essentials" of the royal dynasty, and synecdochically, it could substitute for all government affairs.[52] Moreover, the character 祀 (*si*) is homonymous with 嗣 (*si*),[53] the heir; hence in this context it becomes a euphemistic reference to the Heir. Therefore, the couplet indicates that the Heir showed intimacy with worthy men, his assistants.

Since the first line has such implication, logically the next line should bear the meaning that the worthy attendants were attached to the Heir. Fortunately, besides its literal meaning of "fragrance" or "joss stick," the character 香 (*xiang*) is homonymous with 相 (*xiang*), which can, if used as noun, be glossed as assistant, that is, the worthies around the Heir. To substantiate this point and make clear Wen's punning techniques, we can look at the following lines in Wen's "Melody of Damozhi" (達摩支曲, j. 2, WFQ) which employ similar homonymous puns:

The musk, even though it is smashed into powder, will not abandon its fragrance,	搗麝成塵香不滅，
And the lotus, even when it is broken into pieces, will not forsake its silk.	拗蓮作寸絲難絕。

Occupying the fifth syllable of both lines, 香 (*xiang*, fragrance) and 絲 (*si*, silk) combined are a homonymous pun on 相思 (*xiangsi*)—love yearning (metaphorically, political loyalty). This is a frequently used pun in the poems of Li Shangyin and Wen Tingyun, both of whom followed the examples of the Music Bureau poems of the southern dynasties.[54] Making 香 and 祀 pun on 相 (attendant) and 嗣 (the heir) in the case at hand is, therefore, only a variant use of the 相思 (*xiangsi*) pun.

The Boshan Censer came into use in the Han Dynasty as a special adornment-utensil for the nobility. It is a nine-layer incense censer in the shape of Mount Bo (Boshan) located in the sea, with carvings of strange birds, rare beasts, and other wonders on its body and water in its nethermost layer. Legend has it that the Western Queen Mother sends a Boshan Censer to Emperor Wudi.[55] It appears that the term does not have anything special to do with the Heir. The last difficult question, then, is how the Boshan Censer could become a metaphor for the Heir in this context. In sources prior to the Tang, we locate the following texts for comparison with Wen's usage of the term.

1. During and after Han, in various dynasties, a Boshan Censer became an indispensable article in the officially regulated adornment-utensils of the Heir Apparent. The Song Dynasty encyclopedia *Taiping* Yulan[56] quotes "The Memorial of Presenting Miscellaneous Articles" (上雜物疏) by Emperor Wu of the Wei: "The Imperial Heir had four censers of pure silver." It also quotes from "The Former Anecdotes of the Eastern Palace of Jin" (晉東宮舊事): "When the Heir Apparent was appointed and set up, he had in his possession one brass Boshan Censer" (皇太子初立，有銅博山香爐一枚).
2. There are some remaining precedents in pre-Tang literature in which the Boshan Censer refers to the Heir Apparent. Examples are "Song of the Boshan Censer" (詠博山香爐詩)[57] by Liu Hui (劉繪, 458–502): "On the upper part is carved the Crown Heir of Qin / Who, riding a crane, is soaring to the blue cloud" (上鏤秦王子，駕鶴淩青煙). And the Zhaoming Heir Apparent, Xiao Tong (蕭統, 501–531), the compiler of *Wenxuan*, once wrote "Rhapsody On the Brass Boshan Censer" (銅博山香爐賦).
3. Even in the Tang Dynasty, there was still type of decoration designed for the carriage and attire of Heir Apparent, which resembled "Mount Boshan in the ocean." For example, "Part Six of the Imperial Heir's Attires" of the "Records of Carriage and Attires" in XTS (24: 517) states: "For the Far-Trip Crown [a special crown for the Heir], it ought to have three shafts plus a golden Boshan." All the evidence suggests that there was a special connection between the Heir and the "Boshan Censer," although the original record of this allusion, from which all the later uses stem, is no longer extant.
4. The Music Bureau poem "Yang Pan'er" (楊叛兒) contains the following lines: "My love is the joss stick plunging into the water / and I am the Boshan Censer" (郎作沉水香，儂作博山爐).[58] These lines employ *xiang* (香, joss-stick) and Boshan Censer as metaphors for the love between lovers. Wen Tingyun was adept at using the love affairs between lad and lass as metaphors for the political relationship between the monarch and the subject. Here the line, "The Fragrance is attached to the Boshan Censer," is just such a recreation from the Musical Bureau model, keeping its original diction *xiang*, "fragrance" or joss stick, and "the Boshan Censer" as euphemisms not for lovers, but for the Heir and himself. This serves to complete our explanation of Wen's metaphor.
5. Furthermore, perhaps out of fear that later readers would fail to understand his meaning, Wen wrote another poem entitled simply "Boshan Censer" (博山香爐, j. 8, WFQ). This poem was written to vent his deep grief and is also connected to Wen's political frustrations. These can be understood from

the title of the poem and inferred from its last couplet, which, yet again, expresses frustration caused by Wen's attendance on the Heir:

I hear say that Yang Zhu had no end of tears to shed, 見說楊朱無限淚，
Which were not, nay, vainly because the road forked away. 豈能空為岐路分？

Yang Zhu wept on coming to the forked way, because it leads to both south and north. Wen sheds tears in the manner Yang Zhu did; he, too, had his own torment to weep over. As we have read in "Hundred-Rhyme Poem": "In my laments and sighs I felt melancholy as did Yang Zhu"—Wen's frustrations are always connected to his political experiences, and especially with the eunuchs, Now, these frustrations are focused upon the Heir as well. Upon noticing that in the second line quoted above there is the character 岐 (*qi*), the very character Wen used as his changed name when participating in the Metropolitan Prefecture Examination (after attending the Heir), we can infer that the "Boshan Censer" poem must be a work of extreme complexity, as we will demonstrate.

Now, at last, we have developed and proved our explanation of this couplet. The remaining task will possibly be easier. The following couplet describes the role Wen played in the Heir's miniature court.

69 Auspicious sunshade grew dense on the emerald trees, 瑞景森瓊樹，
A light piece of ice brightened the jade pot. 輕冰瑩玉壺。

At the literal level it is still a vivid portrayal of objects in the palace: the fine jade-like trees growing luxuriously under auspicious sunlight, and pieces of ice placed inside a jade pot and used for dispelling the heat. But, as is the case with many other couplets, a layer of hidden meanings underlies the surface meaning of the language. Emerald trees, besides referring to real objects, refer metaphorically to the attendants around the Heir and a light piece of ice, as a metaphor for a pure and transparent heart, refers to the naiveté and artlessness of the youthful Heir, who, being about ten years old at the time, could be aptly described in this manner.[59]

What is the role Wen played in the Heir's "miniature" court?

70 To my divine-sheep cap, an iron shaft is clasped, 豸冠簪鐵柱，
At the Dragon Head was the Golden bureau. 螭首對金鋪。

The couplets preceding the appearance of the Heir Apparent present a picture of the environment of his court, but from this couplet on, the poet purposely turns the readers' attention to his personal position in this miniature court. As we have seen in the sixty-sixth rhyme, the divine-sheep cap was worn by the Attending Censor. In this context, it refers to the Rectifier in the Editorial Service, the official position assumed by Wen. Since the "Golden Bureau atop the Dragon Head" refers to the Left and Right Historiographers or Diarists,[60] its corresponding position in the retinue of the Heir might conceivably be the Remonstrator (司議郎).

71 The Administrator's calligraphy numbered a thousand scrolls, 內史書千卷，
And the General's paintings, one cabinetful. 將軍畫一廚。

"The Administrator" refers to the Jin Dynasty calligrapher Wang Xizhi, who once held the official position of Administrator of Kuaiji Commandery (會稽內史). "The General" here refers to Gu Kaizhi (顧愷之, 392–467), a well-known Jin Dynasty painter, who held the official position of Tigerhead General (虎頭將軍). Wang Xizhi's calligraphy and Gu Kaizhi's paintings were highly valued as imperial treasures during the Tang times. If Wen were to gain access to or take charge of these imperial treasures during his attendance, his official position must have been similar to that of the Academician of the Academy for the Veneration of Literary Worthies (崇文館學士). What, then, was Wen's official position? Was he a Rectifier, a Remonstrator, or an Academician? If we set aside the exaggerated elements in the poetic language and take into consideration the concrete historical milieu, the three above-mentioned positions could have been held by a single person. The reasons are:

1. Just as there are the Probationary Censors, who, inferior to the Attending Censors, "are not formal officials, and not limited to a fixed number," Rectifiers, as officials for Heir Apparent homologous to the Attending Censors, might also have their alternate members or sinecurists. And, with the precedent that Emperor Taizong promoted Ma Zhou (馬周) from commoner directly to the position of Probationary Attending Censor (監察御史里行),[61] Wen could lawfully have been promoted to a similar position, since he was an imperial relative who enjoyed powerful recommendation, and most importantly, possessed talents and pledged loyalty to the dynasty. All these factors combine to support the objective possibility that Wen could "ascend the heavens with one step" from the status of a commoner.
2. Most of the emperors of the middle and Late Tang eras were short-lived rulers who died before their sons could be established as heirs. Because of the usurpation of state power by the eunuchs, even when the emperor on the throne had sons, very few of them could become Heir in accordance with usual practice. Thus, the position Heir Apparent had lain vacant for many years. Furthermore, Emperor Wenzong's inconsiderate measures toward his son contributed to the unchecked jealousy of Worthy Consort Yang, and as a result of the factional strife, the court officials failed to offer effective protection to the Heir. Consequently, the subordinate official institution of the Heir was far from adequate and complete. Emperor Wenzong, himself only a little more than thirty years of age, desired only

to provide his son with good Confucian instruction, choosing many famous scholars to be his tutors. However, he was not yet ready to let the boy practice to be an emperor.

3. Wen was writing an autobiographical poem, not filling out his own curriculum vitae. Accordingly, we cannot take what he says too literally. Comparing the accounts of his official positions in this poem, with that in the "Epistle Thanking Minister Li of Xiangzhou" ("I already reach hold of the iris ink-paste"), it is highly possible that Wen functioned as an alternate Rectifier, concurrently serving as an Academician, a position approximate to that of a literary assistant with larger than fixed official duties.

72 My eyes were dazzled by the surprising display, 眼明驚氣象，
And my heart, awe-stricken at the grand scale. 心死伏規模。
73 I had never expected to look at the imperial treasury, 豈意觀文物，
If it was useless to carve a *crude jadeite* like me. 何勞琢碔砆。[62]

"To look at the imperial treasury" is a euphemism for Wen becoming a close attendant, an experience that redoubled his allegiance to the Tang Empire. However, not even such an opportunity could alter Wen's fate. He was indeed, as he ironically states here, no jade to be carved—despite all the support he had enlisted, he suffered yet another failure. His untimely death ended all Wen's endeavors to carve out a career through service to the Heir. Wen does not recount directly how the young heir met his end, because, on this occasion, it is unnecessary to relate the sad and complex story.

74 Grasses are luxurious—fit for grazing the *Yaoniao* Steed, 草肥牧騕褭，
Mosses rough—proper for tempering the *Kunwu* Blade. 苔澀淬昆吾。

"Grasses are luxurious" stands for "political conditions are favorable." *Yaoniao*, a spirited steed, is said to appear only when a sage king is ruling, and is hence a metaphor for a successful minister. "Mosses [are] rough" refers to difficult situations. *Kunwu* is the name of legendary sword that could cut jade as easily as cutting butter.

Finally, reviewing his attendance on the Heir, Wen understood that a favorable political environment is requisite if talented men are to accomplish great feats for the empire. He failed, to his dismay, to serve the Heir successfully to the end, because both he and the Heir were born at an unfavorable time. However, Wen was not a man easily dejected, on the contrary, the adversity he encountered made him even firmer of purpose and more fearless in action. Although Wen was forced to endure humiliation for the time being, he was now better equipped to play a role in the political arena, because he had experienced a major political event. Nevertheless, he found it difficult to resign himself to this abrupt failure.

Since we are now in possession of many details of Wen's story, a topic of considerable interest and attraction opens up for us. It was by the recommendation of Li Cheng, through an examination by the Ministry of Personnel, and only after the personal consent of Emperor Wenzong that Wen was chosen to be an attendant of Li Yong, the Heir Apparent. Using this shortcut, Wen entered directly into the service of the highest ruler of the empire. In the literary tropes and historical allusions, we have learned how Wen tried to make the best of his opportunities. Unfortunately, in the Late Tang period, the eunuchs always controlled the imperial succession, and thus the Heir Apparent, as a legitimate successor to the throne who had been set up without the approval of the eunuchs, became their target of attack, and his days as designated Heir were numbered.

There remain many questions to answer: how did the young prince die? What was Wen's attitude toward all the participants in the event? What happened to Wen in the process and how did the events affect his later life (and poetry)? "Hundred-Rhyme Poem" answers only some of these questions, since it was unnecessary and impossible to answer them all, and the poet needed to leave other questions unanswered. What he wanted to recount to those he addressed this poem was the affliction he felt at the time. In searching for answers to these other questions, we must turn to other poems.

Chapter Six

Mystifying Poetry

AN ENIGMA OF THE SPHINX

The following poem is, I venture to say, one of the most perplexing poems in the entirety of Chinese classic poetry, and one of the most enchanting. Had Wen written it in a less mystifying and appealing manner, it would not have survived his own time, still less have been handed down for us to study. Moreover, its explanation is indispensable for a complete picture of Wen's attendance upon the Heir, and for a full view of Wen's life and poetry. It is a full account of the "Heir Apparent Incident," a political poem in the deceptive guise of a love song, with all its imagery, symbolism, and labyrinthine complexity. Most fascinating and surprising is its exquisite verbal structure, in which elegant allusions and diction flow smoothly while intimating an intricate poetic world.

"Twenty-Two Rhymes of the Arched Door" (j. 6, WFQ)

1 To an arched door was attached a net of pearls.
A square latticed-window lay hidden in the thick of green.
2 Into the candle-tray the wick-ash dropped scattered.
Through lowered curtain moonlight filtered covertly in.
3 Powder-white were the bureaus of the Immortal Lad.
Frosty cold came the fulling sounds of the Jade Lass.
4 The home of drunkenness was aloft and aloof [from the world],
And the games of chess were intense and quiet.
5 A pale hand held a crystal-clear fan,
[His] raven tufts were set with a hawks-bill-shell hairpin.
6 On seeing the tile-pines I was aware of my precarious position.
By singing the gardenia I praised two similar hearts' affections.

7 Over trees were arrayed decorations of the Thousand-Years.
From towers were hung needles of the Double Seventh.
8 I rewrote the old words of "White Hemp,"
Into new verses in exchange for yellow gold;
9 When the crying crane tuned the barbarian drum,
And the frightened cicada responded to the precious lute.
10 The dance, I suspect, was hard and could not be easily fulfilled;
The song, modulated, was cut short and hardly audible.
11 Withered in dew, the flower fell a victim of jealousy,
Shaken by wind, the willow was too weak to stand.
12 The bridge stood curved, its two pillars set further apart,
The pond was so swollen 'twas as one oar's length deep.
13 Now the road was cleared for an imperial hunt,
While the yellow banners came to the Shanglin Park.
14 So the spirited hawk presented itself in the feather garden,
And the heavenly horses splashed over the muddy hoof puddles.
15 When Lord Military Storehouse was choosing worthy men,
Sir Literary Garden saw a good omen:
16 The pinkish stalk of the magic iris was flourishing,
The vermilion osmanthus tree is about to become sparse.
17 Then you went back to the jade-like mat behind royal curtains,
Where a lamp shed its glare over the brocade quilts.
18 From the picture you took fright at the "Ferocious Beast,"
In the copybook was written the "Attracted Bird."
19 Now dawn came to the River, shining into the Qin chamber,
It cleared up atop the Hill overlooking the Wei Palace.
20 An Empress Zhao, with a green bag, was encountered,
While there appeared a Wang Shen inside the azure gate.
21 With philosophy and abandon I gave up my lonely indignation,
In my laxity and laziness I was tired of remonstrance.
22 Why on earth is the man, who has fled to the south,
Still chanting his Song of the Sleeping Dragon?

The Qing Dynasty annotator of Wen's poetry Gu Sili quoted a certain Mr. Xu's notes: "This work has the same purport as the previous poem." Actually, "the previous poem" in the book is "Twenty-Two Rhymes on Passing the Huaqing Palace" (過華清宮二十二韻), which takes as its theme the story of Emperor Xuanzong and tries to draw some historical lessons from it, so that its gist is easy to discern, unlike the poem at hand.

Gu then cited Yu Yang's (俞瑒) remark: "This is a work written in retrospect about the author's past wanderings; it picked up the first two characters as its title, thus it resembles such works as Li Shangyin's 'Brocade Threshold'" (錦檻).[1] This poem is indeed an "untitled poem" (無題詩) in that its title tells little about what is told in the poem. Yu Yang's remark demonstrates that he sensed something hidden behind the lines that he could not define, just as another Qing scholar, Du Zhao (杜詔), who disagrees with Xu but also cannot really establish a point of his own.[2]

If we take a closer look at the whole poem, we will find that most of its lines are composed in extremely exquisite parallelism and are permeated with a heavy sentimentality. In the face of its suggestiveness and mystery, any reader would be forced to ponder deeply, although the ordinary reader will not have the means to penetrate the mystery. With the seemingly true-to-life descriptions of a rendezvous, this poem appears on the surface to be a love song; but the poet's mental state reflected in this poem is definitely not lovesickness. For, misleading as the elusive lines are, a reading of the final two couplets will, naturally and logically, deny the love song hypothesis.

We must find a path to go in and then out of the labyrinth of this poem.

Upon reading the twenty-first rhyme, we might very naturally raise questions such as: what is Wen's "lonely indignation" that he had to force himself to give up? And why was he "tired of remonstrance" (with the emperor)? Then at the end of the poem, it is Wen's turn to ask himself: why, as a man who has fled to the south, are you still chanting the "Song of the Sleeping Dragon"? Occurring as it does at the end, this reference manifests the poem's motif and impresses the reader with the author's command of his subject.

The "Song of the Sleeping Dragon," although here referring to this very poem, alludes to the "*Liangfu Yin*" (梁甫吟), originally a Music Bureau topic giving expression of righteous indignation against worldly injustice and serving as a dirge to mourn the dead. The famous statesman Zhuge Liang, it was said, was fond of chanting it in his early years, hence it is referred to after his sobriquet, the Sleeping Dragon.[3] Here, as a finishing touch, the poet suddenly throws away all the sophisticated masks, and displays with vehemence and wrath his true self-image: he is a noble-minded man concerned about and involved in political events. As a result, he has been forced to flee to the south as a refugee. This hearkens back not only to Wen's remark in the long title of "Hundred-Rhyme Poem"—"to betake myself to a far place"—but also to a couplet in that same poem:

82 Between right and wrong—waking or dreaming,
  I was confused, 是非迷覺夢，
From Qin for Wu, I planned a travel. 行役議秦吳。

That is to say, in the winter of 840, Wen was forced to leave Qin (the capital Chang'an) for Wu (roughly the delta of the Yangtze River). In recounting his flight to the south, "Twenty-Two-Rhyme" and "Hundred-Rhyme Poem" are in conformity with each other.

For convenience sake, we will leave for the next chapter a detailed discussion of Wen's experiences directly after attending the Heir. For our purposes here we need simply to point out that as a direct political consequence of serving the Heir, Wen became entangled in various court struggles, which eventually precipitated his escape from the capital and his decision to quit the political arena altogether. From the last two couplets of the poem we shall now trace backward seeking more details to round off the story of Wen's attendance on the Heir. There is something of paramount importance in the twentieth rhyme, which is one of our historical keys to the treasury of Wen's poetic information.

20	An Empress Zhao, with a green bag, was encountered,	綠囊逢趙后，
	While there appeared a Wang Shen inside the azure gate.	青瑣見王沈。

The first line alludes to the story of Zhao Feiyan (趙飛燕) and Beauty Xu (許美人), both consorts of Emperor Cheng of Han (r. 32–7, B.C.). When Beauty Xu gave birth to a son, Empress Zhao was so jealous that she refused to eat, crying and beating her head against a wall. Then she ordered a eunuch, Jin Yan (靳嚴) by name, to send Beauty Xu a letter in a green bag. Upon receiving the bag from Empress Zhao, Beauty Xu put her newborn baby in a straw case, which, together with the letter in the green bag, she surrendered to Jin Yan; immediately Empress Zhao killed the baby.[4]

The allusion to Empress Zhao and Beauty Xu is quite obviously a reference to Worthy Consort Yang and Virtuous Consort Wang respectively, in which Beauty Xu's son is analogous to the Heir Apparent Li Yong. The eunuch Jin Yan certainly has a role to play as well, although it is only a minor one. To remedy this inexactitude, the poet adds a supplementary allusion of Wang Shen to complete his idea. A Jin Dynasty chief eunuch in the court of Liu Cong (劉聰, ?–318), Wang Shen usurped all of Liu's power and persecuted Liu's court officials.[5] "Wang Shen" here is a clear reference to the eunuchs who were dominating the court at Wen's time; although this historical Wang Shen is hardly alluded to by anyone else in poetry. However, the fact that in JS there are three men of this name has baffled the Qing Dynasty scholars who annotated Wen's poems. They mentioned the other two Wang Shens,[6] both irrelevant to the case, but overlooked the eunuch Wang Shen; as a result, their annotation of this line is too far from the point.

Therefore, this couplet imparts that there appeared in the inner palace an imperial consort as merciless as Empress Zhao, who deliberately planned to take the imperial heir's life, and, with the help of a chief eunuch as domineering as Wang Shen, finally attained her goal. The two allusions of this couplet refer to the complete story of Worthy Consort Yang, Virtuous Consort Wang, and her son Li Yong, furnishing strong evidence that Worthy Consort Yang was an accomplice of the eunuchs in murdering the Heir, although neither side is accused of the crime in the standard histories. Thus, Wen's poetry conveys a surprising incident that the histories fail to record.

The Heir was murdered and consequently Wen was forced to flee to the south; this alone suggests strongly that there was a close relationship between the Heir and Wen. Therefore, as inferred from the last three couplets, the whole poem must be a shrouded representation of the Heir Apparent Incident; and the descriptions of the first nineteen rhymes, which appear to be about a love affair, are an elegantly camouflaged political narrative, with subtle and rich implications concealed in every line.

This is both a unique narrative poem and an "untitled" lyric poem. Throughout the poem, imagery and metaphors are gracefully deployed such that they constitute the main narrative in elegant and attractive parallel couplets. As empathized nature, its scenic representations convey the subtle feelings of the poet; meanwhile, as metaphors for particular aspects of the event, the scenic representations "narrate" the complex details of the story. By the same token, it always presents one thing in the likeness of another, never showing clearly what is veiled metaphor and what is simple realistic narration. The import of each line seems either covert or overt. Insofar as it is covert, there are always clues that throw a ray of light on the author's intention, while insofar as it is overt, the subject matter is too elusive to grasp. As a magnum opus in the palace style poems, the structure of this poem can be compared to the architecture of imperial palaces, with their labyrinths and tunnels, myriad windows and countless gates. But in the final analysis, the riddle has a solution, since our historical key can hopefully open the gate to the poetic labyrinth; were it not so, the poet would have written his poem in vain.

Now, let us attempt to decode the cipher and give a detailed explanation of the poem in the order of the original text, couplet by couplet. In cases where problems arise, we will, to avoid too many digressions, set them aside for the moment.

First, we will scrutinize the entrance to the labyrinth.

1 To an arched door was attached a net of pearls. 洞戶連珠網，
A square latticed-window lay hidden in the thick of green. 方疏隱碧潯。
2 Into the candle-tray the wick-ash dropped scattered. 燭盤煙墜燼，
Through lowered curtain moonlight filtered covertly in. 簾壓月通陰。

The two beginning couplets immediately usher the reader into picturesque surroundings, a world of mysterious pomp. The scattered wick-ash of candles is silent testimony to a story to which only the moonlight was witness. Here is an abode of wealth and rank, and yet a haunt of heartbreak, in which flowing water was saturated with the woe of fallen flowers, and the dream of "holding a candle for a night excursion" was ruined.

In the laconic delineation of the scenery, a hidden clue is skillfully planted in advance (*fubi*, 伏筆), which prepares the reader for what is to follow. Simply put, in addition to being a direct scenic description, these opening lines are a covert reference to the Heir Apparent's residence, the *Shaoyangyuan*. Here as a most confidential assistant Wen attended, for about one year, the boy Heir Apparent, Li Yong. The three Chinese characters *Shao-yang-yuan* are not found here, but to conclude that the *Shaoyangyuan* is referred to follows logically from a reading of the whole poem.

Then, the poet gives information about where and when he met his young lord:

3 Powder-white were the bureaus of the Immortal Lad. 粉白仙朗署，
Frosty cold came the fulling sounds of the Jade Lass. 霜清玉女砧。
4 The home of drunkenness was aloft and aloof [from the world], 醉鄉高窈窈，
And the games of chess were intense and quiet. 棋陣靜愔愔。

This represents a social occasion, from which we are given to understand that this is the place and time of Wen's first encounter with Li Yong. The scene is set in one of the "powdered-white bureaus," seemingly in the Department of the State Affairs, where the "Immortal Lads"—bureau directors—are on duty. The time is the beginning of autumn, when the "Jade Lass" fulls her clothes, because "Every year at the beginning of autumn, people heard the Jade Lass fulling her brocade atop Mount Song."[7] As we have already demonstrated, a "powdered-white bureau" here actually refers to an office in the Editorial Service under the Left Secretariat of the Heir Apparent, and the time in question is at the beginning of the autumn of the second year of Kaicheng (837). At this time and in this place, many of those present were inebriated, while others were calmly playing chess. Matched with "the Jade Lass," "the Immortal Lad" in this couplet is also, apart from its aforementioned meaning, a metaphor for Wen himself in relation to the Heir. Here the technique is referred to as "using the feelings of lad and lass to speak about the affair between the monarch and his subjects." Service to the monarch (albeit a young monarch) is compared with wooing of a girl, a well-developed trope that can be dated as far back as the *Songs of the South*. The application of that trope here indicates the close relationship between Wen and the Heir Apparent.

As in the case in "Hundred-Rhyme Poem," Wen lets the "Jade Lass"—the young Heir and the protagonist of the poem—enter the scene in a dramatic pose, which is quite difficult for the readers to identify:

5 A pale hand held a crystal-clear fan, 素手琉璃扇，
[His] raven tufts were set with a hawks-bill-shell hairpin. 玄髻玳瑁簪。

We need not mistake the figure for a female because of the slender and pale hand. It would be in fact normal for a male child born into the imperial family to have an appearance like a girl. Although Wen compares Li Yong to the "Jade Lass," we can recognize him in his feminine disguise. And, the Chinese term "raven tufts" (玄鬢) is mostly used for a child (male or female) about ten years of age, which tallies perfectly with the youthful appearance of the Heir (827–838), an eleven-year old lad at the time (837).

Moreover, "crystal-clear fan" and "hawks-bill-shell hairpin" are also designed to reveal the special identity of the wearer. Made of a glass-like plastic substance called *liuli* (琉璃), the crystal-clear fan was sent as a precious tribute from central Asia to the Chinese emperor, hence originally it was available only to the royal family. Almost equally valuable were hawks-bill-shell hairpins, which were by custom given as betrothal gifts to the consort of an Heir Apparent,[8] and were thus a kind of insignia of an Heir Apparent.

It is out of the question that the figure referred to here should be a consort of the Heir. Only eleven years old at the time, the Heir was too young to have a consort. Emperor Wenzong once did try to choose a consort for him, but "the official and eminent families felt great disquiet about it," as no family was willing to send its daughter on the road to ruin. Regretting that his subjects "were reluctant to become related in marriage to my family," Wenzong could however well understand the reason and "gave up his plan."[9] Furthermore, if we were to explain this figure as a palace lady, or even the consort of the Heir, the complete poem would make no sense at all, as can be seen from any of the remaining couplets, including the one immediately following:

6	On seeing the tile-pines I was aware of my precarious position.	昔邪看寄跡，
	By singing the gardenia I praised two similar hearts' affections.	梔子詠同心。

Tile-pine is a moss-like and drought-enduring plant that grows on the roof-tiles of old houses; here it is used as a metaphor for Wen, who finds himself in a high place on very unstable ground. Gardenia, with its pistil and stamen (心) growing together (actually, pistillate and staminate flowers growing out of the same receptacle), symbolizes the constancy in love in Chinese poetic diction, and here stands for the mutual confidence between the Heir and Wen. Wen compares himself to the tile-pines, because his relationship with the Heir was accidental and lacked a solid foundation. But now something unexpected had happened—he found that the two of them were of one heart and mind, and for a period of time they became inseparable companions.

Now we see what Wen witnessed after he became an aide of the imperial heir.

7	Over trees were arrayed decorations of the Thousand-Years.	樹列千秋勝，

From towers were hung needles of the Double Seventh. 樓懸七夕針。

The palace ladies were following whatever pastimes they could to amuse themselves during the festive season. This couplet has the appearance of a narrative account, but still contains several layers of meanings.

First, the poet reminds his reader once more of the approximate time when he began his service to the Heir Apparent. It happened to be the Double Seventh, the eve of which was believed to be the time when the Weaving Girl and the Herd Boy of the legend had their yearly reunion. This was an occasion when court ladies would hang up needles with nine eyes and attempt to thread them under the moonlight, as prayers for a happy future.[10] Then came the "Thousand-Years Day," the fifth day of the eighth month on the Chinese calendar, which marked Emperor Xuanzong's (玄宗, r. 712–756) birthday, established as a national festival since the year 728.[11] On this day, it was customary for the court ladies to adorn trees with paper flowers and engage in various entertainments.

To pray for happiness on the Double Seventh Eve was just what "the Immortal Lad" and "the Jade Lass" would attempt to do with their "two similar hearts' affections." "Thousand-Years," meaning thousands of years of everlasting good governance, speaks to Wen's wish that the Heir Apparent be free of disasters and the harmonious monarch-subject relationship between the Heir and himself endure as long as possible. However, the Weaving Girl and the Herd Boy themselves meet only briefly; how could they come to the aid of helpless lovers in the human world? Emperor Xuanzong's dream of ruling for thousands of years had long vanished like smoke and fog since his own reign; how could he bless his imperial scions when he could not bless himself? Therefore, this couplet meanwhile implies some oncoming disaster.

It is worth noting that in this couplet the Thousand-Year Day and the Double Seventh Eve are mentioned in reversed chronological order. In other words, the two festivals both fell in the same year of 837. As the time from the autumn of 837, when Wen gained access to the Heir, to the ninth month of 838, when the Heir died, was only a little more than one year, it could not cover two peaceful autumns. This is proved by Wen's experiences.

8 I rewrote the old words of "White Hemp," 舊詞翻白紵，
Into new verses in exchange for yellow gold; 新賦換黃金。

This couplet suggests the role Wen played when he was attending the Heir.

"White Hemp" is a title of a dance melody of the "Music Bureau," matched with words; "Emperor Wudi of Liang made Shen Yue (沈約, 441–513) rewrite its words and retitle it 'Song of the White Hemp of the Four Seasons'" (四時白紵歌).[12] Thus, in his capacity as literary attendant, Wen must have written verses to music that was to be performed in the inner court. In Wen's extant works can be found many poems written during this period that often perplex modern readers. Once we know of Wen's attendance on the Heir, these poems become explicable, as valuable samples of the Late Tang palace style.

Moreover, it is no accident that we find Wen once more playing the role of Sima Xiangru. It was said that Empress Chen, Emperor Han Wudi's consort, asked Xiangru to write a love poem for her. She presented this poem to the emperor in an attempt to win back the imperial favor, paying Xiangru a hundred taels of yellow gold as reward.[13] In the allusion at hand, we can infer that Wen is here referring to his personal experiences of writing poems on behalf of Consort Wang, the Heir's mother, in an effort to dissuade Emperor Wenzong from abandoning her. Thus, we can see, until Wang's death in the eighth month of the third year of Kaicheng (838), Wen had vainly tried to persuade Wenzong not to abandon his old consort (the emperor himself just thirty years of age). However, his efforts were unsuccessful.

Everything bodes ill for the Heir and his mother:

> 9 When the crying crane tuned the barbarian drum, 唳鶴調蠻鼓，
> And the frightened cicada responded to the precious lute. 驚蟬應寶琴。

According to legend, there was a huge drum in the prefecture of Kuaiji, into which a crane flew, which set the drum to beating, such that the noise could be heard all the way to Luoyang.[14] Note that here the crane that flew into the drum is a crying one, so that the sound the drum produces must be sad and heartrending, an ill omen portending some catastrophe. By the same token, the "frightened cicada" that "responded to the precious lute" is a prey to the circumstances under the sway of a "killing mind."[15] Chinese music theory since antiquity has held that all worldly order and disorder, fortune and misfortune are embodied in music. "The way of music is homologous with that of government" (聲音之道，與政通矣)[16] Although, superficially speaking, these two lines are representations of the performances of drum and lute, we sense that amidst the cacophony, an ulterior murderous intrigue was at work—the conspiracy of Consort Yang, aimed at taking the life of the Heir's mother. In the eighth couplet, "new verses in exchange for yellow gold" suggests that the situation might possibly change for the better, but this couplet indicates that things were worsening suddenly. Consort Yang spared no efforts in vilifying her rival, and, as implied in these and following veiled references, fulfilled her plan in the short span of a single year.

> 10 The dance, I suspect, was hard and could not be easily fulfilled; 舞疑繁易度，
> The song, modulated, was cut short and hardly audible. 歌轉斷難尋。

Now not only was the "dance" not easy to fulfill, but also the "song" was "modulated" to another tune, then "cut short and hardly audible." Using singing and dancing as metaphors for Consort Wang's predicament, this couplet insinuates that any hope for her to survive this intrigue was extinguished—as a victim of Yang's slander and Wenzong's fickleness, Consort Wang was eliminated. Neither Consort Wang nor Wen had anticipated that, as the mother of the Heir and a senior imperial consort, she would die so tragically as a result of Consort Yang's bitter jealousy, even though they knew that Yang might succeed in currying more imperial favor. Now that the mother was dead, her son's position was no longer secure. The young heir found himself in an increasingly perilous position and totally defenseless in face of crisis:

11 Withered in dew, the flower fell a victim of jealousy, 露委花相妒，
Shaken by wind, the willow was too weak to stand. 風欹柳不禁。

Here we are given a supplementary account of the political situation. After the death of the Heir Apparent's mother, the child himself fell into an abyss of disappointment. The flower that withered in the chilly dew and the willow that shook in the sharp wind symbolize both Consort Wang, who died, and her son, who would, to Wen's anguish, die soon after. Having succeeded in taking the mother's life, now Consort Yang made an attempt on the son.

The eunuch usurpation greatly weakened the functioning of the government. Factional strife further sapped the empire, and the confused and fatuous Wenzong bestowed his conjugal favors exclusively on a merciless and ambitious consort. All these spelled ruin for the Heir Apparent.

12 The bridge stood curved, its two pillars set further apart, 橋彎雙表迴，
The pond was so swollen 'twas as one oar's length deep. 池漲一篙深。

What are the connotations of this couplet in the concrete context of the poem?

First, from the perspective of scenic description, the pond was swollen because the rainy season had come. Excessive rain, accompanied by the wind and dew mentioned in the last couplet, registers the arrival of another autumn. Comparing this with the "frosty-cold," and "the Double Seventh Eve" and "Thousand Years" representing the previous autumn, we can see that a year had passed since Wen began his service to the Heir.

Secondly, guided by our grasp of the political situation of the time, and enlightened by the clues occurring later in this poem, we understand this couplet as an elaborately designed metaphor. Preceding this couplet, we have learned that Consort Yang was implicated in Consort Wang's death. Following this couplet, we will learn that Yang, in collaboration with the eunuchs, was responsible for murdering Wang's son, the Heir Apparent. In the logical sequence of the poem, this couplet must, therefore, metaphorically represent the situation leading up to the Heir's death.

Thirdly, the relationships among various objects described in this couplet deserve special attention. It was because "The pond was so swollen it was one oar's length deep," that the poet observes how "The bridge stood curved, its two pillars set further apart." And, too, it was because "The pond was swollen" that " 'twas was one oar's length deep"; and because "The bridge stood curved" that "its two pillars [seemed to be] set further apart." The way the scenic objects are arrayed bears the obvious imprint of the poet's empathy. The poet projects his feelings onto the objects he describes—the bridge, the two pillars, the pond, and the one oar—such that all the images become metaphors for the person or group of persons who played a role in the Heir Apparent Incident.

"The curved bridge" stands for Emperor Wenzong who, as the intermediary connecting the imperial consorts Wang and Yang, the eunuchs and officials, Niu and Li factions, and even Wen Tingyun and the Heir, resembles a bridge. But he was not a straight bridge, because he did not have enough wisdom to be termed a good emperor.[17] During the Kaicheng era (836–840), the opposition between the two factions reached its height of intensity. This was due in large part to Emperor Wenzong himself. Therefore, the connotation of "the two pillars set further apart" is transparent: because of Emperor Wenzong's wrong handling of contradictions between the two factions under the eunuchs' power, the two contending factions, Niu and Li, politically became all the more opposed to each other; and their hostility and discord on any political affairs at court, increased steadily. It is the two factions, not the Southern and Northern Offices, which become the two pillars, because Wen was so contemptuous of the eunuchs that he would not regard them as pillars of the court, and absolutely never use comparisons such as this.

Proceeding to the second line, "the pond was swollen" points to the increasing imperial favor shown to the Niu Faction. We ground this reading in the historical reality that in the latter part of the Kaicheng era, the Niu Faction had gained overwhelming superiority over the Li Faction. Connected with this, "one oar's length deep" adds to the rich implication of the line: it was Consort Yang alone who, supported by the Niu Faction, was in high favor with the emperor. Here we ought not to ignore the indelicate overtone (a sexual indelicacy) implied in the line. This is an infelicity in this poem, though it does no harm to the artistic expression of the poem as a whole.

Wen does not directly implicate the eunuchs, but they are involved in the context. The autumn wind and excessive rain symbolize eunuch tyranny. Now, viewing things in the concrete historical milieu, we are able to carefully examine the next two couplets.

13 Now the road was cleared for an imperial hunt, 清蹕傳恢囿，
While the yellow banners came to the Shanglin Park. 黃旗幸上林。

Should the emperor, at this critical moment, be in a mood to go hunting? It would *appear* so! Behold, how he ordered that the road be cleared (of passengers and pedestrians), and, how, with his retinue, he plausibly came to Shanglin, the imperial park.

14 So the spirited hawk presented itself in the feather garden, 神鷹參翰苑，
And the heavenly horses splashed over the muddy hoof puddles. 天馬破蹄涔。

The flying hawk and galloping horses are parts of a magnificent spectacle, the imperial hunt. However, in a context filled with symbolism and metaphors, a direct description seems out of place and therefore strange. If we notice that the term *Hanyuan* (feather garden) is merely another name for *Hanlinyuan* (翰林院, "literary forest academy"), an official institute generally representing important ministers, we then realize that the "spirited hawk" is an accepted metaphor for the censors,[18] bringing the figurative meaning of this couplet immediately to light. Thus, the "spirited hawk" refers to Di Jianmo the Censor-in-Chief, who at the Yanying Palace Conference vehemently and anxiously remonstrated with Emperor Wenzong over his absurd decision to depose his son. Similarly, "heavenly horse" is a metaphor for a particularly important official,[19] who opposed the removal of the Heir by refuting Consort Yang's slander and thus helped prevent Emperor Wenzong from going too far with his extremely foolish actions.

Here we perceive how the poet employs highly suggestive diction, in an effort to prevent the reader from becoming lost in the labyrinth of his poetic world.

A re-reading of the thirteenth couplet in the light of this understanding of the fourteenth reveals that the imperial hunt is a metaphor for the Yanying Conference! The poet substitutes the spectacle of an imperial hunt for that of a palace conference. At first glance, such a reading might seem far-fetched, but the more we examine it, the more we find the metaphoric correspondences to be both appropriate and ingenious. For, in imperial China, it was very common to refer to court officials as hawks, horses, or even hunting dogs of the emperors—metaphors so natural that they can have no pejorative overtone at all. Satisfyingly, we find that historical references and poetic description tally with each other to perfection.

The strong opposition from his subjects served to warn Wenzong, restoring him to his senses. Full of regret for being foolish, he behaved in a manner which led to an improvement in the situations of the Heir and of Wen especially.

15 When Lord Military Storehouse was choosing worthy men, 武庫方題品，
Sir Literary Garden saw a good omen: 文園有好音。

At the Yanying Palace Conference, there was a "Lord Military Storehouse," an influential minister such as Du Yu, who was entitled to recommend qualified candidates for the civil service official examination. This man must have deeply respected Wen's talents and political courage. His recommendation would place our poet Wen Tingyun, a Sima Xiangru incarnate (the prefect of "Literary Garden"),[20] in a position with which he might finally "see a good omen"—a very promising prospect, after years of disappointment.

16 The pinkish stalk of the magic iris was flourishing, 朱莖殊菌蠢，
The vermilion osmanthus is about to become sparse. 丹桂欲蕭森。

As we have discovered, "magic iris"[21] is a Taoist jargon for censors. Here Wen likens himself to the "magic iris" because he had served in the Editorial Service in the Household of the Heir Apparent under the Left Secretariat as a Rectifier, an official post somewhat analogous to that of an Attending Censor, though with lower rank. In any event, when the "Lord Military Storehouse" was choosing worthy men, Wen presented himself as an excellent aide to the Heir, deserving of a more prominent position. "To pluck an osmanthus twig" is a conventional metaphor for obtaining the Presented Scholar degree. "The vermilion osmanthus is about to become sparse," because some of the twigs would be plucked, and with the plucked twigs, Wen would be honored as Presented Scholar.

To sum up, ever since the Yanying Palace Conference, Wen enjoyed the appreciation of a powerful minister and had strong hopes of being accepted as a Presented Scholar in the upcoming examination. This important minister must have been Pei Du or someone under Pei's influence. Here, we find the underlying cause of Wen's attainment of the academic degree "Equivalent to Passing" in the year following Li Yong's death.

In the remainder of the poem, we find other details confirming the particulars of the Heir Apparent Incident.

17 Then you went back to the jade-like mat behind royal curtains, 黻帳回瑤席，
Where a lamp shed its glare over the brocade quilts. 華燈對錦衾。

In this couplet, the Heir's perspective is presented, but, as is the situation throughout the whole event, the poet is also presumed to be a witness. Like the first two couplets of this poem, this one becomes a scenic presentation without ambiguity, once we have an understanding of it in the context of the whole event. It demonstrates the Heir's feelings after being ordered back to his residence, the *Shaoyangyuan*, where despite the luxury and comfort of his surroundings, he spent sleepless nights, because dangers were lurking around him. This is a time of fleeting peace before disaster strikes.

18 From the picture you took fright at the "Ferocious Beast," 畫圖驚走獸，
In the copybook was written the "Attracted Bird." 書帖得來禽。[22]

Highlighting a famous painting and piece of calligraphy in the Heir Apparent's abode, this couplet is a symbolic description of the ominous situation Li Yong faced. We can also understand it as a reflection or afterthought of the Incident on Wen's part.

"Ferocious Beast" refers to a kind of picture believed to have the power to dispel evil spirits; hence the pictures are often used as adornments hung on the wall of a bedroom. In the eyes of the child Heir, the frightening beast in the picture might present itself more as a monster than as something placed there to dispel evil spirits. "Attracted Birds" refers to the handwriting by Wang Xizhi in a letter about the cherry which, because of its delicious taste, *attracts birds*. Here, the poet alludes to the position of the Heir Apparent, a position coveted by many, yet capable of bringing ruin down upon its holder.

19	Now dawn came to the River, shining into the Qin chamber,	河曙秦樓映，
	It cleared up atop the Hill overlooking the Wei Palace.	山晴魏闕臨。

"Qin Chamber" in antithesis to "Wei Palace" here refers to the palace where the Heir lived, while Wei Palace refers to Emperor Wenzong's court. "River" and "Hill" may refer to the Wei River (渭水) and the Mount Zhongnan (終南山), which were close to Chang'an; or they may function together as one term *shanhe* (山河), and stand for the Tang Empire. Note that it is morning, a fine morning possibly betokening peace and prosperity for the empire. However, this was to be merely a fleeting appearance, and, for the Heir, it was similar to a brief pause before the tiger springs on the lamb. Disaster was imminent.

The twentieth rhyme: as previously analyzed, indicates that Li Yong was murdered by the eunuchs in collaboration with Wenzong's favorite Consort Yang.[23] The final outcome, however, was that Yang was herself destroyed by the event, being held in dishonor both for what she had done and for the manner of her death.[24] However, the eunuchs' leading part in the conspiracies remained undetected. Having been involved in this incident from beginning to end, Wen could not bear to keep quiet; and in speaking the truth, he ran the risk of losing his life. For having attended on the Heir Apparent and for voicing his protest against the eunuchs, Wen faced great danger more than once. After a few more desperate efforts, he was forced to leave the capital and flee to the south.

Now for the last two couplets:

21	With philosophy and abandon I gave up my lonely indignation,	任達嫌孤憤，
	In my laxity and laziness I was tired of remonstrance.	疏慵倦九箴。

22 Why on earth is the man who has fled to
the south, 若為南遁客，
Still chanting his song of the Sleeping Dragon? 猶作臥龍吟？

Wen fled to the south and remained there, composing this poem as one of his contributions to the compilation of a veritable history, never admitting defeat or giving up his ambition to aid his country. Far from being a mere dirge lamenting the late Heir Apparent, this poem also presents a vivid account of the complex political situation in Late Tang times, and of the poet's inner world. Because in the entire extant corpus of Tang poetry there are very few reflections of the intrigues of the eunuchs, poems such as this one are all the more significant and valuable to our understanding of Late Tang political history and poetry. Moreover, they also serve to enrich our understanding of Wen's poetic style, with which a seemingly "morally ambiguous" poem can impart a surprisingly complex story.

THEORY GUIDING WEN'S POETIC COMPOSITION

In seeking information about Wen's life, in particular his hidden experiences, we have studied many of his poems. Having abstracted substantial information from the lyric, allusive, and often hyperbolic lines, we find that Wen's poetry is highly sophisticated, to such a degree that his readers are seldom able to understand it easily. The more confidential the affairs he is couching in his verse, the more oblique becomes his artistic expression. Had he not written his poetry under particular political pressure, his obscurity would be difficult to account for. Thus, Wen's literary creations are unique.

Unfortunately, since Wen's death few readers have understood or appreciated the artistic devices he designed for his unutterable political frustrations. It would be rare that anyone, even a scholar, would suspect Wen of having secrets and attempt the concentrated thinking necessary to discover them. Fortunately, once we discover the key to his poetry from examining his life, and grasp the essence of his unique artistry, it becomes possible to explore the richness and complexity of his poetic world. In fact, Wen's poetry is no more ambiguous than the poetry of many of his contemporaries, since the major events, the essential parts of his life, recur repeatedly in his surviving works. Here they are treated from various angles, thus facilitating inquiring studies. Since Wen's poetry is at the same time abstruse and yet explicable, it is imperative that we pay close attention to his artistic technique.

On more than one occasion, Wen mentioned his method of composition, or his literary theory, which (as the natural outcome of his life, providing the key to unraveling his poetry) has never before attracted academic interest, and thus deserves further study.

With respect to subject matter, Wen chose to write about public political affairs in the shape of the private, as expressed in the following remarks (the second of the "Two Epistles Presented to Vice-Minister Jiang" 上蔣侍郎啟二首之二):

> I ruminated over the richness and beauty of Xie Lingyun; I played with the brocade and embroidery of Yan Yanzhi. . . . Though my inborn gifts are not great such that my compositions are no match for the Airs and Elegantiae, my craftsmanship has reached such an extreme degree, that my poetry is very close to the chants and songs (味謝氏之膏腴，弄顏生之錦繡 … 雖天分不多，尚慚于風雅；而人工斯極，劣近于謳歌).

Wen had a predilection for beautiful diction and flowery expression, to such an extent that, whatever he wrote about could, upon first sight at the least, greet the eyes with a flash of beauty. In this regard, masters of parallelism and description, such as Xie Lingyun and Yan Yanzhi, were the models he chose to follow. In Wen's estimation, the masterpieces in *The Book of Songs* are matchless only because they are products of an inborn gift (天分), the natural revelation of the poet's feelings free of any artificial adornment. By comparison, Wen's works are far less natural because they employ too many techniques. Wen seems to have the self-knowledge to enable him to give an honest estimate of his own poetry.

"Chants and songs"(謳歌) is not a general term for poems, but must refer to something special; in this context, in contrast to "the Airs and Elegantiae" (風雅), it refers to *The Songs of the South*, the counterpart of *The Book of Songs* in Chinese literary history. Therefore, the only reasonable explanation of the term is that it alludes to *Lisao*: "Ning Qi intoned his chants and songs / Duke Huan of Qi heard him and took him as his minister" (甯戚之謳歌兮，齊桓聞以該輔).[25] Wen means here that his poems are like Ning Qi's "Feeding the Bull" or *Lisao* itself. They give expression to the pain of an honest man who cherished high aspirations to serve his country but was misunderstood and maltreated by his times. In this sense, to say his works are "something close to the chants and songs" is to claim that his poetry, though seemingly concerned only with the poet's private "debauched" life, in fact teems with references to politics.

With respect to language style, Wen shows his partiality for the ornate in preference to the simple. This is clarified in another of Wen's important self-appraisals (the first of the "Two Epistles Presented to Vice-Minister Jiang").

> As to the way by which the simple and the ornate differ from and transform into one another, and as for the causes for which black or white (colors) come into vogue with the passing of time,[26] I have roughly taken up the approach of my teacher, and I never dare forget his instructions (質文異變之方，驪翰殊風之旨。粗承師法，敢墜緹緗).

Wen here tells us that he has taken his teacher Li Cheng as his exemplar; hence he has a good command of the technique of alternating a simple style with an ornate, and is familiar with the ways in which literary fashions change with the time. We do see in Wen's poetic works a preference for ornate expression with gorgeous diction, difficult tropes, and erudite allusions. But we also find many masterpieces that show Wen to be the master of simple and transparent style. Hence, we have to emphasize the fact that Wen is capable of either straight or circuitous representation, and conversant with both simple and ornate styles. Necessity decided Wen's choice of pattern for expression. And while among Wen's extant works, poems with ornate style are far more numerous than those with simple style, it was the reality of politics that forced him into ornateness and ambiguity.

By "ambiguity," however, I do not mean that Wen failed to convey clearly his ideas, instead I mean that he was proficient at disguising his motifs, thus averting hostile reading as much as possible. At the same time that he was bent on telling the truth, he had to guard against his political enemies. Wen wrote for contemporary friends and future readers discriminating and appreciative enough to know what he was really saying, despite the fact that such works might appear "unreadable" to some would-be critics.

With respect to the motif of his poetry, it is covert while it is overt, or, the covert is in subtle interchangeability with the overt. This artistry of concealment and exposure, deployed for the skillful artistic expression of his innermost feelings, has much to do with the so-called "*xing*" in traditional Chinese poetic theory. It also has as its theoretical basis the literary conception of *The Book of Changes*. The following is Wen's self-confessed indebtedness to this Chinese classic ("Epistle Presented to Secretary Du" 上杜舍人啟):

> I have become rather conversant with the way to choose pertinent diction; and I have attained a passable mastery of the art of making the covert overt (頗識甄藻之規，粗達顯微之趣).

Over and above self-acknowledgment of his skillful control of the various colors and flavors of language, Wen places special emphasis on his adroitness in both hiding and revealing his subject matter. In order to avoid persecution, he had to hide the motifs of his political poems; whereas his fundamental purpose in writing these poems was to assert himself. Without concealment, Wen's works would not have been handed down; but with too much concealment, his true meanings would have been obscured altogether. Here Wen found himself in a predicament, requiring him to have a total command of the artifice of concealing while revealing. "To make the overt covert," a borrowing from the "Attached Words" (繫詞) of *The Book of Changes* (8: 89), is a perfect solution to the problem:

> *The Book of Changes* makes manifest what was in the past and foresees clearly what will be in the future, and consequently the covert

is made overt and the subtle is rendered apparent (夫易彰往而察來，而微顯闡幽).

In contrast to Wen's "ways to choose pertinent diction," his "art of making the covert overt" takes expression in his poetry as a means for hiding but not tarnishing the motifs of his literary creations. Employing camouflage by constantly varying his pictures, he would first attract the reader into his artistic contrivance, and then distract him with a variety of perplexing and even seemingly unreasonable lines. Throughout this process, he would deliberately give clues that would lure the reader into searching for an answer. Wen proved very adept at indicating that there was something hidden while hinting broadly that whatever was hidden could be found out. Such is the ambivalent nature characteristic of Wen's poetry, the dialectic of his artistry.

To illustrate these points, we will analyze two more of Wen's poems, while substantiating our discovery with more details. Although we have unraveled several of Wen's poems dealing with his attendance upon the Heir, there are many others whose tantalizing puzzles await discovery and identification. In Wen's extant works consisting of about 330 *shi* poems, more than 60 *ci* poems and over 20 epistles, there are more than 40 *shi* poems, 20 *ci* poems and 10 epistles focusing on expressing and illuminating his liaison with the Heir. From my research waiting for future criticism or further evidence, I present these works in order of their appearances in WFQ, in the following list:

J.1. Chant for Weaving Brocade (織錦詞), Ode to a Night Feast (夜宴謠), Song of A Screen of (the Heir's) Birth and Blessing (生禖屏風歌), Melody for a Dancing Robe (舞衣曲), Song of Zhang Jingwan Gathering Lotus (張靜婉采蓮曲), Song for the Palace Lady of Xiang (湘宮人歌), Don't Cross the River, My Lord (公無渡河), Song of the Terrace of Yong (雍臺歌), Song of the God of the Marquis of Jiang (蔣侯神歌)

J.2. Ode for the Old City (故城曲), Midnight Air at the Galloping-Horse Tower (走馬樓三更曲), Melody Damozhi (達摩支曲), Song for a Feast of Eastern Xiang (湘東宴曲), Jiangnan Air (江南曲), Regrets for the Passing of Spring (惜春曲)

J.3. Hunting Horses (獵騎), Writing My Heart (寓懷), Poem Composed on Admiring Orchids (觀蘭作), Song for the Double Seventh Eve (七夕歌), Presenting to a Friend (酬友人), Golden-Tiger Terrace (金虎臺), Lord Guo of Handan (邯鄲郭公辭), Ancient Feeling (古意), Two Dirges for the Late Heir Apparent Zhuangke (莊恪太子挽歌詞二首), Two Poems Written at the Western Pool of Heir Apparent (太子西池二首)

J.4. A Spring Day Impromptu (春日偶作), Written at the Wangyuan Post (題望苑驛), Written for the Willow (題柳), The Old Residence of Recluse Li Yu (李羽處士故里), Double Seventh Eve on the Pond (池塘七夕)

J.5. Contracting Malaria in the Middle of Summer (夏中病痁作), The Four White Seniors (四皓)

J.6. Hundred-Rhyme Poem (百韻), Fifty-Rhyme Poem (五十韻), Twenty-Two Rhymes on the Arched Gate (洞戶二十二韻)

J.7. Written at the Temple of Mystical Emptiness (題谷神廟)

J.8. The Boshan Censer" (博山香爐)
J.9. Sent to a Friend, Written on an Evening (晚坐酬友人), Seeing off Bohai Prince to Return to His Country (送渤海王子歸本國), Bitter Jian Flower (苦楝花), Angling on the Pool of the Xue Family (薛氏池垂釣)

Fourteen "Pusaman" (菩薩蠻十四首), Qingpingyue (清平樂, the first of the two)

Epistle Thanking Minister Li of Xiangzhou (謝襄州李尚書啟), Epistle Thanking Prime Minister Hegan (謝紇干相公啟), Two Epistles Presented to Vice-Minister Jiang (上蔣侍郎啟二首), Epistle Presented to Prime Minster Pei (上裴相公啟), Epistle Presented to Prime Minister Linghu (上令狐相公啟), Epistle Presented to Prime Minister Cui (上崔相公啟), Epistle Presented to Minister Feng (上封尚書啟), Epistle Presented to Drafter Pei (上裴舍人啟), Two Epistles Presented to the Academician Secretary (上學士舍人啟二首) (the first), Epistle Presented to Drafter Du (上杜舍人啟).

MORE EXAMPLES

Even though we can proceed on the basis of the already elucidated poems, identifying the motifs of many of the entries in this list will not be easy. We already know when and how Wen gained access to Li Yong, why Wenzong gave his consent to appointing Wen as his son's assistant, what role Wen played throughout, and how Li Yong was murdered. But we have not discussed the consequences Wen had to suffer, nor have we adduced additional details, clarifying Wen's attitudes toward different persons involved. By studying the following poems we will be able to elicit some supplementary relevant information.

SONG OF THE GOD OF MARQUIS JIANG

Marquis Jiang, also called Emperor Jiang (蔣帝), is a title imperially bestowed on one Jiang Ziwen (蔣子文), a legendary figure who, after death, became the God of Mount Zhong (also called Mount Jiang) and the object of popular idolatry, from the end of the Han to the Tang Dynasty.[27] It is Wen Tingyun who first used this New Music Bureau title.[28] This poem seems to recount the story of Jiang Ziwen, but the details of the story betray a worldly concern, which is anything but a eulogy to the deity. Alongside the awe-inspiring and confusing displays of the supernatural, we find that Wen's interest is focused on special figures of the human world, who played a role closely connected with Wen's political life.

Here is the last couplet of the poem:

6 Atop the blue cloud there naturally came the descendant of the black dragon,
Consort Pan, you had better not knot the lilacs.
青雲自有黑龍子，潘妃莫結丁香花.[29]

The suggestion that Consort Pan should not knot the lilacs is a satire on her person, effected by means of an ambiguous metaphor that seems to have a connection with the imperial succession. The implication of this couplet can be explicated as follows:

1. Consort Pan was a devout disciple of Marquis Jiang, and by praying day and night to him, she sought to hold the imperial favor forever. Unable to give birth to a child, she mothered an imperial prince and intended him to succeed to the throne at the expense of Precious Spouse Huang (黃貴妃). Besides, in her worship of Marquis Jiang, she acted in close collaboration with a eunuch, Zhu Guangshang (朱光尚).
2. Comparing these details about Precious Consort Pan with the situation of Worthy Consort Yang, we immediately recognize that Pan is designed as a substitute for Yang. As an imperial consort in high favor with Emperor Wenzong, Yang was as jealous, ambitious, and venomous as Pan; she also mothered an imperial prince, Prince An, in a vain bid to have the Heir Apparent replaced; she took the lives of Virtuous Consort Wang and her son in collaboration with the eunuchs. There are too many similarities between the two for Wen not to be using Pan as a historical counterpart to Yang.
3. "Knot the lilacs" must have to do with Consort Yang's prayers for being blessed with a son, since one characteristic of lilac was to bear seeds (子), *zi*, a pun on "son." Yang's means of attaining her purpose, however, was to show partiality to a certain imperial son, one of many princes. Because the flowers of the lilac by nature grow in clusters, it is not necessary to "knot" them together. The imperial princes, from among whom Consort Pan (or Yang) wanted to select an imperial successor, form, interestingly, a group that "clusters" on the royal family tree. Yang should have had no hand in the matter. This similarity between the lilac flowers and the imperial princes supplies the vehicle for Wen's metaphor, the tenor of which is that it was futile for Yang to show favoritism toward one imperial son at the expense of another.
4. "Descendant of the black dragon" refers to Emperor Wuzong, who, as a result of the inner court struggle and the eunuchs' political conspiracy, came to the throne by a fluke in an unorthodox manner after Wenzong's death. As we have seen, after Emperor Wenzong rejected Consort Yang's request, crowning as Heir Apparent Prince Chen, instead of Prince An, the eunuchs eventually set on the throne yet another imperial heir—Emperor Wuzong. It was he who, in Wen's honorific terms, "naturally appeared atop the blue clouds," as "the descendant of the black dragon," even though he was nothing more than a survivor of the palace coup. If Wuzong is "the descendant," it is clear that "black dragon" stands for an imperial ancestor.

Because the last couplet carries such a burden of worldly concern, the rest of the poem as a whole must conceal in itself, despite its misleading appearances, Wen's attitudes toward the inner working of the Tang court. We can justify this reading by divulging the details of the story, a story with which we are familiar since we already know its major plots, but which we will find strange, since Wen couches it in such a way as to make it unusual and almost unrecognizable.

1 The God of Chu, riding on armored horse with golden bridle-ornaments,
Was agitated from his dragon's pool at night, and set pale billows surging.
楚神鐵馬金鳴珂，夜動蛟潭生素波。

"The God of Chu" refers to Jiang Ziwen who was once given the title "King of Chu of Wuxing" (吳興楚王), a title redolent of "Prince of Guangling" (廣陵王) that Emperor Xianzong (grandfather of Wenzong and Wuzong) bore before succeeding to the throne.[30] The "dragon's pool" refers to the "Black Dragon Pool" (黑龍潭) of Mount Zhong, where a black dragon was believed to have appeared as Marquis Jiang incarnate.[31] Granted that "Chu" in Wen's works often stands for the Heir, or, through the Heir, for the Tang Empire, the "God of Chu" appears on the scene, therefore, as the legitimating might of the Tang imperial power acting to shield the throne from harm. More to the point, as "Sage Emperor" (who effected the "Yuanhe Restoration"), he acts as an imperial ancestor and a guardian deity of his imperial descendants. Hence we see here the god of Chu, with all identities of a Tang imperial ancestor, soaring up on behalf of the Tang Empire from his dragon pool, full of divine grandeur and irresistible wrath.

2 The autumn gust stirring up the waters tolls the death of the Western Emperor,
In front of his temple on the ancient tree is coiled a white snake.
商風刮水報西帝，廟前古樹蟠白蛇。[32]

A storm—a great political disturbance—results in the death of the Western Emperor, who, now as a slain dragon, takes the image of a white snake, and coils itself (mortally wounded) around the tree in front of the temple of its ancestor, the God of Chu. This couplet thus suggests the death of Emperor Wenzong.

Both "Western Emperor" and "white snake" have pejorative meanings. The former is a sobriquet for the monarch(s) in Chang'an, which belonged to the Qin Kingdom in ancient times, while the latter is an image symbolic of the Qin Dynasty on the verge of downfall. Wen is not unaware of the disparaging undertone of these two terms, but he uses them euphemistically in this poem, to voice criticism of Wenzong, who had a considerable share of responsibility for the death of his son, and who in his subsequent desperation, died a tragic death. Meanwhile, Wen not merely refers to the Tang Dynasty capital with the unspoken term "Qin," as was explicit in "Hundred-Rhyme

Poem," he reluctantly applies an overtone: the Tang Dynasty was approaching its end.

3 The Red Hatchet of the King of Wu cut the cloud array, 吳王赤斧砍雲陳，
And in the Painted Hall was a forest of halberds and frosty blades. 畫堂列戟叢霜刃。

The King of Wu, in accordance with the revelation from Marquis Jiang, carried out a massacre "in the cloud array," and brought about a bloodbath in the "Painted Hall." This couplet hints at the purge conducted by Wuzong in which Consort Yang, Prince An, and Prince Chen were all put to death.

The "King of Wu" (not Chu) does not refer to Marquis Jiang, but to Emperor Wuzong in the guise of Jiang. We suggest that the reason Wen had Wuzong play the role is that he believed or at least pretended to believe, that Wuzong's massacre at the beginning of his reign was sanctioned by the deity of a former sage emperor of the dynasty. The "Red Hatchet" was a symbol of Wuzong's ironhanded policy, while at the same time it is the name of an immortal.[33] "The cloud array," an array as untouchable as the clouds, is a metaphor for the scramble for the succession within the royal clan, provoked by Consort Yang and aggravated by the eunuchs. Therefore, the meaning of the first line is: in order to clear up the untenable situation created by Wenzong, Wuzong "cut the Gordian knot" in an effort to assert himself as the orthodox successor of the throne. As a result, the "Painted Hall" was turned into a forest of halberds and frosty swords, that is, all those who lived there were killed. As the residence of the imperial consorts and princes, the Painted Hall deserves close scrutiny.[34] If the words were only referring to a common boudoir, the connotation of "Painted Hall" in ordinary cases, why does the place contain so many weapons that it resembles an arsenal?

Although Wen retained his affection for his late young lord, he had no choice but to pledge allegiance to Wuzong. Wuzong had mounted the throne through a palace coup staged by the eunuchs, and it might be suspected that he cherished friendly feelings toward Li Yong and also his attendants. That is why Wen felt the need to represent all Wuzong's political measures in positive, though ambiguous, language.

Notwithstanding this, Wuzong, in a sense, did exact vengeance on Worthy Consort Yang on behalf of Li Yong and Virtuous Consort Wang. If Wang's soul in the nether regions had the ability to sense, how would she react to the changes in the human world? Here Wen offers a poetic answer to this question:

4 The Goddess of Mount Wu conveys her feeling with a touch of sad strings,
And, amidst the clangorous notes of bells, fingers her temple hairs.
巫娥傳意托悲絲，鐸語瑯瑯理雙鬢。

The Goddess of Mount Wu (巫山神女) was the legendary fairy maiden who offered herself to King Xiang of Chu. Here, she appears as the incarnation of Consort Wang. The "notes of the bells" is a dance melody that originated from the Han Dynasty, played in the performance of "Bell Dance." Since a wooden bell (木鐸) was used to give orders to the whole country, the performance of the bell dance is in accordance with Virtuous Consort Wang's capacity as an imperial spouse.[35] Possibly, in her lifetime, Wang was adept at both lute and bell dance. In Wen's imagination, Wang strikes a pose. She plays the lute and then performs an elegant bell dance to express her feelings—she was grieved and perplexed, perhaps feeling a mixture of gratitude and anxiety, and as a wronged and loyal imperial consort subsequently rehabilitated, she feared that the cruel slaughter of Wuzong instigated by the eunuchs would be the ruin of the empire.

5 The Xiang smoke was swept green and the Xiang mountains stood slanted,
At sunrise in the east the divine ravens were flying.
湘煙刷翠湘山斜，東方日出飛神鴉。

After Wuzong came to the throne, the Tang Empire for a time assumed a fresh appearance and a new political equilibrium, with a peaceful and thriving atmosphere temporarily prevailing. Xiang, a river of the Chu region, equates with "Chu" which in Wen's poetic diction is a metaphor for the Tang Empire. The divine ravens at sunrise are emblematic of the imperial authority and heaven-blessed prosperity. Then, as explained above, this entire poem distils down to the aphorism stated in the last couplet: that Marquis Jiang has his own choice for the imperial succession, and all of Consort Pan's (Yang's) attempts are in vain.

In addition to a complementary account of Wen's incisive attack on the eunuchs in other poems, this poem shows clearly his political attitude toward the participants in the Heir Apparent Incident. Wen, of course, sided with Li Yong and his mother; but in addition to showing his submissive loyalty and support, he also expressed veiled criticism directed toward Emperor Wenzong. To Consort Yang, Wen's stance is one of castigation and satire, mixed with sympathy for her tragic end, because she was to be put to death once she outlived her usefulness. To Emperor Wuzong, the "orthodox" successor to the throne, ruling with an iron hand and having the potential to become a catastrophic force in the poet's political or even physical life, Wen dared show nothing but an awe-stricken allegiance.

MELODY DAMOZHI (達摩支曲)[36]

---

1 The musk, even though it is smashed into powder, will not abandon its fragrance,

And the lotus, even when it is broken into pieces, will not forsake its silk.
搗麝成塵香不滅，拗蓮作寸絲難絕。

The first couplet, as we have quoted earlier, gives expression to a grief or yearning deeply imprinted in Wen's heart. However, if isolated from the context, it reads like an aphorism of a love song.

2 The red tears of Wenji, the spring over the Luo River,
The white hair of Su Wu, and the snow atop the Heavenly Mountain.
紅淚文姬洛水春，白頭蘇武天山雪。

Finding the beginning inadequate to manifest his emotions, and fearful lest readers misread it as an expression of lovesickness, the poet complements two more allusions, to guide our scrutiny into his anxieties and anguish concerning his political life.

Cai Wenji (蔡文姬),[37] the daughter of Cai Yong, was captured by northern horsemen and made the wife of the chieftain of the Huns, giving birth to two children, staying in the north until Cao Cao offered to send for and ransom her back, forcing her to leave her own flesh and blood and return alone. For Wenji, to return was her dream, but to part forever from her sons was a sorrow that tore her heart to pieces. Su Wu,[38] a Han Dynasty court official, was sent on a mission to the Huns and was detained in the north for nineteen years; he was made to tend the sheep in the snow, and was told he would only be permitted to return if he-sheep could give birth to lambs. Despite all this, he never yielded. Here Wenji's torment reminds us of Wen's awkward situation. We can imagine how reluctantly and painfully Wen gave up his pursuit of official career through the "Eastern Palace" avenue; meanwhile, he had to confront the consequence of having attended the Heir, becoming a more sensitive political figure, a "forbidden meat" (禁臠) that neither the Li nor the Niu Faction would wish to "touch" by offering him employment. On the other hand, Su Wu's unswerving loyalty to his country makes him an exemplar of political constancy even to modern Chinese. Likening himself to Su is Wen's self-affirmation that his loyalty to the Tang remained unchanged, despite the humiliation he had suffered.

3 Don't you see Gao Wei "*sans soucis*" [39] buried himself in a sea of flowers,
But after his carousals by Zhang River only the dewdrops, pure and chilly, remained.
君不見無愁高緯花漫漫，漳浦宴餘清露寒。

4 Once together with his aides and assistants he was taken prisoner,
Before he could play the Nomad flute he was all in tears.
一旦臣僚共囚虜，欲吹羌笛先汍瀾。

After broaching the topic in such a powerful and impressive beginning, Wen turns to the main subject, which seems to be one of "meditating on an ancient site" (懷古) and which takes the form of a lament for Gao Wei. In his poetic representation of the historical events concerning Gao, however, Wen does not dwell on the causes for the fall of this young and naive monarch, nor does he endeavor to draw a historical lesson from it. Instead, after showing before us a forlorn scene, he deplores the anguish the monarch and his subjects felt in their confinement:

5 His former subjects' temple hairs turned an untimely frost-white. 舊臣頭鬢霜華早，
What a pity his heroic ambition died amidst bouts of drunkenness. 可惜雄心醉中老。
6 From time immemorial springs return but never the bygone dream, 萬古春歸夢不歸，
Amidst the winds and rains of Ye City forlorn grasses reach to the sky. 鄴城風雨連天草。

The image Wen painted of those "former subjects" is of men who became victims of their lord's downfall, just as slaves were buried along with their deceased master. This forms an exact self-portrait of Wen after the Heir's death. A reading of the end of this poem will fully convince us of this insight. For, if the second last couplet seems to be still something spoken for Gao Wei's "former subjects," the last couplet throws off Wen's mask and reveals his own keenly felt pain, not in the guise of any other roles.

If we notice that the carousing Gao Wei indulged in took place near the Zhang River at Linzhang, that is, Ye City, we can immediately, with a smile of understanding, commune with our poet. It was in Ye City that Cao Zhi feasted and enjoyed the company of his attendants before finally suffering imperial persecution from his brother, Cao Pi. Cao Zhi did have his "former subjects" who were put to death after Cao Pei took the throne,[40] and also others friends, who must have lived in disgrace after Cao Zhi was placed under house arrest. In understanding this poem, however, it does not really matter if the "former subjects" referred in the context served Gao Wei instead of Cao Zhi. Because, in the final analysis, Wen grafts a "twig" of one event into a "trunk" of another historical fact—he subtly substitutes one thing for another—making his historical allusion both ambiguous and all-embracing. In any case, what he stresses is an identification of himself with such "former subjects." He empathizes with the "former subjects" and projects all his emotions onto them, because the lifelong frustration and sorrow of the "former subjects" were in tune with Wen's innermost feelings. These feelings were those of a confidential assistant who had once placed his hopes on Li Yong, only to lose them forever. Wen's originality lies in that he is also able to conceal his own affairs behind the guise of historical events, in contrast to the general practice of using the historical events to illustrate feelings. This is one more pattern of his "making the covert overt."

Now we know something about the Heir Apparent Incident, and armed with this knowledge, we can unravel more of Wen's baffling works. This incident is, however, only the prelude to a political career filled with dramatic events. We will deal with these events in the following chapters.

Chapter Seven

Changing Name and Taking the Examination

After the Heir Apparent's death, Wen was forced to seek assistance from Prime Minister Pei. Recognizing Wen's worth during his attendance upon Li Yong, Pei attempted to support him by facilitating his passing of the civil service examination. The result was that, in the autumn of the fourth year of Kaicheng (839), Wen took the Metropolitan Prefecture Examination and was conferred the academic title "Equivalent to Passing," yet finally "failed to pass." For all his efforts, he found himself once more completely frustrated, and was forced to flee to the south. To illustrate these details, we will examine the political situation after Li Yong's death in search of further information.

"EQUIVALENT TO PASSING" YET "FAILED TO PASS"

We first review a portion of Wen's "Epistle Presented to Prime Minister Pei":

> With my name secretly listed for arrest, I could hardly benefit from imperial favor. Together with the embers I am to be thrown away [like a burned zither], and compared with insects [that also have their share of imperial favor], I am more hopeless.

Wen had come to a most critical turn in his life. The eunuchs would conspire against him more determinedly because of his former role as a most confidential assistant of the Heir Apparent, and of his present status as a potential witness to their crimes. As a man of outspoken nature, Wen would have undoubtedly divulged what he knew to his friends and foiling the eunuchs' attempt to keep their murder of the Heir a secret. As a result, filled with fresh hatreds and old enmity for Wen, the eunuchs impatiently sought to take his life. It was under such circumstances that Wen's name was put on the blacklist for arrest, forcing him to desperately attempt to escape. In his "Epistle Presented to Drafter Pei," Wen alluded once more to this state of affairs, revealing what he had to do in order not to fall victim to the eunuchs:

> Since I have no longer an "eastern way host" to depend upon, and the southern airs could not last through to the end, I felt like as though I had fallen into an abyss and was cast adrift on a vast sea. I did not know how I could find one to seek refuge with, nor did I see where I might ask for lodging. By risking the lives of Sun Song's hundred domestics, I clung to my precarious existence; and like the singular case of Wang Zun, I came to bay amidst the scandalmongers (某自東道無依，南風不競；如擠井谷，若泛滄溟，莫知投足之方，不識棲身之所。孫嵩百口，系以存亡；王尊一身，困于讒佞).

After the Heir died and Wen lost his "eastern way host," he was facing a life-threatening situation such that "the southern airs cannot last through to the end."[1] Wen likened himself to Zhao Qi (趙岐, 110?–201), while at the same time he regarded Drafter Pei as a Sun Song (孫嵩). Wen used this analogy because, in order to escape arrest by the eunuchs, Zhao had once sought asylum with Sun Song, who said: "I am Sun Binshi (賓石, his style) of Beihai, and with *the hundred domestics* of my family, I will certainly help you." He then hid Zhao in his double partition wall.[2] Wen's predicament was also similar to that of Wang Zun who once suffered from malign rumors in the court.[3] Here the allusion to Zhao Qi becomes more meaningful than it first appears to be once we realize that Wen changed his name to Wen Qi when taking the examination, in token of his admiration for Zhao and his determined opposition to the eunuchs. Here we see a vivid picture of the insecure life Wen led under the eunuchs' political persecution. For him the main problem was now how to escape with his life rather than how to search for political advancement.

Under such circumstances, how could Wen take part in the civil service examination? It was impossible for Wen to take the examination openly. But Wen was not a man easily reconciled to failure. By means of unstinting effort he was able to enlist the help of a few ministers. What ensued from this was another climax in his life: he was permitted to sit for the Metropolitan Prefecture Examination under a changed name and was recommended by the Metropolitan Prefecture (achieved the academic title "Equivalent to Passing"). However, he then was rejected by the Ministry of Ritual ("Failed to Pass" after all). To be accepted as "Equivalent to Passing" was no ordinary success. It illustrates Wen's unremitting tenacity in his struggle against adversity and his appeal to his contemporaries for social justice. Before proceeding to the details of how Wen changed his name, we need to clarify the degree to which a recommendation from the Metropolitan Prefecture spelled political success at the time.

In the Late Tang times, among the Presented Scholars, that is, the so-called "Scholars Presented as Local Tribute" (鄉貢進士), those recommended by the Metropolitan Prefecture were considered special. In "Metropolitan Prefecture Recommendation" (京兆府解送) of the *Tangzhiyan* (2: 13), we read:

> The Divine Prefecture Recommendation is the so-called "Equivalent to Passing." Ever since the eras of Kaiyuan and Tianbao, all the first ten candidates in order of excellence have been so designated. It is required that the title be well deserved, to help to promote the Confucian teachings. The Examination Administrator shall make his choice among them, and he might even accept all, or at least seven or eight out of ten [as Presented Scholars]. If things differed from this, the Metropolitan Prefecture would address an official letter to the Examination Administrator's office asking for the reasons why the recommendations were denied (神州解送，自開元天寶之際，率得以在上十人，謂之等第。必求名實相副，以滋教化之源。小宗伯倚而選之，或至渾化；不然，十得其七八。苟異于是，則往往牒貢院請落由).

From this we can elicit three important points:

First, to be recommended by the Metropolitan Prefecture meant having a much better chance to be passed as a Presented Scholar than via the "local tribute" in general. Such was the case because the Metropolitan Prefecture, the capital area, was where the final decision was made concerning the final acceptance of Presented Scholars. Here, most candidates strove to influence the decision-making process, by "paying respects to and asking favor from patrons of authority and power" (造請權要), or, in the parlance of that time, they tried "to straighten the key links" (通關節)[4]—to smooth away obstacles and get powerful support on their path toward achievement of the Presented Scholar degree. As a result of such mechanisms, "Those having gained [the recommendation] soared to the Heavenly Precincts and advanced toward 'the Orchid Ministries'—for these, it was actually the beginning of 'six month's ascension'" (得之者搏躍雲衢，階梯蘭省，即六月沖霄之漸也).[5] This recommendation thus became a direct route to advancement followed by many candidates, because of its high proportion of accepted Presented Scholars to the recommended candidates.

Second, this recommendation was definitely not easy to obtain, but once it was obtained, it would not be easily denied by the Ministry of Ritual, since the Metropolitan Prefecture might address inquiries to the Examination Administrator about why any candidate it had recommended was denied. To be recommended by the Metropolitan Prefecture was the expected outcome of the "straightening" of all "key links," thus in due course, it was very naturally considered "Equivalent to Passing" as a Presented Scholar.

Third, in the fourth year of Kaicheng, among all candidates recommended by the Metropolitan Prefecture, only Wen was rejected. This was a remarkable exception to the general rule, and must have had its unique causes. Given the power of the eunuchs, to become a Presented Scholar one would also have to "straighten the key links" with them, or at least not be at odds with them, for although the eunuchs were not in direct charge of examination matters, their influence over the acceptance or rejection of the candidates should not be discounted. Wen's failure certainly had to do with the eunuchs' unwillingness to let him succeed. By investigating Wen's particular case, apart from understanding his special efforts to obtain a Presented Scholar degree, we can also see his deeply rooted connections in the central bureaucracy, and, above all, the workings of the eunuchs, serving to always thwart his efforts.

The Metropolitan Prefecture Recommendation was so controversial that, during the Late Tang times it was not always in effect.[6] Gaining the chance to be recommended, Wen surmounted numerous difficulties; after failing to be accepted as a Presented Scholar, he experienced new frustrations. Such was the tragicomedy of Wen's life. Preparing to sit for this examination, Wen had to study the classics extensively, as expressed in "Hundred-Rhyme Poem" in the following passage:

11 It was indeed seeking fish by climbing a tree, 定為魚緣木，
And for a second rabbit, by the stump I'd vainly waited. 曾因兔守株。
12 Up to "five wagonfuls" were piled my books, 五車堆縹帙，
Within "three footpaths" I closed my strung gate.[7] 三徑闔繩樞。
13 I then joined company with many an eminent soul, 適與群英集，
Only for the offer of a good price, I stipulated. 將期善價沽。

It was of course after his attendance on the Heir that Wen seriously began his preparations for the Metropolitan Prefecture Examination. He buried himself in books behind a closed door, with a view to looking for "the offer of a good price."[8] Normally, people with great talent would be almost assured of success. However, in Wen's case, this might not happen.

In order to be recommended for the Metropolitan Examination, Wen of course had to "straighten the key links." After Pei Du's death in the spring of 839, powerful assistance from this source was no longer available. Consequently, Wen must have sought special favor from other authorities, especially the Governors of the Metropolitan Prefecture (京兆尹), who supervised the examination. In extant sources there is some evidence that this is what he did. Prior to becoming "Equivalent to Passing," Wen had requested help from men such as Vice-Minister Jiang (Jiang Xi, 蔣系), Drafter Academician Zhou (Zhou Chi, 周墀), and Prime Minister Cui (Cui Gong, 崔珙).[9] All of these men might have assisted in Wen's efforts to obtain the title "Equivalent to Passing," as is suggested in the following passages.

In the "Epistle Presented to Drafter Academician" (上學士舍人啟), we read:

> Now, having been recommended by the Divine Prefecture, I am to compete with other men of letters for excellence; however, holding in vain my inkstone and mat, I do not know where to go (今乃受薦神州，爭雄墨客。空持硯席，莫識津途).

We see that after Wen was recommended by the Metropolitan (Divine) Prefecture (839), he was at a loss about what to do next. While in his second "Epistle Presented to Vice-Minister Jiang," Wen wrote:

> I once visited you with the calling card of a student, and presented you with a letter to a teacher. I was flattered to be in your good graces and won others' high praise. Then I sought in the literary garden for recognition and subjected myself to the Divine Prefecture's selection. I was subsequently able to express my gratitude to you with a bundle of fresh fodder,[10] like a decayed broom just refurbished (頃常撰刺門人，投書齋師。蒙垂盼飾，致在褒稱。既而文圃求知，神州就選。遂得生芻表意，腐帚生姿).

Apparently Jiang had appreciated Wen's talent, and helped him to be recommended by the Metropolitan Prefecture. That is why, when recalling the past in this epistle, Wen still cherished a heartfelt gratitude for his help. The same event was recounted in his "Epistle Presented to Prime Minister Cui" (上崔相公啟):

> When I came for your Bright Mirror and looked up to your Great Excellency. . . . It surpassed my wish that you would help an awkward orphan like me and take pains to recharge me with hope and life. You chose and promoted me from the mud and dust, and raised me up to hazy heavens. . . . Thus for a time I was revived at the Dragon Gate, no longer a cornered fish; and like an oriole soaring out from his valley, was enabled to be in company with those flying on high.[11] . . . Nevertheless, I have vainly rejoiced in the occasion of your changing the music scale,[12] but have not yet seen any omen that I can offer my devoted service (既而竊仰洪鈞，來窺皎鏡……豈謂不遺孤拙，曲假生成。拔于泥滓之中，致在煙霄之上。遂使龍門奮發，不作窮鱗；鶯谷翩翻，終陪逸翰。空乘變律之機，未得捐軀之兆).

Again this passage makes reference to the fact that, having surmounted all political difficulties, Wen had succeeded in becoming "Equivalent to Passing." It also shows that Prime Minister Cui had rendered Wen great service directed toward gaining this academic title. However, after this initial achievement, Wen fell short of success in the decisive final stage, because more influential support was lacking. Therefore, we can infer that it was after Wen became "Equivalent to Passing" (in the autumn of 839), and before Wen finally gave up his hope (in the winter of 840), that he presented this epistle to Cui. Since it happened to be "the occasion of changing the music scale" (Cui had just ascended to the Prime-Ministership), Wen hoped to enlist Cui's assistance one more time; but to his frustration, he "vainly rejoiced in the occasion," because Cui could help him no further. According to the "List of Prime Ministers" of XTS (72: 2795), Cui Gong was appointed Prime Minister in the fifth month of 839, and he was the only appointment to Prime Minister who bore the surname Cui during Wen's attempts to gain the Presented Scholar degree. This Prime Minister Cui addressed here must therefore be Cui Gong.

The friendship between Cui Gong and Wen can be traced to an earlier time, since, while Wen was serving the Heir (837–838), Cui held the post of the Magistrate of Metropolitan Prefecture.[13] We are not deviating far from the truth when we surmise that during Wen's attendance upon the Heir, Cui, as Magistrate of Metropolitan Prefecture under the influence of the so-called "Lord Military Storehouse," had already offered Wen support. Far from just casual kindness, Cui's attitude to Wen was one of political sympathy. He would have had to resist pressure from the eunuchs and bear considerable responsibility in permitting Wen to be awarded the academic title "Equivalent to Passing."

The above examples demonstrate that in order to become "Equivalent to Passing" Wen had fully utilized all his social links to the capital's aristocratic society. But this was not sufficient. Wen still had to surmount the obstacle presented by the eunuchs. To avoid attracting the eunuchs' hostile attention when he was taking the examination, Wen resorted to the drastic step of changing his name.

To clarify Wen's experiences during the course of these events, we shall first elucidate the relevant details related in "Hundred-Rhyme Poem," especially the passage about the examination. Only a close scrutiny of the poetic accounts in this poem can reveal the complete story:

1	All the winged hooves are going before on the way,	逸足皆先路，[14]
	Only I, a cornered dragon, have to weep:	窮蛟獨向隅。[15]
2	Like a stubborn fugitive in *broad-willow* I have escaped,	頑童逃廣柳，
	Now a fatigued horse, in flat wilderness is lying prostrate.	羸馬臥平蕪。

The first two couplets go directly into the subject and establish a strong contrast between what happened to the others and to the poet. All others "go before on the way" to serve their country, but only Wen remains in great distress and danger. In his own ironic term, a "wretched fugitive," he had to take his flight using special means, in his metaphor a *broad-willow* wagon as Ji Bu did[16]—it was by employing this special ruse that he succeeded in escaping with his life. Only subsequent to this was Wen able to recall his painful experiences and compose this poem. Before stating any direct or indirect causes leading to his failure, Wen first presents a picture of the consequences he suffered. This is the start of a long autobiographical poem, recounting all the important events of Wen's life up to the time of its composition, the fifth year of Kaicheng (840).

3 Of the yellow scrolls, who, alas, asks about my erudition? 黃卷嗟誰問，
With the red strings, I amuse myself on this occasion. 朱弦偶自娛。
4 "Deer's Singing" played, for all successful candidates, 鹿鳴皆綴士，
Far from a true man, I should lie low like a female. 雌伏竟非夫。

Since his great knowledge of the "yellow scrolls" (the classics) was not sufficient to earn him the Presented Scholar degree, Wen bitterly uses it to articulate his feelings about the injustice he suffered, that is, to "amuse" himself "with red string." The "red string," on which he played his tune, originally stands for the orthodox music. It is thus an equivalent term for serious literature, and here refers to this very poem.[17] This poem tells the complex story of his efforts and frustrations, and was written both to express his indignation and to "amuse himself," so to speak. In other word, the long poem is the summary of Wen's reflection over his failures. The details of how Wen could have been recommended and yet failed are as follows:

14 Lord She's Dragon pictures are truly bright, 葉龍圖夭矯，
The counterfeit, the Yan rat, will make itself a sight. 燕鼠笑胡盧。

Like Lord She's fondness for dragons,[18] the examination officials, who ostensibly sought talent, were unable to uncover and recommend any true talent, because they could not tell the worthy man from the unworthy. In addition to mistaking a worthless Yan stone for a treasure, those in charge of the examination might even mistake a rat for a jade-enfolding stone.[19] Since they possessed no discernment, how could Wen escape being failed by them?

15 I knew my innate gift to be preordained, 賦分知前定，
And fear of being maligned filled my disappointed mind. 寒心畏厚誣。

Wen was proud of his literary talent, but afraid of the calumny of the eunuchs. He wished to display his literary talent while escaping somehow from the eunuchs' slander. The following couplet suggests a solution to this problem, although in apparently veiled language—very misleading to a reader who knows nothing of his story.

16 I scurried swifter than Qingji, throwing the dust behind, 躡塵追慶忌，
I followed the model of Lu Ban, wielding sword in hand. 操劍學班輸。

To avoid the eunuchs' slander, Wen ran "swifter than Qingji," the ancient warrior who was said to have the legs of a wild beast and to catch flying birds with his bare hands;[20] to show his literary talent, he followed "the model of Lu Ban," an ancient craftsman famous for his ingenious inventions. Logically following the last couplet, this couplet tells how Wen took the examination, and how well he did in it.

The allusion to Qingji is a metaphor referring to Wen's expedient of taking the examination under a changed name. No matter what means he might have used before the examination, it would be impossible for Wen to outrun Qingji, so what sense did it make to say so? In fact, Wen did manage to "run" sufficiently fast to be able, at least for the moment, to outpace the rumors and avoid the eunuchs' slander, participating in and passing the examination. The name change was the only way to accomplish this. It was this logic of his political adventure that Wen interpolated into the allusion to Qingji, almost completely concealing his meaning. But this paraphrase of the metaphor is the key to the hidden tenor of the line. The comparison with Lu Ban stresses Wen's literary talent and excellent performance in the examination. Wen wielded his "sword" skillfully, as Lu Ban had—since Lu was a master in handicraft, just as Wen was a master of literary composition. In this metaphor the master artisan symbolized a surpassing literary talent. In other words, Wen is saying that, as an outstanding literary master of his time, he had the ability to handle the examination topics with great ease and surpassing talent.

17 In the Literary Garden I attended many a candidate, 文囿陪多士，
Taking the Divine Prefecture Examination for the No. 1 place. 神州試大巫。
18 My answer could be "a rare playing of the lute," 對雖希鼓瑟，
So my name was passed off among those who blew the flute. 名亦濫吹竽。
Footnote: Last autumn I sat for the Metropolitan Prefecture Examination and got my name recommended on the supplementary list (原注：余去秋試京兆，薦名居其副).

Here the eighteenth couplet needs some explanation.

Confucius once asked what each of his students would wish to do; when it was his best student Zeng Dian's turn, "the music of playing on his lute died away" (鼓瑟希) before he offered the best answer to the master's question. He "would wash in the Yi River, enjoy the breeze among the rain altars, and return home singing."[21] Wen reversed the original Chinese text 鼓瑟希 to 希鼓瑟, which we translate as "a rare playing of the lute," because of its overtone "ranking among the best," the very meaning Wen wanted to express. Being "passed off among those who blew the flute" refers to the well-known *Hanfeizi* story of Mr. Nanguo, who passed himself off as one of the players in the ensemble by pretending to know how to play the flute, but who was at a loss when called upon to play solo. Here it is a modest way of speaking about Wen's gaining an "Equivalent to Passing" degree. Therefore, this couplet means that because of his excellent performance during the examination, Wen passed.

After all necessary preparations, Wen took the Metropolitan Prefecture Examination; and, as he elegantly declares here, his performances were remarkable and he succeeded in becoming an "Equivalent to Passing" (causing controversies in his lifetime and misunderstandings after his death). Here the footnote verifies the reliability of the record in *Tangzhiyan* (2: 15) about Wen's being equivalent to passing in 839. However, the achievement of this passing degree ultimately resulted in Wen's unexpected failure to pass:

19 [This served] only to make men suspect I desired profit and fame, 正使猜奔競，
Though I took no account of whether I won or lost. 何嘗計有無？
20 A Liu Shan had looked for and found me—it was useless, 劉剡虛訪覓，
So the Wang Ba I imitated was mocked, what a shame! 王霸竟揶揄。

Being thus recommended brought no good fortune. Rather, Wen became deeply enmeshed in troubles. Here we can infer from the context that his temporary expedient, the change of his name, was exposed and he became the topic of gossip. He was in an awkward position and found it difficult to vindicate himself. The recommendation of someone (likened to Liu Shan, very possibly Cui Gong) finally proved fruitless, and despite his loyalty to the dynasty, he was held up for ridicule, as Wang Ba once had been.[22]

21 To buy fealty, someone had burned the tallies, to no avail, 市義虛焚卷，
I was derided at the pass, for having thrown the silk credential away. 關譏漫棄繻。
22 The best remarks (of my friend), by now, I came to believe, 至言今信矣，
And my humble ambition was, for sure, a grief! 微尚亦悲夫。

Allowing Wen to conceal his identity so as to escape the eunuchs' hostile attention was like Lord Mengchang's acquiescence in allowing Feng Xuan, his retainer, to burn the tallies "to buy fealty" for him, even though it proved to be fruitless. Wen found it difficult to fulfill his long-cherished ambition, and his imitation of Zhong Jun became ridiculous.[23] Only when he finally understood the reality of his failure did Wen realize he had underestimated the political difficulty of gaining the Presented Scholar degree. He could only lament all his previous efforts and honestly deal with his humiliation.

23 Let me tune the pitch for the White Snow aria, 白雪調歌響，
And enjoy dancing by the Rain Altar in the pure breeze. 清風樂舞雩。
24 I could not raise my shoulders [to adulate anyone] affectedly, 脅肩難黽免，
But I had to scratch my head, sighing in agony. 搔首易嗟吁。[24]

Metaphorically, the "White Snow," an exquisite tune, which few were able to sing, stands for the lofty moral principle Wen would still adhere to, isolated as he was in his political stand. Regarding himself as a first-rate Confucian scholar as Zeng Dian had been, he would take delight in following Zeng's example of noble reclusion and poverty.[25] Unable by nature to "raise his shoulders," to win the favor with those in power, especially the eunuchs, he had to resign himself to a petty, lowly, life lived in depression.

Wen's predicament was partly due to the unfairness of the selection:

25 To vie for winning I was not a competent man, 角勝非能者，
But to choose the worthy, was it really by archery? 推賢見射乎。
26 When the "horn pitcher" contains in it more dread and fright, 兕觥增恐悚，
The "cup" will lose its share of water, little and slight. 杯水失錙銖。

Wen confesses here that he was not competent enough in the examination, because it was more of a political rivalry than a competition of literary talents. If the best candidates are not picked out from the examination, so, by analogy, he asked whether or not the most worthy man was decided by "archery."[26] Just as wine is poured into each cup from the "horn pitcher," the degree is conferred to each candidate by the Examination Administrator. If the "pitcher" is filled with "dread and fright"—as the official quarters were frightened by the threatening eunuchs and swayed by political prejudices—then "the cup will lose its share of water"—the candidates unavoidably become the victims of unfair judgments and lose what they might have deserved. In other words, because "the examination officials were afraid of the eunuchs," Wen was rejected.

27 The white target has been withdrawn, no longer red and bright, 粉垛收丹采，
While the golden whistling arrows, I have to hide. 金髇隱仆姑。
28 Letting drop my bowcase, I was ashamed of finishing the cup, 垂橐羞盡爵，
Raising the goblet, they insulted me for curving the bow. 揚觶辱彎弧。

29 Clumsy [as I am], I should not talk of drawing
a tiger, 虎拙休言畫，
Nor wish to imitate [the action of] slaying a
seldom-seen dragon. 龍希莫學屠。[27]

Though his performance in the examination was superior, Wen was forced to quit the competition and conceal his talent. He found himself humiliated and under suspicion. As a Chinese proverb states, "failure to draw a tiger makes it, instead, resemble a dog"—Wen's allegiance to the court was, contrary to his expectations, distorted as disloyalty and he had made a spectacle of himself in spite of his loyalty. "Slaying dragons" means something impractical, which might be an allusion to Wen's plan to annihilate the eunuchs, which Wen was forced to abandon.

To sum up this portion of "Hundred-Rhyme Poem": after the Heir's death, Wen tried everything he could to achieve the Presented Scholar degree. As an expedient, he changed his name and succeeded in having his name recommended. Unfortunately, his behavior was purposely misconstrued, and everything turned against him. Even those who had been friendly to him could no longer help. In trying to circumvent the eunuchs in order to take and pass the examination, Wen had met with bitter failure.

THE CHANGE OF NAME

Now we can concentrate on clearing up misunderstandings about Wen's name change.

The information drawn from the above passage places in a clearer light Wen's experiences in the examination. But some points require further clarification. For example, did Wen *really* change his name merely for the purpose of taking the Metropolitan Examination? Our elicitation of this important matter seems too simple to be convincing. We should not, after all, attach too much importance to the information drawn from a single poetic couplet. Interpreted in isolation, the sixteenth rhyme allows explanations other than we have offered, thus we must provide more proof. We need to determine what new name he took, and why he assumed such a name. At the very least, we have a responsibility to give a more detailed consideration to such a problem.

The question of Wen's change of name arises when we study the records in the two *Tang Histories*. Wen's Biography in JTS (190: 5079) says:

> His original name is Qi, and his style name Feiqing. . . . His younger brother was Tinghao (本名岐，字飛卿，…… 弟庭皓).

And Wen's Biography in XTS (91: 3787) has exactly the same record at this point:

> His original name is Qi, and his style name Feiqing. His younger brother was Tinghao (本名岐，字飛卿，弟庭皓).

Here we discern a problem. To state that Wen's original name is Wen Qi is to affirm that the name Tingyun was used only as the changed name. But since Tingyun had a younger brother named Tinghao, how could it be that the elder brother changed his name to be in conformity with his young brother, when the brothers in a family always shared a character in their names? If Wen never changed his name, his biographies in the two *Tang Histories* do not need to mention Wen's "original name," but if Wen really did change his name, their records are obviously implausible. That Wen did undergo a name change is frequently mentioned and mishandled in the notes and anecdotes written about him between Tang and Song times; we have quoted some of them earlier and shall study them further. The discrepancies in the two *Tang Histories* can serve as a starting point for our further studies, which will substantiate our arguments with more details concerning when and why Wen changed his name.

The *Beimeng Suoyan* account indicates that the change of Wen's name took place as a consequence of the Jianghuai Incident. The *Yuquanzi* record reveals that the Jianghuai Incident happened right before Wen was about to follow the local recommendation [and thus take the examination]. Conceivably, the change of name might have something to do with the local recommendation. Wen's first "following of the local recommendation" was, without a doubt, his following of the Metropolitan Prefecture Recommendation in 839. Preferential as it was, this examination was merely a kind of local recommendation. It is because of this that we affirm that Wen's change of name happened in 839, just before his participation in the Metropolitan Examination. And it is on this inference that we ground our argument that in "Hundred-Rhyme Poem" (written in 840) there must be some record to that effect. This recommendation would, for many years thereafter, qualify Wen to take the Presented Scholar examinations held by the Ministry of Ritual, as he later did in the Dazhong era (847–860).

On the other hand, however, as far as we can determine, in all of the extant works of Wen's contemporaries, Wen was addressed as "Feiqing" or "Tingyun." For example, Li Shangyin's "Hearing Zhuming's Death, Mailed to Feiqing with Tears" (聞著明兇問哭寄飛卿), Ji Tangfu's "Seeing off Wen Feiqing to Be Defender of Fangcheng" (送溫飛卿尉方城), Zhang Hu's poem with the same topic, Duan Chengshi's "Teasing Feiqing" (嘲飛卿) and "Eight Letters to Wen Feiqing" (與溫飛卿書八首).[28] All of these were apparently written after the year 839, indicating that after that date Wen's name remained Wen Tingyun. Even the official edict composed by Pei Tan (裴坦, fl. 830–860) in the year 859—"Edict for Demoting Wen Tingyun as Defender of Suixian" (貶溫庭筠隋縣尉制)[29]—addressed Wen as "the Former Local Tribute Presented Scholar Wen Tingyun," rather than Wen Qi, although it was under the name Wen Qi that Wen took the Metropolitan Prefecture Examination and was registered as a qualified "Local Tribute Presented Scholar." This is a clear indication that even those in official quarters regarded Wen's true name as Tingyun, despite his ruse in changing his name to Qi.

Regarding this problem, Xia Chengtao once surmised, "After Wen was insulted [in Jianghuai] he changed his name to Qi, and soon resumed his original name [Tingyun]" (390). This is not far from the truth, except that it lacks completeness. What really happened is that Wen changed his name to Qi solely to gain the Presented Scholar degree, and, when the name change was divulged and he met with failure, it was no longer necessary to keep the changed name. Actually, even if he really had succeeded in passing, employing this ruse, everyone would have recognized Wen Qi as the famous and infamous Wen Tingyun! Wen Qi was a makeshift name assumed for taking the Metropolitan Examination and nothing more. It is no wonder that none of Wen's contemporaries used it in formally addressing him. This changed name, however, was recorded in the "Records for the Equivalents to Passing of the Devine Prefecture" (神州等第錄) under the heading "Equivalent to Passing but Failed to Pass." Wang Dingbao's *Tangzhiyan* presents for the modern reader an access to the hidden truth.

We have already mentioned that Wen likens himself to Zhao Qi, changing his name just to Wen Qi, using the same character Qi (岐). This was not accidental. In Wen's extant works, we can find other examples where Zhao Qi is alluded to, all of which indicate that Wen's use of this character in his name was a deliberate allusion. For example, in the first of his two "Epistles Presented to Vice Minister Jiang," Wen wrote:

> What kind of person was Yue Shifu that you appreciate the essays he left behind; how could Zhao Taiqing make a fool of me since I respectfully follow the example that he set up (越石父彼何人也，夙佩遺文；趙臺卿敢欺我哉，敬承餘烈).

By the allusion to Yan Ying, who rescued Yue Shifu, Wen expressed his gratitude for Jiang's appreciation, likening himself to Yue Shifu; then he showed his reverence for this ancient model, Zhao Taiqing (style of Zhao Qi).

Another example is found in Wen's "Epistle Presented to Drafter Du": "Out of the carriage of Sun Bin [Shi], you stooped to recommend me, the ordinary man" (孫賓〔石〕車上，欲引凡姿). Wen likens Drafter Du to Sun Song, with the implication that he himself was a Zhao Qi looking forward to Du's protection and promotion, in the face of the eunuchs. The reason why Wen took Zhao Qi as his model and encouraged himself by invoking Zhao's spirit was very clear: Zhao also firmly opposed the eunuchs. According to "Biography of Zhao Qi" in HHS, Zhao Qi's original name was Jia, with the style-name Binqing (玢卿); it was only in his later exile that he changed his name. He named himself Qi, and, as he was born in the Censorate (御史臺), he styled himself Taiqing (臺卿). Zhao had been a child prodigy and versatile writer,[30] as was Wen. All these coincidences directly inspired Wen to adopt Zhao's name as his own, with the implication that as a man of rectitude, he was opposed to the eunuchs.

Since Wen for a time changed his name to Qi, it is likely that he also gave himself a new style-name corresponding to the new name Qi. We have indeed found some records indicative of a style-name for Wen other than Feiqing, in a poem of Li Shangyin, Wen's intimate friend. We will see what the following poem by Li Shangyin reveals:

"MISSING AND THINKING ZAIMENG FEIQING"
(有懷在蒙飛卿, *Yuxisheng Shiji Jianzhu*, 2: 524)

Now frequently transferred at minor posts with diseases,	薄宦頻移疾，
Formerly for long you lived in oblivion and isolation.	當年久索居。
Your lament resembles that of Area Commander Yu [Xin],	哀同庾開府，
And your emaciation is as that of Minister Shen [Yue].	瘦極沈尚書。[31]
When the city is green with new shades of distant trees,	城綠新蔭遠，
The River is pure and the afterglow is faint.	江清反照虛。
To express my yearning, I resort only to my brush and ink,	所思惟翰墨，
Following the ancient model I look forward to a pair of carp.	從古待雙魚。[32]

The title of the poem is somewhat problematic. In his annotation, the Qing Dynasty scholar Feng Hao (1719–1801) quoted *Beimeng Suoyan* with some uncertainty:

> Wen Tingyun is styled Feiqing. Some say "Yun" (雲) should be "Yun" (筠), [and his] style [should be] Zaimeng (溫庭雲者，字飛卿；或雲作筠，字在蒙). . . . It cannot be ascertained (無考).[33]

But in any version of *Beimeng Suoyan* (*juan* 10) extant today, the text that corresponds to the above-cited passage reads:

> Wen Tingyun is styled Feiqing. Some say "Yun" (雲) should be "Yun" (筠), [and his] style . . . original name should be Qi (溫庭雲，字飛卿；或雲作筠，字舊名岐).

Apart from Li's poem, the *Beimeng Suoyan* text Feng Hao quoted is the only source available to us that documents that Wen has anything to do with Zaimeng. Feng Hao lived in an earlier time than we do, and he may have seen a version of *Beimeng Suoyan* that is not available to us. Compared to the passage Feng quoted, the present versions of *Beimeng Suoyan* have some key characters missing, which results in the ungrammaticality of the sentence. With these missing characters reinserted, we have a restored text as follows:

> Wen Tingyun is styled Feiqing. Some say "Yun" should be "Yun", [and his] style name [should be] Zaimeng, while his original name is Qi (溫庭雲，字飛卿；或雲作筠，字在蒙。舊名岐).

Such is the original text of *Beimeng Suoyan*, valuable even though it contains mistakes. In trying to explain the title of Li's poem, we must not commit the blunder of taking "Meng" as a place name.[34] Likewise, to suppose Zaimeng to be the style of another person proves to be untenable. We agree with the *Beimeng Suoyan* record, and take Zaimeng as Wen's style. Feng Hao's comment on it ("It cannot be ascertained") only serves to suggest once more that Zaimeng is not the style of any other person, but a style name that matches Qi. The *Beimeng Suoyan* record cannot be totally groundless; it must have its earlier sources, and contains many grains of truth.

If we understand Zaimeng in the title of the poem as another style-name that Wen adopted, then, grammatically it is apposite to Feiqing, that is, both Zaimeng and Feiqing address the same person. Accordingly, the meaning of Zaimeng is rendered immediately transparent, as is the title of the poem. Feiqing has the literal meaning of "an honorable man in flight" or "a man of soaring ambition." Addressing Wen as Zaimeng-Feiqing is equivalent to calling him a frustrated man of rare gifts and bold strategy, who resembled a bright pearl thrown into darkness, or a swan pinioned and no longer able to soar on high. In such familiar banter we can sense the intimacy and sympathy of a bosom friend. There are, indeed, no precedents for addressing a friend using the old and new style-names together, but neither is there any reason to believe that Li Shangyin, who happened to have such a friend bearing such style names, could not contrive to do so.

A careful reading of the poem itself that adheres closely to its title supports this inference. The poem expresses Li's deep concern for Wen, and attests to the depth of friendship between the two most talented and unlucky poets of their time. Most noteworthy is how Li's poem strictly keeps to the title words line by line, a basic requirement for the composition of any Chinese classic poem.

In the first couplet, Li expresses his compassion and understanding (such concerns account for *youhuai*, 有懷) of the injustices and hardship Wen suffered, both in his present official transfers and in his former lonely reclusion (such distresses spell *zaimeng*, 在蒙). He then focuses on Wen's poetic endowments in relation to his personal feelings (a yearning for Wen, again *youhuai*), likening Wen to Yu Xin and Shen Yue, both most brilliant poets (such men are *Feiqings*, 飛卿) in adversity (although they were *zaimeng*). Next, in a symbolic depiction of the scene Li remembers Wen with longing (again *youhuai*), blocked as they are from each other (*zaimeng*). In the last couplet, longing becomes yearning for Wen's letter (*youhuai*).

The above explanation of Li's poem does no more than explain it in the manner that Li composed it: starting (起)—entering into the topic; proceeding (承)—further elaborating the connotations of the topic; turning (轉)—shifting to another aspect of interest intrinsic to the topic; and responding (和)—eliciting the poetic conclusion. The emphasis throughout is on an exploration of the implications of the title: Li's yearning for (*youhuai*) a frustrated (*zaimeng*) talented spirit (*Feiqing*). These feelings expressed in the poem are clearly addressed to one person, and one person only—Wen Tingyun. Li plays with the meanings of Wen's two style-names, which encapsulate the ambivalent quality of Wen's official career with its lofty ambition and persistent adversity. The phrasing of the title is redolent of Li's poetic style and his profound friendship with Wen. We therefore reject the hypothesis that the poem might address two persons at the same time.

Now we can discuss Wen's names and style-names.

Comparing the records in the *Beimeng Suoyan* with those of the two *Tang Histories*, we raise the following questions: Is Wen's name Tingyun (庭雲) or Tingyun (庭筠)? Is his style name Feiqing (飛卿) or Zaimeng (在蒙) or both? What is Wen's original name?

Before attempting answers, we must understand how Chinese literati had a name matched with a style-name. As a universally accepted practice this began about the era of Emperor Wudi of Han (r. 140–87 B.C.). The name (名), or taboo (諱), was something to be avoided when addressing its bearer. Instead, the style-name, or the courtesy name (literally expressing character[s], 表字), was used in place of the name when addressing the person politely. Thus, the style name expressed the connotation of the name and its use could avoid the inconvenience of directly addressing a person by his name. Depending on different eras and aesthetic tastes, the ways in which people matched name with style-name differed. Often, people would make some changes in their own name or style-name, for a variety of reasons.

We will concentrate on finding out how Wen's style-names, Feiqing and Zaimeng, match with his given name Tingyun (庭筠), Tingyun (庭雲), and Qi (岐). Once this question is answered, the others can be readily solved.

Since "Feiqing" means "a man of soaring ambition," that is, one who can fly as high as the clouds (*yun*), it does somewhat "express" the meaning of "*yun*" (雲, cloud). Similarly, the name-character *yun* (筠) is a synecdoche for the bamboo, which, with its strong joints *jie* (節), a homonym for *qijie* (氣節), moral integrity, can also grow as high as the clouds and symbolizes the lofty moral principle of noble men. Thus, it is a more elegant and implied meaning for "Feiqing" to convey. Therefore, between the style-name Feiqing and either of the two homonymic characters *yun* (雲 and 筠),[35] there exist solid semantic connections. We have no reason to reject either one.

With Zaimeng, the case becomes different. There is no meaning whatsoever in it that has to do with *yun* in either form. The only possibility left is that it is a style-name for Wen's changed name, Qi, if it is a style-name at all. As Feng Hao has already involuntarily suggested, Zaimeng is Wen's style-name and thus can be understood as matching Qi. But before we can agree, we must provide a convincing proof of this assumption. Starting from the most frequently used meaning of the character *meng*—to be covered (with something from light or justice), we will trace back to its ultimate definition—as one of the names of the Sixty-four Diagrams in the *Book of Changes*. Granted *meng* as a name of Divination, the phrase "*zaimeng*" acquires its complex but suggestive connotations: a state of being endangered or frustrated, but still in hope of changing for the better by surmounting all difficulties. However, to make it match the name character Qi, we must proceed to further clarifications.

Actually, the compound expression *Zaimeng* does occur, although extremely rarely. What is most fascinating is that it appears in the "Rhapsody on the Meng Spring,"[36] by none other than Li Cheng, Wen's beloved teacher. There we can trace its original meaning and uncover the basic clue as to why Wen chose it as his style-name:

> At the foot of the Eastern Mountain, there is a Meng Spring. It has no good fortune to devote itself to irrigation, but boasts its freshness and transparency in vain. Empty and bright, it is like a mirror; lucid and clear, it is simply itself. It's good to be accustomed to *Kan* as its virtue, and why should it stop in front of *Gen* and go no further.[37] . . . Moreover, were it silted up, it would stop, while when it is dredged, it flows through. It can go either farther or nearer, regardless of whether it flows west or east. With the balance of the four seasons' breezes, it possesses in silence its pretty algae; subject to coverings of overlapping gloom, it was blocked from a pure air. . . . All others have to depend on people and ask favors from them; only this spring remains intact in its existence of "*meng*."
> (蒙彼東山，山下有泉。運未逢于畎澮，色空濟于澄鮮。虛明可鑒，澹泊自然。宜習坎以為德，胡止艮而莫前。且大壅則止，理則通。能致遠邇，任決西東。荷四氣之平均，潛生麗藻，處重陰而蒙蔽，尚阻清風。彼皆因人而有托，此獨居然而在蒙).

This rhapsody is a profound representation of Li Cheng's philosophy and his feelings about how to deal with but not to mix into the corrupt world. Li did this by means of *yongwu* (咏物), that is, personifying the Meng Spring as an ideal character who retains his lofty virtue in defiance of the hardship and dangers of life. This passage brims over with the wisdom of the *Book of Changes*. Its first sentence alludes to the following:

> Meng: A danger presents itself at the foot of the mountain. To face the danger and stop, that is Meng. A spring wells up at the foot of the mountain, that is Meng. Thus the superior man fosters his character by thoroughness in all that he does (山下有險，險而止，蒙。山下出泉，蒙，君子以果行育德).[38]

These remarks illuminate the fundamental purport of Li Cheng's rhapsody, especially the term *Zaimeng*. As Wang Bi explained the term *Meng*:

> If one retreats, he will fall into dire straits; if he advances, the mountain is blocking his way, and one is at a loss as to where to go—such is the meaning of *meng* (退則困險，進則閡山，不知所使，蒙之義也).

Therefore, Zaimeng means to be in the state of being *meng*, that is, finding it difficult either to go ahead or to retreat. It also implies that, even in such a plight, a noble man can be at ease, with his personality intact. We suggest that such were the meanings of the term *Zaimeng* that Wen had in mind when he adopted it as his style-name. He borrowed the term from Li Cheng, as a token of his own tenacity of purpose under political pressures, demonstrating at the same time his admiration for his teacher.

This example provides a case in point for our further reflection. When investigating Wen's secret attendance upon the Heir, we discovered that Li Cheng was Wen's teacher. Now we see evidence in Wen's behavior of the influence of his teacher. If the course we are pursuing concerning Wen's life were not in accordance with what happened in reality, we could never be able to uncover interconnected evidence of the puzzle such as this.

Now we turn to the meaning of the character *qi* (岐) that Wen used as his changed name. In "Hundred-Rhyme Poem," we have read:

In my laments and sighs I felt melancholy, as did Yang Zhu.	悲嘆似楊朱。

And in the "Boshan Censer", we have also read:

I hear say that Yang Zhu had no end of tears,	見說楊朱無限淚，
Which were not, nay, vainly because the road forked away.	豈能空為路岐分？

In both cases Wen avails himself of the allusion to Yang Zhu, who "wept on coming to the *forked road*, for it could lead to both south and north." Here we must see Yang Zhu as more than the embodiment of a frustrated Wen Tingyun. It is suggestive that Yang Zhu's tears were shed on the "*forked road*" (岐路), a term that literally contains the very character Wen used for his changed name, *qi*. In this expression, Yang Zhu's weeping is not only a symbol of Wen's political frustration in general, but it points directly to the causes and effects of his change of name, marking the climax of his troubles. Substituting *qi* for "forked" [road], we find that the poetic implication of the couplet becomes doubly rich.[39] The character *qi*, apart from its literal meaning "forked way," signifies the crucial turn in Wen's political career, in the face of which Wen was determined to advance courageously and deliberately, regardless of any new frustrations and dangers. Now we see clearly that the character Qi as Wen's name has connotations that tally with those of *meng* that are couched in the *Book of Changes*. We cannot but conclude that Qi and Zaimeng as name and style-name are, in the full sense, an ideal pair.

Wen adopted Zaimeng as his style-name, to match his name Qi. The name and the style-name bring into relief each other's connotations: even faced with the power and the importunate pursuit of the eunuchs, Wen would never admit defeat. As shown in the above examples, Wen's distress was always linked to his frustration under eunuch dominance, both throughout the Heir Apparent Incident and during the examinations. The accounts of *Tongxin* and *Beimeng Suoyan* indicate that Wen's name change resulted from the whipping he received, and thus it was also connected with the Jianghuai Incident. In summary, Wen's name change was connected to all his past political experiences and profoundly affected his future life career.

Upon examining the two homonymic characters *yun* (筠) and *yun* (雲), again in Li Cheng's works, we find something that corroborates the account in *Tongxin*.

Tongxin asserts that Wen's original name was Qi, and the name change from Qi to Tingyun (庭雲) resulted from a whipping by his senior relatives. This account certainly departs from the historical truth. But its serious argument that "other books" should refer to Wen as Tingyun (庭雲) instead of Tingyun (庭筠) poses a question in earnest: which is the right name? The answer to this question will provide us with more messages about his life.

As our analysis above demonstrates, the two characters *yun* and *yun*, besides being homonymous, both match with the style-name Feiqing. As it is, there is nothing in the shape or literal meanings of the two characters that would cause them to be confused with each other, thus we cannot impute the discrepancy to the error of block-printings during the circulation of Wen's works. Nor is it likely that contemporary writers just invented the name on Wen's behalf. No. Such a subtle name choice could only have been Wen's own, just like his choice of the name Qi and style-name Zaimeng.

At the examination in the twelfth year of Zhenyuan (796), which he passed as the first candidate, Li Cheng had composed a poem and a rhapsody both of which were entitled "The Bamboo-Arrow Has Its Cuticle" (竹箭有筠).[40] From the latter we read:

> People observing the rites is just like the bamboo-arrow having its cuticle. . . . If only it has its constant nature, the hardy bamboo fears no shifts of the seasons; never changing his mind, a man of virtue is always concerned about keeping the Way. The bamboo cannot protect its joints without its cuticle, nor can people be established as the model of the time by abandoning the rites. The wise teachings of the former sages are the lasting lessons for the generations to come. . . . When it springs up as a shoot, it has already a protective

> sheath enveloping its body; and when its sparse stalks grow, as expected, it towers above the cloud in due time. . . . Therefore we know that my observing ritual resembles my having disciples; and the bamboo having the cuticle is just like my having my skin. . . . (喻人有禮，如竹有筠。苟常其性，寒竹何患于時移；不易其心，志士常懷于道在。竹無筠無以固其節，人舍禮何以法于時。伊先哲之善喻，作後代之元龜。苞本之時，已包周身之防；疏莖之勢，更叶淩雲之期。是以禮之于己，如我有徒；筠之于竹，如我有膚……)

The whole of Li's rhapsody focuses on the key word *yun* (筠, cuticle), with *li* (禮, rites) as its motif. Personified as a noble man, the bamboo-arrow with its cuticle has a sense of honor and shame. The cuticle of the bamboo offers protection to its joints. In like manner, the rites enable the noble man to protect his own rectitude. The bamboo shoot's armor-like envelope is emblematic of the wisdom of a noble man that protects him in the chaos of the times, while the lonely and straight pole towering above the clouds symbolizes the worthy man who achieves his ambitions. Finally, Li concludes that the cuticle has more importance to the bamboo than do the rites to himself, by comparing the former with having skin and the latter with having disciples. Having skin, of course, is more vitally important than having disciples. Here we discover why Wen took *yun* (筠) as his name—he must have been a student on particularly close terms with Li Cheng.

It is clear that Wen took all the meanings of "*yun*" in Li's rhapsody when making a revision in his name. Such a habit of substituting a homonym for one's existing name persists even today in China and cannot be taken as a formal change of name. Although we do not know the exact time Wen did this, it must have been some time after he became Li's student. Considering that *yun* (雲) was also quite well known, the substitution of *yun* (筠) could not have been made very early in Wen's life. Therefore, in deference to Wen's own decision, we will call him Wen Tingyun (溫庭筠).

We now are aware of how Wen tried to pass the civil service examination and how he failed to become a Presented Scholar. Throughout, it was always the power of the eunuchs that thwarted his plans and ruined his chances. The official histories fail to yield veritable records about many important affairs involving these eunuchs. By comparison, miscellaneous notes and anecdotes, works such as *Yuquanzi*, *Tongxin*, and *Beimeng Suoyan*, biased though they be, contain much that is true, when examined using a discriminating historical approach.

WEN'S AFTERTHOUGHT

Turning to the relevant passage of "Hundred-Rhyme Poem," we will complete our account of the whole story (rhymes 75–85) by connecting it to other affairs.

75 My yearning for home is of a bird nesting on the southern branch, 鄉思巢枝鳥，
The passage of time, like the sun crossing the cloud-crevice. 年華過隙駒。[41]
76 Harboring gratitude [to emperors] I vainly accompany my shadow, 懷恩空抱影，
For I have no chance to devote myself to repay the imperial grace. 酬德未捐軀。
77 Among my compeers I've been honored as a good friend, 時輩推良友，
Of my pedigree I have carried on an honest fame 家聲繼令圖。
78 To present myself I grieve my wings were too short, 致身傷短翮，
With head high, you looked back at me, a worn-out horse. 驤首顧疲駑。

In Wen's nostalgia, he laments over the passage of time while he regrets his unrealized dream. He was unsuccessful both in serving his country and in reglorifying his family. A social literary man with an honest family fame, as he was, Wen failed because, in his own terms, his "wings" were "too short," that is, he lacked a powerful mediator to help him, although his failure can more properly be attributed to his particular family circumstances and personality.

79 Now Ban and Sima are galloping forth side by side, 班馬方齊鶩，
While Chen and Lei are, also, driving neck and neck. 陳雷亦并驅。
80 In the past, each of you told his wishes, 昔皆言爾志，
By now I likewise regard my disciple with awe. 今亦畏我徒。
81 The energy I possess, to the Altair and the Plough can soar, 有氣干牛斗，
But where is the man, to really know the precious *Lulu* sword? 無人辨轆轤。

"Ban and Ma", that is, Ban Gu (32–92) and Sima Qian (?–145 B.C.), both great historiographers, refer to people to whom Wen addressed his poem. Lei Yi (雷義) and Chen Zhong (陳重), good friends famous for their mutual friendship in their official careers,[42] also refer to Wen's companions. Many of those who "in the past" each "told his wishes"—Wen's classmates under the same teacher, or even his own students—were pushing forward in their official careers and were "regarded with awe"[43] on Wen's part. Wen likened his talents to legendary precious swords such as *Lulu*[44] that emit a purple light to the Altair and Plough Constellations, though no one in power could really appreciate it. The crux of the problem is implied in the lines that follow:

82 Coming as guest, the green-ant, I poured. 客來斟綠蟻，
Trying to ransom a wife, on the blue-beetles, I trod. 妻試踏青蚨。
83 By incessant aspersions, even [flesh and] bones are destroyed, 積毀方銷骨，
And I fear that a slight blemish would spoil the whole gem. 微瑕懼掩瑜。

As we have pointed out, Wen squandered his money to ransom the singer and eventually married her. After that he was forced to face the consequences of his marriage, opprobrium from orthodox literati and the calumnies of eunuchs. Wen confesses here that the marriage was for him similar to a "slight blemish" obscuring the splendor of the whole gem. That is to say that the resultant rumors brought thorough ruin to his official career. Here Wen attributes his failure to the Jianghuai Incident, which ushered in a lifetime of nightmare—the eunuchs' ubiquitous influence, from which he was never successful in freeing himself.

84 As the snake-spears are still involved in shifting wars, 蛇矛猶轉戰，
"The [one in] fish disguise" is in detainment and thrall. 魚服自囚拘。
85 By such tricks *they* intended to delude the world, 欲就欺人事，
But how can the ghost's execution be dodged? 何能逭鬼誅？

The snake-spears (a metaphor for the Tang state army) are still involved in shifting wars, against the recalcitrant military satraps. "The one in fish disguise,"[45] meaning Emperor Wenzong, was "in detainment and thrall"—under virtual house arrest. At the time Wen composed this poem, Wenzong had already died; the new emperor Wuzong established by the eunuchs was facing a situation hardly any better than that of Wenzong, especially at the beginning. These and similar facts all reveal that the eunuchs were plunging the Tang Empire into political crisis. This is Wen's indignant accusation: although *they* [please note that the pronoun *they* is inserted pending translation and absent in Chinese original] might succeed in deluding the world, how could *they* evade the execution at the hands of ghosts?[46] *They* would have to pay the price for their clandestine evils.

In summation, frustrated as he was, Wen retained his political nerve and verve. He attributed all his failures to, and aimed his veiled attacks at the eunuchs, exhibiting a laudable political courage and insight.

86 Between right and wrong—waking or dreaming, I was confused, 是非迷覺夢，
From Qin to Wu, I planned a journey. 行役議秦吳。
87 In the piercing cold the wind was wailing, 凜冽風埃殘，
In the desolation, plants were withered. 蕭條草木枯。
88 Reluctant departure made me heartbroken, 低回傷志氣，
Braving the cold, my skin and flesh were frostbitten. 蒙犯變肌膚。
89 Only the cries of migrating wild geese were heard, 旅雁惟聞叫，
When a hungry falcon came to me without being called. 飢鷹不待呼。
90 The shuttle of my dream was hastened like the cries of crickets, 夢梭抛促織，
The cocoon of my yearning heart was modeled on those of spiders. 心繭學蜘蛛。

As a consequence, Wen had to seek political refuge in the south. Wen was aware there was no way to justify himself, since right and wrong confused together. On his way back from Chang'an to Wu in the piercing cold, he was downcast. He grieved over his precarious life, and was impatient for a chance to serve his country. Painful memories combined with hopes crowded into his dreams, leaving him sleepless. Despite his knowledge of what was really happening, he was forced to imitate the spider and envelop his heart in a cocoon—the basic cause of this poem's uniquely dense and ambiguous language.

91 How can *their* tricks, again, be hard to foresee? 寧復機難料？
But wasn't such petty faith too trifling to be trusted? 庸非信未孚？
92 Furious and wild, I'm a tiger shot by an arrow, 激揚銜箭虎，
In doubt and fear, I'm a fox listening on the ice. 疑懼聽冰狐。

Wen anonymously asks the eunuchs: are not your tricks known even to all? Then he directs an undefined criticism at an individual by asking: "Isn't such petty faith too trifling to be trusted?" Very possibly, Wen's involvement in the inner court struggles might have a subtle bearing upon the political susceptibility of the new emperor Wuzong. By all accounts Wen was infuriated at the eunuchs' machinations, but he had to be on his guard against further attacks from them. He portrays himself as a wounded tiger or suspicious fox.

93 For saving myself, I will dig one more "burrow," 處己將營窟，
Such is my heart that tallies with that of the sage. 論心將合符。

94 Don't say that I am in my "brother's" grace, 浪言輝棣萼，
Where can a remote kinsman like me entrust his life? 何所托葭莩？
95 From a tall tree an oriole can seek friends with his warbling voice, 喬木能求友，
In a dilapidated nest an Owl vainly scares *Yuanchu*, with a rotten rat. 危巢莫嚇雛。[47]
96 I'd rather assume a lofty demeanor as a leading figure, 風華飄領秀，
Than bow to shirt and skirt with the Poetry and Rites. 詩禮拜衾襦。[48]

Faced with a critical situation, Wen had to prepare multiple means of survival for himself. His retreat, he declares here, tallied with the Sage's teachings. When he was in need, however, not only did his "brothers" fail to help him, but even his status as an imperial relative had proved futile. Though he failed, Wen had made friends with quite a few successful men during his efforts for a Presented Scholar degree.[49] Likening himself to a *Yuanchu* that unwittingly scares the owl devouring its rotten rat,[50] Wen was declaring to the political speculators that he would not compete with them. As a first-rate writer of his time, Wen had his own peculiar insight, and the manner in which he chose to behave was sometimes contrary to the hypocritical teachings of orthodox Confucianism. Wen directs doubt and irony toward their "statesmanship," as revealed in the allusion contained in the last line. He charges that their major principles and great learning are nothing more than means to rob, using *Zhuangzi's* poignant sarcasm:

> The Confucianists sack tombs with [what they learn in] the *Book of Songs* (Poetry) and the *Book of Rites*. The major Confucian spoke down: "Day is breaking in the east, how is our business going on?" The minor Confucian answered: Not yet take off the shirt and skirt, but there is a pearl in the mouth, as is said in the *Book of Songs*: "Green, green is the wheat, / growing on the slope of the hill. / When alive offered nothing for the relief, / why after death keep in mouth a pearl (儒以詩禮發冢，大儒臚傳曰"東方作矣，事之如何？"小儒曰："未解裙襦，口中有珠。詩不言乎：青青之麥，生于陵陂。生不布施，死何含珠為？").

97 When I recline on a pillow, my feelings are immensely bitter, 欹枕情何苦，
In the same boat, how can their Way, from mine, differ? 同舟道豈殊。

98 Let me abandon myself to caressing melilotus and angelica, 放懷親蕙芷，
Though my retirement is not yet at the "mulberry and elm" year. 收跡異桑榆。[51]
99 As a gift to my distant friends, I break off a willow twig, 贈遠聊攀柳，[52]
And I will cut the bulrushes to make a letter. 裁書欲截蒲。
100 Gazing into the air, endless tears blurring my eyes, 瞻風無限淚，
I turn my head back, and faltered. 回首更踟躕。

The more Wen thought about his failure, the more he wondered why people in the same boat could have different Ways, and why someone had turned against him by divulging the "secret" of his name change. Now, although not yet in his old age, he had to return to his old reclusive way of life. At the very end, Wen expresses his affection for his friends and his reluctance to leave, looking back at Chang'an in tears.

After a painful reflection on the causes and consequences of his failure, Wen still retained feelings of anger and pride and, of course, sorrow and distress. For the time being, however, he had to return to the south, leaving political life behind.

We must stress repeatedly the constant, deliberate persecution imposed on Wen by the eunuchs. Again, it was the eunuchs' persecution that drove Wen to seek political refuge. Emperor Wuzong mounted the throne during the terror of a palace coup launched by the eunuchs. To guarantee his claim to be a legitimate emperor, upon being enthroned, he would, of his own volition, follow the eunuchs' advice. That is why, without any hesitation, he executed Worthy Consort Yang, Prince An, and Prince Chen shortly after his ascension. Wuzong simply could not show any favor to Wen, all the more because Wen had pledged allegiance to the Heir.

From another perspective, the ups and downs of Wen's political career can, to some degree, be taken as a barometer of the political struggles between eunuchs and court officials on the one hand, and the Niu and the Li Factions on the other. For example, the Heir Apparent's death was a result of the court officials' defeat in their rivalry with the eunuchs; at the same time, the Heir's death evinces that the Niu had gained the upper hand over the Li Faction. By the same token, Wen's failure was a part and parcel of the Li Faction's failure in its struggle against the eunuchs. Members of this faction were Wen's major supporters during his efforts to pass the examination. All through this process, however, in order to meet the demands of the changed situation, the eunuchs had aided the Li Faction in their rise to full power at the expense of the Nius. Therefore, at the same time that the Li Faction was losing the war against the eunuchs, it was winning a battle over the Niu Faction. Despite the fact that Wen for a time sided with the Lis, they could not help Wen upon coming to power, because it would not be wise to promote such a politically sensitive figure and entail the risk of offending the eunuchs.

Therefore, throughout the Huichang era, Wen could not attempt any civil service examination. Confining himself mostly to the Wu and Yue regions, he might have found some minor local post, or else lived a semireclusive life on his inherited estates awaiting his opportunity. For him this was a period of political hibernation, during which he never forgot his ambition. His whereabouts during this period, however, are not a central concern of this study.

Chapter Eight

Highlights during the Dazhong Era

COMPLICATIONS IN WEN'S FRUSTRATED EFFORTS

Wen did not return to the capital until the last years of the Huichang era,[1] when Emperor Xuanzong (r. 847–860) ascended the throne, with the "support" of the eunuchs.

A son of Emperor Xianzong (r. 806–820) and an uncle of both Wenzong and Wuzong, Xuanzong cherished a bitter hatred for his nephew Wuzong, rooted in the oppression and humiliation he had suffered at the latter's hands. In addition, he harbored the utmost loathing for Li Deyu, the powerful Prime Minister throughout Wuzong's reign and head of the Li Faction. The Huichang era was remarkable for its military feats and civil successes, which paved the way for the last period of relative stability of the Tang Empire. However, while benefiting from what had been achieved by his predecessors, Xuanzong purposely abandoned most of the important policies pursued in the Huichang era and implemented a set of measures of his own. One of the results was that those who formerly could not take the civil service examination at all, such as Wen, now faced more favorable circumstances. Most conspicuously, Xuanzong offered particular patronage for the recruitment of Presented Scholars. According to Wang Dang's *Tangyulin* (4: 134), he even called himself a "Local Contributed Presented Scholar" and inscribed the title on a pillar in his palace. Sun Qi's *Beilizhui* (1: 2) described the situation with the following remarks:

> The Dazhong Emperor was fond of Confucian statecraft, and he set the greatest store by the civil service recruitment. Thus the Presented Scholar degree became popular on an unprecedented scale (大中皇帝好儒術，特重科第，故進士此道尤勝，曠古無儔).

Hence, there appeared a glimmer of hope that Wen might be able to remount the "dragon's gate." However, the policies Xuanzong adopted did not mean a rehabilitation of Wen's case. Despite a drastic shift in the political balance within the decision-making circle, an insurmountable obstacle—the eunuchs' bitter hostility—still prevented him from passing.

As a consequence of Xuanzong's ascension, the Niu Faction took over power from the Li Faction for the final time, even though the eunuchs' political control remained as powerful and persistent as ever before. In dealing with the eunuchs, the Niu Faction, too, had to exercise extreme caution. Seen from the perspective of the factional conflicts, the new state of affairs was only marginally better for Wen's political prospects than the old one. Despite his constant efforts in campaigning for patronage, as a politically sensitive figure, Wen could please neither faction. Nor was it easy for him to make any progress in the political crevice between the factions. Put in his own words ("Epistle Presented to the Vice-Minister, Salt and Iron Commissioner"), Wen was in an awkward situation such as this:

> I, with the common quality of cogongrass and reeds, and from a debased stock like that of Zhu or Teng, have given up a life of ploughing and weeding in my humble town, and come to observe the rites and music in the Metropolitan capital (某菅蒯凡姿，邾滕陋族，釋耕耘于下邑，觀禮樂于中都).

In Wen's metaphor, once people have silk and hemp for clothing, they will treat him as though he was "cogongrass and reeds"[2] (wild grasses of tough fiber), and will throw him away. For him to earn official standing in the aristocratic society and between the vying factions could be compared to small feudal states such as Zhu or Teng maintaining a precarious existence between the contending powers of Qi and Chu.[3] Despite his remaining family influence and his good relationships with some figures in office, Wen's efforts had little effect. In the factional struggles of the time, Wen subordinated himself to neither group, although he had to appeal more than once to members of both for help. And even though on more than one occasion he enlisted the support of (or more accurately, was employed by) one faction, to his dismay, it happened at the expense of offending someone on the opposite side, nullifying his endeavor. This is the second cause of Wen's repeated failures.

Nevertheless, Wen's efforts were not entirely fruitless. From the commencement of the Dazhong era, it took him more than ten years on an extremely tortuous path, before he finally "succeeded" in earning himself a mere and bare Presented Scholar degree.

From Wen's epistles presented to various ministers during the Dazhong era (such as his "Epistle Presented to Prime Minister Linghu," "Two Epistles Presented to Vice-Minister Jiang," "Epistle Presented to Minister Feng," "Epistle Presented to the Vice-Minister, Salt and Iron Commissioner," "Epistle Presented to Secretary Du," and "Epistles Presented to the Prime Minister"),[4] we are able to obtain a full picture of Wen's unremitting efforts. He tried everything he could, appealing to any minister who might help open up a way to an official career. Although things sometimes appeared fairly hopeful for our poet, the official he was dealing with would sooner break faith with Wen than take substantial steps to help him. For, in the complex political struggles under the control of the eunuchs, a minister who did try to redress Wen's injustice would endanger his own career and fall victim to yet another injustice. Such was the lesson the political realities had taught any Late Tang official to whom Wen might appeal.

To make better use of limited space, we will bypass a lengthy textual and factual investigation of the above-mentioned epistles, and proceed directly into his biographies in the standard histories to determine the reasons for Wen's repeated failures.

One of the defects of Wen's biographies is that their authors rely on the information provided by unofficial histories, but fail to discriminate between what is true and what is false in them. In the face of the perplexing first-hand information, in addition to being misled by the contradictory Tang sources, the biographers were too constrained by their own factional and hierarchical biases to do Wen justice. If Wen's biographies fail even to give a clear account of such basic information as Wen's names and style-names, we cannot expect much from their accounts of Wen's life. However, in order to repudiate the slander, which has found general acceptance among later generations, and to clarify Wen's experiences during the Dazhong era, we will undertake a study of these biographies.

In fact, Wen's biographies in the two *Tang Histories*, apart from some comments written in a contemptuous tone, present concrete details for only three events in Wen's life, all of which are frequent topics in unofficial histories written between the Tang and Song dynasties. The first of these concerns Wen's performances in the Presented Scholar examinations in the Dazhong era, namely, the cheating incidents in which Wen took the examination on others' behalf and suffered repeated failures. The second is a garbled version of the Jianghuai Incident, misdated as in the middle of the Xiantong era (860–873) and related to Linghu Tao. The third relates how Wen rushed about seeking an official position in the Xiantong era, the last decade of his life. Since these amount to no more than a sketchy account of Wen's alleged experiences during the Dazhong era and later, Wen's biographies in the two *Tang Histories* are both incomplete and inaccurate. We will concentrate here first on Wen's performances in the examinations.

The following comprises the first few lines of Wen's biography in JTS (190: 5078), which, after introducing the name, recounts his basic experiences during the Dazhong era:

> In the beginning of the Dazhong, he took the Presented Scholar Examination. Due to his painstaking studies and practices, he was particularly conversant with the compositions of poetry and rhapsody. On his first arrival at the capital, he was appreciated and held in high esteem by many men of eminence (大中初，應進士。苦心研習，尤長于詩賦。初至京師，人士翕然推重).

The record attests to Wen's literary attainment and fame, a fact even the biased Song biographers did not deny. However, it contains a serious mistake in chronology. The correct way of expressing the fact is that, in the beginning of Dazhong era, on Wen's arrival (rather than on his *first* arrival) at the capital, he *once more* took the Presented Scholar Examination. By beginning Wen's biography in this manner, JTS produces the false impression that Wen just embarked on his life career at the time, which accounts for a fallacy in determining Wen's birth year, calculating that it occurred much later than it really did.[5] Even if the remaining details were all correct, a biography that begins from the time when its subject was already fifty years of age is, to say the least, incomplete.

The biography continues as follows:

> But his behavior as a scholar was improper and impure, and he disregarded small niceties. He was capable of matching the music of stringed or wind instruments to obscene and florid words; and he often drank and gambled with the dissolute sons of high-ranking officials, such as Pei Cheng, Linghu Hao, and their ilk, carousing for a whole day at a time. Therefore, for many years, he failed to pass the Presented Scholar Examination (然士行塵雜，不修邊幅。能逐弦吹之音，為側艷之詞。公卿家無賴子弟裴誠、令狐滈之徒，相與蒱飲，酣醉終日。由是累年不第).

This passage (the only account in the biography dealing with Wen's taking the examination) emphasizes Wen's repeated failures, only to leave readers with the misrepresentation that never in his entire life did Wen pass the Presented Scholar Examination. To reveal the false nature of the preceding account, we will examine both the causes of Wen's failures and the end results of all his efforts.

As we have seen clearly from Wen's life up to now, the only reason Wen's biographers might have for condemning his behavior as "improper and impure" is their distorted grasp of the Jianghuai Incident. It was chiefly because of Wen's unconventional marriage with a singer-prostitute and the many rumors that were spread on account of it that Wen's fame was tarnished. As for Wen's disregard for "small niceties," this was characteristic of the Late Tang literati, and not a viable reason to account for his failures. In the eyes of the biased and snobbish Song Dynasty historiographers, to neglect "small niceties" was virtue in a powerful figure, but spelled ruin for insignificant man such as Wen. For someone like Wen, moreover, skill in music and expertise at composing verses labeled "obscene and florid," could be taken as "evidence" of misdeeds and a cause of failure. Obviously, as the products of fabrication, these reasons must not be credited.

As for the problematic claims that Wen often drank and gambled with the dissolute sons of high-ranking officials, the logical confusions contained in them can attest to their fallacy, as is evident from the following story in Fan Shu's *Yunxi Youyi* (65–66): Pei Xian (裴諴)[6] and Wen were good friends because of their shared fondness for poetry, music, and humor. Zhou Dehua, a famous singer, sang the poems of many celebrities of the time at a party, but she refused to sing either Wen's or Pei's version of "Branches of the Willows" and embarrassed both on the spot. Frankly speaking, we cannot give full credit to this story, nor can we credit the reputed sensitivity of a legendary singer, although very possibly this anecdote is one of the sources upon which Wen's biographers drew. Pei Xian's poems written for the occasion were particularly indelicate:

The sole ovary of lotus seeds none could eye, 獨房蓮子沒人看，
To pick a lotus on the quiet will exhaust all my might. 偷折蓮時命也拚。
If anyone has a reason and asks you why, 若有所由來借問，
Tell him the lotus stealer is a low-ranking official guy. 但道偷蓮是下官。

Any connoisseur of poetry can surely see that this is written in the worst of taste. "Sole ovary of lotus seeds" and "low-ranking official guy" (lower organ) are obscene homophones, punning on sex. The poem is an indecent joke, a nakedly sexual depiction and nothing more.

Wen's poem, subjected to the same censure, however, is a model of poetic originality:

In the bottom of the well, I light a lamp—deeply illuminate it: 井底點燈深燭（囑）伊，
With my lad, I like "long travel," not "encircling chess." 共郎長行莫圍棋（違期）。[7]
A dainty die with red beans engraved in it, don't you know, 玲瓏骰子安紅豆，
Is a love yearning that penetrates to the bone? 入骨相思知不知？

"The bottom of the well" is a "deep" place to "light a lamp" and "illuminate it"; "deeply illuminate it" (深燭伊) puns on "affectionately exhort him" (深囑伊). Thus, "In the bottom of the well I light a lamp" spells the message "affectionately exhort him" by means of homophonic puns. How does the lass express her love to the lad? Certainly there is something more to the point, behind the seemingly irrelevant remark of the second line. Substituting "miss the date [for return]" (*weiqi*, 違期) for its homophone, "encircling chess" (*weiqi*, 圍棋), as the poet's note suggests, we will understand "with my lad I like 'long travel'" in a new light—the so-called "long travel" is no longer merely a game name, as is encircling chess, it spells its very connotation in our English translation. Thus, the second line as a whole is the lass's extortion that she would go with her lad in the long travel, (and if she could not) her lad must not miss the date for return.

In the second couplet, the die, a small cube bearing different numbers (from one to six) of spots, fits for the poet's artistic imagination because of its two traits. First, it is made of bone; and second, engraved into the bone, its spots are dyed red and look like red beans, that is, the seeds of love pea and symbol of love yearning. Through such semantic and syntactic links, the red spots that are carved into the bone-made die become the synonym and pun for a love yearning that penetrates to the bone.

Each and every line of this poem can please both the eye and, on reflection, the heart of its reader: the punning homophones and double meanings are handled with masterful dexterity; the images are fresh and rich, teeming with resources and vitality; the poetic taste is refined and delicate. The poem exemplifies Wen's proficiency in poetry, *ci* poetry par excellence, a result of his imitating and surpassing the urban folksongs, drawing from and excelling the Southern Dynasty Music Bureau verses, an artistic creativeness that really deserves to be called original.

A comparison of the two works immediately brings to light their great differences in taste and quality. Pei's composition can hardly be called a poem. However, even though Pei's work is "indecent," composing such works never prevented him from having a moderately successful official career, as is recounted in *Yunxi Youyi* and other sources. In addition, we can be sure that Pei would have functioned more as a friend contributing to Wen's success than a bad companion adding to his failures. But Wen's poems scarcely ever have the kind of indelicate implications found in Pei's example. Otherwise, as "a scholar without virtue" presenting a target to hostile gossips, Wen would have been subjected to much greater moral censure than he was. Neither his "indecent" poems nor his friendship with Pei could have been a serious obstacle to his gaining the Presented Scholar degree.

Wen's associating and drinking with Linghu Hao and thus failing to pass is also a fiction. Linghu Hao was the son of Linghu Tao (803–880) and grandson of Linghu Chu (765–836), whom Wen also knew personally.[8] It was during Linghu Tao's long tenure as Prime Minister (850–859) that Wen failed to pass as a Presented Scholar. In the meantime, Linghu Hao became a "White-robe Prime Minister," notorious for assuming and abusing his father's power, but never rendering Wen any help. The two men had totally different backgrounds and careers, and the baseness of one of them had no effect on the other. Linghu Hao was said to have frequented the pleasure quarters of the capital, as was then the vogue (see Sun Qi, 41). This is perhaps one of the reasons JTS puts his name in Wen's biography, seeking to draw attention to Wen's debauched way of life. However, Linghu Hao, too, was a man of letters, who had much more to do than merely idle away his time in drinking all day. The problem with JTS is that, piecing together scattered disparaging accounts concerning Wen, it tends to portray most of Wen's friends unfavorably, or else to regard indiscriminately people of ostensibly bad repute as Wen's friends.

Therefore, the biography gives no sound reasons to account for Wen's repeated failures. The self-righteous biographers hardly offer anything plausible, and their sketchy biographies are full of inconsistencies and contradictions. But then the question is raised once more: what caused Wen's repeated failures? We have no need to determine or discover other "right" answers, because, as we have repeatedly stressed, the cause was always the opposition presented by the eunuchs.

We thus have good reason to discredit the tale told in JTS, concerning the reasons why Wen failed to pass the examinations so many times. We will also disprove the notion that Wen *never* did acquire the Presented Scholar degree, a fallacy for which we hold JTS responsible. To this end, we can cite as evidence the following clear and exact sources.

It is in *Tangzhiyan* (2: 16), under the subtitle of "Pass the Presented Scholar Examination Only Long after Becoming Equivalent to Passing" (為等第久方及第) that we find: "Wen Qi fled helter-skelter as a commoner" (溫岐濫竄于白衣). We are given to understand that after a long period of frustrations earning no official position, Wen, with great difficulty at last, procured a Presented Scholar degree. Wen's biography in JTS stresses his numerous failures but ignores the record that he finally did achieve a very special and narrow pass.

In Wen's "Epistle Presented to the Censor-In-Chief" (Xu Shang), he also related in clear terms that he had gained the Presented Scholar degree indeed. Had he not really done so, it would have been ridiculous for him to refer to himself in the following manner:

> It was by hanging burned reeds to illuminate the characters and weaving rushes to make writing paper that I succeeded in acquiring the state examination degree and benefited with an imperial salary (懸蘆照字，編草為資。遂竊科名，才沾祿賜).[9]

When, then, did Wen gain the degree? We must look into Wen's biography in XTS (91: 3788) for the information JTS fails to include:

> As a man of marvelously quick wit, he often made compositions for others. Toward the end of the Dazhong era, he sat for the examination held by the government. As the invigilation was especially exacting, Tingyun was unhappy about it; but he presented a memorial of more than a thousand characters, while having stealthily helped eight persons. Those in power held him in contempt for his behavior, and appointed him Defender of Fangshan County (庭筠思神速，多為人作文。大中末，試有司，廉視尤謹。庭筠不樂，上書千餘言，然私相占授者已八人。執政鄙其所為，授方山尉).

In XTS, this passage comes after an account similar to that found in JTS about Wen's repeated failures in the examinations. It is a supplement to Wen's experiences in the period, the only supplement contributed by XTS that improves JTS. Here, the first point calling for our attention is that the repeated blows dealt to Wen by fate incited him to a kind of abnormal protest. Knowing he was far superior to those who had passed while he was always rejected, Wen decided to give vent to his discontent by helping others to pass and thus voicing his protest. To do Wen justice, he was determined to fight to the end of his life against the eunuchs' persecution, letting his actions serve as a denunciation of the imperial state machine that had buckled under the pressure of the eunuchs' power.

Here, however, the story becomes quite baffling: it is strange that Wen should achieve his goal of gaining a position merely by using fraud in the examinations. This is almost like saying that the more he cheated, and the more those in power held him in contempt, the higher the position he would attain! We must quote additional details concerning Wen's performance in his examination-related activities before we are able to shed more light on this problem.

Records in *Tangzhiyan* (13: 146) also confirm the story that Wen cheated in the examinations by mischievously helping others:

> In the year when Vice-Minister Shen[10] from Shanbei held the position of Examination Administrator, knowing that Feiqing used to be fond of helping others, he specially called him to be examined in *front* of (instead of behind) his carrel curtain. It so happened that Feiqing was unhappy on this day, and in the evening asked that the door be opened to let him out, whereupon he submitted a memorial of over a thousand characters. Some said that he had secretly managed to help eight candidates (山北沈侍郎主文年，特召溫飛卿于簾前試之，為飛卿愛救人故也。適屬翌日庭筠不樂，其日晚間請開門先出，仍獻啟千餘言，或曰潛救八人矣).

Similar records can be found in *Beimeng Suoyan* (4: 29) and later *Tangshi Jishi* (54: 822) with more details added. Among them, *Tangzhiyan* and *Beimeng Suoyan* are earlier sources. All verify the credibility of the record that Wen's eccentric cheating efforts in the examinations had become out of control and created troubles for the authorities. Evidently, it was not that Wen's cheating caused his failures, rather, it was that his repeated failures provoked his cheating. *Beimeng Suoyan* contains the following account of the same fact:

> Moreover, in every year's examination, Tingyun often wrote for others. When Vice Minister Shen Xun was Examination Administrator, he put Tingyun in a seat not adjacent to those of the other examinees. On the following day, he told Tingyun in front of the examination carrel, "There have been a number of examinees attain-

> ing their goal with the aid of the essays and rhapsodies written by you, Academician.[11] This year the examinations are in my charge, and I will permit no interference from you, Academician. Mind yourself about this." Therefore he rejected him and Wen always failed (庭筠又每歲舉場，多為舉人假手。侍郎沈詢知舉，別施鋪席授庭筠，不與諸公鄰比。翌日于簾前請庭筠曰：向來策名者，皆是文賦托于學士；某今歲舉場中，并無假托學士。勉旃。因遣之。由是不得意也).

It can be imagined that, prior to the ninth year of Dazhong, Wen had already annoyed the examination officials by cheating many times. What is represented in the above account, and incorrectly put forward as the basic cause of his failure, is only one instance among many acts of persistent mischief on Wen's part.

From the following record of *Dongguan Zouji*,[12] we find a full and exact account of how, by writing on other examinees' behalf, Wen caused consternation among those concerned with the examinations.

> In the beginning, Pei Shen was concurrently in charge of supervising the candidates and presiding over the two special examinations, the Erudite Literatus and the Preeminent Talent. In that year there were a great number of Presented Scholars vying for these honors. . . . Shen was of a lenient and beneficent nature, and it was rumored that the topic of examination rhapsody had been divulged. The Registered Presented Scholar Liu Han was the son of Liu Xi, Magistrate of the Metropolitan Prefecture. In accordance with the established rule, the examination of Erudite Literatus chose only three candidates, but Han was among them. Those who had failed to pass complained that Han had known the rhapsody topic by way of Shen and then asked the writer Wen Tingyun to compose the rhapsody for him. After Han was chosen, an incessant racket of protest was made, and words of the affair reached His Majesty (初，裴諗兼上詮，主試宏拔二科。其年爭名者眾……諗寬豫仁厚，有賦題不密之說。前進士柳翰，京兆尹柳熹之子也。故事：宏詞科只三人，翰在選中。不中者言翰于諗處先得賦題，托詞人溫庭筠為之。翰既中選，其聲聒不止，事徹宸聽).

For convenience's sake, we will call this contretemps the Dazhong Ninth Year Incident. Ever since Wen had renewed his attempts to gain the Presented Scholar degree in the beginning of the Dazhong era, he had experienced many frustrations. In his repeated failures, he had acquired the "dishonorable" habit of aiding other examinees who were also taking the examinations. His actions in this respect precipitated a dramatic climax in the Dazhong Ninth Year Incident. By now Wen's voice was loud enough to get a nationwide hearing, and those in power could no longer ignore the question Wen raised by his actions: were the examinations controlled by the eunuchs or court officials loyal to His Majesty? In fact, Wen succeeded at this time in enlisting quite extensive support and sympathy from within the literati-officials' group. Some officials, whose sense of righteousness had not yet been obscured by the ruthless and chaotic realities of the times, were inspired by Wen's actions to stand up for social justice. Of course, enabling some to pass with assistance was not fair to those who lacked such assistance. But people might as well ask: since those aided by Wen could pass even the Erudite Literatus examination, one of the most difficult and advanced examinations, what were the special reasons that always served to prevent Wen from passing as a mere Presented Scholar?

The Dazhong Ninth Year Incident at the time had far-reaching consequences. It was recorded in JTS that because the candidates for the Erudite Literatus examination had learned the topic ahead of time, the Vice-Minister of the Ministry of Ritual, Pei Shen, was impeached by the Censorate and demoted.[13] This irregularity was even taken as a manifestation of Heaven's warning against human injustice: "At an earlier time, the Imperial Astrologer reported to His Majesty that the Literature Star had dimmed, presaging that there would be troubles in the examinations. Now what the Astrologer had reported proved true."[14] Wen's persistent efforts created turmoil and at last succeeded in shocking the ruling clique. As we have stated before, the fundamental political situation at the time remained largely unchanged. The eunuchs still exercised close control over court power and had the emperor in their hands. Despite his efforts, Wen could not rehabilitate himself and remained in disgrace for a long time. No Examination Administrator dared pass him, since the eunuchs were so opposed to him. Under such circumstances, Wen's underhanded performances amazed the world. This had the effect of appealing his case forcefully to those in power who had hitherto ignored it, and demanding a reasonable settlement.

There were undoubtedly disputes among those in power about the disposition of Wen's case. For them, never to pass Wen or never to punish Wen for his cheating was equally annoying, in view of the ambivalent responses such actions evoked. They could no longer fail him, confronted by the troubles Wen made. But to pass Wen, in addition to offending the eunuchs, was to defy the imperial dignity, because Wen's cheating was, after all, a violation of the law. After about three or four years' suspension, in the thirteenth year of Dazhong (859), Pei Tan, the then Secretariat Drafter, issued the following edict on behalf of the emperor.

"Edict for Demoting Wen Tingyun as the Defender of Suixian County:"[15]

Imperial behest to the Local Tribute Presented Scholar Wen Tingyun: At early age you followed the local representative and had long since

> built up a great reputation. You have vainly boasted of your unrestrained talent, which can scarcely suit the needs of the time. Therefore we exile a Qu Yuan by the banks of the Xiang River, and banish a Jia Yi at the marshes of Changsha. You can look forward to the day when the imperial mat will again be moved forward to you, and there is no hindering you from wielding your brush. Your appointment to Defender of Suixian County, Suizhou Prefecture is approved (敕鄉貢進士溫庭筠：早隨計吏，夙著雄名；徒負不羈之才，罕有適時之用。放屈原于湘浦，竄賈誼于長沙。尚有前席之期，未爽抽毫之思。可隨州隨縣尉).

The most interesting remarks in this imperial edict to demote Wen Tingyun is that it likens Wen to Qu Yuan and Jia Yi, traditionally the typical worthy court officials well known for their great talent, loyalty, and the injustice they suffered. Qu Yuan, the author of *Lisao*, was said to have been demoted to the banks of Xiang River. Jia Yi, toward whom the Han Emperor Wendi in an audience moved his mat forward (inquiring only, however, about the ghosts and spirits, but not about the people), was demoted to Changsha.[16]

The following points connected with this action merit our consideration:

First, as a result of Wen's numerous participations in and failures of the examinations, especially his notorious episodes of cheating, and in view of the nationwide repercussions of his behaviors, those in power finally agreed to confer the Presented Scholar degree on him, as a concession to outraged public opinion. What makes this action confusing is that the conferral of the Presented Scholar degree was made public simultaneously with a demotion. Whatever demotion could be imposed upon Wen at the moment was at the same time an official appointment that, as a rule, was conferred only upon those who had passed the Presented Scholar Examination and become a Presented Scholar. Wen's pass, however, presented itself as a very particular case.

Secondly, the imperial edict announcing the conferring of the degree is accompanied by the emperor's command that Wen be appointed as Defender of Suixian County.[17] This appointment was intended as a demotion brought about by Wen's lack of restraint. Demoting Wen to a remote county post would at the same time be acceptable to the eunuchs. Despite this, the edict is still confusing without further explanation. Prior to the Late Tang times, it was normal for a successful Presented Scholar to begin his official career with a lowly post such as Defender or something similar. How, then, had things progressed to the point that appointing a recently passed Presented Scholar, not yet possessing official standing, to the post of Defender, could amount to a *demotion*? We shall deal with the underlying reasons immediately below.

Thirdly, Pei Tan's "Edict Demoting Wen Tingyun" sounds more like an official eulogy than an imperial censure of Wen for his faults. The only expression of censure, that Wen "can scarcely suit the needs of the time," is painfully accurate—with his unruly and unconventional character and his stubborn defiance of the eunuchs, Wen was born in the wrong time and his talent was doomed to be wasted, in spite of his desire to cure the maladies of his country.

Fourthly, the contradictory implications of the edict have their historical context. As we have seen, to meet the political demands of the contending sides, the drafter Pei Tan was facing a painful decision, and he was at pains to redress the balance in Wen's particular case. In *Tangzhiyan* (11: 121), there is a passage concerning this:

> Among those in power, there was one who had an aversion to Wen and reported to His Majesty about his making trouble in the examination carrels, and Wen was demoted to Defender in Suizhou. At the time, it was Secretariat Drafter Pei Tan who was to draft the imperial edict. Pei, hesitating and flustered, held his writing brush for quite a while, before he consulted an old clerk by his side, on the promotion and demotion in question. The clerk replied: "Your Excellency ought to make some terms of reproach. Why? A Presented Scholar presenting a memorial [to His Majesty] is hardly inferior to an Assistant Prefect or Aide Magistrate of superior prefectures." Only then did Tan feel relieved. Therefore there appeared in his edict metaphors such as "Banks of the Xiang River" and "Marshes of Changsha" (執政間復有惡奏庭筠攪擾場屋，黜隨州縣尉。時中書舍人裴坦當制，忸怩含毫久之。時有老吏在側，因訊之升黜。對曰：舍人合為責詞，何者？入策進士，與望州長、馬一起資。坦釋然，故有澤畔長沙之比).

Here an old clerk conversant with the general rule governing official appointments came to the rescue of Pei Tan, who was at a loss as how to draft the edict. For the first official appointment of a successful Presented Scholar, however minor the position might be, the edict ought to be filled with praise and encouragement. In Wen's case, however, the appointment was disappointing and repulsive, as Pei Tan was fully aware. It defied common sense to use only positive language in an edict announcing such an appointment, while it was also contrary to the established rule to employ terms of reproach when appointing a Presented Scholar at the time. Since the old clerk pointed out bluntly the crux of the matter, namely, Wen's attainment of Presented Scholar degree was more a demotion than a promotion, Pei Tan need no longer hesitate as how to balance his praise and blame. Consequently, Pei Tan criticized Wen as one who "can scarcely suit the needs of the time"; then, to make up for this, he likened Wen to Qu Yuan and Jia Yi. This accounts for *Dongguan Zouji*'s meaningful comment after quoting the edict:

> His Majesty (Xuanzong) is a wise lord, yet Tingyun, quite unexpectedly, is demoted just because of his talent. . . . Isn't it because His Majesty attached so much importance to literature that he thought literature is a consummate art and became stingy when granting the

> degree? It is really something we cannot ask and know (上明主也，而庭筠反以才廢。豈以文學為極致已靳于斯，遂于祿位有所愛耶？不可得而問矣).

To put it bluntly, Pei Tingyu had in mind something that would be awkward to disclose, since he was unable to blame either Emperor Xuanzong or Tingyun. It could only be the eunuchs!

The old clerk's remark suggests that, at least during a period covering the Dazhong era, the Presented Scholar degree had risen to such an unprecedented height that most of those who succeeded in achieving it had much better official prospects than had been true hitherto. In the light of this development, Wen's passing was purposely undervalued. Indeed it was no more than a trick or an expedient resorted to in order to deceive the public. Nevertheless, the truth remained that Wen had passed, although in essence he was demoted. Pei Tan's edict, however, was and is taken as evidence of Wen's failure, and the clear evidence to the contrary in *Tangzhiyan* has been left unaccountably neglected.

In handling Wen's case in this manner, Pei Tan was making an effort to soothe his own conscience. However, he was nevertheless the dupe of those who manipulated the events behind the scenes, as is evidenced by the following passage in *Tangyulin* (7: 244):

> During the reign of Xuanzong, Wen was demoted to Defender of Suixian County. The edict said: "We send into exile a Qu Yuan to the banks of the Xiang River, and demote a Jia Yi to the Marshes of Changsha." This was Drafter Pei's remark which men of the time found laughable (宣宗時，謫為隨縣尉。制曰"放騷人于湘浦，移賈誼于長沙"。舍人裴坦之詞。世以為笑).

Dongguan Zouji also records that "noble men held up Pei's remarks to ridicule." People seemed to have ignored the dilemma Pei faced when drafting the edict: he was exposed to both criticisms from the public and pressure from his superiors. Not knowing the real story, those who mocked Pei generally held the preconception that Pei ought to be speaking on behalf of the state dynasty, whereas the allusions to Qu Yuan and Jia Yi do imply that Wen is considered a talented man wronged by the officials responsible, which is a free confession that the official quarters were in the wrong. He was thus held up to ridicule. However, thanks to Pei's conscience, we have in hand a picturesque literary sample reflecting realities that would otherwise have been even more difficult to discover.

The following weird and yet interesting poem cannot be omitted from our discussion. It may be the only extant poetic proof of Wen's "cheating," if our paraphrase of the poem is substantially correct. Here we will see how mischievous Wen Tingyun can be—it is not surprising at all that he has been misunderstood.

"On a Casual Topic" (偶題, j. 7, WFQ)

A peacock is sleeping in the tall tree,	孔雀眠高樹，
A cherry is touching the short eaves.	櫻桃拂短檐。
The painting shines with a golden sheen,	畫明金冉冉，
The *zheng* murmurs from a plucker of dainty jade.[18]	箏語玉纖纖。
A fine drizzle does no harm to the candle [light],	細雨無妨燭，
A gentle cold cannot be stopped from entering the curtain.[19]	輕寒不隔簾。
I would like to send a bolt of red brocade,	欲將紅錦緞，
To Jiang Yan by means of appearing in his dream.[20]	因夢寄江淹。

The allusion to Jiang Yan in the last couplet of this poem declares in unequivocal terms Wen's wish to use his outstanding aptitude to aid those literary men who could not write well. It also reflects Wen's conceit and condescension in so doing. According to Wen's habitual practice of manifesting the motif of a poem only at its end, the lines that precede the last couplet must be a veiled account paving the way for the Jiang Yan allusion, although it is very difficult to substantiate this hypothesis. However, if the poem as a whole is to make sense, intrinsic connections with the ending poetic conclusion must underlie all the other lines, even though, literally, these lines seem to be quite clear and to involve no identifiable poetic allusions. To this purpose, we strongly suggest that Wen's forte, the employment of punning homophones, is at work here.

The images of candle (*zhu*, 燭) and curtain (*lian*, 簾) in the third couplet, the former for lighting and the latter for separating the examinees from one another in their assigned carrels, serve to direct our attention to the examination environment. Most remarkably, "candle" (*zhu*) was often used in classic Chinese poems (including Wen's) as homonym of "to tell" (*zhu*, 囑). In order to determine the punning implication of the whole couplet, in addition to substituting "to tell" for "candle," we must also find out correspondingly what other key words the couplet might pun on or refer to. "Fine drizzle" (*xiyu*, 細雨) and "gentle cold" (*qinghan*, 輕寒), although at first glance seeming to speak about the weather, must also have some link with the punned "candle" and "curtain." Reconsidering Wen's behavior of aiding others during the examinations, we derive the following solution, which seems more reasonable than we first hoped.

"Fine drizzle" puns on "whispers" (細語),[21] that is, whispers exchanged among the examinees; while the Chinese term for "does no harm to" (無妨) also means "does not matter." So, the whole line of "Fine drizzle does no harm to the candle [light]" may have a punned meaning as "It does not matter to *tell* others in whispers" (細語無妨囑). In like manner, "gentle cold" (輕寒) puns on "short letters" (輕函),[22] or something similar to notepapers with answers written on them. Thus, "A gentle cold cannot be stopped from entering the curtain" (輕寒不隔簾) can mean "Notepapers (messages) cannot be hindered from passing on (secretly) through the curtains" (輕函不隔簾). In other words, the perfunctory invigilation could not prevent candidates in different carrels from transmitting messages to one another "through the curtains."

Insofar as we can imagine a metaphorical reading of the first couplet, we find that the peacock sleeping leisurely in a tall tree becomes a humorous image of Wen himself, a brilliant talent overlooking the examination affairs from a superior vantage point. The cherry, as we have explained in "Twenty-Two Rhymes of the Arched Door," presents itself as something attractive, say, the desired Presented Scholar degree. "Short eaves," a term we have encountered before in "Hundred-Rhyme Poem," here stands for a small and somewhat contemptible arena for the exercise of Wen's literary capacities, the civil service examination system as a whole.

Thus far three couplets out of the four have been paraphrased and the motif of the poem has been almost completely exposed, but as yet a tolerable explanation of how the second couplet uses homophones has yet to be propounded.[23] To avoid straining its meaning, we can proceed no farther without more solid evidence. At any rate, only by paraphrasing the couplets in the light of the puns discerned above are we able to make the last couplet, as a logical conclusion of the whole poem, stand on firm ground. It is obvious that leaving the allusions in this poem unsolved serves to perpetuate the misinformation found in the records in the two *Tang Histories*.

To sum up, after Li Yong's death in 839, more than twenty years elapsed before Wen was finally awarded the Presented Scholar degree, along with the minor post of Defender of Suixian County (the lower ninth rank). This was a position much lower than the ones he had held in the Cassia Area, and a position which could be attained without possessing a Presented Scholar degree. It is understandable that Wen was unable to rest content. Therefore, having earned the degree, he embarked upon new efforts to obtain a better position more in keeping with his talents. Such efforts consumed the last years of his life.

After Wen was demoted to Suixian County in 859, according to JTS:

> When Xu Shang was in charge of the garrison of Xiangyang,[24] Wen went there to depend on Xu, who assigned him the post of local inspector[25] (徐商鎮襄陽，往依之，署巡官).

From this time forward, as a man of more than sixty years of age, Wen continually directed appeals through those in power to the throne. The extant records reveal that he finally succeeded in finding a position in the capital, Instructor of the State Sons' University (國子助教). Shortly after, as a result of his sympathy for literati of humble origins, he was once more sent into exile, and died while in exile.

We do not have space to cover every detail of Wen's experiences during this period, because confirming these details presents a whole series of challenging problems. We will, however, consider one additional example showing the result of Wen's efforts in the third year of Xiantong (862), when he was demoted to Defender of Fangcheng. This example is the following poem by Ji Tangfu (紀唐夫, fl. 862):

"SEEING OFF WEN FEIQING TO BE DEFENDER OF FANGCHENG"
(送溫飛卿尉方城, QTS, 542: 6257, YUNXI YOUYI, 47)

Why, in a bright age, do you frequently weep over your jade?	何事明時泣玉頻？
In Chang'an, you cannot see the Apricot Garden in spring.[26]	長安不見杏園春。
Though the Phoenix Edict came down, conferring on you a degree,	鳳凰詔下雖沾命，
"The Parrot" with its brilliant talent brought upon you mischief.[27]	鸚鵡才高卻累身。
Please drink Green Wine, to assuage your pent-up rage,	且飲錄醑銷積恨，
Don't refuse the Yellow Ribbon, trailed in the dust of journey.[28]	莫辭黃綬拂行塵。
How can Fangcheng be as distant as Changsha?	方城若比長沙遠？
But it's still a thousand hills and ten thousand streams away.	猶隔千山與萬津。

Ji likened Wen, with his unrecognized talent and loyalty to the empire, to the heartbroken Bian He whose priceless jade was left unappreciated, and to the outspoken Ni Heng whose daring spirit invited ruin. Though Wen had at last narrowly passed as a Presented Scholar, he did not benefit from the degree, for upon attaining it he received only demotions. All these misfortunes, Ji points out, occurred because of Wen's unrestrained character, a character that did not allow catering to the influential. In his efforts to comfort Wen, Ji suggests that he pour the Green Wine to assuage his grief, and that he make the best of a bad situation, by accepting the demotions. For, in Ji's words, Fangcheng was after all not as far away as Changsha, the place to which Jia Yi, with whom Wen often identified, had been demoted.

As a very insightful summary of Wen's life, Ji's poem expressed public sympathy with Wen, and was very popular in Wen's day. *Tangzhiyan* (11: 121) records: "When Wen went to the post of Defender of Fangcheng, men of letters and poets vied with one another in addressing him with poems as a farewell gift. Ji Tangfu's poem was the most outstanding"

(庭筠之任，文士詩人爭為辭送。惟紀唐夫得其尤). *Yunxi Youyi* (47) also comments: "Either that Tingyun became Defender, or that Ji Tangfu won fame, was a result of his literary compositions" (庭筠作尉，紀唐夫得名，蓋因文而致也). These provide evidence that Wen was popular among those who were out of power and had a sense of justice, and unwelcome among those who were in power and had reacted against this same sense. Depreciation of Wen's character while ignoring this telling fact, therefore, indicates acceptance of the historical biases.

THE TRUTH OF THE FOURTEEN PUSAMAN

In chapter 4, we quoted accounts in the two *Tang Histories* that are a misrepresentation of the Jianghuai Incident—not only misdated as happening in the Xiantong era, but also mistaken as relating to Linghu Tao. Now we need to clarify Wen's relationship with the Linghu family, and, if possible, clarify the basic causes leading to the aforementioned fallacy in the standard histories.

In records such as *Tongxin* or *Yuquanzi*, which form the earliest sources about the Jianghuai Incident (836) and Wen's change of name (839), the two affairs, which in reality occurred three years apart, were already intermingled. After initiating this confusion, these two sources of information about Wen's life were quoted over and again, gradually and firmly establishing the false impression.

In other sources, such as Wang Dingbao's *Tangzhiyan* (11: 121), we read:

> During the Kaicheng years, Wen Tingyun became notorious because of his talent, but he rarely limited himself to small niceties, and made his compositions a kind of commodity. Men of good taste held him in contempt. Before long, among those in power, there was one who had an aversion to Wen and reported to His Majesty about his making trouble in the examination carrels (開成間，溫庭筠才名藉甚。然罕拘細行，以文為貨，識者鄙之。無何，執政間復有惡奏庭筠攪擾場屋).

Despite the correct statement that Wen became notorious in the Kaicheng era, Wen's experiences at that time are confused, blended together with affairs occurring more than twenty years later in the Dazhong era. Similar mistakes also appear in Ji Yougong's *Tangshi Jishi* (54: 822). Most probably, confusion occurred because the authors made no distinction between Wen's two different behaviors when dealing with the examination: changing his own name in order to sit for the examination and assuming someone else's name to take it. The former behavior was Wen's attempt to escape the eunuchs' hostile supervision and earn himself the degree, the latter, as we have pointed out, can be regarded as his special way of protesting long years of injustice. In any event, records in *Tangzhiyan* and elsewhere have only succeeded in creating more confusion.

The authors of the two *Tang Histories* failed to make discriminating use of the above-mentioned sources. Faced with various distorted reports already circulating and wishing to establish their own version of Wen's life, they bungled the disposition of their sources. As a result, the standard histories, which were originally intended to excel the anecdotal sources in accuracy, instead yield a glaring counterfeit, inferior in its authenticity to all earlier accounts of Wen's life.

According to the editors of *Siku Quanshu Zongmu Tiyao*, the fundamental causes of the mistakes in the two *Tang Histories* are as follows:[29]

> Ever since the Changqing (821–824) era, the state historiographers had been no longer functioning [as a result of the chaos of the time], and there were no reliable records [for composing the biographies]. [Liu] Xu et al. (the authors of JTS) had to avail themselves of miscellaneous fictions or biographies in other sources, which, after some rearrangements, were compiled into the biographies of their works (長慶以後，史失其官，無復善本。煦等自采雜説，排纂成之).

These were the circumstances under which JTS was edited, and thus it is small wonder that there are serious errors in the biographies of many of the men of the time, especially men such as Wen.

Most of the crucial events in Wen's life occurred just after the Changqing era. These events, although they were closely connected to the corresponding political situations, were enveloped in the shadow of the struggles between the Southern and the Northern Offices and the strife between the Niu and the Li factions. Even though some of the anecdotes about the factional strife occasionally mentioned some aspects of Wen's life, more often than not, owing to the limited quantity of sources and the prejudices of their authors, their accounts of Wen's actions appeared, on the whole, confusing and incredible. When the sources were contradictory, they left readers totally ignorant of what to believe. This is the congenital deficiency afflicting all of Wen's biographies.

What is more, while attempting to gather more information from Wen's own surviving works in an effort to make up for the scarcity of historical materials, the biographers were faced with an extremely ambiguous poet whose works were laden with allusions to the behind-the-scenes affairs of the political arena, which posed great difficulties for the historiographers composing his biography.

Because neither JTS nor XTS contains a reasonable account of Wen's life, it is incumbent upon modern scholars to come up with one. The misinterpretation of the Jianghuai Incident by the two *Tang Histories* resulted from a failure to make effective use of historical materials and from an overemphasis on the factional strife, resulting in the neglect of the struggle between the court officials and the eunuchs. The picture the Song historiographers offered of the Incident therefore is totally inaccurate, ignoring the maneuvering eunuchs and illuminating only one individual of the Southern Offices—

Linghu Tao. As we discerned before, other interested persons such as Yao Xu, Han Yi, Linghu Chu, and Li Shi, are ignored altogether.

The Jianghuai Incident occurred only a few years after Linghu Tao had passed his Presented Scholar examinations,[30] making him unable to play a role in the Incident. His implication in the Incident may have resulted from his being mistaken for his father Linghu Chu, who became Salt and Iron Commissioner, following the murdered Prime Minister Wang Ya. Since Li Shi and Han Yi, both officials in the Salt and Iron Monopoly Bureau in the same period, were implicated either in the Sweet Dew Incident or in the Jianghuai Incident, it would not be surprising that Linghu Chu might also have become the target of rumors during the event. In the Song historiographers' meager biography of Wen, it would not be uncommon for the father to be mistaken for the son. On the other hand, Linghu Tao rose to power in the Dazhong era, the time when Wen suffered his successive failures, and so Wen might have directed complaints against him then. Since Linghu Tao frustrated Wen's good friend Li Shangyin,[31] he would have been capable of treating Wen in much the same manner. It might be from this that Wen's biographers seem to have drawn their inferences.

Actually, before the Kaicheng era, Wen could for a time have been possibly connected with Linghu Chu. According to Wen's remark in his "Epistle Presented to Prime Minister Linghu (Tao)": "I cherish a feeling to ask favor from my family's old friend" (蓋牽求舊之情). Therefore, I suggest that Wen's friendship with the Linghus began much earlier, during his acquaintance with Tao's father, Linghu Chu. After Linghu Tao ascended to the prime ministership (in 850), Wen was initially accepted as a distinguished guest at Linghu's mansion, when he came to the capital once more. As Xin Wenfang's *Tang Caizizhuan* has it (8:135): "Wen frequented the study of Prime Minister Linghu and was very favorably accepted" (出入令狐相國書館中，待遇甚優).

This being the case, why was Linghu Tao not able to help Wen to become a Presented Scholar? On Wen's part, he could not have been contented with being the Prime Minister's idle guest. On Linghu Tao's part, he could not even allow his own son Linghu Hao to pass during his long tenure as Prime Minister, for fear of hostile responses from among the court officials. In Wen's case, the situation was more complex. When the two men were on good terms with each other, Linghu simply was not able to help. Later, when there appeared problems in their friendship, he was neither willing nor able to help. He was unable to help because Wen was a thorn in the side of the eunuchs. He was unwilling to help because Wen had a sharp tongue and often satirized the abuses of the time. Whether in good humor or bad, he frequently laid bare contradictions that Linghu Tao tried to cover up. In the eyes of many people in authority, Wen exhibited no understanding of the political affairs of the time, and talented poet though he was, he was regarded as incapable of accomplishing anything. Therefore, Wen's friendship with the Linghus was not merely a question of personal relationships, but was tainted by the factional strife and shadowed by eunuch power. As to the degree of the deterioration of their relations, it was possible that Wen might pass Linghu's mansion without asking for an audience (as JTS states), or that Linghu could cold-shoulder him as an unwelcome guest. Whatever might have happened between them, they were not enemies, and Linghu should not be held responsible for Wen's career failures.

Now we are able to study the background and nature of the Pusaman series.

This is a question of lasting controversy and fascination and of considerable importance in Chinese literary history. We will attempt to reach a new conclusion through a restudy of the series, as a natural and logical outcome of our examination of Wen's life and poetry. Sun Guangxian's *Beimeng Suoyan* (4: 29) says:[32]

> Emperor Xuanzong liked the singing of Pusaman. Prime Minister Linghu Tao took and secretly presented to His Majesty Wen Tingyun's twenty compositions to the tune. Linghu warned Wen not let the affair leak out, but soon after, he told others. Because of this, Linghu became estranged from Wen. Thereupon Wen remarked, "In the Hall of the Secretariat there sits a general," satirizing Linghu for his lack of learning (宣宗愛唱菩薩蠻詞。丞相令狐綯假溫庭筠手撰二十首密進。誡令勿泄，而遽言于人，由是疏之。溫亦有言"中書堂內坐將軍"，譏相國無學).

In studying this record, we find the following points meriting our attention.

First, we must stress that this record is trustworthy. The Tang emperors often ordered their literary servants to compose poems to be matched with music and sung in the inner court. There are numerous similar examples: Li Bai wrote "Qingping Yue"; Wang Jian (王建) presented one hundred "palace verses" (宮詞); Yuan Zhen's poems were popular among the palace ladies, who nicknamed him "Talented Literatus Yuan" (元才子); Bai Juyi, while holding the position of Hanlin Academician, composed at the emperor's order some palace-style verses.[33] It was not strange that the Dazhong emperor ordered his Prime Minister to gather words to sing to Pusaman, his favorite tune.

Responding to the imperial order, Linghu Tao, having the wisdom to recognize Wen's talent, chose Wen as the right man to carry it out. As his attendance on the Heir had demonstrated, Wen was adept at composing exquisite palace-style poems. Linghu Tao's submission of Wen's Pusaman poems indicates how much he appreciated Wen's aptitude for writing; he must have also sympathized with Wen in his depression, and regarded Wen as his confidential retainer. But why did he present the compositions to the emperor *secretly* and warn Wen not to reveal any details of the affair?

Generally, during the Tang Dynasty, presenting poems to the emperors to be sung in the palaces was never a clandestine activity, nor did the emperors keep such presentations a secret from other officials. A court official who received the imperial commission to create such poems was not doing anything wrong if he divulged the affair to the public. Moreover, if the verses were to be sung in the palaces and thus brought into fashion, it was only natural that the name of the author would be publicized, just as in the cases of Li, Wang, Bai, and Yuan. In Wen's case, there must have been reasons for the secrecy.

In considering Linghu Tao's personal background and situation, we must first determine whether it was possible that he wished to take credit for the authorship of Wen's works, as a means of currying more imperial favor. Though this possibility can be easily inferred from the surface story, this was definitely not the case. According to his biographies, Linghu Tao ascended to the prime ministership by dint of his partisanship, as the son of Linghu Chu, one of the most influential leaders of the Niu Faction. In his capacity as an expert politician rather than an outstanding literatus, he was already in high favor with Xuanzong, a favor on no account earned, or in need of buttressing, by his literary talent. On the contrary, as the leading Prime Minister throughout Xuanzong's reign, he had been recommending eminent poets to His Majesty, because this was part of his official obligations and he wished to show that he was a competent and conscientious Prime Minister. Examples include his recommendation to Emperor Xuanzong two famous poets, Li Qunyu (李群玉) and Li Yuan (李遠),[34] the latter of whom, as we know from the title of "Hundred-Rhyme Poem," was Wen's good friend. There is no reason to believe that Linghu wished to plagiarize Wen's works.

Obviously, Linghu Tao's secrecy suggests that he wished to utilize Wen's literary talent without letting the affair be publicized. Nobody at the time dared to promote Wen because of the risk of provoking the eunuchs' political hostility. Even Xuanzong and this influential Prime Minister harbored enormous fear of the eunuchs.[35] Inevitably the eunuch's rage would be aroused if Wen's compositions were allowed to circulate in the palaces under his own name. The works would enjoy great popularity and bring credit upon Wen, their foe, a man driven by the desire to avenge himself and to rehabilitate himself for the injustices they had visited on him. In his compositions, whatever their form, Wen asserted himself by literary means, both overt and covert, investing them with deeply personal feelings stemming from the frustrations of his political life. We have seen such assertions in many of his representative works. Could the Pusaman series be an exception?

Noticing that Wen composed the Pusaman poems while he was still on good terms with Linghu, that is, in about the middle of the Dazhong era, we realize that he was at the time impatient to rid himself of political pressures from the eunuchs, which had frustrated him for so many years. Now that his poems would be circulated in the palaces and he could use them to serve the emperor directly, he, very understandably, thought his chance had come. Unlike Linghu Tao, who desired only to delight the emperor with exquisite works while attaching little importance to who the author was, Wen desired to give voice to his feelings using his poems. It is small wonder that he, as the author, would not keep his identity hidden. To meet the demand of the emperor, he tried to his utmost to cater to the palace taste, bringing into full play his consummate literary skills in an attempt to court imperial favor. At the same time, he used the opportunity to give vent to his painful feelings and to bare his heart to His Majesty, in the same way as if he were presenting a memorial or rhapsody (獻賦), to explain himself. In these circumstances, a group of most exquisite, delicate, subtle, and circuitous Pusaman *ci* poems were brought into being. However, the revelation that Wen was the author of these poems created troubles, and sowed discord between the two friends, one a Prime Minister and the other a commoner.

As Chinese literary appreciation and comments for more than a thousand years have evidenced, without knowing the authorship of the Pusaman poems, even Wen's contemporary connoisseurs could not readily sense the deep implications contained in the series. They could at most reach an understanding that the author, as a frustrated man of letters, was very proficient at representing the life and mentality of the palace ladies. To readers of later generations, who have remained ignorant of the hidden aspects of Wen's life, Wen's masterpieces are most attractive and baffling, and a matter of lasting controversy. They are attractive because of exquisite design and sentimental mood. They are baffling because they challenge pedestrian reading with aesthetic mystery. From the perspective of palace-style poetry, as Chen Tingchuo, the representative of the Changzhou School, suggests, "The fourteen Pusaman of Feiqing, all modeled on and changed from *Lisao*, are a consummate exemplar of all times. It is mistake if the reader only appreciates the freshness and beauty in them" (飛卿菩薩蠻十四首，全祖離騷，所以獨絕千古。徒賞其芊麗，誤也).[36] In Chen's terms, Wen's masterpieces in the Pusaman series, with their picturesque depiction of the palace-lady and penetrating revelations of her mentality, "have reached an unattainable height, and none of the later writers can compose anything comparable to them" (已臻絕詣，後來莫能為繼). However, because this series of poems is more densely conceived, it transcended the palace style and was enduringly appreciated by later generations of readers.

We have every reason to take the fourteen pieces as a series. The techniques of composing *shi* poems in series had matured since Du Fu's time, though it was Wen who was among the trailblazers in composing such series in the domain of *ci* poetry, expressing his personal feelings while covertly telling his story. Wen's Pusaman series originally contained twenty pieces. Each poem in the series had to conform to the form of "palace-style verse" and be easy to sing. At the same time, each poem in the series had to be independent and the series as an artistic whole had to possess a consistent style. To put into the series the aesthetic burden of a lifetime, with every line saturated with feelings, and especially, with experiences imprinted on the poet's mind by life, required amazing elaboration.

It can be imagined what the various responses were after "Wen told others" after the series was circulating inside and outside the palaces.

Firstly, in so doing, Wen contravened Linghu Tao's wishes, and invited trouble from the eunuchs. Secondly, the eunuchs would certainly not be content to let the matter rest. Since what had been done could not be undone, several pieces of the series, most probably the less veiled ones, were taken out of circulation in an attempt to cope with censure from the eunuchs. What we have available today are only fourteen Pusaman pieces, like a Venus without arms; and it is challenging to imagine what the original arms were like.

Another question can be raised: "Were these compositions (the fourteen pieces) presented as a series to the throne during Wen's lifetime or were they simply an ensemble of all his works under the same topic composed at various moments of his life?"[37] This seems easy to answer, for, in *Jinlianji*, there is another Pusaman piece (starting 玉纖彈處珍珠落, see WFQ, 228), which, despite being about a palace lady, was never compiled with the fourteen pieces under discussion here. Moreover, the fourteen Pusaman poems first appeared as a series in *Huajianji*, a collection edited by Zhao Chongzuo in the third year of Guangzheng of the Latter Shu Dynasty (940), only some seventy years after Wen's death. From any perspective, it is impossible that the fourteen Pusaman poems could have been combined without a definite purpose. They form an inseparable artistic unity. In the series, from the beginning to the end, the narrative threads, subjective feelings, the thought of image, linguistic style, the prototype (of *a* palace lady) and even the mood and diction, are all consistent with one another.

Politics and love are the dominant concerns running through Wen's whole life. Wen is an "orthodox" figure, because all his life he never gave up his ambition to serve his country and secure his fame for later generations, employing his literary talent, loyalty, conscientiousness, and integrity. At the same time, Wen is also an unorthodox figure, because, driven by true love for the object of his affections, he acted like a man of modern times, regardless of the so-called niceties and decencies and in defiance of the social conventions of his day. Politics intruded into his private life, but on the other hand it was his private life that ruined his political career. Private love affairs and public political affairs were uniquely interwoven throughout his life, finding expression in Wen's peculiar technique: "using the feelings between the lad and lass, to speak about the affairs between monarch and his subjects" (以兒女之情，言君臣之事). Grounding ourselves on our observations in chapter 6, we can further define Wen's representative and characteristic poetic style: his preference for ornate appearances, in the shape of private love affairs, as vehicles for subtle ideas and feelings about his political experiences. The "Twenty-Two Rhymes of the Arched Door" has provided a most convincing example of this style. In Wen's extant works, there are other examples even more revelatory of this style, for instance, many of the poems on the topic of the Heir Apparent. Before explicating the labyrinthine Pusaman series, let us study the following poem:

"JIANGNAN AIR" (j. 2, WFQ)

1	My abode is on White-Fern Bank,[38]	妾家白蘋浦，
	Every day I board a Hibiscus skiff.	日上芙蓉檝。
2	Row upon row, bending over my oars,	軋軋搖槳聲，
	I move the vessel amid the wild-rice leaves.	移舟入茭葉。
3	The stream is long, the wild-rice deep,	溪長茭葉深，
	Try as you can, it's hard to find me.	作底難相尋。
4	To keep away from the lad and not let him see,	避郎郎不見，
	I watch the wild-ducks swim and dip.	鸂鶒自浮沉。
5	I pick the duckweeds, duckweeds without root,	拾萍萍無限，
	I collect the lotus, lotus with seeds.[39]	采蓮蓮有子。
6	I would rather die as a lotus flower,	不作浮萍生，
	Than live as a floating duckweed.	寧為藕花死。
7	There is a riding lad near the bank,	岸傍騎馬郎，
	In black gauze cap, a purple-roving-rein in hand.	烏帽紫游韁。
8	With unspoken sorrow and a forced smile,	含愁復含笑，
	I turn away, to look for Cross Pond.[40]	回首向橫塘。
9	I used to live in Jinling riverside,	妾住金陵步，
	In front of my door was Red Bird Ferry.[41]	門前朱雀航。
10	With colored tassels decorating my bed-curtains,	流蘇持作帳，
	And Hibiscus timber making the house beams.	芙蓉持作梁。
11	In and out went my carriage of golden calf canopy,	出入金犢幰，
	My brothers were all court celebrities.[42]	兄弟侍中郎。
12	In years past I learned to sing and dance,	前年學歌舞，
	To make sure I would obtain my lad's affections.	定得郎相許。
13	My eyebrows, dim and nice, curved like distant hills,	連娟眉繞山，
	My waist, slender and dainty, hardly thicker than a handspan.	依約腰如杵。
14	The phoenix pipe was so mournful it seemed to sob,	鳳管悲若咽，
	The simurgh string with its fragile chord was about to speak.[43]	鸞弦嬌如語。
15	My fan is thin, the red powder on my face shown through,	扇薄露紅鉛，
	My silk robe is light, weighed down with golden threads.	羅輕壓金縷。

16 The bright moon shone over the Southwestern Palace, 明月西南樓，
Where the pearled-curtains were hooked with hawks-bill-shell.[44] 珠簾玳瑁鉤。
17 Bright waves in my eyes are capable of captivating smiles, 橫波巧能笑，
While my curved moth eyebrows knew no grief. 彎蛾不識愁。
18 After the flower withered, the fruits were left on the tree, 花開子留樹，
And when grasses grow, their roots would be attached to clay. 草長根依土。
19 Had I known the Golden Ditch was this far away,[45] 早知金溝遠，
Why would I have married myself off to my lad? 何事歸郎許？
20 But I won't follow the example of White Flower Yang, 不學楊白花，
And shed tears like showers of rain, day after day.[46] 朝朝淚如雨。

This is a Music Bureau verse of a considerable narrative content. We will first take an overall look at the story employed by the poet in his depiction of the heroine.

At her first appearance, as a native of the "White-Fern Isle," the lotus-gathering lady is paddling her dainty "Hibiscus" skiff into the depths of the water grasses to hide herself. She is a devoted lover who would rather die for her affection than indiscreetly change her resolution. When a riding lad with "purple-roving-rein in hand" comes in sight on the bank, she purposely turns away from him, and then recounts a story of her glorious past: she used to live in an extremely rich family at the capital Jinling and was in great favor with her beloved and eminent husband; but great joy turned to sorrow: she was reduced, with regret, to her old way of life. The life of the heroine can be divided into three stages: early maiden days, happy married days, and present reflective days. Each of these "stands for" a period in Wen's life: early years before serving in the court, attendance of the Heir, and forced retreat to the south in the Huichang era.

Ambiguity enters this story when we try to discern the identity of the lady's husband. But toward the end of the poem, we read: "Had I known the Golden Ditch was this far away / Why would I have married myself off to my lad?" The Golden Ditch, the name of an imperial ditch, is used synecdochically here as a substitute for the imperial palaces or the royal family. Thus, this lady's former husband is a member of the royal family living in the imperial palace, as we can guess, at the moment.

When we trace back a little farther, we find that the evidence becomes clearer: "The bright moon shone over the Southwestern Palace / Where there were the pearled-curtains, hooked with hawks-bill-shell"—here there is no doubt that the lady in her former days lived in one of the palaces. The second line is even reminiscent of the *Shaoyangyuan* in "Twenty-Two Rhymes of the Arched Door," the residence of the Heir Apparent. It is no wonder that her surroundings were so sumptuous and luxurious.

Is her late husband really an Heir Apparent? One more clue in the poem will bring home the inference that he is. Why does the lady under the poet's writing brush "turn away" from the "riding lad" who holds the "purple-roving-rein"? It is because the riding lad is *not* the imperial crowned prince, as can be seen clearly in the following folksong which first used the special term "purple-roving-rein":[47]

Green, green are the poplars on the imperial way,	青青御路楊，
There are your white horse and a purple-roving-rein.	白馬紫游繮。
Since you are not the imperial crowned prince,	汝非皇太子，
How can you gain the sweet dew libation?	安得甘露漿？

As a poetic clue, this offers much food for thought. It is evident that the man the lotus-gathering lady turns away from is one who is "not the imperial crowned prince." In other words, the man she devotes her affections to is none other than the Heir.[48] As to why the lady lived in Jinling, the ancient capital of the Six Dynasties, instead of Chang'an, this substitution is one of Wen's frequently used tropes to demonstrate rather than obfuscate his true meaning.

It might seem strange that a beautiful lady, having served in the palace, should have come back to her native place in the Yue region to engage once more in lotus gathering.[49] We only know of the actual occurrence of the reverse: there had been a famous beauty Xi Shi (西施) who was sent from the Yue countryside to the Wu palace. The lady in question here even has had the remarkable experience of serving an imperial Heir, though she is reluctant to speak about his death. Put in the context of the Late Tang times, such a tale is hardly imaginable. Even if such a situation were possible, Wen's life experiences give the poetic subterfuge away. Wen finds it convenient to give expression to his feelings through such a story. The title of a Music Bureau topic provides him more freedom to compose poetry so as "to await collectors of poems" (以俟采詩者).[50] Like the director of a film, he compels his actress to play the part he intends her to play. As a result, the beautiful lady was from the Yue region like Xi Shi and, like Wen, went into the palace in the service of the Heir Apparent, and then returned to her old way of life. Thus, she became a "refurbished version" of Wen's life. It becomes obvious that the lotus-gathering lady is an embodiment of Wen's self-image, and the story of her entering the palace and coming back to Yue hints obliquely at Wen's attendance upon the Heir and return to Jiangdong. In view of this, we infer that this poem must have been written during the Huichang era.

Closer scrutiny of each line uncovers the metaphorical details. One more example is: "The phoenix pipe was so mournful it seems to sob / The simurgh string with its fragile chord was about to speak." If we recall the legend (see chapter 5) that Qiao, the Heir Apparent of King Ling of Zhou, liked playing the *Sheng* to imitate the cry of the phoenix, we immediately perceive the overtone of the so-called "phoenix pipe," that the lady's husband is a crowned prince. As to the "simurgh string," it suggests a heartrending music. In the mournful notes of the flutes and chords, we sense the lady's deep grief connected with her vain attempts to retrieve her failure. This is a figure for the grief resulting from Wen's futile efforts to find any remedy for his situation.

Therefore, by pursuing the trail of poetic implications in the poem and comparing the narrative details with Wen's actual experiences of attending the Heir, and by then taking into consideration the blank spaces in the poem's narrative structure, we will come to realize the poem's ingenuity and grasp its hidden motifs. Having realized this, it is worth our while to glance back at the image of the lotus-gathering lady. Among the elements constituting the image, some characteristics are unrealistic or idealized; and while some individual aspects may be realistic, the combined effect is surrealistic. A lady might have served in the palace, and she might have lived in the Yue region, but it is inconceivable that she could, after the remarkable event of having served an Heir in the royal palace, come back to Yue region still in the prime of life. Despite this, seen in its entirety, the image of the lotus-gathering lady possesses many realistic characteristics. Her peculiar experiences and mentality mirror exactly the poet's life experiences; to such a degree that even concrete particulars in the poet's political career were made manifest through the dramatic performance and exposure of the lady's inner world. The unrealistic, idealized characteristics or the realistic, specific ones are the different sides of the same coin. The poet secretes in his poem a seemingly inscrutable riddle that forces the reader to think deeply in order to arrive, after painstaking labors, at an answer.

We remember that in "Twenty-Two Rhymes of the Arched Door" Wen likened himself to the "Immortal Lad" and the Heir to the "Jade Lass." Here, with reference to the same affair, he changes his part, taking on the female role. Historically, in pre-Qin Chinese poetry, there is a tradition of likening courtship of a girl to serving one's monarch. In poetry after the Tang Dynasty, as a result of the centuries-old moral demand that a wife serve her husband and that an official serve his monarch, it was more frequently the case that the poet likens himself to the woman. It is true that a court official was more subject to the wanton domination of his monarch than a woman was to the fickleness of her husband. In Wen's poetry, however, even though he might assume the part of a woman, that role could hardly muffle his spirited, masculine voice. Nevertheless, pursuing the narrow artistic path of "using the feelings between the lad and lass, to speak about the affairs between Monarch and his subjects." Wen had arrived at an extreme point that was at the same time both an insurmountable peak and a dead end. With respect to sublimity of verbal beauty, richness of imagery, and profundity of subject matter, we can say that Wen has really reached an insurmountable peak. However, faced with the narrative details cloaked in dense and subtle metaphors and allusions, readers could not always follow the ideas Wen meant to express. Such poetry, more often than not, was too obscure for uninitiated readers to fathom. In this sense, we opine that Wen has proceeded too far down his literary path and has encountered a dead end.

Now we are ready to attempt an overall explanation of the Pusaman series.

In the current state of studies of this series, four theories exist. Zhang Huiyan (1761–1837) and the Qing Dynasty Changzhou School of *ci*-poetry represented by him maintained that the series must have a deeper theme than it exhibits on the surface (that is, it has *jituo*),[51] something concerned with the author's political experiences. From the sixteen *ci* poems Zhang selected for discussion from Wen's works, including the Pusaman series, Zhang claimed that the Pusaman series contains a motif in which "a scholar laments not meeting his lord" (此感士不遇也). As to the artistry used in the series, Zhang felt that "there are flashbacks along with the unfolding of every stanza" (用節節逆敘). Throughout the series runs the main thread of a dream, just as the series "opens with a scene of waking from the dream" (從夢曉領起). In this multi-act dream all the hidden yearnings of the heroine are implied, with an idea (as lofty as that) of *Lisao*'s "original raiment"[52] (離騷初服之意)—a token of Qu Yuan's innate virtue. Scholars represented by Wang Guowei (1877–1927) were very opposed to Zhang's theory;[53] some of them even said that Wen "was nothing more than a frustrated literary man, so how could he have had such breadth of vision as to bewail the times and pity the people?"[54] In order to discredit the *jituo* theory, even the authorship of the series was groundlessly denied. The third theory was represented by Professor Shi Zhecun, who thought that the "hidden-motifs" theory could be justified as a kind of normative reading, in that it fits with Chinese literary tradition. However, he continued, "It is a mistake to suppose that Wen had the intention to express his 'hidden motifs' when he set brush to paper."[55] A fourth approach is to enjoy and value this series without bothering to discern whether or not it has any hidden motifs at all, and, perhaps to make the readings easier, simply to regard the poetry as "purely objective."[56] These four theories share a common shortcoming: none of them is based on a sufficient understanding of Wen's life and Wen's literary theory. Although few critics have endorsed Zhang's theory, we will see that he was basically correct. The only fault we find in him is that he raised his theory without making an adequate investigation of Wen's life.

Our general understanding of the series, not conforming to any of the above theories, can be summarized in the following two points:

First, we should observe the series as an entirety not only as a lyric but also as a narrative. As we weave the narrative threads together, we will see the story that the series tells. We find that the heroine is a frustrated court lady as beautiful as Xi Shi. Originally, she "took residence in the curve of a Yue stream" (家住越溪曲, No. 9). She and her husband "Met each other in the season of the peonies / But too soon were we forced to part" (相見牡丹時，暫來還別離。No. 3). She had to return to her native place in the south of the Yangtze River: "From the painted tower no more news was heard / Amid the fragrant herbs, by the southern bank of the River" (畫樓音信斷，芳草江南岸。No. 10). She cherished a heartrending memory of the past: "In those days I knew to treasure myself / but the past events I cannot bear to recollect" (當年還自惜，往事哪堪憶？No. 12). Now that "The messages from the jade gate are scarce" (玉關音信希。No. 4), she can only lament the miserable status that "Wu Palace in my old country was far away" (故國吳宮遠。No. 14), and that "When I was yearning for you, I dreamed no dream" (相憶夢難成。No. 8). There is no mistaking the inferences that all these particulars are strikingly similar to the experiences of the lotus-gathering lady in "Jiangnan Air," and it is irresistible to infer that the two poems share the same subject matter. We also find in the case of this lady a three-stage life similar to that of the lotus-gathering lady: her early years, service at the court, and forced retreat to the south, hence yet another version of Wen's life, although the narrative details here are scattered through the series, serving to divert the reader's attention from discovering the story itself.

Secondly, the series is more than a palace-style poetic account of the yearning lady's feelings; it is also a political allegory for the frustrated Wen Tingyun. Throughout the series, the man who is the object of the heroine's affections, like the lad in "Jiangnan Air," never appears on the scene. There are, however, enough hints to suggest that he is no ordinary lad but a substitute for, or an incarnation of, the late Heir. As more examples will reveal, there are many clues in the series serving to bring out the hidden motifs, so many that they cannot merely be unintentional revelations of the author's persona. Meanwhile, when reading the poem, we cannot rest content with enjoying the beauty of the heroine and being touched by the affective power of the images surrounding her. Instead, we must probe into the depths of her inner world, to determine why we involuntarily respond to the poem with sympathetic inspiration. In Wen's poetry, the surface appearance of the poem often serves to create an ambience that at the same time moves and baffles the reader. Only by penetrating the surface can we completely discover the buried aesthetic treasure. In illustrating these points, the following serves as our first example:

In my languorous dream, I recall the Golden Hall,	閑夢憶金堂，
Facing a courtyard covered with luxuriant daylilies.	滿庭萱草長。(No. 13)

Understood literally, when the lady dreams of her past in "the Golden Hall," the moving sight of the palace courtyard with its exuberant daylilies appears before her eyes. To grasp the figurative meaning of this couplet, we must trace the implications of the Chinese term *daylilies* (萱草), *Hemerocallis*. It was also known in ancient China as *yinan* (宜男), "good-for-bearing-sons herb," or *wangyou* (忘憂), the "forgetting-sorrow herb." In the *Book of Songs*, we have: "Where can I get a daylily / To plant behind the house" (焉得萱草，言樹之北); Kong Yingda's annotation reads: "The daylily makes people forget their sorrow."[57] According to *Yiwen Leiju* (81: 1396) quoting Zhou Chu's *Fengtu Ji*: "*Yinan* is the name of an herb . . . with flowers like those of the lotus. Wearing it (at the belt) is good for a pregnant woman, who will be sure to give birth to a boy." In the same page of the book is also found Xiahou Zhan's (夏侯湛, of the Jin dynasty) "Rhapsody on the *Yinan* Flower" (宜男花賦) and Cao Zhi's "Hymn for the *Yinan* Flower" (宜男花贊). In the former, these lines occur:

Superior to all other herbs, it grows tall and graceful,	冠眾卉而挺生兮，
Imbued with the virtue of wood at the *Shaoyang*.	承木德于少陽。
. . . Served as the luxuriant adornments of the imperial harem,	……充後宮之盛飾兮，
It ascends the inner chamber of the Purple Subtlety.	登紫微之內堂。

Here, very suggestively, Xiahou Zhan attributes to the daylily the virtue of wood, one of the Five Elements corresponding to the direction east. This reminds us the eastern palace, where Heir Apparent resides. Xiahou located the virtue of wood in *Shaoyang*, not accidentally identical with *Shaoyangyuan*, the Heir Apparent's residence: *Shaoyang* is a term equivalent to the eastern palace, and thus to the Heir Apparent.[58]

Briefly put, "daylily" has a wide range of meanings encompassing matriarchal affection, matrimonial harmony, imperial conjugal love, and finally the blessings from Heaven for the imperial prince. In Wen's unique diction, it becomes a poetic substitute for, or at least a reminder of, the Heir Apparent.

Wen uses the same designation on another occasion in his "Song on a Screen of [the Heir Apparent's] Birth and Blessing" (j. 2, WFQ): "Good-for-bearing-sons herb, being as it is an inner palace-herb / Cannot be as red as the thousand fruits of the cherry" (宜男漫作後庭草，不似櫻桃千子紅). Professor Zhan Antai, who hypothesized that Wen had served the Heir Apparent Zhuangke, provided this poem as one of his proofs. "If the *yinan* herb could not even compare in redness to the cherry's thousand seeds, is this not to say that the Heir Apparent was in a condition worse than that of the other princes?"[59] Professor Zhan's conjecture is well made, but he has failed to support his inference with stronger proofs.

Now we can understand "Facing a courtyard covered with luxuriant daylilies"—the "court lady" recalls with nostalgia the days when the Heir

Apparent and his mother both enjoyed imperial favor. These are the feelings that Wen imparts to the lady's "languorous dream," as a part of recollection of the "Golden Hall." In reality, this was his own dream.

The next example contains the far-flung explanation of the term *painted tower* (畫樓). This term is used several times in the series, as in the following couplets:

For long I've been yearning for the painted tower, where,	畫樓相望久，
Beyond the balustrades, were drooping the silky willows.	欄外垂絲柳。(No. 4)
From the painted tower, no more news was heard,	畫樓音信斷，
Amid the fragrant herbs, by the southern bank of the River.	芳草江南岸。(No. 10)
A spring love sickness is felt to the depths of my heart, amid	春恨正關情，
The remaining drippings of the clepsydra in the painted tower.	畫樓殘點聲。(No. 14)

If "the painted tower" were the place where the court lady now lives, she would not say, "For long I've been yearning for" it, nor that she hears "no more news" from it. But if it was her boudoir in days past, why, in her present longing, does she say that she hears "The remaining drippings of the clepsydra in the painted tower"? In this series, even such common terminology forces us to seek out some deeper meaning.

We will read "painted tower" in conjunction with similar usage in "Song of a Screen of [the Heir Apparent's] Birth and Blessing Prayer" and "Song for the God of Marquis Jiang." In the former, we have "The Painted wall in the gloomy Hall of the Nine Sons" (畫壁陰森九子堂), and in the latter, we have "In the Painted Hall was a forest of halberds with frosty blades" (畫堂列戟叢霜刃). It is not far-fetched to understand "painted tower" (畫樓) as a variant or a synonym for "Painted Hall" (畫堂), which is short for "Painted Hall of the First Abode of the Heir Apparent," an inner-palace residence where the imperial sons and consorts lived since the Han Dynasty.[60] Since "painted hall" can have the special reference to "Painted Hall of the First Abode of the Heir Apparent," we have no reason to exclude "painted tower" from similar usage, as they are under ordinary circumstances interchangeable terms referring to the heroine's boudoir.

Only by tracing the term's connotations to their root can we reach the hidden information it contains. Understanding it merely at its face value, however, we can still feel its rich connotation with all its links in the context, although at a relatively superficial level. For, after all, Wen was writing in the palace style, and he must in the first place be able to cater to the palace taste, which did not value a show of erudition. We know that Wen seldom completely exposes his intention, instead, he always keeps it somewhat disguised; allowing for his onstage performance with his persona disguised as a palace lady, his choice of words such as "painted tower" becomes understandable. The term both retains its underlying definition (as the residence of the Heir Apparent) and fits well in with a palace-style poetic environment.

Hence, we emphasize once more that while we can read Wen's political experiences and feelings into the series, we must also treat it as characteristic of palace poetry. What we have here is a poetry that is both pleasing to the eye and appealing to the mind.

Our third example is the following couplet:

Simurgh mirror and the flowering twig,	鸞鏡與花枝，
This feeling of mine, who can get to know it.	此情誰得知。(No. 3)

The simurgh mirror alludes to a tragic story:[61] It was said that a king obtained a simurgh and tried to make him sing. Despite the golden cage and delicate food the king offered him, the bird was increasingly grieved and refused to sing. When placed before a mirror, however, he thought he had met another simurgh, and, watching his image in the mirror, he sent forth a sad cry that resounded through to the skies. Then, with a last struggle for life, he died. The image has a strong sentimental burden, that of losing one's "understanding friend," and, in "Simurgh mirror and the flowering twig," implies that the husband of the lady was dead, otherwise she would not be in such a melancholy mood. The mirror before her and her own beautiful image in it bring out in stark relief a grief that, in view of the story alluded to, can be understood as occasioned only by the death of her husband. That the "husband" of the "lady" was none other than the Heir Apparent will be adduced, as we employ more inferences. The court lady is a revelation of the poet, who designed this image to stand and to speak for himself.

Besides the above examples, as Zhang Huiyan suggests (p. 1): "The blue palace gate, the golden hall, the old country and the Wu palace disclose subtle hints to the effect that there are hidden motifs" (青瑣金堂故國吳宮，微露寓意). Indeed, every line and every term in the series is rich with treasure waiting to be uncovered. Even the names of flora and birds are emblematic of affections and tragic happenings. Willow (柳, *liu*), appearing eight times in the series, on various occasions, is charged each time with the yearning of separation. Other plants, such as apricot (杏, *xing*, a token for passing the Presented Scholar degree), pear (梨, similar to, 李, plum, and also the royal surname), cordate telosma (夜合, *yehe*, symbol of happy married life), daylily, bamboo (竹, metaphorical substitute for a noble man), and fragrant herbs (symbolic of worthy gentleman) all abound in literary suggestiveness. Birds such as the mythical phoenix (鳳凰, *fenghuang*, imperial consort), simurgh (鸞鳥, *luanniao*, frustrated nobleman), mandarin duck (鴛鴦, symbol of conjugal love), cuckoo (杜鵑, *dujuan*, spirit of tragedy), oriole (黃鶯, *huangying*, a sign of getting the Presented Scholar degree), and swallow

(燕, the messenger of spring or political favor), wild duck (鸂鶒, *jichi*), partridge (鷓鴣), kingfishers (翡翠) appear throughout the series. Each of these has some symbolic import related to the concrete experiences of Wen's life.

To sum up, in this series Wen assumes the persona of a beauty, speaking through her about his life experiences and feelings up to the Dazhong era. The brilliance and inventiveness of the series lie in that Wen not only subtly places all his political experiences into the narrative of a frustrated court lady, but also depicts her in complete and authentic detail—with all her apparel, makeup, moods, yearnings, and dreams. We suggest that Wen's own life, a political life frustrated to a considerable degree by his marriage with a singer-prostitute, enabled him to gain a deep insight into both his own feelings and those of the opposite sex. He differed from many of his contemporaries in that he regarded the woman not as a temporary object of pleasure, but as a human subject sharing a fate similar to his own. Fusing his own character and personality with that of the heroine, he was able to sympathize and empathize with her. The Pusaman series is a consummate example of this practice since the poet's personality and spirit merge with those of the court lady, to such a degree that the empathizer and the one empathized with are almost indistinguishable. At the same time, barriers of time and space, past and present, night and day, and dream and reality become blurred, causing all description and narration to have a single referent—Wen's feelings and the experiences that underlie his feelings.

Limited by space, we will examine only a few specimens:[62]

Within beaded crystal curtains are cool porcelain pillows,	水晶簾里玻璃枕，
And warm scented mandarin-duck brocade that courts dreams.	暖香惹夢鴛鴦錦。
On the river bank, willows appear smoke-like,	江上柳如煙，
Wild geese wing across the waning moon in the sky.	雁飛殘月天。
A lotus-silk skirt in a light hue of autumn,	藕絲秋色淺，
And a headpiece of colored lace, in cunning pattern.	人勝參差剪。[63]
In each temple are flowers fragrant and red,	雙鬢隔香紅，
Waving over the hair in a gentle breeze, a jade pin.	玉釵頭上風。(No. 2)

The first couplet of the first stanza (the first four lines) depicts a very sumptuous boudoir. The cool porcelain pillows and mandarin-duck brocade (quilt) are not only objects that once coaxed our heroine into her dreams in the former days, they are the images that emerge in her present dream—of a past when she was in possession of such items. "Mandarin-duck brocade" also appears in "Weaving Brocade" (j. 1, WFQ), written for the Heir Apparent. In that poem, it is the emblem of the weaving lady's affections for her husband, a metaphor for Wen's loyalty to the Heir. But here it is the token of the heroine's enduring love. Even paying no attention to all this background information, we are still ushered into a highly suggestive ambiance where the exquisiteness of the objects throws into relief the captivating beauty of the heroine, even before she appears on the scene.

When we read the next couplet, we find to our puzzlement that the scene now shifts to a vast natural setting by the River. Zhang Huiyan was correct in considering it to be a dreamscape of the heroine (3), although he failed to point out that the first couplet is also what emerges from her dream, a dream about her past experience in the palace. Since both the first and the second couplets are but parts of a deliberately designed dream, we need to consider the foundation of reality on which it is constructed and take the shift from inside the palace to the banks of the River. This is actually an oblique reference at Wen's returning to the south from the capital after serving the Heir Apparent.

A dream, in its own right, can defy logic. The poem becomes all the more true to life because the dream is in a jumble, despite the controlling logic of the poet, which governs the whole of the series. Whether this reality is his heroine's dream or his own, given literary expression, these are at least Wen's own creations. In fact, it is in lines such as the description of the dreamscape that Wen ignores the confinements of palace poetry, revealing himself as a writer whose ultimate concern is politics. For Wen, putting this unforgettable memory into his lady's dream is an irresistible dictate of his innermost feelings rather than a spontaneous revelation of his mind.

It is not until the second stanza that we have a direct description of the heroine. Time and again, we are struck by the realistic and vivid depiction of her beauty (internal and external), conventionally understood as a metaphor for the virtue and ability of an honest subject. The lady is now living in widowhood, as bereft as an honest subject who has lost his lord. Every line hints at her loneliness. For example, "lotus-silk" (藕絲) in line five, puns on "yearning for spouse" (思偶); her spouse, in any event, never materializes, but serves only as a foil to set off her beauty and sorrow. In comparison to the content of the dream (expressed in the first stanza), the image of the heroine (described in the second stanza) in her daytime dress seems a little pale. This is because, a dream, dreamed at night, is emblematic of her past; while awakening from the dream—her status during the daytime—stands metaphorically for her present situation. Her dream might have been a nightmare, or a reverie. Whatever the case, her awakening causes her to suffer her bereavement anew. Most of the fourteen poems of the Pusaman series follow this pattern, in which past and present, night and day, and dreaming and waking are interwoven and also interdependent.

Employing the same approach, we find the next example easier to fathom:

Stamen's gold brightens the forehead, limitlessly fair,	蕊黃無限當山額，
In nightdress, inaudible laughter, from behind gauze windows.	宿妝隱笑紗窗隔。
We met in the bloom of the peonies;	相見牡丹時，
Only too soon we bid each other farewell.	暫來還別離。
To the golden-stem is attached a hairpin of emerald,	翠釵金作股，
Atop the hairpin, frozen in flight, are two butterflies.	釵上蝶雙舞。
Who knows the innermost secrets of my heart?	心事竟誰知？
Flowers covering the branches in the moonlight.	月明花滿枝。(No. 3)

As was the case in the last example, this poem starts with a scene in the woman's dream, a scene of better days, persisting in her memory. We see her dressed in her best, enjoying wedded bliss with her husband. His appearance in the dream, however, is only implied. To her regret, she met him at a late stage in her life, and their married life together was too brief. They met during "the bloom of the peonies," namely, toward the end of spring.[64] This suggests, metaphorically, that the woman was at this time no longer young. Considering Wen's age when he served the Heir—forty (837)—we find the seasonal metaphor precise and effective. The shortness of the marital union figuratively refers to the brevity of Wen's encounter with the Heir. We can see once more that all Wen's emotions relating to his political experiences are fully articulated by the image of the court lady. Examples like this are too numerous to ignore.

As is the established pattern, the second stanza shifts to the lady's makeup and her activities when she is awake. The image of "two butterflies" on her hairpin symbolizes a perfect couple in a happy marriage. But they are "frozen in flight" and cannot actually fly together. Here are precisely the lady's "innermost secrets," which no one around her is aware of or cares about. Throughout her sleepless nights she can only empathize with the flowers that bloom in the moonlight.

Here the literary technique of "using the feelings between the lad and lass, to speak about the affairs between monarch and his subjects" has reached a peak of perfection. The image is a highly realistic and picturesque representation of the court lady in her disappointment and lovesickness, while it is also subtly and nimbly expressive of the poet himself, cherishing the memories of the dead Heir, which are combined with his political frustrations. Wen's mastery of this traditional artistry is faultless; no one in Chinese literary history, either before or after, traveled as far along such a cryptic artistic path as Wen has. It is no wonder that few readers of later generations have been able to reach the innermost recesses of his hidden meanings. It is also not surprising that many scholars believe that he is only writing about a court lady, and not about himself.[65]

To do Wen justice, however, we ought to say that he is *indeed* writing about a court lady, *so as* to write about himself. We must agree that the lady imaged in his portrait is true to life, but this is no reason to infer that he is only writing about the lady. On the contrary, behind every line and every word describing the lady, there is a hidden import relating to himself. This is where the Pusaman poems surpass conventional palace poetry and where Wen distinguishes himself as a master of *ci* poetry. When we say that there are hidden motifs in Wen's *ci* poetry, we mean that hidden behind the apparently "fragrant and gorgeous" diction devoted to a woman, are a disguised political career and, in addition, allusions to many major events and his responses to them.

The following example (No. 6) can more clearly illustrate this point:

In the moonlit jade tower, I always think of him,	玉樓明月常相憶，
The silken willows were delicate, the spring is lethargic.	柳絲裊娜春無力。
Over the grasses growing lush and green outside the gate,	門外草萋萋，
I sent you off, hearing the horses neigh.	送君聞馬嘶。
By the painted drapery patterned with golden kingfishers,	畫羅金翡翠，
Fragrant candles melt into tears.	香燭銷成淚。
Amidst the falling blossoms, the plaints of the cuckoo,	花落子歸啼，
Behind her green-gauze window, her remaining dream was dazed.	綠窗殘夢迷。

The moonlit jade tower and silken willow always haunt the lady's dream. The former, as we have seen repeatedly, is located somewhere in the palace. The image of "silken willows" is an image saturated with the sense of reluctance to part company with someone. In Wen's poetry in particular, it is a cipher used frequently to symbolize his yearning for the Heir Apparent.[66]

The first line in the next couplet, while presenting a general parting scene from the dream, also alludes to "Summons for A Recluse" in the *Songs of the South*:

A prince went wandering and did not return,	王孫游兮不歸，
In spring the grasses grow, lush and green.[67]	春草生兮萋萋。

Who was this prince? Since "Summons for the Recluse" was composed by one of the retainers of Liu An (劉安, 179–122 B.C.), the Prince of Huainan (淮南王), in a mournful endeavor to "summon the soul" for him after his death, the "prince" refers naturally to Liu An,[68] employing him as an allusive surrogate here for the prince Wen had served. In reading Wen Tingyun we cannot afford to neglect such oblique implications.

"I sent you off, hearing the horses neigh" hints back to another poem of Wen's, the second of "Two Dirges for the Late Heir Apparent Zhuangke":

On the dusty road the capital people feel resentful,	塵陌都人恨，
In the frosty suburbs the mourning horses neigh sadly.	霜郊賵馬悲。

This is no ordinary horse, but a "mourning horse." Hence "I sent you off" in this context can also mean as "I took part in your funeral procession" or "I sent you off [to the nether world]." It is not out of the context to see a covert expression of Wen's sad recollection of the late Heir's funeral ceremony in this reference.

Of course, the reader can read something different into the couplet, depending on personal experience rather than knowledge of these hidden allusions, because, in accordance with modern hermeneutical theories, the work is, in its own right, an open artistic world to explore. However, the aesthetic standards of the Late Tang literati, governing the reading or composition of poetry, were far from free and open. Here we are seeking to reveal Wen's original motivation, formed during his own course of life in this era, as he set about creating this series. When we attempt to elicit Wen's own motives for writing, it is therefore not applicable to give free rein to imagination.

Turning to the second stanza of poem No. 6, again the images are so arranged as to voice the lady's present desire in contradistinction to her past dream. "Golden kingfishers," like the image of the two butterflies in the previous example, symbolize an unrealized marriage, our heroine's vanished dream. "Fragrant candles melt into tears" is similar to Li Shangyin's "The candle will not dry its tears until it turns to ashes" (蠟炬成灰淚始乾), and both lines refer to a sorrow that the lover's life would be dedicated to hopeless love. Now the cuckoo is heard again amidst the fallen flowers drifting away with the flowing water; as Li Shangyin put it, "Emperor Wang's amorous heart in spring is entrusted to the cuckoo" (望帝春心托杜鵑).[69] The cuckoo, spirit of tragedy, with its bleeding beak and grievous cries, now laments the heroine's heartbreaking dream. The more she thinks, the more she dreams; the dream is broken, and only some debris "remain"; causing her thought to be confused, and her dream to be "dazed." Here dream and reality, past and present, what was yearned for at night and sought after during the daytime are all merged into one, by a yearning and anxious mind. This poem is more a revelation of Wen's inner world than that of the court lady, even though it is always presented in the guise of the latter.

The next example (No. 12) will present more indications to confirm this point:

Willow floss, piled up, covered the ground of the south garden,	南園滿地飛輕絮，
Sadly I listened to the torrents of rain in the Pure Bright season.	愁聞一霎清明雨。
After the rain, was the slanting sun,	雨後卻斜陽，
Apricot blossoms, withered and fallen, were more fragrant.	杏花零落香。
Silently I made up my sleepy face,	無言勻睡臉，
About the pillow, behind the folding screen.	枕上屏山掩。
The time of day is nearing dusky twilight,	時節欲黃昏，
Listless and alone, I leaned by the gate.	無聊獨閉門。

The first stanza is a recollection or dream of some particular moment in her past, while the second stanza returns to her present situation. Her past always haunts her present dreams, while her present concerns are the consequences of her past.

The spring season's splendor has nearly ended. The willow floss, completely fallen, covers the ground. A shower typical of the Pure Bright season adds to her sorrow. In Chinese tradition, this pessimistic picture toward the end of spring may awaken in a beautiful woman regretful feelings of having spent her youth in vain and can be used as a metaphor for a noble man's aspiration to serve his country before it is too late.

During the Late Tang times, all the successful candidates who had passed as Presented Scholars would gather in the Apricot Garden to congratulate one another. So there may be more hidden import in Wen's apricot blossom image, related to his experiences in the examination. For example, in representing his frustration at his failure to pass, one of Wen's poems says: "I know I have no access to the Apricot Garden / To my chagrin, in front of my horse, red blossoms are all over the branches" (知有杏園無計入，馬前惆悵滿枝紅).[70] Now, after the wind and rain had passed and it had turned fine again, the apricot blossom in the slanting sun was devastated, though it still kept its fragrance. On the surface, this is a description of what happens in the natural world. But essentially, it gives at the same time an account of what happened in Wen's life. Thus, behind the metaphorical guise is revealed to us how, following the trials and tribulations of a political accident, the situation had become calm once more; and how Wen, now an old man, failed again and again to be passed as a Presented Scholar, even though his reputation as an honest and talented man was widespread.

The second stanza serves to compare the lady's past frustration with her present distress. Wen seems to fear that he is putting too much of himself into the series, so now he turns back again to the beauty herself, with her languorous air. Why is she so downcast? Her own answer is that: "The time of day is nearing dusky twilight / Listless and alone I leaned by the gate." The meaning is that she is growing old. Clearly, in the Dazhong era (847–860) Wen was already well into his fifties (birth year 798). His life had been wasted in pursuit of official recognition—in his striving for a Presented Scholar degree and an official post. This tragedy of a "worthy man" bears a strong resemblance to that of the abandoned beauty in her enduring sorrow.

To sum up, the Pusaman series is definitely closely connected with Wen's unique experiences and, indeed, contains "hidden motifs." As we have demonstrated, there are many allusions closely connected with the major upheavals in Wen's life. If it had not been for his efforts to arrange clues in all kinds of disguises throughout the series, we could never have discovered them so easily. Because, however we try to force the language, we cannot create a story out of nothing. Our reading of the series, however, is not meant to deny the traditional readings. Rather, it can enrich these readings by taking into account more of the writer's personal background and general poetic style. This study has concentrated on Wen's life rather than his poetic style, thus we have not concerned ourselves with the complex hermeneutic theories of the modern West. In seeking to excuse myself, I hope that my "creative reading" is one roughly consistent with Wen Tingyun's original creative process.

It is equipped with the clarified information about Wen's life that we come to this new understanding of the Fourteen Pusaman *ci* poems. Taking into consideration the background against which the Pusaman series was composed, we employ Wen's own poetic techniques to fathom his poetry and find that this series is much more than merely a group of palace-style poems. In the fourteen poems themselves, their shared leading actress, melancholy mood, and evasive and eager manner combine to point to a hidden common motif. Looking more carefully into each line, examining the metaphors, analyzing the subtle shades of meanings in every word and allusion, we find implications in every line that suggest that these are more than typical palace-style poems. It is no accident that throughout the series we find messages redolent of the details of Wen's life. Put together, these messages spell out all of Wen's relevant experiences, although not explicitly and chronologically. Here Wen is not merely describing love, but is writing about political affairs under the guise of love. Although we should not take the poems as exclusively autobiographical, rich autobiographical elements can be found in them. We must forsake the barely viable theory that this series consists only of an objective, palace-styled description of a court lady. In addition to being such a description, the series is also Wen's lamentation for his own life, a life characterized by an unyielding pursuit of love and truth.

In concluding, we will add one additional argument. As mentioned earlier, Zhang Huiyan, and later Chen Tingchuo, put forth the theory that the fourteen Pusaman poems must contain some hidden motifs related to Wen's personal experiences. Rejecting this theory, however, some of the modern treatments of this series identify it as nothing more than an objective and picturesque description of a court lady. In doing so, however, they fail to offer a convincing account of the series' aesthetic contents. Wang Guowei, an outstanding critic, once commented on Zhang's theory: "How obstinate was Zhang Gaowen (Zhang's style name) in making his running commentary! The fourteen Pusaman poems by Feiqing are nothing more than impromptu creations possessing some undefined mood, how can there be any special hidden motifs in them?" (固哉張皋文之為詞也！飛卿菩薩蠻十四首，不過一時興到之作，有何命意).[71] In Wang's view, Zhang's mistake was that he used "the hereditary approach to the *Book of Changes* handed down from his family" (說易家法) to study the literary pattern of Wen's *ci* poems. Broadly speaking, it is perhaps best that academic approaches to philosophical texts such as the *Book of Changes*, not be employed in research on literature. Different objects of study require different study approaches. Aside from the fact that Zhang Huiyan was indeed an expert in the study of the *Book of Changes*,[72] the point needs to be made that Wen Tingyun was much influenced by this text. Indeed, the *Book of Changes* was a source of literary inspiration for countless generations. For the study of literature in general, and Wen's *ci* in particular, we should avail ourselves of as many approaches as possible; why, then, should we exclude an approach related to that used in the study of the *Book of Changes*? Our only regret is that Zhang Huiyan did not make an analytical study of Wen's life, leaving it for modern scholars to undertake.

Conclusion

It is by the "mutual evidence" of history and poetry that we have picked our way through the distorted reports in extant sources and reconstructed the substantial information relating to Wen's life. That is to say, guided by a general understanding of the historical background, we have undertaken a study of Wen's poetry, and facilitated by concrete details found in this poetry, we have obtained a fuller grasp of the historical background. In this sense, to understand Wen's life is to fathom his poetry, and vice versa.

Born into an aristocratic clan in decline and related to the imperial family by marriage, Wen had, from childhood, received a Confucian education and become determined to contribute to the restoration of a powerful state dynasty and the retrieval of his family's glory. Because of the ongoing conflict between Wen's family and the eunuchs, and because of Wen's unyielding integrity, the power-entrenched eunuchs would not allow any political advance on his part. Moreover, Wen was unable to find a source of opportunity for political promotion in either of the two political factions existing in his time. Consequently, even in his attempts to find a livelihood under local patrons, Wen suffered severely from the eunuchs' persecution. The whole Jianghuai Incident, and especially his marriage to a singer-prostitute, should be highlighted. The whole story reflects how both eunuch power and social convention worked against him, turning an unconventional marriage into a scandal. Rumors were spread in Wen's lifetime by the eunuchs. Tales were recorded and retold by many authors after his death, and, worst of all, were taken up by the Song Dynasty historiographers. For our poet, this amounted to a political "frame-up" consigning to him a notoriety that has lasted for more than a thousand years. Thus, Wen's path to a favorable official career in his lifetime was blocked not by his "moral failings," but for most part by the hostility of the eunuchs. Comparing Wen with many of his eminent contemporaries, we find the claims that Wen was to any degree "immoral" to be dubious. On the contrary, we suggest that his affection for a singer-prostitute evinces a remarkable humanity transcending class and gender bias in a manner extremely rare for his time. His unremitting resistance to the eunuchs exhibits a political courage and tenacity, making Wen one of the most admirable men of his time. The choice of Wen as attendant of the Heir Apparent makes it clear that he was regarded as a man of great talent and honesty by most of his contemporaries, including the emperors. Emperor Wenzong exerted great care and effort in selecting "honest and serious literati and court officials to be mentors and attendants" for his son.[1] In the face of these historical records, all the slander of the eunuchs and the censure of the Song Dynasty historiographers, as well as their later echoes, collapse completely.[2] Wen's attendance upon the Heir and his political stance in connection with each of the interested parties in the Heir Apparent Incident speak eloquently as to what kind of man he was. Furthermore, we are able to justify Wen's behavior in changing his name in order to sit for the examination. He was forced to do so, because it was the only way he could take, much less pass, the examination. This ruse, marking the crux of Wen's protracted efforts to elude the eunuchs and pass the examination, was a typical instance of the Late Tang times, characteristic of the strife between the "Southern Office" and the "Northern Office." It also illustrates the degree to which Wen struggled with adversity. As to his "cheating"—his taking the examinations for others—this was not blameworthy. It was an "abnormal" form of protest engendered in a normal but frustrated individual. If Wen is to blame for anything, it is perhaps that he was too persistent in his desire to realize his political ambitions.

In summation, all Wen's involvements in the political troubles of his day, taken as a series, present us with: a man who was true to himself as well as to others; a soul who revolted against social injustice and prejudice; a figure who defied brute force and the entrenched authority; and a poet who had concern for the fate of his country and the well-being of his people. Of course, Wen was not perfect. Because he was not perfect, and never pretended to be, he was a genuine and sincere man, in no sense inferior to any poet of eminence in Chinese history.

The following series of causes and effects, contained in several case studies, serve to verify and complement one another, and thus confirm themselves forcefully.

In dealing with Wen's "Two Dirges for the Late Heir Apparent Zhuangke," we discerned Wen's particular relationship with the Heir Apparent. Then, from the "Epistle Thanking Minister Li of Xiangzhou," we found that Li Cheng was Wen's teacher and that it was Li who introduced Wen to Emperor Wenzong to be attendant of the crowned heir, thus confirming Wen's liaison with the Heir in more detail. Having rediscovered and complemented this event, we were enabled to successfully expound a long obscure passage in "Hundred-Rhyme Poem," once more finding strong evidence to confirm our initial discoveries. Later we exposed at length the riddle of the Sphinx posed by the "Twenty-Two Rhymes of the Arched Door," and continued to fill in the blanks surrounding this special event, even though some uncertainties still remained. Discovering that Zaimeng, Wen's self-chosen style-name, is a term borrowed from an essay by none other than the above-mentioned Li Cheng, and was adopted to betoken both the poet's reverence for his teacher and his enmity against the eunuchs, caused us to be both amazed and amused at the coincidence of history and literature. Our efforts were thus directed toward discovering more details of the coincidence rather than merely proving that it happened. The two findings—that Minister Li of Xiangzhou was Wen's teacher Li Cheng and that Wen's style name was Zaimeng, a term coined by Li Cheng—could not be completely incorrect because, in each case, we had followed a strict sequence of logical inferences. Even if we were inadvertently mistaken in some way, it is improbable that two such mistakes would both point to the identical person, from a multitude of options in each case. Therefore, the life experiences of Wen Tingyun form a kind of logical sequence, in which all terms are interdependent and serve to confirm one another. Determination of a key link in the chain enables us to follow the links on either side and arrive at the complete and accurate story comprised of all those links. It is this logic that has given me a sense that I am at least not totally in the wrong; it has also encouraged me to track down the clues until I can discover something substantial.

For all our "discoveries," however, there are still a number of questions that require further investigation. I have repeatedly imputed Wen's repeated failures to the eunuchs, but I have not ascertained who the particular eunuch(s) might be. It is quite clear that Wen could not have the energy and strength to confront the eunuchs *en masse*, although the eunuch or eunuchs he regarded as his sworn enemy must have been sufficiently influential to be able to block his way to any easy advancement. Since Wen had to change his name to take the examination of the year 839, whereas from the beginning of Dazhong (847) onward he was able to take the examinations openly as many times as he wished, the particular eunuch opposed to him must have quit the political arena during the Huichang era (841–846), even though his influence continued to be felt in the succeeding years. Therefore, I conjecture that Wen's particular enemy was the arch-eunuch Qiu Shiliang, or someone with comparable position. Qiu was the chief person responsible for the massacre of the court officials in the Sweet Dew Incident; he also plotted the assassination of the Heir Apparent and drove Emperor Wenzong to his death. He had more than enough power to take Wen's life if Wen were to seriously offend him or to dare to come within his reach by venturing onto the political stage. After Li Yong's death, Wen was forced to conceal himself in Drafter Pei's house to escape arrest. Similarly, after his name change was divulged, he was faced not only with failure, but also with a threat to his life that forced him to flee. Taking all this into consideration, in all probability, Qiu was the prime architect of Wen's ruin. It is true that a minor eunuch would be too insignificant to influence the decision-making process (such as the choice of successful Presented Scholars), and thus would have not been able to spoil Wen's political career altogether. Nevertheless, we lack conclusive evidence to pinpoint Qiu as Wen's personal adversary.

Turning our attention to the eunuchs' activities, we find that in specific historical situations, there were different factions even among the eunuchs. As a powerful social force unwelcome to the traditional literati, the eunuch-clique must have had a much more complex history than the orthodox historiographers present. To our regret, the standard histories only provide extremely scanty records for very few arch-eunuchs, from which we even cannot determine how they combined together, still less how they inflicted blows on Wen. Considering all these factors plus Wen's radical stance toward them, we can only confirm their state of mutual animosity. Beyond a doubt, it was the eunuchs who were ever ready to find fault with Wen, at the slightest provocation. But that is as far as we can go.

Another problem we have not fully explicated is Wen's political relations with the Niu and the Li factions, a problem essentially subordinate to the problem of the eunuchs. Since we cannot focus our efforts on identifying the partisanship of every individual with whom Wen came into close contact, we are still lacking a complete grasp of the various situations Wen encountered. To our relief, guided by the wealth of information preserved in Wen's works, which demonstrates that he belonged to neither faction, we could possibly commence a more detailed study of the factional strife of the Late Tang times from a fresh perspective. There is certainly much to discover.

I must point out that other important aspects of Wen's life remain to be explored. I have no space to deal with them in this particular study. For example, Wen was much concerned with the defense of the frontier and the life of the people, as is evidenced by many of his extant works. His final tragic ending itself speaks strongly and eloquently to his personality as well as his political orientation: he died in exile as a direct consequence of his speaking out on behalf of some literati of humble origin during his tenure as Instructor in the State Son's University, an official post gained only after a lifetime of effort.

Reconstructing Wen's life has also enabled us to reach a new understanding of his poetic style, its formation and its expression.

Born into the Late Tang times, when the dominant literary trend favored ornateness and sophistication, as a young poet in the southeastern region Wen accepted the influence of a style represented by Yuan Zhen and termed licentious and sumptuous. During his long years of travel all over the country in search of patrons, Wen developed a more mature artistic style, which he employed both to represent nature and to express himself with appealing power. He constantly drew from his brilliant predecessors, poets such as Du Fu, Han Yu, Bai Juyi, and especially Li Bai. He also received more direct instruction from his teacher Li Cheng. His attendance on the Heir Apparent enabled him to add more exquisiteness and artistic charm to his poetry, as he catered to the palace taste. Following this period, his poetic style underwent a radical change. In a life filled with political dangers and frustrations under the eunuchs' reign of terror, he fulfilled his poet's duty to record what he witnessed in life, concealing what he wanted to say behind an ornate artistic expression without tarnishing his motifs. To use his own terms, he had the ability "to make the overt covert." Such is Wen's poetic style, presenting itself as political (affairs) in the guise of private (love). It was Wen's particular path of life that caused his unique style of poetry to take such a shape. As for the puzzling beauty of Wen's poetry, even the authors of JTS, without really understanding him, described his style as "pure and surpassing."

This study focuses on rediscovering Wen's life through his poetry; as such, it is not an all-encompassing study of his poetry. Nevertheless, we are still able, to make a few summary remarks about the major characteristics of Wen's poetic style as measured against the general trends of the Late Tang poetry's development and as compared to some of the most influential Tang poets. After the High Tang, often called the golden age of Chinese poetry, it became very difficult for poets to open up new prospects or to explore new realms for their poetic creations. As we know from the Tang literary history, in the Yuanhe era (806–820), an era that compares favorably with or even surpasses the High Tang, there were two major poetic schools—one headed by Bai Juyi and Yuan Zhen, the other represented by Han Yu and Meng Jiao—each having a great number of followers. In a sense, the two poetic schools respectively inherited "the mantle and alms bowl" of Li Bai and Du Fu, but each deviated from its models considerably, as a consequence of "the general tendency of Yuanhe that advocated strangeness" (元和之風尚怪).[3] No Late Tang poet was able to detach himself from the trends of his time. Wen must have also been influenced considerably by the two poetic schools (patterns), when developing his own pattern. As seen from the examples we have utilized in reconstructing his life, Wen was a versatile poet who excelled in composing almost all the poetic subgenres that were in use in his day. In Wen's poems there are indeed a variety of aesthetic expressions and artistic techniques, which intermingle and defy a simple stylistic classification. Our typology for Wen's poetry is divided, therefore, according to his attitudes during the composition, rather than types of versification. Thus, Wen's poems can be divided into three categories.

1. Poems composed extemporaneously and quick-wittedly (率意之作) to represent his mood at a particular moment: most of this group are straightforward, natural, and simple but elegant verses bearing the clear traces of Bai Juyi or Yuan Zhen, although they inherit in the long run Li Bai and the Music Bureau folksong of the Six Dynasties.
2. Poems composed with great elaborateness and deliberation (刻意之作) and grave themes. In this category, among others, are the "Hundred-Rhyme Poem" and the "Twenty-Two Rhymes on the Arched Door," which have totally beguiled Wen's readership, in a manner contrary to what he originally intended. After unraveling them, however, we find that none of the artistic techniques used by him are abnormal, except for the fact that many of his allusions are too archaic for ordinary readers to understand. And, unlike other poets, even in long regulated poems (排律), the most serious

and highly sophisticated of the poetic genres, Wen sometimes resorts to homophonic puns. In general, this category of his poems exhibits the traces of influence from Han Yu and, still earlier, from Du Fu.

3. Poems written with great pain, and yet poems in which he takes pride (得意之作), such as his Music Bureau verses and the Pusaman series: these are Wen's representative works. Poems of this category reach such a consummate unity of content and form and of truth and beauty that the later Chinese writers viewed them with fascination and yet found themselves incapable of duplicating them. These poems appear simple, but they are rich with implication. At first appearance they seem to be poems about women; under scrutiny, however, they present their deeper references concerning political affairs. Viewed simply from the perspective of love poetry, they are already matchless, and they have enjoyed a high reputation mainly as love poetry. It is not strange that some critics have been at a loss when they have been presented with another layer of the truth implied in Wen's poetic language. In these works, the "fragrant" diction and gorgeous lines contrast in perfect harmony with the subtle mood and deeply hidden motifs. With the language uttered and the meanings unuttered, Wen's serious subject is made manifest amidst minute objects. These kinds of masterpieces have enabled Wen to make a special poetic contribution in Chinese literary history, establishing the role of a new poetic subgenre—*ci* poetry. Such a contribution could only have been made by a poet of unique personality and artistic character, a poet such as Wen Tingyun.

Qian Zhongshu has pointed out that Wen is one of the few Late Tang poets who rid his poetry completely of the influence of Li He (790–816).[4] We suggest that Wen, while exhibiting the same extraordinary talent as Li He, was, in comparison, a poetic genius more full-fledged and more developed in profundity and dimension. After all, Wen saw much more of life than the short-lived and somewhat abnormal young poet Li He. In its quest for the true, the good, and the beautiful, his poetry is more immersed in deeply felt life experiences and insistent worldly concerns, exhibiting a positive outlook on life combined with admirable courage in facing all the hardship presented to him by fate. In his brave sufferings and struggles, we see the undying spark of life.

In contrast with his counterpart Li Shangyin, while both share a style with subtle motif, puzzling trope, and elegant diction, Wen's poetic voices are more masculine and powerful, infused with the spirit of *Yang* rather than *Yin*. Most of Li's "untitled" poems are filled with so much feminine tenderness that the reader becomes unable to discern a controlling masculine mind. On the contrary, in Wen's poetry there is an unrestrained and heroic spirit that reveals Wen Tingyun (the director), even though he has assumed the role of a woman. Wen's heroines behave in a uniquely characteristic manner. This is not a problem of artistic superiority or inferiority between the two poets.

This difference results directly from the two different political lives of the two men. Wen's was one of drastic rise and fall while Li's was much less tumultuous.

What is the intrinsic relationship between Wen's personality and the personae depicted in his works? It is no longer necessary to disparage his works to find conformity between a debauched person and a licentious style. Nor is it necessary to attempt to enhance his personality in accord with a favorable assessment of his poetry. Rather than divorcing his works from his life, or simply dubbing many of them "ambiguous" or "aestheticist," we are able to base our understanding on our discoveries and recognize in Wen's work a unity of politics and literature, reality and art. As a master of Chinese poetic language, Wen chose to write ambiguously, because without ambiguity he could not protect himself and his poetry. However, his "ambiguity" differs from the usual connotations of that term in that it conveys hard and clear-cut events, disguised by historical allusions and literary tropes. As a result, his political poems have survived the vicissitude of time and are eminently worthy of attention.

Therefore, we can state that, despite the conventional disparagement of him, Wen has his own praiseworthy idiosyncrasies—a consistent style as well as an insistent personality, both in its sentiments and in its elegance. He was an honest man and outstanding poet whose work is not only understandable but also capable of touching our emotions.

In reality, over the past millennium, Wen has never lacked for admirers, including those critics who basically denied his personality. When we browse through the voluminous "poetry talk", we find that from the Song Dynasty onward, quite a few of his extant poems are cited as exemplars of the best *shi* poetry.[5] Furthermore, Wen has been acclaimed as the first great literati *ci* master and the founder of the Graceful and Restrained (*Wanyue*, 婉約) School of *ci* poetry.

After the death of these two major poets, the poetic reputations of Wen and his good friend Li Shangyin underwent a drastic change. Originally the two enjoyed equal fame in poetry as well as in prose. They were paired as Wen-Li. Pi Rixiu (皮日休, 834–883), their younger contemporary, once remarked that "Wen Feiqing and Li Yishan are the laureates of recent decades" (近代稱溫飛卿李義山為之最).[6] And Chao Gongwu's (晁公武) *Junzhai Dushuzhi* (4: 8) records that Wen's poetry enjoyed fame equal to that of Li Shangyin. In the Song Dynasty, even orthodox critics thought that Wen and Li were a match for each other: "Compared with each other, Wen and Li each has his superior and inferior points."[7] The two of them have been thus ranked as equals in poetic fame from their own time to the present. Literary appraisals such as this, presenting the general response from generations of readers, cannot be easily denied. However, the evaluation of the two poets began to differ in recent centuries. The "Biography of Li Shangyin" in JTS (190: 5078) stresses that "Li Shangyin's literary compositions are pure and beautiful but

Tingyun's surpass them" (詩思清麗，庭筠過之), but the same text in a different version just says the contrary by adding one word—"Li's compositions are pure and beautiful and surpass Tingyun's" (詩思清麗，視庭筠過之).[8] The tendency has continued to grow until today when Wen's reputation is almost overshadowed by that of Li Shangyin.

Later critics are entitled to prefer one poet at the expense of another, depending on the criteria specific to their own times. Nevertheless, without a correct understanding of the poet's works, they are not really qualified to discuss in involved language what the poet and his poetry should or should not be like. How can we accept their critical judgments of a poet whose works they have never fully fathomed? Faced with the consistently depreciatory appraisal of Wen still at work today, we can still feel the injustice done to him in his lifetime. Another factor contributing to the substantial difference in the current literary appraisals of Wen and Li is that for Li's extant works there exist two annotations of considerable academic quality—*Yuxisheng Shiji Jianzhu*, by Feng Hao, and *Li Yishan Shi Jianzhu*, by Zhu Heling and Qu Fu; the only existing annotation for Wen's works, *Wen Feiqing Shiji Jianzhu*, by Zeng Yi et al., is a woeful failure. One additional reason for Li Shangyin's better posthumous reputation could be that in their lifetimes, Li was "unluckier" than Wen, since he never had the chance to directly serve the highest ruler of the empire. As a result, he did not become involved in the secret political machinations at the top, as did Wen. Li was outside the "Besieged City" from which Wen could not escape, and he remained outside all his life, as it were, like an onlooker without a net positioned at the edge of a pool longing vainly to fish.

Subsequent to Feng Hao and Zhu Heling's relatively successful studies of Li Shangyin's works, first Chinese scholars, then Western scholars in their wake, have produced an immense number of publications on Li Shangyin—something we can term a "Li Shangyin craze." On the other hand, both groups have been largely indifferent to Wen's works. I do not wish to stress Wen's poetic achievements at the expense of Li's, rather, I feel that Li's poetic achievements have been overemphasized to the detriment of Wen's accomplishments. I have sought in this study to restore Wen's reputation as a major poet in the history of Chinese literature, a reputation in no way inferior to Li Shangyin's.

My next question is: how can we account for the fact that Wen's collected works, very easy to obtain for any scholar or even casual reader, have been able to conceal his many secrets in black and white terms for more than a thousand years?

Even a poet whose life is clear and whose works are easy to understand can receive totally different appraisals made through a variety of approaches. It is understandable that appraisals of an unrecognized and secretive poet such as Wen Tingyun will vary tremendously. Fundamentally speaking, in the declining ages of imperial dynasties since the Song, few scholars spent enough time on studying our poet, or even suspected that a noteworthy personality could be discovered in him. If they found anything in Wen's works that they could not understand, either unwilling or unable to make further study on our poet, whose typical behavior is against Confucianism, they just left it as it was. In any event, the fact is that Wen Tingyun has up to now not been adequately studied, as is the case with many other poets.

In the study of any poet, there are two components of equal importance: the study of the life and the study of the poetry. The more remote the poet's time from our own, the less we are likely to know about his life, hence the more reliance we will have to place on his works. If the works are burdened with lengthy scholiums by earlier scholars, apart from trusting them to be better equipped with knowledge concerning the poet's life, or at least to have more of the linguistic lore necessary to explain the poet's language, we cannot completely accept their conclusions because we know their views are colored by the biases of their own time. In Wen's case, to our regret, little can be accepted from the Qing annotators, who scarcely had access to any more source materials than we do, and whose scholarship is so obviously deficient that they cannot fathom Wen's profundity.

Penetrating and successful analyses of poetry presuppose an accurate grasp of the poet's psychological realities, which ensues from a deep insight into the circumstances of the poet's life. The study of Wen Tingyun undertaken here, however, has taken the opposite course. The singularity lies in the fact that it is in Wen's own poetry rather than in any other sources that the hidden truths of Wen's life are to be found. Although my discoveries must await general acceptance, I feel encouraged that I have uncovered some important events in the poet's life, and that once having been ascertained, they will not change; unlike the explanation of his poetic style, which, subject to the theoretical approaches taken, can be more flexible and variable. An analogy can be made with the computer in front of me: once the hardware is manufactured, various softwares may be installed in it. It is my wish that the hardware of Wen's actual life, which I have fashioned in this study, will remain compatible with the software that has been and will be written for his poetry.

Appendix

"Hundred-Rhyme Poem" (abbr. for the following title)

開成五年秋，以抱疾郊野，不得與鄉計偕至王府，將議遐適，隆冬自傷。因書懷奉寄殿院徐侍御、察院陳、李二侍御、回中蘇端公、鄠縣韋少府，兼呈袁郊苗紳李逸三友人一百韻

This long title spells out the complex situation Wen encountered in the winter of 840. He had to abandon his efforts to attain the Presented Scholar degree and took flight to the south. All those addressed in the title were friends who knew Wen's story; some of them even shared with him the experience of attending the Heir Apparent.

1 All the winged hooves are going before on the way, 逸足皆先路，
Only I, a cornered dragon, have to weep. 窮蛟獨向隅。
2 Like a stubborn fugitive in *broad-willow* I have escaped, 頑童逃廣柳，
Now a fatigued horse in flat wilderness is lying prostrate. 羸馬臥平蕪。

Unlike his friends, after the political storm, Wen still could gain no opportunity to advance in the world, but instead had to flee for his life (rhymes 1–2).

3 Of the yellow scrolls, who, alas, asks about my erudition? 黃卷嗟誰問？
With the red strings I amuse myself on this occasion. 朱弦偶自娛。
4 "Deer's Singing" played, for all successful candidates, 鹿鳴皆綴士，
Far from a true man, I should lie low as a female. 雌伏竟非夫。

Now that he was rejected, nobody cared about his insight and talent. He could only use this poem ("the red string") to "amuse" himself, namely, to give vent to his complaints. Compared with those who were honored with the Presented Scholar degree, Wen felt all the more humiliated (3–4).

5 The [ancestral] enfeoffment in the forlorn wild is left waste, 采地荒遺野，
And our fief by the old capital has long been divested. 爰田失故都。

Poet's footnote: My forefathers were dukes and ministers of the state dynasty, and after helping (the first emperors) effect the Heavenly Mandate, they were enfeoffed in the commanderies of Bing and Fen (原注：余先祖國朝公相，晉陽佐命，食采于并汾也).

6 Having lost the sheep, I still toss the dice, 亡羊猶博塞，
Letting go the horse, I weary of shouting for stakes. 放馬倦呼盧。

Wen tells us that his forefathers had rendered outstanding service to the royal family in founding the Tang Dynasty, but the lineage has now lost its past glory. Wen then hints at what had led to this state of affairs, suggesting that the family's tradition of honesty and outspokenness had brought disgrace to his forefathers and now was the cause of his own failures (5–6).

7 For generations the Wens partook of the Zhou emoluments, 奕世參周祿，
As family tradition, we used to follow the Lu Confucians. 承家學魯儒。
8 Witness of our family feats: the remaining swords and courtboots, 功庸留劍舄，
Inscribed on imperial plates and basins: our ancestors' admonitions. 銘誡在盤盂。

Wen next gives a proud description of his clan's glorious past with its privilege and prestige. We may take Wen's statements as somewhat hyperbolic (7–8).

9 For statecraft, I have good designs, 經濟懷良畫，
As regards retreat and advance, far-sighted plans. 行藏識遠圖。
10 Not in a position to sound the Jade of Chu, 未能鳴楚玉，
In vain I desire to hold the Pearl of [Marquis] Sui. 空欲握隋珠。

Wen then expresses his aspiration and capacity to serve his country and lord. However, his talent and his loyalty were not yet recognized (9–10).

11 I was indeed seeking fish by climbing a tree, 定為魚緣木，
And for a second rabbit, by the stump I'd vainly waited. 曾因兔守株。

Wen here drops a very subtle hint about his first performance in the capital political arena—his attendance on the Heir Apparent, which, despite his sincere efforts, had proved to be an impassable road for realizing his high political ambitions.

12 Up to "five wagonfuls" were piled my books, 五車堆縹帙，
With three footpaths I closed my strung gate. 三徑闔繩樞。
13 I then joined company with many an eminent soul, 適與群英集，
Only for the offer of a good price, I stipulated. 將期善價沽。

However, Wen was enabled to pursue the ordinary course for entering officialdom—sitting for the Presented Scholar Examination. To this end, he studied very hard to prepare for it, and looked forward to a chance to stand out among his fellow candidates (12–13).

14 Lord She's dragon pictures are truly bright, 葉龍圖夭矯，
The counterfeit, the "Yan rat" will make itself a sight. 燕鼠笑胡盧。

Even before his participation, he felt apprehensive that the examination administrators would not be able to distinguish the worthy and true talent from the unworthy and false, although he hoped that his talent would be accepted in any event.

15 I knew my innate gift to be preordained, 賦分知前定，
And fear of being maligned filled my disappointed mind. 寒心畏厚誣。
16 I scurried swifter than Qingji, throwing the dust behind, 躡塵追慶忌，
And followed the model of Lu Ban, wielding sword in hand. 操劍學班輸。

Despite his excellent literary talent (as preeminent as the handicraft of Lu Ban), he must avoid the slander from the eunuchs (by running faster than Qingji, a miraculous racer!). He changed his name in order to take the examination (15–16).

17 In the Literary Garden I attended many a candidate, 文囿陪多士，
Taking the Divine Prefecture Examination for the No. 1 place. 神州試大巫。

18 My answer could be "a rare playing of the lute," 對雖希鼓瑟，
So my name was passed off among those who blew the flute. 名亦濫吹竽。

Poet's footnote: Last autumn I sat for the Metropolitan Prefecture Examination, and got my name recommended on the supplementary list (原注：余去秋試京兆，薦名，居其副).

As expected, he passed the Metropolitan Prefecture Examination and became "Equivalent to Passing" (17–18).

19 [This served] only to make men suspect I desired profit and fame, 正使猜奔競，
Though I took no account of whether I won or lost. 何嘗計有無。
20 A Liu Shan had looked for and found me—it was useless, 劉剡虛訪覓，
So the Wang Ba I imitated was mocked, what a shame! 王霸竟揶揄！
21 To buy fealty, someone had burned the tallies, to no avail; 市義虛焚卷；
I was derided at the pass, for having thrown the silk credential away. 關譏漫棄繻。
22 The best remarks (of my friends), by now, I came to believe, 至言今信矣，
And my humble ambition was, for sure, a grief! 微尚亦悲夫！

The repercussions, however, created a sensation. Wen became the topic of gossip. Those vying with him never hesitated to smear his reputation, while those who once helped him could do nothing now. Wen's allegiance to the empire was deliberately made the target of ridicule. Faced with this situation, he was forced to confess failure. Evidently, Wen "failed to pass" because of the revelation of his name change (rhymes 19–22).

23 Let me tune the pitch for the White Snow aria, 白雪調歌響，
And enjoy dancing by the Rain Altar in the pure breeze. 清風樂舞雩。
24 I could not raise my shoulders [to adulate anyone] affectedly, 脅肩難黽免，
But I had to scratch my head, sighing in agony. 搔首易嗟吁。
25 To vie for winning, I was not a competent man, 角勝非能者，
But to determine who is the worthy, was it really by archery? 推賢見射乎？

It was against his nature to serve the eunuchs with servile flattery, and accepting or rejecting examinees was in no sense based on fair play. Wen had to employ philosophy to console his frustration. This is the price he had to pay for his pride (23–25).

26	When "the horn pitcher" contains in it more dread and fright,	兕觥增恐悚，
	"The cup" will lose its share of water, little and slight.	杯水失錙銖。
27	The white target has been withdrawn, no longer red and bright,	粉垛收丹采，
	While the golden whistling arrows, I have to hide.	金髇隱僕姑。
28	Letting drop my bow case, I was ashamed of finishing the cup,	垂橐羞盡爵，
	Raising the goblet, they insulted me for curving the bow.	揚觶辱彎弧。
29	Clumsy [as I am], I should not talk of drawing a tiger,	虎拙休言畫，
	Nor imitate [the action of] butchering a (seldom-seen) dragon.	龍希莫學屠。

Next, Wen hints at the political causes of his failure—that the officials in charge of the examination feared the eunuchs and that the succeeding monarch, Emperor Wuzong, showed distaste for him (26–29).

30	In a life of whirled-up fluff, I was used to leisure,	轉蓬隨款段，
	Let me weed the grass to erect my earthen shelter.	耘草辟墁墟。
31	I received my academic lessons in a village called Zheng,	受業鄉名鄭，
	I hid myself with my wisdom in a vale named Fool.	藏機谷號愚。
32	Of the simple style or the refined, I had an equal command,	質文精等貫，
	Tune of lute and lyre each responds to my ready hand.	琴筑韻相須。
33	I built my dwelling adjacent to the vast fields,	筑室連中野，
	By cutting the bulrush close to the Upper Fertile Land.	誅茅接上腴。
34	I have flowers of weeds interlacing the bamboo-hedge,	葦花綸虎落，

	And gnarls of pines embellishing the pillars and beams.	松瘦斗欒櫨。
35	I conversed with the warbling orioles in tranquility,	靜語鶯相對，
	Or shared a nap with the divine cranes at their ease.	閑眠鶴浪俱。
36	When stamens were ample, overworking the powdered-wings,	蕊多勞粉翅，
	And intoxicating aroma made bee's whiskers break.	香酷墜蜂鬚。
37	The fragrant herbs were redolent of the Three Islands,	芳草迷三島，
	And lucid ripples were similar to those of the Five Lakes.	澄波似五湖。
38	There were jumping fish frolicking out of the waterweeds,	躍魚翻藻荇，
	And gloomy egrets slumbering beneath the bulrushes.	愁鷺睡葭蘆。
39	Nesting on the dim islet were wild-ducks,	溟渚藏鸂鶒，
	Perching before my quiet screen, partridges.	幽屏臥鷓鴣。
40	I toiled and moiled for the field care,	苦辛隨藝植，
	My "sweetness and fat" depend on the farm's products.	甘旨仰樵蘇。
41	Laughing and muttering, I pointlessly held oranges in my sleeve,	笑語空懷橘，
	In poverty and in grief, I, too, leaned against a *wutong* tree.	窮愁亦據梧。
42	Able yet to be content with a half dinner of beans,	尚能甘半菽，
	I dared not slight the green sheaf.	非敢薄生芻。
43	My angling rock was covered with green moss,	釣石封蒼蘚，
	And the fragrant paths, decorated with purple calyces.	芳蹊豔絳跗。
44	I planted the orchids encircling the parcels,	樹蘭畦繚繞，
	And passed through bamboos, by a winding road.	穿竹路縈紆。
45	My loom shuttle is unlike that of *the mulberry lady*,	機杼非桑女，
	And my grove and garden differ from *the wood slave.*	林園異木奴。
46	I looked out warily for the red carps, stretching out my rod,	橫竿窺赤鯉，

And was on watch for the black cormorant,
holding camouflage. 持翳望青鶘。
47 I yearned for the taste of watercress at the "*the Semi-circular Pool*," 泮水思芹味，
I found the source of "*ricefield rent in Langye Commandery*." 瑯琊得稻租。

Circumstances forced him to retreat to his old way of life, of which he now provides a lengthy poetic description, a display of his skill in composing pastoral poetry (rhymes 30–47). He tells the readers of his diligent studies under a famous tutor (30–32), his taste for and pleasure in enjoying nature as a recluse (33–39), his cultivation of his personality and development of his moral principles (40–44), his financial status in reclusion (45), his aspiration ever since his adolescent years to serve his country (46), and his reputation as a precocious talent in the National University of Luoyang (47).

48 The light rattan cane was gnarled and bumpy, 杖輕藜臃腫，
My lotus attire was disheveled and shabby. 衣破芰披敷。
49 I was sad for the shrike with its fragrant spirit, 芳意憂鶗鴂，
And empathized with the cicadas in their mournful chirps. 愁聲覺蟪蛄。
50 The noisy swallows were shrieking on the short eaves, 短檐喧語燕，
While a hungry squirrel fell from a tall tree. 高木落飢鼯。
51 Urged by pressure, I had to leave my calm solitude, 事迫離幽墅，
And driven by destitution I ventured upon the frightful way. 貧牽犯畏途。

It was both his eagerness to serve his country and his desire to support his family in need after his father's death that caused him to embark on his precarious official career (rhymes 48–51).

52 In my loves and hates I took precautions against Du Kui, 愛憎防杜蕢，
In my laments and sighs I felt melancholy, as did Yang Zhu. 悲嘆似楊朱。

To his dismay, the eunuchs—the nightmare of his life—threatened him from the very outset of his social life (52).

53 Traveling for a living, I often passed by the country of Wei, 旅食常過衛，
And tarrying in my journey, I almost crossed the River Lu. 羈游欲渡瀘。

54 On the frontier I lamented "the Song of the
Protector-General," 塞歌傷都護，
By the border I meditated on the horn "Tune
of *Chanyu*." 邊角思單于。
55 At the military fords lances and spears were
clashing, 堡戍摽槍槊，
In the River Pass boats and ships were blockaded. 關河鎖舳艫。

Thus, instead of going to the capital, Wen was froced to travel all over the country, including the frontier, in order to avoid encountering the eunuchs directly (53–55).

56 I venerated the august bearing of General Big
Tree, 威容尊大樹，
And tried to shun *Autumn-Tu*, the law and penalty. 刑法避秋荼。
57 From afar I gazed back beyond a thousand leagues, 遠目窮千里，
And my returning heart flew to the Nine
Highways. 歸心寄九衢。

At the end of this period of travel, Wen went to the capital to rehabilitate himself—as is intimated here, he had already suffered a great injustice (56–57).

58 To enjoy sound sleep, the price is to suffer long
depression, 寢甘誠繫滯，
To be served free soup, I have to act with caution
and attention. 漿饋貴睢盱。
59 I keep a calling card in my pocket even though
I am far-famed, 懷刺名先遠，
To help the time, very few appreciate my Way. 干時道自孤。
60 By molars and incisors I was repeatedly
recommended and praised, 齒牙頻激發，
With umbrella and bookcase my road was yet
rugged and rocky. 簦笈尚崎嶇。

Wen recounts his unsuccessful efforts in the capital to secure a position. In spite of the recommendations on his behalf, nothing resulted. Apparently, his political orientation and personality made it not easy for him to be accepted at the time (58–60).

61 The lotus mansion and the Marquis' gates valued
my talents, 蓮府侯門貴，
Thus, to the Frost Terrace came the consent of the
royal mandate. 霜臺帝命俞。

62 Now the steed's hooves began to run swifter than a gale, 驥蹄初躡景，
And the roc's wings were about to spiral up to the zenith. 鵬翅欲搏扶。
63 Having stayed on duty, I returned on my dapple horse, 寓直回驄馬，
Sitting in different sections, we faced the dusky crows. 分曹對冥烏。
64 The Hundred Spirits attended, as it were, enjoying offerings, 百神歆髣髴，
Isolated Bamboos were sending notes, dim and lost. 孤竹韻含胡。
65 In Phoenix Hall we stood in lines to each side, 鳳闕分班立，
From egret rows with swords erect we paced forward. 鴛行竦劍趨。
66 At confidential behest, we butted against evil, 觸邪承密勿，
On behalf of the royal plan we maintained the law. 持法奉訏謨。
67 With jades clanging we strutted up and down, 鳴玉鏘登降，
And the pendants' sounding lingered faintly on. 衡牙響曳婁。
68 His Worship showed intimacy with Heshi's Jade, 祀親和氏璧，
The Fragrance was attached to the Boshan Censer. 香近博山爐。
69 Auspicious sunshade grew dense on the emerald trees, 瑞景森瓊樹，
A light piece of ice brightened the jade pot. 輕冰瑩玉壺。
70 To my divine-sheep cap, an iron shaft is clasped, 豸冠簪鐵柱，
At the dragon head was the Golden Bureau. 螭首對金鋪。
71 The Administrator's calligraphy numbered a thousand scrolls, 內史書千卷，
And the General's paintings, one cabinetful. 將軍畫一廚。
72 My eyes were dazzled by this surprising display, 眼明驚氣象，
And my heart awestricken by the grand scale. 心死伏規模。

However, unexpectedly, with the recommendation of a Prime Minister and the consent of the emperor himself, Wen gained an opportunity to serve the Heir Apparent. This is one of the major secrets of Wen's life, and one of the most ambiguous passages in this poem. The passage here provides a detailed description of how he served the Heir Apparent and what he witnessed during his attendance (61–72).

73 I had never expected to look at the imperial treasury, 豈意觀文物，

If it was useless to carve a *crude jadeite* like me. 何勞琢碔砆。
74 Grasses are luxuriant—fit for grazing the Yaoniao Steed, 草肥牧騕褭，
Mosses are rough—proper for tempering the *Kunwu* Blade. 苔澀淬昆吾。

A hard as he tried, all his efforts came to naught. Time was not favorable (73–74). The information implied, which was unnecessary to point out to those addressed in the title of the poem, is that the Heir Apparent died as a victim of the eunuchs.

75 My yearning for home is of a bird nesting on the southern branch, 鄉思巢枝鳥，
The passage of time, like the sun crossing the cloud-crevice. 年華過隙駒。
76 Harboring gratitude [to the emperor] I vainly accompany my shadow, 銜恩空抱影，
For I had no chance to devote myself to repay the imperial grace, 酬德未捐軀。
77 Among my compeers I've been honored as a good friend, 時輩推良友，
Of my pedigree I have carried on an honest fame. 家聲繼令圖。
78 To present myself, I grieve my wings were too short, 致身傷短翮，
With head high, you look back at me, a worn-out horse. 驤首顧疲駑，
79 Now Ban and Sima are galloping forth side by side, 班馬方齊鶩，
While Chen and Lei are, also, driving neck and neck. 陳雷亦并驅。
80 In the past, each of you told his own wishes, 昔皆言爾志，
By now I likewise regard my disciples with awe. 今亦畏吾徒。
81 The energy I possess, to Altair and Plough can soar, 有氣干牛斗，
But where is the man to really know the precious Lulu sword? 無人辨轆轤？

At this point, once more taking up the thread of return, Wen laments his bad luck. He could not "repay the imperial grace," and seeing that many of his friends, including his students, were well advanced in their official careers, he sighed mournfully over his frustrations and the waste of his talent (75–81).

82 Coming as a guest, the green-ants, I poured 客來斟綠蟻，
Trying to ransom a wife, on the blue-beetles, I trod, 妻試踏青蚨。
83 By incessant aspersions, even [flesh and] bones are destroyed, 積毀方銷骨，
And I fear that a slight blemish would spoil the whole gem. 微瑕懼掩瑜。

The fundamental cause of his failure was his marriage with a singer-prostitute and the slanders from the eunuchs on that pretext, as implied back in rhyme 56 (82–83).

84 As the snake-spears are still involved in shifting wars, 蛇矛猶轉戰，
The "[one in] fish disguise" is in detainment and in thrall. 魚服自囚拘。
85 By such tricks they intended to delude the world, 欲就欺人事，
But how can the ghost's execution be dodged? 何能逭鬼誅？

It was the eunuchs who had done all the mischief clandestinely—they seized control of the emperor and threw the country into confusion—at least Wen believed that they did. And it was also the eunuchs who forced Wen into such a difficult situation. Here the poet addresses the question to the eunuchs by referring to their crimes instead of their names (rhymes 84–85).

86 Between right and wrong—waking or dreaming, I was confused, 是非迷覺夢，
From Qin to Wu, I planned a journey. 行役議秦吳。
87 In the piercing cold the wind was wailing 凜冽風埃慘，
In the desolation, plants were withered. 蕭條草木枯。
88 Reluctant departure made me heartbroken, 低回傷志氣，
Braving the cold, my skin and flesh were frostbitten. 蒙犯變肌膚。
89 Only the cries of migrating wild geese were heard, 旅雁唯聞叫，
When a hungry falcon came to me without being called. 飢鷹不待呼。

Wen went back to Wu from the capital in the cold winter. Here the migrating wild geese and hungry falcons are self-portraits of himself (86–89).

90 The shuttle of my dream was hastened like the cries of crickets, 夢梭抛促織，
The cocoon of my yearning heart was modeled on those of spiders. 心繭學蜘蛛。
91 How can *their* tricks, again, be hard to foresee? 寧復機難料？
But wasn't such petty faith too trifling to be trusted? 庸非信未孚？
92 Furious and wild, I'm a tiger shot by an arrow, 激揚銜箭虎，
In doubt and fear, I'm a fox listening on the ice. 疑懼聽冰狐。
93 For saving myself, I will dig one more "burrow," 處己將營窟，
Such is my heart that tallies to that of the sage. 論心若合符。

Fearing the danger around him, and angry at the eunuchs' evils, Wen wanted to have his say, but he could not speak out openly, and had to be careful of his life (90–93).

94 Don't say that I am in my "brother's" grace, 浪言輝棣萼，
Where can a remote kinsman like me entrust his life? 何所托葭莩？
95 From a tall tree an oriole can seek friends with his warbling voice, 喬木能求友，
In a dilapidated nest an Owl vainly scares *Yuanchu*, with a rotten rat. 危巢莫嚇鶵。
96 I'd rather assume a lofty demeanor as a leading figure, 風華飄領袖，
Than bow to shirt and skirt with the *Poetry* and *Rites.* 詩禮拜衾襦。

Helpless but unyielding, Wen still keeps his pride and shows some skepticism of sanctimonious Confucian doctrines (94–96).

97 When I recline on a pillow, my feelings are immensely bitter, 欹枕情何苦，
In the same boat, how can their Way from mine differ? 同舟道豈殊？

Wen once more expresses his deeply felt sorrow, using a confusing rhetorical question by means of which he blamed somebody who betrayed him (97).

98 Let me abandon myself to caressing melilotus and angelica, 放懷親蕙芷，
Though my retirement is not yet in a "mulberry and elm" year. 收迹異桑榆。

99	As a gift to my distant friends, I break off a willow twig, And I will cut the bulrushes to make a letter.	贈遠聊攀柳， 裁書欲截蒲。
100	Gazing into the air, endless tears blurring my eyes, I turn my head back, and faltered.	瞻風無限淚， 回首更踟躕。

Wen ends the poem with a reference to his reluctant and forced withdrawal, accompanied by all his frustrations and sadness (98–100).

Notes

INTRODUCTION

1. See Pulleyblank, 24–74 and Twittchett, 1, 374–681.

2. The eight Tang emperors who reigned from 806 to 888 were all installed on the throne and subsequently murdered by the eunuchs. See Zhao Yi: 383–88.

3. See Song Minqiu, 326, "*Amnesty Edict on Changing the Era Title to Tianfu (901)*": "In the seventh year of Dahe, the seventeen households of Wang Ya and others were all executed under the false accusation of treason. These loyal men acted on the secret order of Wenzong, were unjustly condemned . . . , and should be rehabilitated in rank and reputation."

4. For Liu's biographies, see JTS, 190: 5064–77 and XTS, 178: 5293–5307.

5. For Han's role in this revitalization, see Hartman.

6. For Liu's role, see Chen, *Liu Tsung-yuan and Intellectual Change in T'ang China.*

7. For a Western study of Li Ao, see Barrett.

8. For a Western study of this topic, see E. Zurcher, *The Buddhist Conquest of China.*

9. See chapter 8, Pei Tingyu's comment on why Xuanzong could not grant Wen a degree.

10. See Zhang Huiyan, *Cixuan*, 1; Xue Xue, *Yipiao Shihua*, 675–717, in *Qing Shihua.*

11. "Princely Establishment" refers to the Ministry of Ritual, which was to administer the Presented Scholar Examination that Wen failed to pass because of political reasons. Xu [Shang] (徐商), Chen [Gu] (陳蝦), Li [Yuan] (李遠), Yuan Jiao (袁郊), and Miao Shen (苗紳) are all well-known literati-officials or famous poets of the time. Su (蘇), Wei (韋), and Li Yi (李逸) are unknown. 端公, is an unofficial reference to the Attending Censor. To avoid digressions we will not discuss these men in this study.

12. These "discoveries" are the summary of my intermittent deliberations and studies for a long time; some of them were published in Chinese, see the Bibliography of this book. However, I will corroborate my arguments with many more proofs, in addition to those already used in bearing out the basic contour of the events.

CHAPTER ONE. FAMILY BACKGROUND

1. See JTS, 190: 5079–81 and XTS, 91: 3188–89.

2. See Li Jifu, *Yuanhe Junxianzhi*, 8–9; or XTS, "The Geographical Records," 39: 1003.

3. Ever since the time of Wen He (溫何, of the Western Han Dynasty), down to Wen Xu (溫序, of the Eastern Han Dynasty) and Wen Xian (溫羨, of the Jin Dynasty), an eminent clan had lived in Qi; see *Shiji*, 18: 937; JS, 44:1268.

4. This alludes to "Surging forward are the Jiang and the Han Rivers / Main-threads of the southern country" (滔滔江漢，南國之紀). See *Maoshi* The Fourth Month (13: 462) and Waley Arthur, no. 140.

5. Wen's connection with Li Shen will be clarified in chapter 2.

6. For Shan Tao and Ji Shao's biographies, see JS, 43: 1223 and 89: 2298, 49: 1369.

7. See DKJK, 16: 4 and XTS, 181: 5347.

8. An annotated translation of this epistle is in chapter 2.

9. King Xuan of Qi (齊宣王) appointed seventy-six Jixia Academicians in order to let them comment on the affairs of the state. See *Shiji,* 70: 2300, "Hereditary Eminent Clan of Tian Jingzhong" (田敬仲世家).

10. See JS, 92: 2378.

11. Wen's poems indicating his nostalgia or special link with the Yue district include the following, all in WFQ, "Jiangnan Air" (江南曲, j. 2), "Ode of Su Xiaoxiao" (蘇小小歌, j. 2), "Ode of Burning the Wild Grass" (燒歌, j. 2), "Ode of Qiantang" (錢唐曲, j. 2), "Written in the Villa of Senior Li" (李先生別墅, j. 7), Inscribed in the Temple of Mount Xiao" (題蕭山廟, j. 7), "The Seclusion of Recluse Chen"* (陳處士幽居, j. 7), "Seeing Off Secretary Guo of Bingzhou"* (送并州郭書記, j. 7), "Inspired by Some Happenings before the Cold Food Festival"* (寒食節前有懷, j. 8), "Inscribed in He Zhizhang's Former Residence" (題賀知章故居, j. 8), "Responding with Respect to Senior Li"* (敬答李先生, j. 9), "Mailing to Senior Cui" (寄崔先生, j. 9), "Bidding Farewell to a Friend on the River"* (江上別友人, j. 9), and "Lodging in a Monastery of Fengqu" (宿灃曲精舍, j. 9), etc. Those marked with "*" are especially related to Tonglu in Muzhou (睦州).

12. We identify this Grand Master Cui as Cui Xian (崔咸, ?–834); see JTS, 190: 5059, XTS, 177: 5273, and Gu Xuejie: 218.

13. For the allusion to Xie Lingyun as Xie the Guest, *see Shipin* (詩品), "Xie Lingyun, the Magistrate of Linchuan of the Song," in Ding Fubao, *Lidai Shihua Xubian*, 9.

14. See "The Category of Literature" of *Congshu Jicheng Chubian* (叢書集成初編文學類). Dong Fen, date unknown; see also Wang Chongmin, 502.

15. The poet's note: "In the Fishing Isle of Yan Guang, there are an eastern terrace and a western terrace" (原注：嚴光釣渚有西臺東臺).

16. The poet's note: "In Tonglu there is Nine Li Isle" (原注：桐廬有九里洲).

17. See Wei Qingzhi, 3: 61.

18. *Wenyuan Yinghua* (223: 1116) designates this poem as one composed by Fang Gan (Wen's younger contemporary), to which I do not agree, since two other sources

attribute it to Wen and it fits quite well with the internal evidence I find in Wen's entire works.

19. See XTS, 91: 3783.

20. See Cen Zhongmian, "*Yuanhe Xingcu*an Sijiaoji," 351–52 and XTS, 72: 2661–65.

21. All are marked with "*" in the table. See XTS, 83: 3644–59, "Biographies of the Princesses," and Wang Pu: 6: 63–64, "Princesses" (公主).

22. See XTS, 83: 3659. Princess Song'guo did not die until well into the Yuanhe era. She seems to be Wen Tingyun's aunt, if not his mother.

23. Emperor Gaozu, Liu Bang, said to Consort Qi (戚姬), "Please perform a Chu dance for me, and I will sing a Chu song in turn" (為我楚舞，吾為若楚歌), when both knew that it was impossible to substitute the Prince Ruyi (born of Qi) for the Heir Apparent (born of Empress Lü). See *Shiji*, 55: 2047, "Biography of Marquis Liu" (留侯列傳). Here it hints at the tragedy of Virtuous Consort Wang and her son; see chapter 5.

24. Zhang Fang, an imperial relative, often accompanied Emperor Yuan both when going out incognito and sleeping. See HS, 1395, 2654–57 and 3721–33.

25. See HS, 18: 677–720, Chronology for Imperial Relatives, Marquis of Royal Blessing (外戚恩澤侯年表).

26. For Wen Zao's biographies, see JTS, 165: 4312 and XTS, 91:3784.

27. For an annotated translation and analysis of this epistle, see chapter 3.

28. See XTS, 91. 3784.

29. See XTS, 91: 3781.

30. For a detailed discussion of the text of this epistle, see chapter 2.

31. In ancient China, before starting to lecture, one was to *pull down the drapery* (下帷) in the room, hence the term came to mean to study Confucian doctrines; and by analogy, to "sew up the broken drapery" means to restore the declining Confucianism.

32. See Legge, *Texts of Taoism*, 273 and Watson, *Chuangtzu*, 202–203. The line also refers to an axiom: "It is not too late to repair the pen when the sheep has bolted" (亡羊而補牢，未為遲也). See Liu Xiang, 17:556.

33. 牧 might originally be 放, as the similarity of the two Chinese characters could easily cause such confusion. A second reason for this speculation is that 牧馬 involves no allusion whatsoever to match 亡羊.

34. See *Shangshu*, 11: 84 and Waltham's translation, *Shujing*, 121.

35. "Shouting for stakes" refers to the game called *Shupu*: tossing the five black-white dice on a chessboard, the player shouted for the highest prize, *Lu*: the dice all black.

36. See "Watching the Chess Game" (觀棋, j. 9 WFQ) for another example.

37. See *Wenxuan*, 43: 600–603.

38. Li Shangyin's "Thinking of Zaimeng Feiqing" (有懷在蒙飛卿, *Yuxisheng Shiji Jianzhu*, 2: 524); Ji Tangfu's "Sending Wen Feiqing to Be the Defender of Fangcheng" (送溫飛卿尉方城, QTS, 542: 6257), Zhang Hu's poem of the same topic (QTS, 511:

5837), Duan Chengshi's "The Eight Letters to Wen Feiqing" (與溫飛卿書八首, QTW, 787: 10391), and Pei's *Dong'guan Zouji* (5: 17) all praise Wen's personality.

39. For Wang Zun, Lu Ji, and Xie Lingyun's being orphaned in their childhood, see respectively "Biography of Wang Zun" in HS, 3226–38, "Biography of Lu Ji" in SGZ, 1328–29, and "Biography of Xie Lingyun" in SS, 1743–88.

40. Wen is Yanbo's "distant scion and orphan" (裔孤). But the term was mistakenly "corrected" to "distant scion" (裔孫), to conform to the record in XTS. See Ji, *Tangshijishi*, 53: 822.

41. For Zhang Ping's biography, see JS, 75: 1992 and NATW, 119.

42. "Falling and rising" is a case of *pianyi fuci* (偏義復詞); that is, despite the parallel juxtaposition of the paired antonyms, stress is put on one of the pair, while the other has only a structural function.

43. For Xiang's biography, see JS, 49: 1374–75. For his rhapsody, see *Wenxuan*, 16: 22.

44. See Denis Twitchett, 600–609.

45. Wang Chong, *Lunheng*, 74: "Somebody says Heaven lets the five grains grow so as to feed the people, and produces silk and hemp so as to clothe them. This is as good as saying that Heaven serves the people as if it were the like of farmers and mulberry-ladies" (或說天生五谷以食人，生絲麻以衣人，此謂天為人作農夫桑麻之徒也).

46. *Wood Slave* alludes to Sheng Hongzhi's (盛弘之, of the Jin Dynasty) *Jingzhouji* (荊州記; see Shuofu, j. 61 for its extant text): Li Heng had planted a thousand orange trees in Longyang Isle, he bade his son on his deathbed, saying: "On my isle there are a thousand *Wood Slaves*, with which you will get a thousand bolts of brocade" (李衡于龍陽洲種橘千株，臨死敕其子曰：吾洲里千頭木奴，歲可得絹千匹).

47. That Minister Liu Director of the Palace Library is Liu Yuxi is attested by Cen (*Tangshi Yushen*, 4: 251) and Bian (*Congkao*, 295–96); we will provide more proofs.

48. Liu Yuxi was a good calligrapher; see Zheng Qiao, 73: 751. Bao Zhao (鮑照, 422–465) once remarked that Xie Lingyun's five syllabic poetry is like a lotus just blooming with a natural charm. See NS, 34: 877.

49. Ma Rong (馬融, 79–166), a master of Confucianism, gave lectures before a crimson gauze screen. See HHS, 58: 1952.

50. Jia Yi's (賈誼, 200–168 B.C.) "Preface to Rhapsody on the Owl (鵩鳥賦序), speaks about an evil omen, an owl that flew into his room. See *Wenxuan*, 13: 198–200.

51. Shan Tao said: "When Ji Kang is drunk he leaned crazily like a *jade mountain* about to collapse." Zhong Hui said to Emperor Wendi: "Ji Kang is a *sleeping dragon* and should not be promoted." See NATW, 14: 309 and JS, 49: 1370.

52. "The Nine-Plain" was a cemetery, where the Grand Master of the Jin Kingdom, Zhao Dun, was buried; Zhao once said, "If the dead should come to life again, whom am I to go with" (死者如可作，吾誰與歸). See *Liji*, 10: 1316.

53. "Whitewashed office" refers the bureaus under the Department of State Affairs (尚書省), where Liu Yuxi once had an office.

54. When Yin Hao led an army into Luoyang to *renovate the imperial tombs*, his soldiers rebelled, and he was then discharged from all of his posts. See JS, 77: 2043–48.

55. Liu was descended from the Huns, though he claimed to be the offspring of the Han Dynasty Prince of Zhongshan, Liu Sheng (中山靖王劉勝). See Bian, *Nianpu,* 1–3. Here the Jingkou Liu was descended from Prince Yuan of Chu, Liu Jiao (楚元王劉交), HS, 37: 1921–27), as were the Liu-Song imperial clan and Liu Dan. This is Wen's complimentary version of Liu's family stock.

56. See Bian, *Nianpu*, 40.

57. Liu Yuxi's "Watching A Chess Game" (觀棋歌, QTS, 356: 4005) shows that Liu was indeed a good chess player.

58. Xie An (謝安, 320–385), the Jin Dynasty Prime Minister, organized the counterattack against Fu Jian's (苻堅, 338–385) invasion from the north. When the Jin army defeated Fu, Xie was playing chess and did not look surprised at all. See JS, 79: 2072–77. Here "Xie" refers to Pei Du, who kept the company of quite a few famous literati of his time, including Liu and Wen; see his biography discussed in chapter 2.

59. Upon hearing the song: "In the morning, I set out from Xiangyang / In the evening I lodged by the Big Dike / Many girls of the Big Dike / Are pretty as flowers, to their lover's surprise" (朝發襄陽城，暮至大堤宿。大堤諸女兒，花艷驚郎目), Prince Sui, Liu Dan (隨王劉誕) of the Liu-Song composed "*Xiangyang Yue* (襄陽樂); see YFSJ, 48: 705.

60. Mr. Liu, the poet Liu Yun (柳惲, 465–517), here refers to Liu Yuxi by the homonymic nature of their surnames. See LS, 21: 331–32 for more information about Liu Yun.

61. See Wang Mingsheng, 77: 1205–209

62. See "Postscript to *Jinlianji*" (跋金奩集), in *Lu You Ji*, 26: 2243.

63. See Bian, *Liu Yuxi Congkao*, 296.

64. Zhang Hua (張華, 232–300) and his friend Lei Huan found a pair of precious swords and each took one. After Lei's son obtained the sword, it changed into a dragon and leapt into the surging waves, when he was crossing a river. See JS, 36: 1068–77.

65. For Yang's biography, see JS, 79: 2077.

66. "The lower party" (下黨), translated as "junior party," keeps the meaning of "lower" (下) with respect to generations.

67. See Bian, *Nianpu*, 105.

68. See HS, 55: 1799,"Biographies of Eight Princes of Emperor Zhang" (章帝八王傳).

69. See HHS, 67: 2185–86, "Biographies of the Imprisoned Factionalists" (黨錮列傳).

70. For Li's biographies, see JTS, 167: 4372 and XTS, 131: 4511; Li's relations with the two Lius, see Bian, *Nianpu*, 36–103 and *Congkao*, 73–75. See also chapter 5.

71. "Li Cheng, on the 27th of the Ninth month of the 20th year of the Zhenyuan era (804), was promoted (to Hanlin Academician) from the position of Investigating Censor. On the 17th of the third month of the 21st year of Zhenyuan (805), he was appointed to the concurrent post of Vice Director of the Bureau of the Waterways and Irrigation. On the twenty-third day of the third month of the first year of the Yuanhe era (806), Li was transferred out of the Hanlin Academy and appointed

Magistrate of Suizhou." See Ding Juhui's "Chongxiu Hanlin Xueshi Biji," 3375 in *Zhibuzu Congshu.*

72. See *Liu Yuxi Ji*, 40: 403.

CHAPTER TWO. WEN'S BIRTH YEAR

1. For Zhu Yu, see HHS, 78: 2526, "Biographies of the Eunuchs"(宦者列傳).

2. See *Shiji*, 68: 2229 and *Sanguozhi*, 21: 604–605.

3. See *Mengzi*, 16: 2682, "King Hui of Liang" (梁惠王).

4. See *Zuozhuan*, 1: 2019, "Duke Zhao the First Year" (昭公元年).

5. See *Liji*, 9: 1305, and *Zuozhuan*, 45: 2057, "Duke Zhao the Ninth Year."

6. See Li's "Rhapsody on Striking the Bell in the Palace" (鼓鐘于宮賦), QTW, 632: 8107.

7. Du Yu's annotation and Kong Yingda's sub-annotation (疏) to *Zuozhuan*, as well as Zheng Xuan's annotation and Kong's sub-annotation to *Liji* hold that what Du Kui did serves as a model that embodies the Confucian rites and morals. Defying the traditional exegeses, Li Cheng regards this passage as a misrepresentation of the *Book of Rites* and Wen followed his teacher in using the topic to attack the eunuchs, by means of innuendo.

8. See *Wenxuan*, 14: 23.

9. See *Zuozhuan*, "Duke Zhuang the Ninth Year," 8: 1766.

10. See Xia, 383–424, Gu, *Wenxue Lunji*, 188–260. Xia and Gu, both pioneers in studying Wen's life, had collected a wealth of firsthand information.

11. Basing his argument on the line in "Hundred-Rhyme Poem": "Though my retirement is not in a mulberry and elm year" (收迹異桑榆), Xia infers that "it means that Wen was not yet an aged man; but at the time he was at least about thirty. If we subtract thirty from 840 (when the poem was composed), Wen's birth year falls in the Yuanhe era of Emperor Xianzong (806–820). Since the Yuanhe era has fifteen years, we can suppose it for the time being to be in the middle, i. e., the seventh year of Yuanhe (812)." See Xia (389).

12. It was two years after Ji Kang wrote the "Letter for Breaking Off Relations with Shan Juyuan" (in which he says "My son is eight years of age") that he was executed. Hence, Ji Shao's biography states that he "became an orphan at the age of ten."

13. Out of many possibilities Gu decides Li Deyu to be the "Chancellor Li," without strict logical inference. Then, he guesses that "since in the fifth year of Kaicheng (840) Li's age (787–849) is fifty four, Feiqing was *probably* twenty nine, and that the difference of Li's and Wen's age is about twenty-five years." See Gu, *Lunwenji*,190.

14. The conclusions about Wen's birth year that differ from Xia's are: 801 (Chen Shangjun), 817 (Liu Kaiyang), 824 (Huang Zhenyun), 827 (Wang Dajin), and 798 (Mou).

15. The Marquis of Sui saved a badly wounded snake. Later on the snake got for him a pearl, which thus was called the pearl of the Marquis of Sui. Bian He got a jade-enfolding stone and presented it to the kings of Chu. The first two kings, however, thought that He was deceiving them and had his feet cut off. The third King, however,

had the "stone" carved and found therein a most precious treasure, named the Jade of Heshi. See Gao You's exegesis to "Lanmingxun," *Huainanzi* (*Ershierzi*, 6: 1231). Lord Cang and Doctor Bianque are both well-known ancient doctors; see *Shiji*, 105: 2785.

16. "The year of Having the Way" alludes to the age at which Guo Tai (郭泰, 128–69) died, i.e., forty-two years. "Having the Way" was originally the name given to a kind of civil recruitment in the Han Dynasty for men of moral value. Toward the end of the Eastern Han, however, this system became so corrupt that many of those who really "had the way," men such as Guo Tai, refused to take part. Guo was thus universally respected with the title "Having the Way Guo" (郭有道). Cai Yong (蔡邕, 132–92), a well-known writer of epitaphs, composed the "Epitaph for Having the Way Guo" (郭有道碑文), after Guo's death "at the age of 42," saying: "I have written epitaphs for so many individuals, all of whom are unworthy of my compliments, save Having the Way Guo, who truly need not be ashamed of my praise." See HHS, 68: 2225–331 and *Wenxuan*, 58: 800.

17. "Kong Lin" refers to Kong Linzhi (孔琳之, 369–423), who, like his grandfather Kong Qun, was famous for selflessness when he held the office of Palace Aide to the Censor-In-Chief. See NS, 27: 731 and SS, 56: 1559. Zhang Dai might be the grandson of Zhang Yue (張說, 667–730), a Prime Minister of the Kaiyuan (712–740) era, see XTS, 31: 1750; it is also possible that the source this Zhang Dai refers to is no longer extant.

18. "To put the classics across the knees" (橫經) is a kenning for studying hard.

19. From "my teacher" we can infer that it was when Wen was studying in the Luoyang National University that he met his lifelong teacher Li Cheng.

20. Wen offered no account of what reduced him to a traveling orphan, except that he had to give up his studies and face a harder life.

21. "Chumo" is the style name of Wu Yinzhi (吳隱之). It was said that Wu was so frugal and incorruptible that he had no bedclothes for the winter. See NATW, 23. "Xiuling" is the style-name of Wang Huzhi (王胡之), who once lived in extreme poverty and want. Tao Fan, who was serving as Magistrate of Wucheng Prefecture [Zhejiang], sent him a boatload of rice as a present. See NATW, 174. Note the punning nature of the two names: "Chumo" can mean living in reclusion, and "Xiuling" means long years.

22. "Shoot blood" is an allusion to *Shiji*, 3: 104, "The Yin Annals" (殷本紀): The Emperor Wuyi (帝武乙) filled leather bags with blood and shot upward at them, calling it "*Shooting Heaven*" (射天). The meaning of this term in this context is "blaspheming the emperor," and because of this, Wen states that "it is indeed an unjust charge." For tonal reasons, the poet used "shoot blood" (射血) instead.

23. "Prime Minister Liu" refers to Liu Youqiu (劉幽求, 655–715), who helped Emperor Xuanzong do away with the usurping Princess Taiping and inaugurated an era of prosperity. See JTS, 97: 3039 and XTS, 121: 4327. Duke Xu Su refers to Su Ting (蘇頲), (670–727), who was also a Prime Minister during Xuanzong's reign and was famous for his elegant style in writing imperial edicts. See JTS, 88: 2880 and XTS, 125: 4399.

24. According to HHS, 60: 2004, Cai Yong, with a piece of *wutong* wood he rescued from the embers, made "a zither with a burned end." (焦尾琴), which produced beautiful musical sound. This is alluded to by Liu Yuxi's "Epistle Presented to Du, Minister of Works" (上杜司空啓, see Qu Tuiyuan, 18: 450): "Like a half-burned lonely *wutong* I wish

to be taken back from the embers"(孤桐半焦，冀見收于煨燼), while Liu's remark is alluded to by Wen's. "The Dance Song of Great Joy" (大豫舞歌), a eulogizing Music Bureau song of the Jin Dynasty (YFSJ, 52: 757) says: "[The imperial] beneficence reaches trees and grasses, and the royal grace was given even to the insects" (仁及草木，惠加昆蟲).

25. While on the road, Yan Ying (晏嬰, ?–500 B.C.), Chief Minister of the Qi Kingdom, came across the worthy man Yue Shifu (越石父) being taken prisoner; he untied from the right yoke of his carriage a horse for the latter's ransom, and accepted him as a distinguished guest. See *Shiji*, 62: 2134. Lord Mengchang's (孟嘗君) retainer, Feng Xuan, chanted and tapped at his sword to express his grievances. The lord met all his demands and moved him from a second-class room to the best guesthouse. See *Shiji*, 75: 2531.

26. Wen's travels will also be dealt with in chapter 3.

27. Wen's experiences in the Huai River valley (836) will be discussed in chapter 4.

28. Wen's service to the Heir Apparent will be studied in chapter 5.

29. Wen's examination performance will be discussed in chapters 7 and 8.

30. According to Pei Du's biography in XTS, 14: 4433, after he died, Wenzong asked if he had any letters left behind for him, Pei's family presented his draft which only shows Pei's concern about the imperial succession and says nothing about his own affairs.

31. That Wen abruptly turns to speaking about Emperor Xuanzong might indicate the close relation of the latter with the Wen clan, as was proved in chapter 1.

32. That the examination was held before the tenth month of the year can be inferred from Wen's "Poster in the State Son's University" (榜國子監).

33. For Pei Du's biographies, see JTS, 170: 4413–35 and XTS, 173: 5209–19.

34. The role Pei Du played in the Yuanhe Restoration is universally recognized. For a representative English work on this topic, see *The Cambridge History of China*, 611–20.

35. If we take the whole Late Tang period for our survey, there was another Prime Minister, Pei Xiu (裴休, –864, JTS, 177: 4593–94 and XTS, 182: 5371–72), who, for all his connections with Wen on other occasions, does not fit in the situation related in the epistle. Pei Xiu was Prime Minister from 852 to 855 when Wen definitely did not have an urgent crisis like the one related here. Xia and Gu both held that this Pei was Pei Xiu.

36. See Wu Tingxie, TFZNB, 4: 427.

37. My understanding of these poems agrees with that of Wang Mingsheng, who also took the poems as evidence that Wen enjoyed Pei's friendship; see *Eshubian*, 77: 1211.

38. "A cloth-robe commoner from Dan Yang" is a self-styled title of Tao Hongjing, who later became prime minister; see LS, 51: 742–44. "Lotus-isle" (蓮渚), originating from Wang too, is a euphemism for prime ministership, which Pei actually held until very old.

39. For Dou Xian's biography, see HHS, 23: 812; For Du Yu's Biography, see JS, 34: 1030.

40. For Han Yu's writing, see QTW, 561: 7205–7207; for Duan's, see QTW, 617: 7918.

41. When a cabman vomited on the Prime Minister's carriage, Bing Ji (邴吉, ?–55 B.C.) said that it was no more than spoiling a carriage-mat. See HS, 74: 3142–52.

42 Xun Kai was said to leave wherever he sat a fragrance lasting for three days; see WFQ quotes Liu Yiqing. "The State's Fragrance" is also another name for the orchid, a symbol of the noble man. Yu Liang (庾亮 289–340) once ascended the Southern Tower, joining his subordinates there to enjoy the moonlight; see JS, 73: 1915–24.

43. Before his death, Duke Zhou put in a golden case letters and memorials to be presented to King Cheng (of the Zhou Dynasty), see *Shangshu*, 13: 195.

44. The Yan Terrace, i.e., Gold Terrace (黃金臺), was believed to be the spot where King Zhao of Yan (燕昭王, ?–279 B.C.) accepted worthy men by placing a great mass of gold on it; see Liu Xiang, 1065–66.

45. For the sake of his old mother, Mao Yi accepted an official appointment; but after his mother's death, he refused the government's offer of higher offices. See HHS, 27: 946. A group of influential men collected donations for Ruan Xiu's wedding, and many failed to donate their shares simply because they were not famous enough. See JS, 49: 1366–67.

46. "Zhongxuan" was the style of Wang Can (王粲, 177–217), who led a vagrant life until he was well into his thirties, see SGZ, 21: 597-99. "Zhuge" should refer to Wang's contemporary Zhuge Liang (諸葛亮, 181–234), who married late, see SGZ, 35: 911–30.

47. There are different identifications of this Li. Gu Sili (WFQ, 6: 129): Li Wei (李蔚, fl. 840–870); Xia (389) and Gu Xuejie (188–191): Li Deyu; Chen and Mou: Li Shen.

48. For the exact meaning of this couplet, see chapter 7.

49. See Wang Dingbao, *Tangzhiyan*, 2: 151–16. Wen Qi, Wen's assumed name, will be explained in chapter 7.

50. Legend has it that all carp move against the river until they arrive at the Dragon Gate, which they vie to jump over so as to transform themselves into dragons. See WFQ, 113.

51. See *Maoshi*, 9: 405; for the translation, see Waley, No. 183.

52. XTS, 44: 1159–62: "Records of Selection and Recommendation" (選舉志), "Every year in the middle of winter, the commanderies, the counties, the institutes and the universities recommend those who have finished their studies to the Department of State Affairs. Those who were not recommended by institutes or universities were called the provincial contributions. All of them . . . presented themselves to the commanderies and the counties. After the examination, the administrator of the capital, in accordance with the etiquettes of the District Symposium (鄉飲酒), had audience with their subordinate clerks . . . offering lamb to the spirits and singing the poem of the "Deer Singing" before they ranked themselves with the young and older officials in order of seniority." For the District Symposium, see *Yili*, 8: 980 and Steele, *The I-Li*, 74.

53. See *Wenxuan*, 23: 336, Liu Zhen (劉楨, ?–217), "Presented to Leader of the Court Gentlemen for Miscellaneous Uses" (贈五官中郎將).

54. For the time when Li Deyu was appointed Prime Minister, see XTS, 72: 2449; for when Li Shen was appointed Prime Minister, see XTS, 72: 2480; for Kong's edict, see Lu Xinyuan, *Tangwen Shiyi*, 30: 442.

CHAPTER THREE. BEFORE THE YEAR OF "HAVING NO DOULTS"

1. Cheng Gong (? –76) and Zhong Hao (103–163), both Confucian officials of the Eastern Han and famous for their fierce allegiance to the dynasty, refer to Xu Shang, the subject of this epistle. For the two men's biographies see HHS, 27:944 and 56:1826–29.

2. See *Maoshi*, "Wave of the Pan", 21: 610–12 and Waley, No. 250: "Merry the waves of the Pan [semi-circular pool] / Come, pluck the watercress"(思樂泮水，薄采其芹).

3. When Li Baiyao (李百藥, 565–648) was seven years old, he heard someone read an essay by Xu Ling (徐陵, 507–583) to "Reap the rice of Langye"(刈瑯琊之稻), while none but Baiyao knew what it alluded to. See Li's biographies, JTS, 72: 2571 and XTS, 102: 397. WFQ cites *Shishuo* [世說, should be *Xushishuo* (續世說) instead, by Kong Pingzhong, 孔平仲, of the Southern Song] about the anecdote, though the "rice of Langye" alludes to *Zuozhuan* (48: 384) and Du Yu's annotation: "The Monarch of Yu engaged himself in registering the rice field (鄅人藉稻)"; "The Kingdom of Yu is situated in present Kaiyang County of Langye Commandery "(鄅國在瑯琊開陽縣南). For Xu Ling's essay, see Yan Kejun, juan 10, the line not found.

4. Xin Wenfang (8: 135) says: "Having a gift for quick-witted literary composition, Wen could finish a ten-thousand-character essay impromptu" (才思捷給，能立馬萬言).

5. This description, from rhyme 30 to 46, is just prior to rhyme 47—Wen's attending the university, which was, as we have just discussed, only an episode of his long reclusion.

6. When Liu Xiang (劉向) was reading at night, there came a spirit *Taiyi* with a rattan cane. See HS, 36: 1928. For the "gnarled and bumpy" ailanthus in *Zhuangzi*, see Legge, *Texts of Taoism*, 174. "Lotus attire" alludes to *Lisao*: "I made a coat of lotus and water chestnut leaves / And got lotus petals to make myself a skirt." See Hawkes, 25.

7. "Shrike's fragrant spirit" alludes to *Lisao*: "Beware lest the shrike sound his note before the equinox / Causing all the flowers to lose their fine fragrance." See Hawkes, 32. Cry of the shrike signals the fading of all flowers; see Wang Yi: 64. "The cicada" alludes to "Summons for a Recluse": "At the year's evening, comfortless / The cicada sings with a mournful chirp." See Hawkes, 119. The summer cicada, a reminder of the ephemeral human grandeur, was unable to distinguish spring from autumn. See Watson, *Chuangtzu*, 25.

8. "Yang Zhu weeps on coming to the forked road, for it can lead to both the south and the north; Mo Zhai grieves on seeing the dyed silk, for it can be either white or black." See *Huainanzi Shuolin*, 17: 1288. For more implications of this couplet, see chapter 5.

9. See Feng Hao, 2: 524, also quoted in chapter 7.

10. See Quan Deyu (權德輿, 759–818): "Preface to Seeing off Yunsan, the Superior Man" (送雲散上人序), QTW, 483: 6426.

11. See TFZNB, 5: 782–83 and JTS, 166: 4336.

12. "Pass the country of Wei" and "Cross the River of Lu" allude to Confucius's trouble and Zhuge Liang's (諸葛亮) "Memorial to the Throne on Leading the Army out to Fight" (出師表) respectively; see *Shiji*, 47: 1905 and *Wenxuan*, 37: 516–17. Crossing the River Lu means to travel at the southernmost end of Shu.

13. The "Song of Protector-General Ding" is a Music Bureau song singing of the hardship of wars. See YFSJ, 45: 659. "Chanyu" (Khan in later time), title for the chieftain of the tribes to the north of China, is also title of a horn tune spread into China from the north.

14. See Shiji, 129: 3261, The "Gazette of Business and Goods" (貨殖列傳).

15. See Xu Jian, 20: 677, Fu Xuan's (傅玄, 217–278) "Rhapsody on the Date Tree"(棗賦).

16. From Wei River, Sanggan River is far in the northeast and cannot be reached by a westward journey; hence the Sanggan here can only be a symbol of the (western) frontier.

17. "Smiling westward," seeking distinction at the capital, alludes to Huan Tan's (桓譚) *Xinlun* in *Shuofu*, j. 59: "He who hears that it is happy in Chang'an will smile westward."

18. The "Shanglin Park" is the ancient Imperial Park located in the east of Luoyang. The Middle Bridge was on the Wei River, which flows through Luoyang.

19. "Setting-Sun Pavilion" was a famous sightseeing spot in Chang'an.

20. "Staff of Han" refers to Su Wu (蘇武, fl. 100–70 B.C.), who, as a diplomatic envoy with a tally staff, the symbol of Han state dignity, was sent to the north, where he was detained for nineteen years among the Huns, but never lost his loyalty to Han. See HS, 54: 2459. "Dagger of Wu" is a sword made in Wu famous for its sharpness; here synecdoche for the Shu general's military talent.

21. Both Guan Ying and Han Xin (? –196 B.C.) were Liu Bang's generals installed as marquises, though with different abilities. See HS, 95: 2667 and *Shiji*, 92: 2609.

22. See ZZhTJ, "The Fourth Year of Dahe" (830), 244: 7868–69.

23. In Chinese tradition, *Dujuan*, the cuckoo, was a tragic symbol. It was said that the bird wept blood from its beak, and that its cries sounded the words "better be back" (不如歸去), hence it was also called Zigui (子歸)—you [must] return.

24. Wenjun was the mistress of the famous poet Sima Xiangru (司馬相如, 179–118 B.C.). See *Shiji*, 117: 2999. Here the name might be a metaphor for a loyal and talented court official.

25. Another legend has it that after King of Shu, Du Yu, died, his soul transformed itself into *Dujuan*. "The fragrant herbs" are used as metaphors for worthy court officials, as in *Chuci*. The "lovelorn tree," another name for the "red pea," is traditionally regarded as a symbol for the affection of lovers, and here a metaphor for the loyalty of a court official.

26. "Home-yearning men" might refer to the demoted ministers and dethroned emperors. It so happened that there did exist in Chengdu a "Home-yearning Terrace" (望鄉臺).

27. Wang Ji recommended his uncle Wang Zhan (王湛, 249–295) to Emperor Wudi (r. 265–290). See JS, 42: 1205. Xie An recommended his nephew Xie Xuan (謝玄,

343–388) to the position of Military General. See JS, 79: 2072–86. The two allusions both imply a relationship of uncle and nephew between the so-called Prime-Minister-Duke and Wen.

28. Kong Li (孔鯉, 532–483 B.C.) once passed the court and his father Confucius taught him a lesson; see *Lunyu*, 16: 2522. The Ruans who were poor, including Ruan Xian (阮咸) and his uncle Ruan Ji, lived in the southern alley. See JS, 49: 1359–63 and NATW, 375.

29. At the end of the year, candidates were busy preparing for the spring examination.

30. "The Metropolitan Port" here refers to Luoyang (located on the Luo River).

31. "Season the soup" (調羹) is a borrowing from *Shangshu* (10: 175) as a metaphor for holding the prime ministership: "Be to me as the salt and the prune in making agreeable soup." For the translation, see Waltham, 98.

32. "Twining creeper" (葛藟) is a term from "Drooping Boughs" (樛木), see *Maoshi*, 1: 278 and Waley, No. 163: "In the south is a tree with drooping bough / The twining creeper binds it" (南有樛木，葛藟纍之). The poem is explained in *Zuozhuan* "Duke Wen the Seventh Year" (19: 1845), "The clans of dukes are the branches and leaves of the royal family. . . . As the twining creeper can protect its trunk and root, the noble man thus takes it as a metaphor." "The pepper-plant" (椒聊) alludes to "The seeds of the pepper-plant / overflowed my pint-measure" (椒聊之實，繁衍盈生), see *Maoshi*, 6: 362 and Waley, No. 8.

33. The musician Zhong Yi, a native of Chu in the south, once fell prisoner to Jin, and when the Marquis of Jin asked him to perform a piece of music on his zither, Zhong played the southern music. See *Zuozhuan*, "Duke Cheng the Ninth Year" (26: 1905). Gu Ti used to kneel and weep when reading letters from his father. See his biography in SGZ, 52: 1228. By alluding to Gu, Wen extends to Wen Zao, his foster father, the wish to be offered an official position near the capital and thus the opportunity to be near to him.

34. The term *xianggong* (相公), translated as Minister-Duke or Prime Minister, can refer to such official positions as the Director or Vice Director of the Chancellery (門下侍郎 or 僕射), the Grand Councilor (中書令), the Censor-in-Chief (御史大夫), the Examination Master (座主), and Commissioner Prime Minister (使相), depending on the context.

35. See Feng Yan; see also Shuofu, j. 45.

36. For the two works, see *Daizokyo*, j. 54, No. 2126 and 2127.

37. For Zongmi's biographies, see Shi Daoyuan, 13: 18–19 and Zan Ning, 6: 13a.

38. See Qu Tuiyuan, 24: 743 and QTS, 365: 4118. "Sending a Poem, Congratulating Minister Wen for His Quelling the Mutiny in Xingyuan" (美溫尚書鎮定興元，以詩寄賀).

39. See *Yuanhe Xingcuan* quoted above and XTS, 83: 3659, "Genealogical Lists for the Prime Ministers."

40. See Gu Xuejie, 245.

41. "Eastern Woods" refers to the "Monastery of Eastern Woods" (東林寺) on Mount Lu.

42. Ruan Ji (阮籍) met Sun Deng (孫登) at Mount Sumen. See JS, 49: 1359–62. "Scholars of Mount Sumen" thus refers to Wen and his friend. "The south-eastern Peak" is another name for the Five Old Men Peak (五老峰), in the southeast of Mount Lu.

43. See QTW, 872: 11507. It is first quoted by Huang Kunyao in his *Wen Tingyun* (30).

44. "Duke of Zanhuang" refers to Li Deyu, who, in the seventh year of Dahe (833), was demoted to Aide Prefect (長史) of Yuanzhou, near Mount Lu. See Fu Xuanzong, 216. Li once was Commissioner of Zhexi from 822 to 829 and of Jian'nan-Xichuan from 830 to 832. See TFZNB, 5: 774–75 and 4: 663–64. In both cases Wen may have had access to him.

45. About this topic, see Xu Tao's essay.

46. See Pei Xiu: "The Epitaph of the Chan Master of Gui Peak" (圭峰禪師碑銘, QTW, 743: 9730–32), *Chuanxin Fayao* (傳心法要, Taisho, *Daizokyo*, No. 2012, 48: 370–87), "Sending off the Senior Zongmi to the Cottage Temple of Mount Zhongnan" (送宗密上人歸草堂寺, QTS, 563: 6530), and Liu Yuxi: "Sending Zongmi Returning to the Cottage Temple of Mount Zhongnan" (送宗密上人歸南山草堂寺, *Liu Yuxi Ji*, 29: 981). Wen's relation with Pei Xiu, can be seen from the explanation of "Epistle Presented to the Vice-Minister, the Salt and Iron Commissioner," which was presented to Pei, see chapter 4.

47. The Eastern Peak, or the Gui Peak (圭峰) is a peak of Mount Zhongnan.

48. Dai Yong (378–441) was a recluse-scholar in Tonglu, whose father Kui and brother Bo were Buddhist laymen. See NS, 75: 1866. Zhi Dun (314–366) was a Buddhist master, and "Army Commander" was an official post held by Zhi Dun's lay friend Wang Qia (王洽).

49. When Bodhidharma died, Song Yun met him on Onion Ridge, saying that he was going to the Western Heaven. See Shi Daoyuan, 3: 9.

50. "White-Lotus Association" is the association presided over by the monk Hui Yuan (慧遠, 334–416). See Taisho, *Daizokyo*, No. 2126: 250, *Sengshilue*. Here it refers to the association gathered around Zongmi.

CHAPTER FOUR. WEN'S MARRIAGE—A CASE OF SCANDAL

1. For Wang Ya's biographies, see JTS, 169: 4401 and XTS, 179: 5317.

2. See QTW, 608: 7803.

3. Zhuge Liang lived in Nanyang before he began his official service; Yang Xiong was a native of Chengdu in Sichuan; see HS, 56: 2358.

4. According to "Biography of Ruan Yu," in a planned outing with his friends, Liu Shan chose Anshi Isle, instead of Mount Fang. See JS, 49: 1368. Mount Fang is (in Jiangning County) near Yangzhou, and so must be Anshi's Isle.

5. See XTS, 179: 5317 and Wang Pu, 87: 1592 and 1600.

6. Wang Ya was Military Commissioner of Jian'nan Dongchuan Circuit from 820 to 823. See TFZNB, 1001–1002.

7. "To set a sparrow-net by the door" alludes to "Biography of Zheng Dangshi" (鄭當時), meaning that there are very few visitors to the house. See HS, 50: 2323.

8. When Wang Dao was about to cross the Huai River, he asked Guo Pu (郭璞, 275–321) to divine for him. Guo said: "All is well, no harm. The River Huai is dry and the Wang clan extinguished" (吉，無咎。淮水絕，王氏滅). See Gu Sili's annotation quoting *Genealogy of the Wang Clan* (王氏家譜), also JS, 65: 1760, "Biography of Wang Hui."

9. Before Guan Fu suffered clan extermination, there was a folksong: "The Ying River is pure, the Guan clan is secured; the Ying River is turbid, the Guan clan is extinguished" (穎水清，灌氏寧；穎水濁，灌氏滅). See *Shiji*, 107: 2845, "Biography of Guan Fu."

10. An old Chinese tradition assumes that, when an important statesman dies, his star in the heavens crashes down. "The ink immortal" refers to Wang Ya, a good calligrapher.

11. "Raven Robe Alley," located south of the Qinhuai River (near Yangzhou), is where the Jin Dynasty eminent Wangs and Xies lived. It may refer to the quarters where Wang Ya lived, either in Yangzhou or in Chang'an.

12. "River-crossing boat," a metaphor for royal minister, is from *Shangshu,* 10: 174; see Waltham, 96: "Suppose me crossing a river, I will use you for a boat with its oars."

13. The "General Big Tree" is the designation the army men used to address Feng Yi (馮異, ?–31); see HS, 17: 639. *Tu* (荼) or *sonchus oleraces*, is a bitter-tasting wild herb, used here as a metaphor for harsh and exacting orders and regulations.

14. "Nine Highways" refers to the capital Chang'an, where the emperors live. Many things pertaining to the emperor were as a rule marked with the number NINE.

15. For Yao Xu's biographies, see XTS, 124: 4388–89; Tan Yao: 14: 30A.

16. See ZZhTJ, 246: 7939.

17. See XTS, 206: 5843.

18. "The beam of the wagon is closer to the yoke," because the wagon is on the down slope. Here Wen compares a carriage on a down slope to his worsening situation.

19. "To take a look at the string and the bow" means to participate in the competition of the examination. "The former era of our dynasty" can only refer to the Dahe era (826–835), when Liu Fen failed to pass the examination because his violent castigation of the eunuchs created a sensation. See JTS, 190: 5064 and XTS, 178: 5293.

20. Guo Fan was a famous Jin Dynasty recluse who owned no land; see JS, 94: 2446.

21. Min Zhongshu (閔仲叔) was too poor to afford pork, and so every day, he bought only a piece of pig liver. The governor of Anyi thus supplied Min's daily need. See HHS, 53: 1740. "The rib of chicken" is here an ironic metaphor for Wen's learning, which Wen could neither throw away nor use to find a position. For the source see SGZ, 1: 1.

22. "A desolate oak tree standing by the village shrine" is a term from *Zhuangzi*, a metaphor for great and useless talent. See Watson, 59–61.

23. When Duke Wen of the Jin (晉文公) returned to his own country after his banishment, he threw away his mats. Jiufan said: "The mat is something you used for

a long time to sleep on, but now you throw it away"; and, bowing, he requested to quit (service of the Duke). The Duke then took back the thrown mats. See *Hanfeizi*, 11: 1157, in *Ershierzi*.

24. "To angle together while pouring one's heart" evidently refers to the past friendship between Wen and Han, although it also contains an unidentified allusion.

25. "Prime Minister during a time of peace" might refer to Wang Ya, Commissioner of the Salt and Iron Monopoly, though all references to him must be very equivocal.

26. Prime Minister Wang Jian ordered that kerchief boxes be prepared as prizes, and that those who won in the competition for composing couplets be given more of the gifts. See NQS, 39: 681. The kerchief box might metaphorically refer to the contents of a letter. Here, the text is corrupt and at least one sentence is missing.

27. "A hard-pressed monkey who finds a tree" alludes to Li Chong's (李充) remark: "Does a hard-pressed monkey fleeing through the forest have the leisure to pick his tree?" See NATW, 67. "A fish in a dry rut who flings itself into a stream" alludes to *Zhuangzi*; see Legge, *The Texts of Taoism*, 1311–41.

28. Cheng Xiao (程曉, fl. 260), antithetical with Shan Tao, must also refer to some historical figure of the Wei or the Jin Dynasty. Since Wen regarded Cheng as his enemy, we can quote only the following sentence: "During the era of Jiaping, Xiao assumed the official position of Vice-minister of the Yellow Gate Ministry" (黃門侍郎), and understand it to be an insinuation about the eunuchs. See SGZ, 14: 425, "Biography of Cheng Xiao."

29. See Hu Sanxing's notes to ZZhTJ, 237: 7560. "Since the era of Dali, the Salt and Iron Transportation Commissioners had set up an inspection office in Yangzi County of the Yangzhou Circuit and established the official post of the Imperial Deputy."

30. "The moose-deer shed their horns" and Kong Yingda's annotation: "The moose [Pere David's deer] is a wild animal of *Yin*, that, in its lewd impulse, loiters about in the marshes; the deer is a wild animal of *Yang*, that, in its lewd impulse, loiters about in the mountains." See *Liji*, 17: 1383 and Legge's translation, *The Li Ki*, SECT. IV, 305.

31. It alludes to *Lisao*: "I had tended many an acre of orchids / And planted a hundred rods of melilotus"; and "All your ladies were jealous of my delicate beauty / they chatted spitefully, saying I loved wantonness." For the translation, see Hawkes, 23 and 25.

32. See Feng Jiwu, 369.

33. See Li Fang, *Taiping Guangji*, 488: 4012–17. Actually the scholar Zhang of the story was Yuan Zhen himself while Yingying was his cousin. See Wang Bijiang, 140–44.

34. See Birrell, *The New Songs of Jade Terrace*, a translation of Xu Ling's *Yutai Xinyong*, "A Peacock Southeast Flew" (孔雀東南飛), 1: 53.

35. Other poems in Wen's works on the same topic may include "Song of Spring Field" (春野歌) and "Ode of Three Islets" (三洲詞, j. 2, WFQ).

36. See QTS, 584: 6769.

37. See Zhangsun Wuji *Tanglü Shuyi*, 4: 257, "Household Marriage" item 39: "Marriage of Elders and Betters with the Mean and the Low." "Artisans, musicians, miscellaneous households, official households, private retainers, female tenants and public and

private slaves must be married to those of the same rank." "In cases where the official households or the miscellaneous households marry with good citizens in defiance of the law, the penalty is 100 lashes or two years of banishment." "Scholars, peasants, artisans and merchants are called the good citizens; those who have been involved in some crime and are forced to do service for the government are called miscellaneous households, and those in still lower position are the slaves."

38. See chapter 2 (26–28) of *A Dream of the Red Chamber* (trans. Yang Hsien-Yi and Gladys Yang); in an argument Jia Yucun (賈雨村) responds to Leng Zixing (冷子興).

39. Only the two *Tang Histories* take the Jianghuai Incident as having occurred in the Xiantong era, Wen's late years; all other sources upon which they draw take it as having happened in Wen's earlier years. "Guangling" was Yangzhou, where Linghu Tao (令狐綯, 795–872), after being dismissed from the prime ministership, occupied the position of Military Commissioner of the Huainan Circuit from 862–869, see TFZNB, 735–36.

40. Linghu Tao was Prime Minister from 850 to 860. Whether Wen became Presented Scholar or not during this period is quite another problem, as I shall discuss in chapter 8. Linghu Hao did frequent the pleasure quarters, see Sun Qi, *Beilizhi*, 41.

41. Passing Linghu's mansion without a visit was regarded as discourteous, because Wen had once been under Linghu's patronage.

42. Comparing this statement with Wen's "Epistle Presented to Bureau Director Han of the Ministry of Personnel," we can understand to what degree Wen's request for help from Han was misinterpreted by his biographers.

43. Here again we have vivid details that sound more like fiction than history. Linghu had indeed something to do with the incident. See chapter 8.

44. Wen's "immoral behavior" in Yangzhou was made known in the capital, several thousand miles away, as a result of Wen's attempts to rehabilitate himself.

45. The affirmative and narrative tone of Wen's biographers, with many a small detail given but no causality supplied for the major events in Wen's life, is specious but not true. Notice here that the depreciatory tone of his biographers undergoes an unnoticed change: now Wen was to clear himself of the *false* charge against him. That is to say, all the accusation laid upon him is fabrication and vilification. How else could false charges exist for Wen to clear himself of? The contradictory accounts give the story away.

46. Wen received a beating from a patrolling soldier *before* Wen served in the secretariat of Xu Shang (860). See Ruan Yue, 4: 27, and Xia, 410.

CHAPTER FIVE. SECRET ATTENDANCE UPON THE HEIR APPARENT

1. See Legge: *The Texts of Taoism*, 202–203.

2. See SGZ, 10: 301.

3. See Zhan, in Xia Chengtao, 520–21.

4. Sources on the Heir Apparent Incident include: "The Annals of Emperor Wenzong" (JTS, 17: 522; XTS, 8: 229), "The Annals of Emperor Wuzong" (JTS, 18: 583;

XTS, 8: 239), "Biographies of the Scions of the Eleven Emperors" (十一宗諸子傳, XTS, 82: 3633–35), "Biographies of the Two Sons of Emperor Wenzong" (文宗二子傳, JTS, 175: 4540), Biographies of Yang Sifu (楊嗣復, JTS, 176: 4555; XTS, 174: 5238), Li Jue (李珏, JTS, 173: 4503; XTS, 182: 5359), Zheng Tan (鄭覃 JTS, 173: 4489; XTS, 165: 5066), Chen Yixing (陳夷行, JTS, 173: 4494; XTS, 181: 5345), and Pei Du, etc.; also see ZZhTJ, *juan* 246; Fan Zuyu, *Tangjian*; Wang Fuzhi, *Du Tongjian Lun*.

5. The following is an incomplete list of those famous scholars who served the Heir, drawn from "Biographies of the Scions of the Eleven Emperors" and other sources: He Yuanliang (和元亮), Yu Jingxiu (庾敬休), Zheng Su (鄭肅), Dou Zongzhi (竇宗直), Zhou Jingfu (周敬復, JTS, 175: 4541); Chen Yixing (陳夷行), Gao Yuanyu (高元裕, JTS, 177: 5285; JTS, 171: 4452); and Wei Wen (韋溫, ZZhTJ, 245: 7929).

6. See ZZhTJ, 246: 7936. At the time, there was a rumor about the event: Li Yong (only twelve years of age) plotted to murder his father, and so he was executed. See Enin, 1: 9.

7. Wenzong died at the age of thirty-three, because of mental breakdown, or more likely as a result of poisoning, as had been the case with Emperor Xianzong. Had the eunuchs not ensured that Wenzong would die at a scheduled time, how could they have chosen the Imperial Fraternal Heir to succeed him in such a planned fashion, despite the fact that there was a new Heir Apparent, Prince Chen, already established?

8. See Ouyang Xun, 16: 291: "The Great Star of the Heart Constellation is the Heavenly Emperor; and its Front Star, the Heir Apparent" (心之大星，天皇也；其前星，太子也).

9. For example, see Gu Xuejie, *Wenxue Lunji*, 218.

10. See JTS, 175: 4540.

11. "Shaohai" is related to an heir apparent, see Xu Jian, 10: 229. For the uses of the term *Western Garden*, see Cao Pi, "Poem on the Lotus Pool" (芙蓉池詩, *Wenxuan*, 27: 311): "Riding my chariot I went for a night tour / Carefree I rambled in the Western Garden" (乘輦夜行游，逍遙步西園). and Cao Zhi, "Poem on Public Feast" (公宴詩, *Wenxuan*, 20: 282): "In a cool night I toured in the Western Garden / With 'official caps and flying canopies' following me" (清夜游西園，冠蓋相追隨).

12. 博望, Bowang Park, or 望苑, Wangyuan, was a park Emperor Wudi built for his Crowned Heir Li (戾太子), who in the end fell victim to slander. See HS, 63: 2741–49.

13. See *Shiji*, 55: 2048, "Biography of Marquis Liu" (留侯列傳).

14. "Eastern Mansion" (東府) would have been Eastern Palace (東宮), the Heir's palace, were it not for the tonal requirement that the second syllable bear an oblique sound.

15. "The place where the jade is buried" alludes to *Zuozhuan*, 46: 2070, "Duke Zhao the Thirteenth Year": King Gong of Chu (楚共王) decided to let gods choose his successor from among his sons; he buried a jade in the palace courtyard, and ordered that the one among his sons who prostrated himself just over the jade be set up as heir.

16. See Ouyang Xun, 44: 790.

17. For King Wen's story, see *Liji*, 20: 1403.

18. See WFQ, 257, quoting *Tongxin* (桐薪), an already lost book.

19. "An altar oak-tree" is something big but good for nothing. "Void-space village" refers to "a tract where there is nothing else," cf., Zhuangzi's advice to Huizi, to plant an Ailanthus tree, in Legge, *The Texts of Taoism*, 174 and 217.

20. "The decorated boat" alludes to the story of Liu Shan (劉剡) and Zhang Ping (張憑): Liu invited Zhang to enter his own boat and recommended him to the emperor; see NATW, 119 and JS, 75: 1992. Cassia garden refers to the Cassia Area, the Editorial Service under the Left Secretariat in the Household of the Heir Apparent.

21. "The Orchid Gate," or the Orchid Terrace, is another name for the Censorate. "Palace Aide to the Censor-In-Chief" is concurrently in charge of the Secretariat of the Orchid Terrace." See Xu Jian, 12: 291 and 295.

22. Both "ascending (your) hall"(登堂) and "being recorded and registered"(著錄) mean to be the disciple of someone. The former alludes to a remark of Confucius: "As to You, he has ascended the hall, but has not yet entered the chamber." See *Lunyu*, 10: 2499. The latter is a phrase from "Biography of Zhang Xing," "Zhang has a far-reaching reputation; the number of his disciples coming from far away and being recorded and registered reaches almost ten thousand." See HHS, 79: 2552.

23. "A sheep-horn" is an epithet for whirling and rising wind, having its origin in *Zhuangzi*. It means rapid advancement in one's official career.

24. See HS, 45: 984.

25. For Yu's poem, see Ouyang Xun, 69: 1202; for Zong's poem, see ibid, 29: 521.

26. For more information about the two men concerned, see Lu Qinli, 1554 and 2357.

27. See Yu Xin: "Eulogy to Wudi of Han's Gathering Books" (漢武聚書贊): "Stamped on a paper strip with iris-paste, and sealed in a jade box" in Ouyang Xun, 12: 232.

28. See Tao Hongjing, 5: 14.

29. See Shangguan Yi: "Presented to Duke Gaoyang" (和贈高陽公), in QTS, 40: 507.

30. See TFZNB, 4: 636–37.

31. See ZZhTJ, "The First Year of Yongzhen (805)," 236: 7929.

32. Both "an aide in the Man-Barbarian headquarters" and "clerk of Jingzhou Prefecture" allude to *Shishuoxinyu*; see NATW, 415 and 135. "While Hao Long (郝隆) was serving as Huan Wen's (桓溫) aide to the Commandant of the Southern Barbarians, there was a gathering at which every one composed poems. . . . After drinking three dipperfuls (of forfeit), he seized a brush and wrote: 'The *Juyu* leaps in the clear pool.' Huan Wen asked: 'What on earth is a *Juyu*?' Long replied: 'The Man Barbarians called fish Juyu.' Huan asked: 'Who ever heard of using the Man language to compose poetry?' Long replied: 'I came a thousand *li* to serve under your Excellency's command, and only got to be an aide in the Man-Barbarian headquarters, so how can I avoid using the Man language?' " "Xi Zuochi's (習鑿齒) ability as a historian was extraordinary. Huan Wen valued him highly, and even before Xi was thirty employed him as keeper of the central documents in his administration of Jing Prefecture. In his letter of thanks on receiving the appointment, Xi said, 'if I had never met your Excellency, I should have remained in Jing Prefecture a perpetual clerk, and nothing more.' "

33. See *Maoshi*, 19: 587 (昊天有成命) and Waley, No. 219 (High Heaven Had a Firm Charge), for my translation of "宥密".

34. Yang Xiong, 2: 6: "Were the disciples of Confucius to make use of the rhapsody, Jia Yi would ascend the hall and Xiangru would be able to enter the chamber." Song Yu is a reputed disciple of Qu Yuan; source of this allusion is unavailable, or it has no source.

35. See Lao Ge, *Langguan Shizhu Timing Kao*, 2: 29a and 22: 18a. For more biographical information about Feng Ao, see XTS, 177: 5287 and JTS, 168: 4392.

36. See XTS, 59: 1522, "Records of Art and Literature."

37. See Xu Song, DKJK, 18: 11a.

38. See *Langguan Shizhu Timingkao*, 7: 21 and 15: 20.

39. See JTS, 165: 4305 and XTS, 163: 5023, "Biographies of Liu Zhongying" (柳仲穎).

40. See Cui Gu (崔嘏): "Edict Appointing Hegan Qi as Inspection Commissioner of Jiangxi Circuit" (授紇干㚖江西觀察使制), QTW, 726: 9472.

41. See Shen Xun (沈詢): "Edict Appointing Hegan Qi as Military Commissioner of Lingnan Circuit"(授紇干㚖嶺南節度使制), QTW, 723: 9426.

42. See JTS, 177: 4593 and XTS, 182: 5371, "Biographies of Pei Xiu."

43. For Pei's biographies, see JTS, 163: 4268; XTS, 148: 4772. After Li Yong's death, for a time Wen had to hide himself at Pei's; see chapter 7.

44. For "dapple horse" and "dusky crows," see HHS, 37: 1258 and HS, 83: 3398.

45. See *Wenxuan*, 11: 168: Wang Yanshou's (王延壽) "Rhapsody on Lingguang Palace of Lu" (魯靈光殿賦): "As if the ghosts and spirits were there" (若鬼神之髣髴).

46. See *Zhouli*, 22: 789.

47. "Phoenix Hall" is an unofficial title for the Secretariat (中書省) or, more commonly, a reference to royal palaces in general. "Egret row" refers to the strict alignment of officials at court audience, perhaps because egrets have good discipline when moving.

48. "Pendant" (衡牙) is a small pendant hung at the lower end of the jade adornment. According to the text of *Zhouli* (30: 1482), 衡牙 should be 衝牙. But in either *Peiwen Yunfu* (3500), or WFQ, the quotation is 衡牙; even though 衝牙 is the correct form.

49. See JS, 25: 768.

50. "Heshi's Jade" does have to do with a crown prince; see HS, 65: 2841. Among Dongfang Shuo's (東方朔) works recorded are "Reproaching Heshi's Jade" (責和氏璧), "The Crown Prince's Birth" (皇太子生賦), "Blessing Prayers for the Crown Prince" (生禖), and "Screen" (屏風), all of which provide interesting contrasts with Wen's "Song of a Screen of [the Heir Apparent's] Birth and Blessing Prayers" (生禖屏風歌 j. 1, WFQ). During Wen's lifetime, Dongfang's works might yet have been extant, and "Reproaching Heshi's Jade" might have been a reproach of the attendants of the Heir, Li (戾太子), who fell victim of slander (HS, 63: 2741), using Heshi's Jade as a metaphor for Li's attendants. Wen likened Li to the Heir; see j. 4, WFQ, "Written at the Wangyuan Post" (題望苑驛).

51. See Zuo Qiuming, *Guoyu*, 18: 579,

52. See *Shangshu*, 12: 189.

53. The Tang pronunciations of 祀 (*zi*) and 嗣 (*zi*) are identical with each other. See Karlgren: *Analytical Dictionary of Chinese and Sino-Japanese*, 241–42.

54. For example, see YFSJ, 46: 677, "Song of Reading the Music" (讀曲歌): "I was grieved to see the weaving of the spider / Looking for silk until dawn" (愁見蜘蛛織，尋絲直到明). Herein "Looking for silk" (尋絲) puns on "thinking over it" (尋思).

55. See Xu Jian, 25: 606.

56. For our evidential citations, except otherwise noted, see *Taiping Yulan*, 703: 3138–39.

57. See Xu Jian, 25: 606.

58. See YFSJ, 49: 720.

59. "Ice in jade pot" stands for the purity and innocence of mind, as can be seen from Bao Zhao's poem "A Song on the White Hair Wedlock" (白頭吟): "As straight as a red silk string, as pure as a piece of ice in a jade pot" (直如朱絲繩，清如玉壺冰); see *Wenxuan*, 28: 404; also Wang Changling's (王昌齡) "Seeing Off Xin Jian on the Lotus Tower" (芙蓉樓送辛漸): "A piece of icy heart in a jade pot" (一片冰心在玉壺); see QTS, 140: 1420.

60. "On each side of the palace-hall, at the second dragon head, i.e., the spot where the dragon heads are hollowed, the Left and the Right Diarists stand when court audiences take place, with ready ink and brush [to write], and they are called the Golden Bureaus on the Dragon Head." See Wang Pu, 56: 963. "Dragon Head" is ornamental stone column lined up along the two sides of palace hall.

61. See Ma Zhou's Biography, JTS, 74: 2612 and XTS, 98: 3894.

62. *Wufu* (碔砆), which we tentatively translate as crude jadeite, is a type of jade-like stone.

CHAPTER SIX. MYSTIFYING POETRY

1. See WFQ, 143; for the poem, see Feng Hao, 1: 136.

2. For his comment on the poem, see Du Zhao, 8: 16.

3. For the explanation of this Music Bureau topic, see YFSJ, 41: 605.

4. See HS, 97b: 3973–88, "Biographies of the Imperial Relatives" (外戚列傳).

5. See JS, 102: 2567, "The Annals of Liu Cong" (劉聰載紀).

6. Gu Sili annotated: "JS: One Wang Shen was the Marquis of Boling; another seen in 'Biographies of the Literary Men'; to neither of them is 'Azure Gate' explicable." He ignored, very normally, that in the same JS there is a eunuch Wang Shen, which, although never alluded to by anyone else, exactly accords with Wen's purpose of exposing the eunuchs' plots. According to SGZ, 4: 144, yet another Wang Shen, an accomplice in the murder of Cao Mao (曹髦, r. 254–255), seems also worth considering; however, this Wang Shen, a court official politically representing the Sima clansmen who were usurping at the time, can also be deviously used in place of the term *eunuch* (see chapter 1).

7. See WFQ, 143, quoting XTS.

8. "When an Heir takes a consort, among his betrothal gifts there are a hair-pin of hawks-bill-shell and a carved dressing mirror." See *Taipingyulan*, 703: 3139, quoting Zhang Chang's (張敞) *Jin Donggong Jiushi* (晉東宮舊事).

9. See *Taiping Guangji*, 184: 1379, quoting *Lushi Zashuo* (盧氏雜說).

10. See WFQ, 144, quoting *Jingchu Suishiji* (荊楚歲時記) and *Kaiyuan Yishi* (開元遺事). Those who succeed in threading the needles are believed to be skillful (巧), a word that puns on "happy coincidence" (巧遇), namely, a happy marriage.

11. See JTS, 8: 167.

12. See XTS, 29: 1064, "Records of Music" (音樂志).

13. See Sima Xiangru: "Preface to the Rhapsody on Changmen Palace" (長門賦序), *Wenxuan*, 16: 227.

14. See Ouyang Xun, 90: 1564.

15. When Cai Yong was invited to attend a music party, he stopped at the door listening and saying to himself: "Why is there a murdering mind in the music?" Later the lute player told him: "I saw a mantis stalking a cicada. I was afraid that the mantis would lose his prey. Is this the murdering mind embodied in the music?" See Ouyang Xun, 97: 1678.

16. See *Shiji*, the "Records of Music," 24: 1181.

17. See also "Song of the Double Seventh Eve" (七夕歌, j. 3. WFQ), which uses "the curved bridge" as a euphemism to mean Emperor Wenzong.

18. Examples of such a practice: Sun Bao (孫寶), an Attending Censor, said that "Now the hawks are starting to soar on high, we should also follow the weather and wipe away the evil, to complete our penalty of stern frost." Zhang Tang (張湯), Censor-In-Chief, was nicknamed "black hawk." See respectively HS, 77: 3523 and *Shiji*, 59: 2637–46.

19. For instances of "heavenly horse" functioning as metaphor for outstanding minister, or particularly important official, see *Shiji*, 24: 1178 and HS, 22: 1060–61, "Song of the Heavenly Horse" (天馬歌) and "Song of the Western-most Heavenly Horse" (西極天馬歌).

20. Du Yu received this appellation for his all-embracing erudition; see JS, 34: 1028. Sima Xiangru once was the Prefect of Literary Garden (文園令); see *Shiji*, 117: 2999.

21. Previous to finding a better term, I use "magic iris" to translate the Chinese term "靈芝"; I am unsure whether this legendary magic plant is a type of herb or of mushroom; even though the term in Chinese medicine can be translated as *Ganoderma lucidum*.

22. "Painting of Ferocious Beast" (畏獸圖) was drawn by Wang Yi (王廙); see Pei Xiaoyuan's *Zhenguan Gongsi Huashi* (Book 8, p. 4); "Attracted Birds" (來禽) refers to Wang Xizhi's calligraphy; see WFQ, 6: 146. The painting and the calligraphy, in all probability, were kept at the time as treasure in the imperial hoard; cf. the paraphrases to the seventy-one rhyme of "Hundred-Rhyme."

23. The Qing Dynasty scholar Wang Mingsheng surmised, not without reason, that the Heir must have died as a victim of the eunuchs' power; see *Eshubian*, 77: 1209.

24. See Feng Hao's annotation to "Jingyang Well" (景陽井) of *Li Yishan Shishi* (1: 146): "Heartbreaking is the river outside the Wu king's palace / Lucky enough was

Xishi to be buried in its turbid mud" (腸斷吳王宮外水，濁泥猶得葬西施); Li's poem is an ironic dirge for Yang, who, after being executed, was thrown into Qujiang River. See also Wang Ming sheng (77: 1210), castigating Yang by quoting Li's poem.

25. Ning Qi, when meeting Duke Huan, chanted a song to vent his complaints and show that he was a worthy man not yet meeting his lord. See Wang Yi, 63–64 and Hawkes, 32.

26. "Black or white" originally refers to black or white horses. It was said that the Xia Dynasty set great store by the black, while the Yin by the white; hence the term acquires its meaning of "changed vogue of different times."

27. See WFQ, 25–27.

28. See Ren Bantang, 107.

29. For biographical information about Consort Pan and Precious Spouse Huang, see NS, 5: 151–55.

30. For Jiang's title, see NS, 51: 1269; for Xianzong's early title, see JTS, 14: 411.

31. See WFQ, 26, quoting *Jinlingzhi*.

32. It was said that when Liu Bang rose in arms against the Qin, he killed a white snake, son of the White Emperor and symbol of the Qin Empire. See *Shiji*, 8: 341. The "Western Emperor" thus indicates an emperor ruling in Chang'an, see *Shiji*, 85: 2587.

33. See *Liexianzhuan*, in *Shuofu*, juan 58.

34. Painted Hall, short for the Painted Hall of the First Abode of the Heir Apparent (太子甲觀畫堂) is where Emperor Cheng was born, and where the imperial consorts lived. See HS, 10: 301.

35. For the source of "the Goddess of Mount Wu," see Song Yu (宋玉): "Rhapsody of Gaotang" (高唐賦), *Wenxuan*, 19: 265. "Wooden bell" (木鐸) used in "Bell Dance" (鐸舞) is *to give orders to the whole country*, see YFSJ, 54: 784.

36. "Damozhi" is the title of a Music Bureau verse, see YFSJ, 80: 1137.

37. See HHS, 84: 2800.

38. See HS, 54: 2459 and note 20 of chapter 2.

39. The notorious "*Sans Soucis* Heaven's Son" is the Latter Monarch (r. 565–569) of the Northern Qi, who addicted himself to pleasure-making "by the Zhang River" in his capital Linzhang (臨漳), and brought ruin to his country. See Li Baiyao, 8: 97

40. For biographies of the Ding brothers (?–220), see SGZ, 19: 561–62.

CHAPTER SEVEN. CHANGING NAME AND TAKING THE EXAMINATION

1. See *Zuozhuan*, 33: 1966. "Duke Xiang the Eighteenth Year," "The Musician Shi Kuang divined the result of the war between Chu and Jin by singing the southern and the northern airs, saying: 'The southern airs cannot last through to the end, and are filled with dead voices, so Chu will certainly have no achievement'" (南風不竟，楚必無功).

2. See HHS, 64: 2121.

3. See HS, 3226–38.

4. See Wang Dingbao, 1: 4.

5. See Wang Tang, 2: 13. "Six month's ascension" alludes to the roc in *Zhuangzi* that ascends upwards 90,000 *li*, on a whirlwind, resting only at the end of six months; see Legge, *Texts of Taoism*, 165.

6. It was abolished in 836 and in the next year restored; it was then again annulled in 852, only to be restored in 877; see Wang Dingbao, 2: 13–15.

7. "Five carriages" means great erudition; "three paths," the courtyard of a scholar recluse.

8. Zi Gong said: "There is a good gem here. Should I lay it up and keep it? or should I seek for a good price and sell it?" The Master said: "Sell it! Sell it! But I would wait for one to offer the price." See *Lunyu*, 9: 2490 and Legge, *The Four Books*, 114.

9. For biographies of Jiang Xi, see JTS, 149: 4028 and XTS, 132: 4534; of Zhou Qi, JTS, 176: 4571 and XTS, 182: 5370; of Cui Gong, JTS, 177: 4587 and XTS, 141: 4656.

10. "A bundle of fresh fodder" is a term from White Steed (白駒) of *The Book of Songs*: "With a bundle of fresh fodder / Though you, its master, is as fair as jade" (生芻一束，其人如玉); see *Maoshi*, 11: 434 and Waley, No. 185. Xu Zhizi (徐稚子) once visited Guo Tai and paid tribute to Guo by leaving a bundle of fresh fodder; see HHS, 53: 1749.

11. "Oriole soaring out from his valley" (鶯谷) is a metaphor for obtaining the Presented Scholar degree. It alludes to Felling the Trees (伐木) of *The Book of Songs*: "Leave the darkly valley / Mount the high tree the oriole is caroling / To seek the response of his friend" (出于幽谷，遷于喬木。嚶其鳴矣，求其友聲). See *Maoshi*, 9: 410 and Waley, No. 195.

12. "Changing the music scale by pitch-pipe" was believed in ancient China to be a sign to change the governance; hence referring to a new Prime Minister's taking office.

13. See JTS, 177: 4589.

14. Before the way (先路), a phrase from *Lisao*, meaning to serve the emperor as his vanguard, see Hawkes, 22.

15. In this line, the Chinese character 郊, literally suburb, might have been 蛟, a kind of dragon, antithetical with the horse implied in the first line.

16. *Broad-willow* is funeral wagon with a cover of willow-twigs; by hiding in this, Ji Bu (季布), Xiang Yu's (項羽, 232–202 B.C.) military assistant, escaped Liu Bang's arrest. See HS, 37: 1975.

17. See *Liji*, 19: 1528. "The Records of Music" (樂記): "The *se* of the Solemn Temple has red strings and sparse holes" (清廟之瑟，朱弦而疏越). *Se* is a kind of twenty-five-string plucked instrument similar to a zither; and "Solemn Temple" is the ancestral temple of the ruling house, the most orthodox symbol of the empire in Chinese imperial ages.

18. "Lord She was fond of dragons, so for all adornments in his house he had the images of dragon. But when the Heavenly Dragon heard it and descended for a visit, he was almost frightened to death." See HHS, "The Biography of Cui Yin," 52: 1703.

19. For Yan rat, see *Taiping Yulan*, 51: 250, quoting *Que Zi* (闕子): A foolish man of the Song got a Yan stone and stored it up as a treasure; see also the story about rat and *pu* in Liu Xiang, 201 and Crump, 113: a man from Zhou, who called a dried sea-

soned rat *pu*, went to sell it in Zheng, where people called a jade-enfolding stone by the same name.

20. For Qingji's story, see Zhao Ye, 4: 11.

21. See *Lunyu*, 11: 2500 and compare with Legge, the *Four Books*, 11: 51.

22. Liu recommended Zhang; see chapter 5, note 20. Wang Ba conscripted men in his allegiance to Emperor Guangwu, but was made a mockery of. See HHS, 20: 734.

23. Feng Xuan went to gather rent for Lord Mengchang, but burned up all the tallies, saying he was buying fealty for him. See *Chan-kuo Ts'e*, 189–192. When Zhong Jun (終軍) went westward into the Pass, he threw away the silk credential the clerk offered him, thinking he would not need it when returning as a successful man. See HS, 64: 2814–20.

24. "Scratch my head, pace up and down" is a line from *Maoshi*; see Waley, No. 22.

25. For "White Snow" see *Wenxuan*, 45: 627, Song Yu's "Answering the Questions of King of Chu" (對楚王問). "Dancing by the Rain Altar" refers to Zeng Dian's remark.

26. Confucius once said: "The noble man has no contentions. If he has to compete, shall this be in archery?" (君子無所爭，必也，射乎). See *Liji*, 62: 1689 or *Lunyu*, 3: 2466 and Legge, the *Four Books*, 21.

27. For "drawing a tiger" and "slaying a dragon" see respectively HHS, 24: 827 and Legge, the *Texts of Taoism*, 206.

28. For these poems, see respectively Feng Hao, 2: 524; QTS, 542: 6257; QTS, 510: 5794; QTS, 584: 6766; and QTW, 787: 10391.

29. See DKJK, 22: 1434–35.

30. As shown in our Bibliography, Zhao Qi's *Correct Meanings to Mencius* (Mengzi Zhengyi) is the earliest authoritative annotation to *Mencius* that is still extant and intact.

31. Yu Xin's (513–581) last official post was Area Commander. One of his most famous works is "Lament for the South of the River" (哀江南賦). See *Wenyuan Yinghua*, 129: 590. Minister Shen refers to Shen Yue (沈約, 441–513), who in one of his essays complained that his waist was growing thinner. See LS, 13: 236.

32. "Pair of carp" is a kenning for letters, alluding to "Watering My Horse in the Pool of the Great Wall" (飲馬長城窟): "The guest coming from afar / Bestows on me a pair of carp" (客從遠方來，遺我雙鯉魚) and finds a one-foot letter of silk. See *Wenxuan*, 27: 389.

33. Arguing that one cannot call a friend using a combination of his old and new styles, Gu thought Zaimeng must be the style of someone else. See Gu: *Wenxue Lunji*, 194.

34. It is a dead end to understand "*meng*" as a name of place, as there is no mention of a place at all in the poem and there are too many places bearing the name *meng*.

35. The character 庭 (alternatively, 廷), appearing in both Tingyun and his brother's name Tinghao, marks a generation and has nothing to do with the style-names.

36. See QTW, 632: 8103. There is a Meng Spring in Jingmen, Hubei Province, however, the rhapsody focuses on the symbolic nature of the name, as does its title.

37. Both *Kan* (坎) and *Gen* (艮) are one of the eight trigrams of the *Yijing*. The two constitute image of *meng*, one of the sixty-four hexagrams, with Gen, the mountain, at the top, and Kan, the water, at the bottom. Kan is the symbol of danger, while

Gen, of keeping away from the danger. This line informs the Meng Spring with the personality of a noble man in distress, as is the basic point of the "Attached Words" (系辭) to the Meng Divination in the *Book of Changes*. See *Zhouyi*, 1: 20.

38. See *Zhouyi*, 1: 20. Wang Bi's explanation is on the same page. For the translation, see Wilhelm, *Book of Changes*, 20–21.

39. Another example of Wen's using *qi* as a pun on his name is found in his "My Feelings on Returning to the East" (東歸有懷, j. 8, WFQ): "No end of tears for a high autumn / On my small skiff I come to the end of the forked way" (無限高秋淚，扁舟極路岐).

40. This title alludes to the following: "[The vessel for performing the rites] to the people is like the cutis to the bamboo pole, and the heart [that fears no cold] to the pine and the cypress" (其在人也，如竹箭之有筠也；如松柏之有心也). See *Liji*, 23: 1430. "Bamboo-arrow" was the name of reputed bamboo pole; *yun* (筠), here designates the shiny cuticle of the bamboo pole, hence its more general, synecdochic use for bamboo. For Li's rhapsody, see QTW, 632: 8109.

41. "Bird nesting on southern branch" is an image of nostalgia; a borrowing from "The Nineteen Classic Poems": "The Tartar horse is attached to the northern wind / the Yue bird nests on a southward branch" (胡馬依北風，越鳥巢南枝). See *Wenxuan*, 29: 409. "Crevice-crossing colt" speaks to the swift passing of a man's lifetime.

42. Lei was recommended as an Excellent Talent, but he yielded the honor to Chen. Hence the ballad: "Glue and varnish are closely attached to each other, but less solid than are Lei and Chen" (膠漆自謂堅，不如雷與陳). See HHS, 81: 2686–87.

43. Confucius once said that those (his students) born later than he are to be regarded with awe (後生可畏). See *Lunyu*, 9. 2451 and Legge, *The Four Books*, 118–19.

44. For *Lulu*, 轆轤, name of precious sword, see chapter 1, note 64.

45. See *Wenxuan*, 3: 66, Zhang Heng (張衡, 78–139), "Rhapsody of the Eastern Capital" (東都賦): "A white dragon in fish disguise, is harassed by Yu Ju" (白龍魚服，見困豫且).

46. "The ghost's execution" is a term from *Zhuangzi*. It was said that one who does something evil openly will be executed by man; and who does evil clandestinely, by ghosts. See Legge, *The Texts of Taoism*, 83.

47. *Yuanchu* (鵷鶵), like the phoenix, is a mythical bird of noble quality, who perches on nothing but Wutong tree, eats nothing but bamboo fruit and drinks nothing but pure spring water. Now an owl got a rotten rat, and a *Yuanchu* just passed by him. Fearing lest Yuanchu seize his prey, the owl attempted to scare him away. For the fable, see "Autumn Water" of *Zhuangzi*. Here, evidently, Wen likened himself to *Yuanchu*. See also note 50 below.

48. The archaic form of the character 裙 (*qun*) is 裠, which is easily confused with 衾 (*qin*); the term 衾襦 should thus have been 裙襦, which alludes to *Zhuangzi*; see Legge, *The Texts of Taoism*, 134–35, as quoted in the following paragraph.

49. See note 11 above.

50. When the Yuanchu flew by, the owl, who had just got a dead rat, looked upward and cried "he" (嚇) to frighten him away. See Legge, *The Texts of Taoism*, 391.

51. Melilotus (蕙) and angelica (芷) are fragrant herbs frequently referred to in *Lisao*, here used to represent the reclusive life. "Mulberry and elm" (桑榆) is a metaphor for the evening of life, because, it was said, the sun sets on such trees.

52. To break off a willow (柳, *liu*) twig and send it to the parting ones to *keep them from going* (留, *liu*) is an old Chinese custom. "Cutting the rushes" means setting pen to paper.

CHAPTER EIGHT. HIGHLIGHTS DURING THE DAZHONG ERA

1. Wen has "A Song for the Bingyin Harvest Year of Huichang" (會昌丙寅豐歲歌, j. 2, WFQ), written near the capital in the Bingyin year (846).

2. Cogongrass and reeds (菅蒯) is a term taken from "Duke Cheng the Ninth Year": "Although you have owned silk and hemp, don't throw away cogongrass and reed" (雖有絲麻，無棄菅蒯). See *Zuozhuan*, 26: 1906.

3. For this explanation of Zhu and Teng (邾滕), see *Zuozhuan*, 38: 1996, "Duke Zhao the Twelfth Year": "Compare ourselves to Zhu or Teng" (視邾滕). Du Yu annotates: "If subordinated to both Jin and Chu, it must needs be doubly taxed, and in this manner Lu is likened to small kingdoms" (兩事晉楚，故賦稅重，故欲比小國).

4. Respectively presented to Linghu Tao (850), Jiang Shen (851), Feng Ao (852), Pei Xiu (852), Du Shenquan (杜審權, 856), and Linghu Tao (859 and 862?).

5. See Wang Dajin: "Tan Wen Tingyun Shengping de Ruogan Wenti."

6. The two names Pei Xian (裴諴) and Pei Cheng (裴誠), most probably, refer to the same person; the character 誠 should be written 諴 here, cf. Fang Jiliu et al., *Renming Suoyin*.

7. Chinese characters in brackets, probably annotator's footnote, appear in WFQ (j. 9) in small characters indicating that they are homophones the original terms pun on.

8. For the biographies of the Linghus, see JTS, 172: 4459–68; XTS, 166: 5098–105.

9. "Hanging burned reeds" and "weaving rushes" are set phrases, meaning to study hard. "Imperial salary" here implies that Wen occupied an official position.

10. Shen Xun (沈詢) was the examination administrator for the ninth year of Dazhong (855). See 22: 1429, DKJK, quoting *Nanbu Xinshu*, 73.

11. Shen addressed Wen as "Academician" (學士), a title that cannot be used as an honorific for anybody not possessing it. It would be inexplicable had Wen not indeed held it (during his attendance upon the Heir).

12. See Pei Tingyu, *Dongguan Zouji*, 18. Pei Tingyu was Pei Du's grandson and Pei Shen's (裴諗) son; his records about his father's experiences should therefore be reliable.

13. See JTS, 18: 93, "Annals of Emperor Xuanzong," and ZZhTJ, 246: 8060, "Ninth Year of Dazhong."

14. See Pei, *Dongguan Zouji*, 18.

15. See Pei, 22, and DKJK, 22:1435.

16. For Qu Yuan and Jia Yi, see Wang Yi, *Chuci Zhangju*, 96 and HS, 48:2221–66.

17. The appointment to the position of Defender to Suixian County of the Suizhou Prefecture might have something to do with the official quarters' recognition of Wen's relation with his teacher Li Cheng, who had been Prefect of Suizhou; see JTS, 131: 4511.

18. *Zheng* (箏) is a 25-stringed instrument similar to a zither; a "dainty jade" may refer to the jade plucker or the fingers of the one who plucks the strings.

19. Candidates sitting for the examination worked in separate small rooms like carrels. Candle (*zhu*, 燭, for lighting) and curtain (*lian*, 簾, used for separating the examinees from one another) are synecdochic for the examination hall.

20. It was said that the famous poet Jiang Yan (444–505) once dreamed that a person had him return the bolt of brocade he owed him. After that, Jiang's compositions became increasingly poor. See LS, 14: 247; NS, 59: 1447.

21. 雨 and 語 are homophonic with each other; see Karlgren's dictionary, 363 and 374.

22. 寒 and 函 ([ɣam] and [ɣan]) are identical with each other; see Karlgren, 53.

23. There might be various possibilities, among which I cannot choose a satisfying one.

24. Xu Shang was Military Commissioner of the East Circuit of Shannan (山南東道) from 857 to 860. See TFZNB, 641–42 and 1387, quoting Li Zhi (李騭): "Epitaph of the Magistrate of the Xiangzhou Commandery" (徐襄州碑) from QTW, 724: 9430.

25. Gathered around Xu in Xiangyang were Tingyun, Tinghao (Wen's brother), Duan Chengshi, Zhou You (周繇), Wei Chan (韋蟾), etc.; see *Liu Chongyuan*, 37 and *Ji Yougong*, 54: 822.

26. "Apricot Garden" was, during the Tang, the place in Chang'an where, after passing the examination in spring, the Presented Scholars gathered and congratulated one another.

27. "Phoenix Edict" is a laudatory title for the edict issued by the Secretariat. "The Parrot" refers to Ni Heng's (禰衡) "Rhapsody on the Parrot" (鸚鵡賦, *Wenxuan*, 13: 200). Ni was killed because of his unrestrained and haughty character. See HHS, 80: 2562.

28. 錄醑, also 綠醑, translated here as green wine, was a kind of famous wine. The yellow ribbon was a part of the official uniform for those of the ninth grade position, such as Defender.

29. See Yongrong, 45: 1003.

30. Linghu Tao became a successful Presented Scholar in 830. See DKJK, 21: 1318.

31. See Li's biographies, JTS, 190: 5077; XTS, 203: 5792.

32. Ji Yougong (54: 822), You Mao (4: 79), and Wang Dang (8: 135) have similar records.

33. See *Gu Xuejie Wenxue Lunji*, 247.

34. See QTW, 759: 9971, Linghu Tao's "Memorial for Recommending the Recluse Li Qunyu" (薦處士李群玉狀); and ZZhTJ, 249: 8073, "The Twelfth Year of Dazhong" (858).

35. Xuanzong said that he remained in great fear of the eunuchs, and planned secretly with Linghu Tao to get rid of them. Their discussion, however, was divulged, only making the situation worse. See ZZhTJ, "The Ninth Year of Dazhong," 246: 8055.

36. See Chen Tingchuo, 7.

37. See Xia Chengtao, 405, quoting Li Bingruo's (李冰若) *Xuzhuang Manji* (栩莊漫記).

38. White-Fern Bank (白蘋浦) is a place near to Wen's native town, Tonglu.

39. The lotus with seeds, 蓮有子 may pun on 憐有子, loving someone.

40. Cross-Pond, 橫塘, name of the place where the female lover, often described in the Southern Dynasty Music Bureau verses, lived.

41. Red Bird Ferry (朱雀航) was a famous spot in Jinling, where the eminent Wang and Xie clans once lived; thus it is a mark of distinction.

42. Lines 19–22 are an imitation of the Music Bureau "Mulberry up the Lane" (陌上桑). See *New Songs from the Jade Terrace*, 33.

43. "The simurgh string" is a string broken and rejoined using "string-sticking glue" (續弦膠); it was said the immortals made it by cooking simurgh-beaks and unicorn-horns.

44. "The Southwestern Palace" alludes to Bao Zhao's "Enjoying the Moon" (玩月詩, *Yiwen Leiju*, 1: 8)—"It first appears over the Southwestern Palace / Slender and slim, it looks like a jade hook / Not yet shining on the northeastern steps / Fine and dainty, it is like a moth eyebrow" (初見西南樓，纖纖如玉鉤。未上東北墀，娟娟如蛾眉)—very possibly, here it refers to the *Shaoyangyuan*. For hawk-bill-shell (玳瑁), see "Twenty-two Rhymes" in chapter 6.

45. "The Golden Ditch" refers to an imperial ditch.

46. White Flower Yang, i.e., Yang Baihua, a person whose name a Music Bureau verse took as title, was said to have been a handsome and valiant man of the Western Wei, who fled and surrendered himself to the Liang Dynasty in order to escape the love of Empress Hu. For the loss of Yang's love, it was said, Hu composed the song, see YFSJ, 73: 1039–40.

47. JS, 28: 847, "Records of Five Elements": During the Taihe era (366–371, identical with Wenzong's era title of 825–835), this song was sung among the people.

48. In JS, 28: 847, after the song, the text reads: "Those who understood the song said: White is a color pertinent to the metal. 'Horse' (馬) means the royal surname (司馬). Purple is a color that confuses orthodox red (亂朱). Soon later, Duke Haixi was forced to abdicate. The three princes, not his sons, were then strangled using reins (韁). The day after their death the south sent sweet dew (甘露) as tribute." Thus, without a doubt the folksong Wen alludes to has to do with the death of the imperial heir. "Purple is a color that assumes the place of the orthodox color" alludes to *Lunyu*, 17: 2524. For the translation, see Legge, 148.

49. Since "lotus" (蓮) puns on "love" (憐), "gathering lotus" acquires the meaning of "looking for love," which can be a metaphor for looking for imperial employment.

50. See WFQ, 1: 12, "Song of Zhang Jingwan Gathering Lotus" (張靜婉采蓮曲).

51. For *jituo* (寄托), an untranslatable term, we may use "hidden motifs" as a makeshift.

52. See Zhang Huiyan, 1–4. In the sixteen *ci* poems Zhang selected from Wen's works, including the Pusaman series, he maintained that the series contains a hidden motif.

53. See Wang Guowei, 37 and 93.

54. See Xia Chengtao, 405, quoting Li Bingruo.

55. See Shi Zhecun.

56. See Ye Jiaying: *Jialing Lunci*, 13: 54.

57. See *Maoshi*, 3: 327. For the translation, see Waley, No. 49.

58. See *Wenxuan*, 46: 645, Li Shan's annotation to "The straight person nourishes his virtue at Shaoyang" (正體毓德于少陽) in Yan Yanzhi's (顏延之) "Preface to Poems Written at Curved Stream on the Third Day of the Third Month" (三月三日曲水詩序一首): "The straight person is the Heir Apparent; Shaoyang is the eastern palace."

59. See Xia Chengtao, 520–21.

60. See WFQ, 1: 10, the annotation by Zeng Yi correctly cites "Annals of Emperor Cheng" of HS. cf. chapter 6, note 34.

61. See Ouyang Xun, 90: 1560, Fan Tai's "Preface to the Simurgh Poem" (鸞鳥詩序).

62. For the translations, I have consulted the following sources: Lois, *Among the Flowers*, 37–54; Liu Wu-chi, *Sunflower Splendor*, 248–50; Cyril Birch. *Anthology of Chinese Literature*, 336–67.

63. Lotus-silk, 藕絲, is a kind of fine silk-fabric in a light yellow color, often used as in lieu of feminine apparel made of the material. 人勝 is a kind of paper-made flower that ancient Chinese women often used when dressing their hair.

64. During the Late Tang times, it was the fashion to enjoy the blossoms of the peonies. Emperor Wenzong was fond of doing this, see Qian Yi, *Nanbu Xinshu*, 9. The peony blooms at the end of the third month on Chinese calendar.

65. See Ye Jiaying, *Jialing Lunci*, 13.

66. See "Written at the Wangyuan Post" (題望苑驛), "Written for the Willow" (題柳), and "The Old Residence of Recluse Li Yu" (李羽處士故里), in j. 4 WFQ.

67. For the translation, see Hawkes, 119.

68. See Ma Maoyuan, *Chucixuan*, 257–58.

69. For the translations of the two lines of Li Shangyin, see James Liu, 66 and 52.

70. See "On a Spring Day, I Was About to Return to the East, and Mailed This to the Newly-Passed Presented Scholar, Miao Shen" (春日將欲東歸，寄新及第苗紳先輩, j. 4, WFQ), a poem composed in the Dazhong era.

71. See Wang Guowei, *Renjian Cihua*, 25.

72. See Shanghai Library, *Congshu Jicheng Zonglu*, Book II, 959.

CONCLUSION

1. See JTS, "Biography of Gao Yuanyu," 171: 4452.

2. Here we should point out in passing another example of the personal attacks Wen suffered that related to the eunuchs. *Tongxin* says: "Wen was a man of ugly features and was nicknamed as 'Wen Zhongkui,' which does not match his reputation as a talented literatus" (溫貌甚陋，號溫鍾馗，不稱才名). To nickname Wen as Zhong Kui solely because of his ugliness is too dubious to be believed. In Tang popular legend Zhong Kui was indeed ugly, but he was an expert in catching ghosts and goblins and

thus a guardian deity of the people, so his picture was hung to dispel the evil spirits ever since the first half of the eighth century. Considering all Wen's exceptional experiences against the eunuchs, Wen did survive quite a few unmitigated disasters in "fighting the devil," perhaps in addition to helping others to do so. Thus, calling Wen as Zhong Kui might have to do with his unremitting struggle with the eunuchs, a kind of devil in the eyes of his contemporaries.

3. See Li Zhao, *Guoshi Bu*, 57.

4. See Qian Zhongshu, *Tanyi Lu*, 55, 56, and 62. Hong Kong Longmen Bookstore, 1965.

5. For examples, see Lu You, *Weinanji*; Ouyang Xiu, *Liuyi Shihua* (He Wenhuan, 263–72); Liu Kezhuang, *Houcun Shihua*, 205–206; Qing Dynasty anonymous author, *Buganju Shihua*; Xue Xue, *Yipiao Shihua*; Zhang Huiyan, *Cixuan*; Chen Tingchuo, *Baiyuzhai Cihua*; Wei Hu, *Caidiaoji*, 479–94; Zhao Chongzuo, *Huajianji*, Chapters 1–2 (*Among the Flower*, 37–55).

6. See Pi Rixiu, "Preface to *Songlingji*" (松陵集序), QTW, 796: 10535–36, composed in 869, by which time, most probably, both Wen and Li had died.

7. See Zhang Jie, *Suihantang Shihua* (歲寒堂詩話), 5, He Wenhuan, 5.

8. See WFQ, 253; whether the Chinese character 視 is added by its annotators is uncertain.

Bibliography

Ban Gu (班固, 32–92) et al. *Hanshu* (abbr. HS), 漢書. Rpt. Shanghai: Zhonghua Shuju (中華書局, abbr. Zhonghua), 1976.

Barrett, T. H. *Li Ao: Buddhist, Taoist, or Neo-Confucian?* Oxford, New York: Oxford UP, 1992.

Bian Xiaoxuan (卞孝萱). *Liu Yuxi Nianpu*, 劉禹錫年譜. Shanghai: Zhonghua, 1963

——. *Liu Yuxi Congkao*, 劉禹錫叢考. Chengdu: Bashu Shushe (巴蜀書社), 1988.

Birch, Cyril, comp and ed. *Anthology of Chinese Literature*. New York: Grove Press, 1965.

Birrell, Anne, trans. *New Songs from a Jade Terrace*. London: George Allen and Unwin, 1982.

Cen Zhongmian (岑仲勉). *Tangren Hangdilu*, 唐人行第錄. Beijing: Zhonghua, 1962

——. *Tangshi Yushen*, 唐史餘瀋. Beijing: Zhonghua, 1960.

——. *Langguan Shizhu Timing Xinkaoding*, 郎官石柱題名新考訂. Shanghai: Guji, 1984.

——. "Hanlin Xueshi Biji Zhubu," 翰林學士壁記注補. 49–223, No. 28. Guoli Zhongyang Yanjiuyuan Lishi Yanjiusuo (國立中央研究院歷史研究所): Commercial Press, 1948.

——. *Yuanhe Xingcuan Sijiaoji*, 元和姓纂四校記, No. 29. Guoli Zhongyang Yanjiuyuan LishiYanjiusuo: Commercial Press, 1948.

Chang, Kang-i Sun. *The Evolution of Chinese Tz'u Poetry from Late Tang to Southern Song*. Princeton: Princeton UP, 1980.

Chao Gongwu (晁公武) et al. *Junzhai Dushuzhi*, 郡齋讀書志. Comp. 1151. Rpt. Taipei, 1967.

Charles O. Hucker, Dictionary of Official Titles in Imperial China. Stanford University Press, Standford, California, 1985.

Chen Hongchi (陳鴻墀). *Quantangwen Jishi*, 全唐文紀事. Shanghai: Zhonghua, 1982.

Chen Ruoshui (陳弱水). *Liu Zongyuan and Intellectual Change in T'ang China*. Cambridge: Cambridge UP, 1992.

Chen Shangjun (陳尚君). "Wen Tingyun Zaonian Shiji Kaobian," 溫庭筠早年事跡考辨. *Zhonghua Wenshi Luncong*, 中華文史論叢 18: 245–67. Shanghai: Zhonghua, 1981.

Chen Shou (陳壽, 233–297). *Sanguozhi* (SGZ), 三國志. Rpt. Beijing: Zhonghua, 1959.

Chen Tingchuo (陳庭綽). *Baiyuzhai Cihua*, 白雨齋詞話. Rpt. Beijing: Remin Wenxue Chubanshe (人民文學出版社), 1959.

Chen Yinke (陳寅恪). "Sui Tang Zhidu Yuanyuan Luelungao," 隋唐制度淵源略論稿, Shanghai: Commercial Press, 1946.

Chunqiu Zuozhuan Zhengyi (abbr. *Zuozhuan*), 春秋左傳正義. Annotated by Du Yu (杜預, 222–280) and Kong Yingda. In *Shisanjing Zhushu* (abbr. *Shisanjing*), 十三經注疏, Comp. Ruan Yuan (阮元, 1764–1849), 697–2188. Rpt. Beijing: Zhonghua, 1980.

Collie, David, trans. *The Chinese Classic Work Commonly Called the Four Books*. Florida: Scholars' Facsimiles and Rpt, 1970.

Crump J. I. Jr., trans. *Chan-Kuo Ts'e*. Oxford: Clarendon Press, 1970.

Des Rotours, Robert. *Le Traite des Examens, Traduit de la Nouvelle Histoire des T'ang*, 2nd ed. San Francisco: Chinese Materials Center, 1976.

Ding Fubao (丁福保), ed. *Qing Shihua*, 清詩話. Shanghai: Guji, 1963.

——. *Lidai Shihua Xubian*, 歷代詩話續编, Rpt. Beijing: Zhonghua, 1983.

Ding Juhui (丁居晦). "Chongxiu Hanlin Xueshi Biji," 重修翰林學士壁記, In *Hanyuan Congshu* (翰苑叢書), Book 13, of *Zhibuzu Zhai Congshu* (知不足齋叢書), comp. Bao Tingbo (鮑廷博), 3374–83. Rpt. Taipei: Xingzhong Shuju (興中書局), 1964.

Dong Gao (董誥, 1740–1818) et al. *Quantangwen* (abbr. QTW), 全唐文. Comp. 1814. Rpt. Taipei: Huiwen Shuju (惠文書局), 1961.

Duan Chengshi (段成式). *Youyang Zazu*, 酉陽雜俎. Beijing: Zhonghua, 1981.

Du Mu (杜牧). *Fanchuanshi Jizhu*, 樊川詩集注. Ed. comm. Feng Jiwu (馮集梧). Rpt. Beijing: Zhonghua, 1962.

Du You (杜佑, 735–812). *Tongdian*, 通典, *Wanyouwenku* ed. Shanghai: Commercial Press, 1935.

Du Zhao (杜詔). *Zhongwantang Shi Koutanji*, 中晚唐詩叩彈集. Rpt. Shanghai: Zhonghua, 1982.

Enin: *Rutang Qiufa Xunliji*, 入唐求法巡禮記. Taipei: Wenhai Chubanshe (文海), 1971.

Fan Wenlan (范文瀾). *Zhongguo Tongshi Jianbian*, 中國通史簡编. 6th ed. Beijing: Renmin Wenxue Chubanshe, 1978.

Fan Shu (范攄, fl. 870). *Yunxi Youyi*, 雲溪友議. In *Tang Guoshibu deng Bazhong*, 唐國史補等八種, comp. Yang Jialuo, 1–79. Taipei: Shijie Shuju (世界書局), 1962.

Fan Ye (范曄, 398–445). *Houhanshu* (abbr. HHS), 後漢書. Beijing: Zhonghua, 1965.

Fan Zuyu (范祖禹, 1041–1098). *Tangjian*, 唐鑒. Rpt. Shanghai: Shanghai Guji Chubanshe (上海古籍出版社), 1984.

Fang Jiliu (方積六) et al., eds. *Tang Wudai Wushier Zhong Biji Xiaoshuo Renming Suoyin*, 唐五代五十二種筆記小說人名索引 Beijing: Zhonghua, 1992.

Fang Xuanling (房玄齡, fl. 570–630) et al. *Jinshu* (abbr. JS), 晉書. Rpt. Beijing: Zhonghua. 1974.

Feifel, E. trans. *Po Chu-i as a Censor; His Memorials Presented to Emperor Hsien-tsung during the Years 808–810*. Tokyo: 's-Gravenchehage Mouton, 1961.

Feng Yan (封演). *Fengshi Wenjian Ji*, 封氏聞見記. Rpt. Beijing: Zhonghua, 1958.

Feng Youlan (馮友蘭). *A History of Chinese Philosophy*. Trans. Derk Bodde. Princeton: Princeton UP, 1983.

Frodsham, J. D., trans. *The Poems of Li Ho* (791–817). Oxford: Oxford UP, 1970.

Fu Lecheng (傅樂成). *Suitang Wudaishi*, 隋唐五代史. Taipei: Shijieshuju, 1959.

Fu Xuanzong (傅璇宗). *Li Deyu Nianpu*, 李德裕年譜. Shanghai: Guji, 1980.

Fusek, Lois. trans. *Among the Flower*. New York: Columbia UP, 1982.

Gao Yanxiu (高彥休). *Tangqueshi*, 唐闕史. Rpt. Beijing: Commercial Press, 1949.

Graham, J. D., trans. *Poems of the Late Tang*. Harmondsworth, Eng: Penguin, 1965.

Guo Maoqian (郭茂倩). *Yuefu Shiji* (abbr. YFSJ), 樂府詩集. Rpt. Beijing: Zhonghua, 1979.

Guo Shaoyu (郭紹虞), *Qing Shihua Xubian* (清詩話續編), Shanghai, Guji, 1983.

Gu Xuejie (顧學頡). "Wen Tingym Jiaoyou Kao," 溫庭筠交游考. 216–36. In Gu Xuejie Wenxue Lunji, 顧學頡文學論集. Beijing: Zhongguo Shehui Kexue Chubanshe (中國社會科學出版社), 1987 (abbr: Lunji).

——. "Wen Tingyun Xingshi Kaolüe," 溫庭筠行實論略. 237–60, in Lunji.

——. "A Correction of the Errors in the Old Annotation of Wen Tingyun's Poem 'Inspired by the Old, Pour My Heart by Fifty Rhymes, Presented to Chancellor Li of Huainan," 溫庭筠感舊陳情五十韻獻淮南李僕射詩舊注辨誤. 188–91, in Lunji; also *Guowen Yuekan*, 國文月刊. No. 57, 1947.

——. "Revision and Supplement to 'Biographies of Wen Tingyun' in the two *Tang Histories*," 新舊唐書溫庭筠傳訂補. 192–215, in Lunji, also see *Guowen Yuekan*, No. 62, (1947).

Gu Zuyu (顧祖禹, 1624–1680). *Dushi Fangyu Jiyao*, 讀史方輿紀要, Rpt. Beijing: Zhonghua, 1955.

Hanfeizi, 韓非子. Annotated by unknown author and collated by Gu Guangqi (顧廣圻, 1770–1813), 1116–1308 in *Ershierzi*, 二十二子. Rpt. of 1880 Zhejiang Shuju (浙江書局) version, Shanghai: Guji, 1985.

Hartman, Charles. *Han Yu and the Tang Search of Unity*. Princeton: Princeton UP, 1986.

Hawkes, David, trans. *Ch'u Tz'u: The Songs of the South*. Oxford: Clarendon. Press, 1959.

He Wenhuan (何文煥). *Lidai Shihua*, 歷代詩話. Beijing: Zhonghua, 1981.

Hu Yinglin (胡應麟). *Shisou*, 詩藪. Rpt. Shanghai: Zhonghua, 1958.

Hu Zhenheng (胡震亨) and Ji Zhenyi (季振宜), *Quantangshi* (abbr. QTS), 全唐詩. Comp. 1707. Rpt. Beijing: Zhonghua, 1980.

Hu Zhenheng. *Tangyin Kuiqian*, 唐音癸籤, Rpt. Shanghai: Gudian Wenxue Chubanshe (古典文學出版社), 1957.

Hu Zi (胡仔). *Tiaoxi Yuyin Conghua*, 苕溪漁隱叢話. Rpt. Beijing: Renmin Wenxue, 1962.

Huai'nanzi, 淮南子. Annotated by Gao You, collated by Zhuang Kuiji (莊逵吉, 1760–1813). *Ershierzi*, 1204–1308.

Huang Kunyao (黃昆堯). *Wen Tingyun*, 溫庭筠. Taipei: Guojia Chubanshe (國家出版社), 1984.

Hung, William. *Tu Fu: China's Greatest Poet*. Cambridge: Harvard UP, 1969.

Iwama Keiji (岩間啟二). *Wen Tingyun No Shiika Sakuin*, 溫庭筠詩歌索引. Kyoto: Friend Bookstore, 1977.

Ji Yougong (計有功). *Tangshijishi*, 唐詩紀事. Rpt. Beijing: Zhonghua, 1965.

Karlgren, Bernhard, trans. *The Book of Documents*. Rpt. from The Far Eastern Antiquities, bulletin 22, Stockholm, 1950.

——. *Grammata Serica*, 1940. Rpt. Taipei: Chenwen, 1966.

——. *Analytical Dictionary of Chinese And Sino-Japanese*. New York: Dover, 1974.

Kong Pingzhong (孔平仲, of the Southern Song), ed. *Xushishuo*, 續世說. Rpt. Taipei. Commercial Press, n. d.

Lao Ge (勞格, 1820–1864) and Zhao Yue (趙鉞). *Tang Shangshusheng Langguan Shizhu Timing Kao*, 唐尚書省郎官石柱題名考. Beijing: Zhonghua, 1992.

——. *Tang Yushitai Jingshe Timing Kao*, 唐御史臺精舍題名考. Rpt. Kyoto: Kabushiki kaish (京都株式會社), Chinese Publishing House, 1978.

Laozi, 老子. Annotated by Wang Bi and Lu Deming (陸德明, 556–627). 1–11 in *Ershierzi*.

Legge, James, trans. *Li Ki, or Collection of Treatises on the Rules of Propriety or Ceremonial Usuages*. Books I–XLVI, Vol. XXVII–VIII *of Sacred Books of the East*. ed. F. Max-Muller. Oxford: Clarendon Press, 1885.

——. *The Four Books*. Rpt. New York: Paragon, 1966.

——. *The I Ching*, New York: Dover, 1975.

——. *The Texts of Taoism*. Part II. New York: Dover, 1962.

Levy Dore J. *Chinese Narrative Poetry*, Durham and London: Duke UP, 1988.

Li Baiyao (李百藥). *Beiqishu*, 北齊書. Beijing: Zhonghua, 1973.

Liezi, 列子. Annotated by Zhang Zhan (張湛, of the Jin Dynasty) and Yin Jingshun (殷敬順, of the Tang Dynasty). 194–222 *Ershierzi*.

Li Fang (李坊, 926–996) et al. *Taiping Guangji*, 太平廣記. Rpt. Beijing: Zhonghua, 1961.

——. *Taipingyulan*, 太平御覽. Rpt. Beijing: Zhonghua, 1981.

——. *Wenyuan Yinghua*, 文苑英華. Rpt. Beijing: Zhonghua, 1982.

Li He (李賀). *Li He Shige Jizhu*, 李賀詩歌集注. Annotated by Wang Qi, 王琦. Shanghai: Renmin. 1977.

Li Linfu (李林甫, ?–752). *Tangliudian*, 唐六典, compt. 740s? Sibucongkan. ed.

Li Jifu (李吉甫, 758–814), *Yuanhe Junxianzhi*, 元和郡縣志. Rpt. Beijing: Zhonghua, 1985. of 1880 Jingling Shuju version.

Li Shangyin (李商隱, 813–58). *Fannan Wenji*, 樊南文集. Annotated by Feng Hao (馮浩, 1719–1801) and reexplained by Qian Zhenlun (錢振倫) and Qian Zhenchang (錢振常). Shanghai: Guji, 1988.

——. *Yuxisheng Shiji Jianzhu*, 玉溪生詩集箋注. Comm. Feng Hao. Rpt. Shanghai: Guji, 1979.

——. *Li Yishan Shi Jianzhu*, 李義山詩箋注. Comm. Zhu Heling (朱鶴齡) and Qu Fu (屈復). Yangzhou Yigutang version. Rpt. Beijing: Zhonghua, 1976.

Li Yanshou (李延壽, fl. 630). *Nanshi* (abbr, NS), 南史. Beijing: Zhonghua, 1975.

Li Zhao (李肇, fl. 820). *Tang Guoshibu*, 唐國史補. 1–66 in *Tang Guoshi Bu Deng Bazhong*, 唐國史補等八種.

Lin Bao (林寶). *Yuanhe Xingcuan*, 元和姓纂. Proofread by Cen Zhongmian. *Yuanhe Xingcuan Sijiaoji*, (元和姓纂四校記). Beijing: Commercial Press, 1948.

Liji Zhengyi (abbr. *Liji*), 禮記正義. Annotated by Zheng Xuan and Kong Yingda 1221–1696 in *Shisanjing*.

Liu Chongyuan (劉崇遠, fl. 930). *Jinhuazi*, 金華子. Rpt. Shanghai: Guji, 1988.

Liu. James J. Y. *The Poetry of Li Shangyin*. Chicago: Chicago UP, 1969.

Liu Kezhuang (劉克莊). *Houcun Shihua*, 後村詩話. Rpt. Beijing: Zhonghua, 1983.

Liu Wenqi (劉文琪, 1789–1854) et al. *Jiutangshu Jiaokanji*, 舊唐書校勘記. 1846. Rpt. Taipei: Shijie Shuju, 1971.

Liu Wuchi and Irving Yucheng Lo. *Sunflower Splendor*. Bloomington and Indianapolis: Indiana UP, 1975.

Liu Xiang (劉向, 77–37 B.C.). *Zhanguoce*, 戰國策. 3 vols. Rpt. Shanghai: Guji, 1978.

Liu Xie (劉勰). *Wenxin Diaolong*, 文心雕龍. Ed. Zhou Zhenfu (周振甫). Beijing: Renmin Wenxue, 1965.

——. *The Literary Mind and the Carving of Dragon*. Trans. by Vincent Yu-Chung Shi. New York Columbia UP, 1959.

Liu Xu (劉煦, 887–946) et al. *Jiutangshu* (abbr. JTS), 舊唐書. Beijing: Zhonghua, 1978.

Liu Yiqing (劉義慶, 403–444). *Shishuoxinyu*, 世說新語. Beijing: Zhonghua, 1989.

Liu Yuxi (劉禹錫). *Liu Yuxi Ji*, 劉禹錫集. Shanghai: Renmin, 1975.

Lunyu Zhushu (abbr. *Lunyu*), 論語注疏. Annotated by He Yan (何晏, 190–249) and Xing Bing (邢昺, 932–1010). 2453–2536 in *Shisanjing*.

Lu Qinli (逯欽立), ed. *Quan Xianqin Han Wei Jin Nanbeichao Shi*, 全先秦漢魏晉南北朝詩. Beijing: Zhonghua, 1983.

Lu Xinyuan (陸心源). *Tangwen Shiyi*, 唐文拾遺. Taipei: Wenhai Chubanshe, 1962.

Lu You (陸游), *Lu You Ji*, 陸游集. Beijing: Zhonghua, 1976.

Lüshi Chunqiu, 呂氏春秋. Annotated by Gao You (高誘, of the Han Dynasty) and collated by Bi Yuan, 625–728. *Ershierzi*.

Lü Simian (呂思勉). *Suitang Wudaishi*, 隋唐五代史. Beijing: Zhonghua, 1959.

Ma Duanlin (馬端臨, 1254–1323). *Wenxian Tongkao*, 文獻通考, Rpt. Beijing: Zhonghua, 1936.

Ma Maoyuan (馬茂元). *Chucixuan*, 楚辭選. Beijing: Renmin Wenxue Chubanshe, 1957.

Maoshi Zhengyi (abbr. *Maoshi*), 毛詩正義. Annotated by Zheng Xuan (鄭玄, 127–200) and Kong Yingda. 259–630 in *Shisanjing*.

Mather, Richard B., trans. *A New Account of Tales of the World* (abbr. NATW). Minneapolis: Minnesota UP, 1976.

Meng Qi (孟棨). *Benshi Shi*, 本事詩. Beijing: Gudian Wenxue Chubanshe, 1957.

Mengzi Zhengyi (abbr. *Mengzi*), 孟子正義. Annotated by Zhao Qi (趙岐, 108–201) and Sun Shi (孫奭, 962–1033). 2659–2785 in *Shisanjing*.

Miao, Ronald C. "Palace-styled Poetry: The Courtly Treatment of Glamour and Love." In *Studies in Chinese Poetry and Poetics*, vol. I, ed. Ronald C. Miao, 1–42. San Francisco: Chinese Materials Center, 1978.

Mou Huaichuan (牟懷川). "A New Ascertainment of Wen Tingyun's Birth year," 溫庭筠生年新證. *Shanghai Shifan Xueyuan Xuebao*, 1: 48–53. (1983).

——. "The Investigation and Explanation of Some Problems about Wen Tingyun's Life," 關于溫庭筠生平若干問題的考證和説明, *Shanghai Shifan Xueyuan Xuebao*, 2: 122–28. (1985).

——. "On Wen Tingyun's Secret Attendance upon the Heir Apparent," 溫庭筠從游莊恪太子考論, *Tangdai Wenxue Luntan* (唐代文學論壇), 1: 339–60. Taiyuan. China. 1988.

——. A Detailed Investigation of Wen Tingyun's Changing His Name," 溫庭筠改名案詳審. *Wenshi*, 38: 181–202. Beijing: Zhonghua, 1994.

Ouyang Xiu *Xintangshu* (abbr, XTS), 新唐書. Beijing: Zhonghua, 1978.

Ouyang Xun (歐陽洵, 557–641). *Yiwenleiju*, 藝文類聚. Rpt. Shanghai. Guji. 1982.

Owen Stephen. *The Great Age of Chinese Poetry*, New Haven: Yale UP, 1981.

——. *The Poetry of Meng Jiao and Han Yu*. New Haven: Yale UP, 1975.

——. *Traditional Chinese Poetry and Poetics: Omen of the World*. Madison: Wisconsin UP, 1985.

Pei Tingyu (裴庭裕). *Dongguan Zouji*, 東觀奏記. Jiangyin, *Ouxiang Lingshi* (藕香零拾). 1911.

Pei Xiaoyuan (裴考源, of the Tang dynasty). *Zhenguan Gongsi Huashi*, 貞觀公私畫史. Book 8, *Tangren Shuohui*, 唐人説薈. Shanghai: Saoye Shanfang (掃葉山房), 1910.

Pulleyblank, Edwin. *The Background of the Rebellion of An Lushan*. Oxford: Oxford UP, 1955.

Qian Yi (錢易). *Nanbu Xinshu*, 南部新書, *Aoyatang Congshu*. ed.

Qian Zhongshu (錢鍾書), *Guanzhui Bian*, 管錐編. Beijing: Zhonghua, 1979.

Qu Tuiyuan (瞿蜕園), ed. *Liu Yuxi Ji Jianzheng*, 劉禹錫集箋證. Shanghai: Guji, 1989.

Qu Yuan (屈原) et al. *Chuci*, 楚辭. Annotated by Wang Yi (王逸) and Hong Xingzu (洪興祖): *Chuci Buzhu*, 楚辭補注. Taipei: Zhonghua, 1972.

Reischauer, E. O. trans. *Ennin's Diary: The Record of a Pilgrimage to China In Search of the Law*. New York: 1955.

Ren Bantang (任半塘). *Tangshengshi*, 唐聲詩. Shanghai: Guji, 1982.

Rouzer, Paul F. *Writing Another's Dream—The Poetry of Wen Tingyun*. Stanford: Stanford UP, 1993.

Ruan Yue (阮閱). *Zengxiu Shihua Zonggui*, 增修詩話總歸. Sibu Congkan version.

Shangshu Zhengyi (abbr. *Shangshu*), 尚書正義. Annotated by Kong Anguo (孔安國, of the Han Dynasty) and Kong Yingda. 109–258 in *Shisanjing*.

Shen Deqian (沈德潛, 1675–1769). *Gushiyuan*, 古詩源. Rpt. Beijing: Zhonghua, 1963.

Shen Yue (沈約, 441–513). *Songshu* (abbr, SS), 宋書. Beijing: Zhonghua, 1974.

Sheng Cheng (盛成). "Wen Tingyun." In *Zhongguo Wenxueshi Lunji*, 中國文學史論集, 430–43. Taipei: Zhonghua Wenhua Chubanshe, 1958.

Shi Daoyuan (釋道原). *Jingde Chuandeng Lu*, 景德傳燈錄. Preface by Yang Yi (楊億, 974–1020). *sibucongkan sanbian* ed.

Shi Zhecun (施蟄存). "Du Wen Feiqing Ci Zhaji," 讀溫飛卿詞札記, *Zhonghua Wenshi Luncong* 8: 273–81, Shanghai: Guji, 1978.

Sima Guang (司馬光, 1019–1086) et al. *Zizhitongjian* (ZZhTJ), 資治通鑒, comp. 1066–1068. Rpt. Beijing: Zhonghua, 1958.

Sima Qian (145–? B.C.). *Shiji*, 史記. Beijing: Zhonghua, 1973.

Soloman, B. S. *The Veritable Record of the Tang Emperor Shun-tsung, 805*. Cambridge: Cambridge UP, 1955.

Song Minqiu (宋敏求, 1019–1079). *Tang Dazhaoling Ji*, 唐大詔令集, Rpt. Beijing: Zhonghua, 1959.

Steele, John, trans. *The I-Li, or Book of Etiquette and Ceremonial*. London. Probsthain, 1917.

Sun Fu (孫甫, 998–1957). *Tangshi Lunduan*, 唐史論斷. Taipei: Commercial, 1967.

Sun Guangxian (孫光憲, 900–968). *Beimeng Suoyan*, 北夢瑣言. Shanghai: Zhonghua, 1981, or series No. 2841 in *Congshu Jicheng Chubian*.

Sun Qi (孫棨, fl. 850–880). *Beilizhi*, 北里志. 1–42, in *Tangguoshibu deng Bazhong*.

Taisho Tripitaka. *Taisho Shinshu Daizokyo*, 大正新修大藏經, Tokyo: Society for the Publication of the Taisho Edition of the Tripitaka, 1924–32.

Tan Yao (談鑰). *Jiatai Wuxing Zhi*, 嘉泰吳興志, *Wuxing Congshu* (吳興叢書本).

Tao Hongjing (陶弘景). *Zhengao*, 真誥. From *Tao Hongjing Ji*, 陶弘景集, of the Daozang (道藏) version. Rpt, Yangzhou: Jiangsu Guangling Guji Keyinshe (楊州江蘇廣陵古籍刻印社), 1992.

Tao Zongyi (陶宗儀). *Shuofu*, 說郛, *Wanwei Shantang* version (宛委山堂本).

Twitchett, Denis Crispin. *Financial Administration under the Tang Dynasty*. 2d ed. Cambridge [Eng]: Cambridge UP, 1970.

Twitchett Denis. *The Writing of Official History under the Tang*. New York: Cambridge UP, 1992.

Twitchett, Denis and John K. Fairbank, eds. *The Cambridge History of China*. Volume 3, *Sui and Tang China*, 589–906. London: Cambridge UP, 1979.

van Zoeren, Steven. *Poetry and Personality: Reading, Exegesis, and Hermeneutics in Traditional China*. Stanford: Stanford UP, 1991.

Waley, Arthur, trans. *The Book of Songs*. New York: Grove Press, 1960.

——. *Life and Times of Po Chuyi*. London: G. Allen and Unwin, 1949.

Waltham, Clae, trans. *Shujing* (*Book of History*). Chicago: Henry Regnery Company, 1971.

Wan Man (萬曼). *Tangji Xulu*, 唐集敘錄. Beijing: Zhonghua, 1982.

Wang Bijiang (王辟疆). *Tangren Xiaoshuo*, 唐人小說. Taipei: Wenguang Tushu, 1975.

Wang Chong (王充, 27–97). *Lunheng*, 論衡. Rpt. Shanghai: Renmin, 1974.

Wang Chongmin (王重民). *Quantangshi Buyi*, 全唐詩補遺. Beijing: Zhonghua, 1982.

Wang Dajin (王達津). "Tan Wen Tingyun Shengping de Ruogan Wenti," 談溫庭筠生平的若干問題, *Naikai Daxue Xuebao*, 南開大學學報 2: 48–53. (1982).

Wang Dang (王讜, fl. 1105). *Tang Yulin*, 唐語林. Rpt. Shanghai: Guji, 1978.

Wang Dingbao (王定保). *Tangzhiyan*, 唐摭言. Shanghai: Guji, 1978.

Wang Fuzhi (王夫之, 1619–1689). *Du Tongjian Lun*, 讀通鑒論. Rpt. Beijing: Zhonghua, 756–953. 1980.

——. *Qing Shihua*, Shanghai Guji, 1963.

Wang Guowei (王國維). *Renjian Cihua*, 人間詞話. In *Renjian Cihua Huibian*, ed. Yao Kefu. Beijing: Shumu Wenxian Chubanshe (書目文獻出版社), 1983.

Wang Li (王力). *Hanyu Shilüxue*, 漢語詩律學. Shanghai: Xinzhishi (新知識), 1958.

Wang Mingsheng (王鳴盛, 1722–1797). *Shiqishi Shangque*, 十七史商榷. Rpt. Shanghai: n. d. 1787.

——. *Eshubian*, 蛾術編. Shanghai: Commercial, 1958.

Wang Pu (王溥, 922–982), *Tanghuiyao*, 唐會要. Rpt. Beijing: Zhonghua, 1958.

Wang Qinruo (王欽若, 962–1025) et al. *Cefu Yuangui*, 冊府元龜, 1005–13. Rpt. of 1642 ed., Beijing: Zhonghua, 1960.

Wang Yaochen (王堯臣, 1001–1056) et al. *Chongwen Zongmu Jishi*, 崇文總目輯釋. Taipei: Shijieshuju, 1968.

Wang Yinglin (王應麟, 1223–1296). *Yuhai*, 玉海. comp. Rpt. Taipei: Shijieshuju, 1967.

Watson, Burton, trans. *Records of the Grand Historian*, Hong Kong-New York: The Chinese University of Hong Kong and Columbia UP. 1961.

——. *Chuangtzu*. New York: Columbia UP. 1964.

Wei Hu (韋縠). *Caidiaoji*, 才調集, *Sibu Congkan* ed.

Wei Qingzhi (魏慶之, fl. 1270). *Shiren Yuxie*, 詩人玉屑. Shanghai: Guji, 1980.

Wen Tingyun. *Wen Tingyun Shicixuan*, 溫庭筠詩詞選 ed. Liu Sihan (劉斯翰). Hong Kong: Sanlian Shudian (三聯書店), 1986.

——. *Wen Feiqing Shiji Jianzhu* (WFQ), 溫飛卿詩集箋注. Annotated by Zeng Yi (曾益), Gu Yuxian (顧予咸), and Gu Sili (顧嗣立). Rpt. Shanghai: Guji, 1980.

——. *Wen Tingyun Shixuan*, 溫庭筠詞選 ed. Wu Dunsheng (吳遁生): Shanghai: Commercial Press. 1930. Rpt. Hong Kong: Daguang (大光), 1973.

Wright, Arthur F., and Denis C. Twitchett, eds. *Perspectives on the Tang*. New Haven: Yale UP. 1973.

Wu Tingxie (吳廷燮). *Tang Fangzhen Nianbiao* (abbr. TFZNB), 唐方鎮年表. Beijing: Zhonghua, 1980.

Xia Chengtao (夏承燾). "Wen Feiqing Xinian," 溫飛卿系年. In *Tangsong Ciren Nianpu*, 唐宋詞人年譜, 383–424. Beijing: Gudian Wenxue, 1955.

Xiao Tong (蕭統, 501–531), ed. *Wenxuan*, 文選. Rpt. Chengdu: Zhonghua, 1981.

Xiao Zixian (蕭子顯, 489–537), *Nanqishu* (NQS), 南齊書, Beijing. Zhonghua, 1972.

Xin Wenfang (辛文房). *Tang Caizi Zhuan*, 唐才子傳. comp. 1304. Rpt. Beijing: Zhonghua, 1957.

Xu Jian (徐堅, 659–729). *Chuxueji*, 初學記. comp. in the era of Kaiyuan (712–740). Rpt. Beijing: Zhonghua, 1985.

Xu Ling (徐陵, 507–583), comp. *Yutai Xinyong*, 玉臺新詠. Comp. Wu Zhaoyi (吳兆宜). Beijing: Zhonghua, 1985.

Xu Song (徐松, 1781–1848). *Dengkeji Kao* (abbr. DKJK), 登科記考. Taipei: Jingsheng Wenwu Gongying Gongsi (驚聲文物供應公司). Rpt. of 1888 ed. n. d.

——. *Tang Liangjing Chengfang Kao*, 唐兩京城坊考. Taipei: Yiwen Yinshuguan, 1967.

Xu Tao (徐匋). "Wen Tingyun Cong Zongmi Chanshi Jieshe Shi Kao," 溫庭筠從宗密禪師結社事考. *Wenshi* 28: 312–318, Beijing: Zhonghua, 1987.

Yan Gengwang (嚴耕望), comp. *Tang Pushang Chenglang Nianbiao*, 唐僕尚丞郎年表. Rpt. Beijing: Zhonghua, 1986.

——. *Tangshi Yanjiu Conggao*, 唐史研究叢稿, Hong Kong: Xinya Yanjiusuo, 1969.

Yan Kejun (嚴可均). comp. *Quan Shanggu Qinhan Sanguo Liuchaowen*, 全上古秦漢三國六朝文. Beijing: Zhonghua, 1958.

Yang Xiong. *Yangzi Fayan*, 揚子法言. Commentary by Li Gui (李軌, of the Jin Dynasty), 811–28, in *Ershierzi*.

Yao Silian (姚思廉, 557–637). *Liangshu* (abbr. LS) 梁書, and *Chenshu* (abbr. CS) 陳書. Beijing: Zhonghua, 1973.

Yanzi Chunqiu, 晏子春秋. Commentary by Sun Xingyan (孫星衍, 1753–1818). 557–624, in *Ershierzi*.

Ye Jiaying (葉嘉瑩). "Wen Tingyun Ci Gaishuo," 溫庭筠詞概說, in *Jialing Lunci Conggao*, 迦陵論詞叢稿. Shanghai: Guji, 1980.

——. "The Chang-chou School of Tz'u Criticism," *Harvard Journal of Asian Studies* 35: 102–32. 1975.

Yili Zhushu (abbr. *Yili*), 儀禮注疏. 941–1220, in *Shisanjing*.

Yin Fan (殷璠). *Tangren Xuan Tangshi*, 唐人選唐詩. Rpt. Beijing: Zhonghua, 1958.

Yongrong et al. (永榮), comp. *Siku Quanshu Zongmu Tiyao*, 四庫全書總目提要. Shanghai: Commercial Press, 1932.

You Mao (尤袤, 1127–1194). *Quantang Shihua*, 全唐詩話. *Congshu Jicheng Chubian*.

Yuquanzi, 玉泉子, unknown writer of Tang. Shanghai: Zhonghua, 1958.

Yu, Pauline. "Formal Distinctions in Chinese Literary Theory." In *The Theories of Arts in China*, ed. Susan Bush and Christian Murck, 27–53. Princeton: Princeton UP. 1983.

Yu Shinan (虞世南). *Beitang Shuchao*, 北堂書鈔. Rpt. Taipei: Wenhai Chubanshe, 1978.

Zan Ning (贊寧). *Song Gaocengzhuan*, 宋高僧傳. Rpt. 1884. Beijing: Zhonghua, 1984.

Zhan Antai (詹安泰). "Du Xia Chengtao Xiansheng de Wen Feiqing Xinian," 讀夏承燾先生的溫飛卿系年. In *Songci Sanlun*, 宋詞散論. Guangdong: Renmin. 1980.

Zhang Daren (張達人). *Liu Yuxi Nianpu*, 劉禹錫年譜. Taiwan: Commercial Press, 1974.

Zhang Gu (張固, of the Tang). *Youxian Guchui*, 幽閑鼓吹. Shanghai: Guji, 1958.

Zhangsun Wuji (長孫無忌, ?–659). *Tanglü Shuyi*, 唐律疏議, Rpt. with paraphrases by Cao Manzhi et al. Changchun: Jilin Renmin Chubanshe, 1989.

Zhang Huiyan (張惠言). *Cixun*, 詞選. Rpt. Beijing: Zhonghua, 1957.

Zhao Chongzuo (趙崇祚). ed. *Huajianji*, 花間集. *Sibu Beiyao* ed.

Zhao Lin (趙驎, fl. 837). *Yinhualu*, 因話錄. 1–55 in *Tang Guoshi Deng Bazhong*.

Zhao Ye (趙曄). *Wuyue Chunqiu*, 吳越春秋. *Sibu Congkan* ed.

Wuyue Chunqiu ZhuziSuoyin, 吳越春秋逐字索引. Hong Kong: Commercial Press, 1993.

Zhao Yi (趙壹, of the Qing). *Nianershi Zaji*, 廿二史劄記. Beijing: Zhonghua, 1963.

Zheng Zhenduo (鄭振鐸). *Zhongguo Chatu Wenxueshi*, 中國插圖文學史. Hong Kong: Guwen Shuju, n.d.

Zhongguo Congshu Zonglu, 中國叢書綜錄. Shanghai Library. ed., 1958.

Zhouyi Zhengyi (abbr. *Zhouyi*), 周易正義. Annotated by Wang Bi (王弼, 226–249) and Kong Yingda (孔穎達, 574–648). 5–108 in *Shisanjing*.

Zhouli Zhushu (abbr. *Zhouli*), 周禮注疏. Commentary. by Zheng Xuan and Jia Gongyan (賈公彥, of the Tang Dynasty). 631–940 in *Shisanjing*.

Zhuangzi, 莊子. Commentary. Guoxiang (郭象, 252–312) and Lu Deming, 12–87 in *Ershierzi*.

Zhu Xi (朱熹). *Shijizhuan*, 詩集傳. Rpt. Shanghai: Zhonghua, 1958.

Zuo Qiuming (左丘明). *Guoyu*, 國語. Rpt. Shanghai: Guji, 1978.

Zurcher, E. *The Buddhist Conquest of China*. Leiden: Brill, 1959.

Index

Academician Yuan, 26, 71
Academy of Cassia Fragrance, 101
administer state's affairs from behind curtains, 94, 95
Aide to the Man-Barbarian Headquarters, 106, 256 n32
Airs and Elegantiae, 139. *See also* Maoshi
Altair and the Plough, 169
Amnesty, 2, 239 n3
Ancient Prose Movement, 3
An-Shi Rebellion, 1, 12, 79
Anshi's Isle, 70, 251 n4
Appointed Scholar Zheng, 64
Apricot Garden, 190, 212, 265 n26
archery, 158, 262 n26
Army Commander, 65, 67, 251 n48
ascending (your) hall, 100, 101, 256 n22
Assistant Du, 56, 57
Attached Word, 139, 263 n37
Attending Censor, 113; and Rectifier, 102, 103, 114, 118
attracted birds, 124, 135, 136, 259 n22
autumn-Tu, 72

Ba, River, 59
Bai Juyi, 30, 82, 105, 194; as Attending Censor, 102; in Music Bureau Movement, 3; philosophy, 30; simplicity and vividness, 53; with Pei Du and Liu Yuxi, 42
Ban Gu, 169; Rhapsody on Communion with the Mystical, 34
Bao Shuya, 34
Bao Zhao, 242 n48, 258 n59
Beauty Xu, 126
being recorded and registered, 100, 101, 256 n22
bell dance, 145, 260 n35
Besieged City, 222
Bian He, 36, 190, 244 n15
Bianque, 36, 244 n15
Bianzhang, 61
Bing Ji, 247 n41
Bing (Prefecture), 11
bird nesting on southern branch, 169, 263 n41
Black Dragon Pool, 143
blue-beetle, 170
Bo, Mount, 116
Bodidharma, 251 n49
Book of Change, 139, 165, 214
Book of Songs, 172, 261 nn10, 11. *See also* Maoshi
Boshan Censer, 114, 115, 116, 117
Bowang Park (Wangyuan), 97, 255 n12
broad willow, 154, 261 n16
Brocade City, 58; River, 57
Buddhism, 3, 67
butting against evil, 113, 114
bundle of fresh fodder, 153, 261 n10
burn tallies, 157, 262 n23

Cai Wenji, 146
Cai Yong, 146, 259 n15; zither with burned end, 245 n24; Epitaph for Having the Way Guo, 245 n16

Cao Pi, 97, 147, 255 n11
Cao Xueqin, A Dream of the Red Chamber, 86
Cao Zhi, 97, 147; Hymn for the Yinan Flower, 204; Poems on Public Feast, 255 n11
carry the writing-brush, 100, 101
Cassia, Area, 101, 189; Garden, 100, 101, 102; Palace, 102
Chancellor Li, 20, 35, 44, 46. *See also* Li Shen
Chang'an, 11, 29, 50, 55, 250, 252 n11; Wen came to, 56, 79, 89, 90, 103, 190; Wen left, 171, 173
changing the music scale, 153, 261 n12
Changsha, 185, 186, 187, 190
Changzhou School, 196, 202
chants and songs, 139. *See also* Songs of the South
Chanyu, 54, 249 n13
Chen Gu, 5, 239 n9
Chen Zhong, 169, 263 n42
Cheng Gong, 50, 248 n1
Cheng Xiao, 78, 80, 253 n28
Chengdu, 57, 70, 251 n3
Chu, 106, 107, 108, 176
Chu River, 85
Chumo, 37. See Wu Yinzhi
ci, 1, 4, 7, 140, 202
clerk of Jingzhou Prefecture, 106, 256 n32
clerk of Lujiang, 85
cloth-robe commoner from Danyang, 246 n38
comprehensive mastery, 19
Confucianism, 3, 38, 223, 257 n34, 250 n28
Confucius, 250 n28, 257 n34
congongrass and reeds, 176, 264 n3
Consort Pan, 141, 142, 260 n29
Consort Qi, 241 n23
Consort Wang. *See* Virtuous Consort Wang
Consort Yang, see Worthy Consort Yang
Cross Pond, 198, 266 n40
cross the River of Lu, 54, 249 n12
Crowned Heir Li (Han), 255 n12
crude jadeite, 120
crying crane, 131
Cui Gong, 75, 152, 154, 157
Cui Gu, 257 n40
Cui Qun, 108
Cui Xian, 240 n12
curved bridge, 133
cut the Gordian knot, 144

Dai Yong, 65, 66, 67, 251 n48
dancing by the rain altar, 158
dapple horse, 113
daylily, 203, 204
Dazhong Ninth Year Incident, 183, 84
dead end, 6, 201, 202
decorated boat, 100, 256 n20
devine-sheep cap, 118
Di Jianmo, 94, 134
Director Xun, 43. See Xun Kai
Divine Prefecture, 54, 55, 151, 152, 156, 161
Dongfang Shuo, 257 n25
Dong Fen, *Yanlingji*, 14
Dongting Lake, 64
Dou Xian, 42, 246 n39
Double Seventh, 124, 130, 132, 258 n17
dragon gate, 45, 175, 247 n50
dragon head, 118, 258 n60
drawing a tiger, 159, 262 n27
Du Kui, 33, 244 n7. *See also* Du Zhi
Du Mi, 28
Du Mu, 82, 83
Du Shenquan, 47, 264 n4
Du Yu (King of Shu), 249 n25
Du Yu, 33, 42, 134, 246 n39, 259 n20
Du Zhao, 125
Du Zhi (Kui), 32, 33, 34, 37, 51, 80
Duan Chengshi, 19, 160, 242 n38; Eight Letters to Wen Feiqing, 160, 241 n38; Teasing Feiqing, 160; On the Occasion that Rouqing Annulled Her . . . , 85
Duan Wenchang, 43, 247 n40
Dujuan, 58, 59, 249 n23
Duke Huan of Qi (Kingdom), 34, 138
Duke of Zanhuang, 251 n44. *See also* Li Deyu
Duke Ping of Jin, 33
Duke Ping of Lu, 32
Duke Xu Su (Su Ting), 38, 245 n23
Duke Zhou, 43; golden case, 247 n43
dusky crow, 112, 113, 257 n44

each tells his wish, 169, 262 n21
Eastern Capital State Son's University, 50
Eastern Han Dynasty (Late Han), 15, 31, 52
Eastern Mansion, 98
Eastern Palace, 15, 97, 102, 201, 255 n14; Avenue, 146
Eastern Peak, 65, 251 n47
eastern way host, 150
Eastern Woods, 64, 250 n41
Editorial Service under the Left Secretariat in the Household of the Heir Apparent, 101, 102, 103, 112, 128, 135, 256 n20
Emperor An (Han), 28
Emperor Cheng of Han, 126
Emperor Dezong, 17, 40
Emperor Gaozu (Tang), 12, 16, 17
Emperor Gaozu (Han), 97, 241 n23
Emperor Guangwu, 31, 262 n22
Emperor He (Han), 28
Emperor Jiang, 141
Emperor Jingzong (Tang), 41, 59
Emperor Muzong, 41
Emperor Ruizong, 16
Emperor Shunzong, 25, 28, 59
Emperor Taizong, 15, 119
Emperor Wendi (Wei), 242 n50
Emperor Wenzong, 6, 34, 95, 105, 131, 136, 170; and Consort Yang, 94, 142; and Consort Wang, 132; and his son, 119, 129, 216; and late-year Pei Du, 41, 43; and Wen's appointment, 112, 121, 141; curved bridge, 133; died under house-slaves, 93, 95, 97, 105, 143, 217, 255 n7; enjoy peonies, 267 n64; senior one of, 104; veiled criticism of, 143; Yangying Conference, 94, 134
Emperor Wu (Wei), 117
Emperor Wudi (Han), 116
Emperor Wudi (Han), 116, 131, 164, 255 n12
Emperor Wudi (Liang), 130
Emperor Wuzong, 142, 144, 145, 173; descendant of black dragon, 142, 144; Imperial Fraternal Heir, 95; poltical sensitivity of, 114, 145; set up in palace coup, 34, 173
Emperor Xiaocheng (Han), 102
Emperor Xian (Han), 95
Emperor Xianzong, 2, 3, 41, 143, 255 n7, 260 n30
Emperor Xuanzong (High Tang), 16, 38, 40, 124; dream, 130; close relation with Wen clan, 246 n31
Emperor Xuanzong, 3, 175, 176; attitude toward Wen, 187; fear the eunuchs, 195, 265 n35; like the singing of Pusaman, 194
Emperor Yuan (Han), 17, 102, 241 n24
Empress Chen, 131
Empress Dowager Dou, 28
Empress Wu (Tang), 94
Empress Zhao (Han), 124, 126
eunuch, 1, 40, 133, 192, 215, 216, 218; rampant, 1, 2, 11, 31, 40, 59, 70, 80, 93, 94, 125, 176, 187; and Wen, 3, 5, 39, 151, 168, 171, 181, 217; Wen alluded to, as, 31 (Zhu Yu), 32 (Du Zhi), 33 (Zang Cang), 78, 253 n28 (Cheng Xiao), 80, 253 n28; (Yellow Gate), 126 (Wang Shen); and Heir Apparent, 94, 125, 126; Wen's changed name has to do with, 150, 156, 161, 217

Fan Tai, 267 n61
Fan Zongshi
Fang Gan, 240 n18
Fang Zhi, 28
Fangcheng, 190
Fang, Mount 251, n4
Fangshan County, 181
Fen (prefecture), 11
Feng Ao, 110, 111, 264 n4
Feng Hao, 162, 164
Feng Xuan, 157, 262 n23, 246 n25
Feng'an Alley, 69
Ferocious Beasts, 124, 259 n22
fertile land, 54, 55
fish in a dry rut, 253 n27
five carriages, 261 n7
Five Lakes, 28
forbidden meat, 146
former party of Ganling, 27, 28–9
forsaken mat, 77, 252–3 n23
Four White-haired Seniors from Mount Shang, 97

fox listening on the ice, 171
frangrant herbs, 59, 249 n25
frightened cicada, 131
Frost Terrace (Censorate), 112
Fu Jian, 243 n58
fubi, 128

Gao Wei, 146, 147
Gao Yuanyu, 110, 267 n1
Ganling, 28
Genealogy of the Wang Clan (*Wangshi Jiapu*), 252 n8
General Big Tree (Feng Yi), 72, 252 n13
General Tigerhead, 119
Gold Terrace, 247 n44
golden case, 43, 247 n43
Golden Ditch, 199, 266 n45
Gong, 55
Good price, 152, 261 n8
Governance of Huichang, 2
Grand Master Cui, 14, 52
green-ant, 170
Green wine, 190, 265 n28
Gu (people name), 18
Gu Sili, 124
Gu Ti, 61, 259 n33
Gu Xuejie, 35
Guan Fu, 70, 252 n9
Guan Ying, 57, 242 n21
Guan Zhong, 34
Guangling, 88, 254 n39. *See also* Yangzhou
Guanglingsan, 21
Guanzhong, 52, 54, 55, 62
Gui Peak, 251 n47; Aranya, 66
Guo Fan, 77, 252 n20
Guo Pu, 252 n8
Guo Tai, 261 n10, 245 n16. *See also* Having the Way

Hall of Nine Sons, 205
Han Dynasty, 12, 28, 42, 107, 146
Han, River, 42
Han Xin, 57, 249 n21
Han Yi, 79, 80, 193
Han Yu, 3, 42, 53, 247 n40; Monument for Quelling Huaixi, 43
Hanlinyuan (Hanyuan), 134
hard-pressed monkey, 77, 253 n27
Having the Way, 36, 40, 41; Guo, 245 n16
Hawks-bill-shell, 123, 128, 129, 199, 259 n8
heavenly horse, 124, 134, 259 n19
Heavenly Mountain, 146
Hebei, 13
Hegan, Qi, 108, 110, 111
He'nan (prefecture), 56, 57
Heir Apparent, 95, 99, 103, 107, 119, 136, 142; and Boshan, 117; and Chu Kingdom, 108; and worship (pun), 116; and Yinan; 129; attendance on, 129, 130, 145; death of, 7, 94, 121, 132, 217; designated, 93; gives audience, 114, 118; heavenly counterpart of, 97, 255 n8; officials under, 119; rumor about, 255 n6; shaoyang, 204; scholars who serve, 255 n5; Wen's access to, 6, 40, 47, 79, 80, 129; Wen's attitude toward, 96–8, 99, 145, 167
Heir Apparent Incident, 91, 93, 99, 107, 135; aftermath of, on Wen, 167; extension of Sweet Dew Incident, 96; metaphor for, 133; particulars of, 135; shrouded account of, 92, 123, 127; sources of, 254 n1
Herd Boy, 129
Heng, Mount, 66
Heshi, Jade of, 10, 114, 115, 257 n50
Hezhou, 28
hidden motifs (jituo), 7, 60, 202, 206, 213, 214, 266 n52
High Tang, 219
Hu County, 23, 56, 66
Hua, Mount, 18
Huai River, 37, 39, 40, 70, 76; grew turbid, 70, 252 n8
Huainan, Wen came to, 54, 69, 70, 71, 89; Wen left, 56, 72, 90
Huaixi, 42
Huan Dian, 113
Huan Tan, 55
Huayan Sect, 65
Hui Yuan, 251 n50

Immortal Lad, 123, 128, 130, 201
Imperial Deputy, 73, 74, 79, 253 n29

Imperial Ditch, 31
ink immortal, 71, 252 n10
iris, magic, 124
isolated willow, 71

Jade Lass, 123, 128, 130, 201
jade mountain, 242 n50
Jade of Chu, 115. *See also* Heshi's Jade
Ji Bu, 154, 261 n16
Ji Kang, 21, 22, 25, 242 n51; Letter for Beaking Off Relations with Shan Juyuan, 19, 20, 80
Ji Kang-Shan Tao-Ji Shao, trio of, 20–2
Ji Mount, 14
Ji Shao, 35, 77, 80, 244 n12; with hairs streaming down his forehead, 12, 20, 22, 35
Ji Shao-Shan Tao-Ji Kang, 41, 46
Ji Tangfu, 19, 160, 241 n38; Seeing Off Wen Feiqing to be Defender of Fangcheng, 190–1
Jia Baoyu, 87
Jia Dao, 4
Jia Yi, 25, 186, 242 n50, 257 n34, 264 n16, Preface to Rhapsody on the Owl, 242; banished to Changsha, 185, 186, 187
Jiang, Mount, 141
Jiang Shen, 264 n4
Jiang Xi, 152, 261 n9
Jiang Yan, 188, 189, 265 n20
Jiang Ziwen, 141, 143
Jiangdong, 88, 89
Jianghuai 6, 53, 54, 72, 78, 80, 87, 89, 91
Jianghuai Inciden, 40, 81, 87, 91, 103, 170; aftermath of, 190; details of, 87; misdated as in Wen's late years, 88–90, 254 n39; name change related to, 167; small aftermath of Sweet Dew Incident, 69; serious misunderstanding of, 72–4, 88–9, 90, 177, 178, 192; Wen's account of, 76–9
Jiangnan, 200
Jiangning, 251 n4
Jiangsu, 12
Jiangxi, 64
Jianye, 77
Jiao Zhongqing, 85
Jin Dynasty, 80, 119, 126, 252 n11
Jin Yan, 126
Jingchu Suishiji, 259 n10
Jingzhou, 63
Jinling, 13, 198, 200, 266 n41
Jinlingzhi, 260 n31
Jinyang, 11, 17
jituo, 202, 266 n51
Jixia, 13, 37; date, 45; Academician, 49, 240 n9
junior party of Ganling, 27, 29, 50, 243 n66

Kaiyuan Yishi, 259 n10
kerchief box, 77, 253, n26
King Cheng, 107, 247 n43
King Ling (Zhou), 201
King Nan (Zhou), 95
King of Chu of Wuxing, 143
King of Shu, 249 n25
King of Wu, 144
King Wen (Zhou), 97, 98, 255 n17
King Xiang of Chu, 145
King Xuan of Qi, 49
King Zhao of Yan, 247 n44
Kong Li, 60, 250 n28
Kong Lin (zhi), 36, 245 n17
Kong Pingzhong, 248 n3
Kong Qiu, 106. *See also* Confucius
Kong Wenye, 46
Kong Yingda, 107
Kuaiji, 52, 119, 131
Kui Pefecture, Kuizhou, 25, 63
Kunwu, 120

lad and lass for monarch and subjects, 54, 117, 128, 197, 201, 209
Langya Commandery, 50
Langzhou, 25
Lantian, 30
Lanting, 14
Late Han, 29
Late Tang, 11, 21, 41, 121; aesthetic standards of, 211; factional strife, 2, 29; palace style of, 131; poetry virtuosity, 1, 36, 44, 93, 111; unique poetic sample of, 137

Latter Shu Dynasty, 197
Lei Huan, 243 n64
Lei Yi, 169, 263 n42
Li Ao, 3, 103
Li Bai, 4, 218; Qingping Yue, 194
Li Baiyao, 248 n3
Li Bingruo, 266 n37
Li Cheng, 6, 29, 110, 111, 264 n17; as friends of two Lius, 29–30, 243 n71; as veteran minister, 103, 104, 107; Bamboo-Arrow Has Its Cuticle, 167–8; exemplar of literary writing, 104, 105, 167; recommendation by, 6, 40, 51, 92, 104, 105, 112, 121, 245 n19; Rhapsody on the Meng Spring, 165–6; the way, use Du Kui, 33–4
Li Deyu, 2, 3, 46, 64, 244 n16; appointed Prime Minister, 248 n54; head of Li Faction, 175. See also Duke of Zanhuang
Li Diao, 3
Li Faction, 2, 29, 88; lose power, 176; Niu's superiority over, 133; rise to full power, 173; Support the Heir, 95
Li He, 105, 220
Li Jue, 95
Li Qi, 12
Li Shangyin, 24, 211, 221; address Wen as Zaimeng Feiqing, 165; Brocade Threshold, 125; comparison With Wen, 221–2; friendship with Wen, 22, 52, 162, 163, 164; Hearing Zhuming's death, Mailed to Feiqing with tears, 160; Jingyang Well, 259 n24; Thinking of Zaimeng Feiqing, 19, 160, 162–4, 241 n38
Li Shen, 12, 22, 35, 46, 82, 240 n5, 247 n47, 248 n54
Li Shi, 80, 193
Li Tang (Dynasty), 22, 30
Li Wei, 247 n47
Li Xun, 65, 67
Li Yi, 5, 239 n9
Li Yong, 6, 34, 93, 96; and Wen 129, 147, 189; murdered, 121, 136, 141; Wuzong's revenge on behalf of, 144. See also Heir Apparent
Li Yu, 14
Li Yuan, 5, 196, 265 n34
Li Yuan, 12, see also Emperor Gaozu
Li Zhenggu, 64, 254 n38
Li Zhi, 265 n24
Liang (Dynasty), 26, 42
Liangfu Yin, 125
Liaoning, 13
Liaoxi, 13, 37, 49
Licence and Luxury, 53
Lin Bao, 15
Lin Zhang, 147, 260 n39
Linhu Chu, 79, 180, 193
Linghu Hao, 178, 180, 254 n40
Linghu Tao, 178, 180, 191, 193, 254 n39, n40, 264 n4, 265 n30; present Pusaman to Xuanzong, 194; false reflection of Wen's relation with, 88, 89, 90, 191, 193, 194; recommending, 195, 265 n34
Literary Garden, 153, 156
Literati of Ye City, 97
Literature Star, 184
Liu An, 211
Liu Bang, 260 n31, 261 n16. *See also* Gaozu (Han)
Liu Dan, 243 n59
Liu Hui, 117
Liu Fen, 3, 79, 252 n19
Liu Han, 183
Liu Jiao, 243 n55
Liu Mengde 26. See Liu Yuxi
Liu Qing, 28
Liu Shan, 21, 157, 251 n4, 256 n20
Liu Sheng, 243 n55
Liu Xi, 183
Liu You Qiu, 245 n23
Liu Yun, 25, 243 n60
Liu Yuxi, 3, 24–6, 59, 105, 242 n47; alluded to as Yin Hao, 25; Ballads of Bamboo Branches, 25; carousing with Pei and Bai; Wen Zao, 62; Condolence Essay for the Grand Master Li, 30; Drafter Bai Condescended to Answer My Clumsy Poem . . . , 27–8; Epistle Presented to Minister of Works Du, 245 n24; former party of Ganling, 28, 29; friendship with Li Cheng

and Liu Zongyuan, 29–30; In the Tenth Year of Yuanhe, I was . . . , 27; Inscriptions to My Humble Study, 70; Sending a Poem, Congratuling Minister Wen, 62, 250 n38; Watching a Chess Game, 242 n57; Wen's indebtedness to, 27; Zongmi, 251 n46
Liu Zhen, 45, 247 n53
long regulated poems (*pailü*), 219
Lord Cang, 36, 244 n15
Lord Mengchang, 157, 246 n25, 262 n23
Lord She, 56, 155, 261 n18
Lord Yang, 105
Lord Yu, 43
lotus attire, 51, 248 n6
lotus-isle, 42, 246 n38
Lu (kingdom), 18
Lü An, 21
Lu Ban, 56, 155
Lu Ji, 20, 242 n39
Lu (Kuang), Mount, 64, 251 n42
Lu You, 243 n62, 268 n7
Lulu, 169, 170, 263 n44
Luo, River, 50, 146, 250 n30
Luoyang, 49, 50, 51, 52, 56, 63, 131

Ma Rong, 25, 242 n49
Ma Zhou, 119
Madame Wen, 73, 75
Maoshi (Book of Songs)
Deer Singing, 45, 247 n52; Drooping Boughs, 250 n32; Felling the Trees, 261 n11; High Heaven Had a Firm Charge, 257 n33; Waves of the Pan, 248 n1; White Steed, 261 n10. See also Book of Songs
Mao Yi, 44, 247 n45
Marquis Jiang, 141, 142, 143, 145. See Jiang Ziwen
Marquis Sui, 36
mediating on an ancient site (*huaigu*), 147
Mencius, 32
Meng Jiao, 53
Meng, name of spring, 165, 262 n36; name of divination, 165, 262 n37
Metropilitan Port, see Luoyang
Metropolitan Prefecture, see Chang'an
Metropolitan Prefecture Examination, 45, 75, 118, 149, 150, 152, 157, 160
Miao Shen, 5, 239 n9
Middle Bridge, 56, 249 n18
Miltary Storehouse, 124, 134, 135
Min Zhongshu, 252 n21
Mirror Lake, 14
Mulberry and elm, 173, 263 n51
mulberry lady, 23
Music Bureau, 117, 125
Mu Zhou, 15

Nanguo, Mr., 156
Nanman, 57
Nanyang, 70, 251 n3
National University of Luoyang, 39, 49, 50, 51
nature of moose and deer, 82, 253 f30
New Music Bureau, 141; Movement, 3
Ni Heng, 92, 190; Rhapsody on the Parrot, 265 n27
Nine Highways, 72, 252 n14
Nine Li Isle, 240 n16
Nine Plains, 96, 242 n50
Nineteen Classic Poems, 263 n41
Ning Qi, 138, 260 n25
Niu Faction, 2, 29, 88, 94; different attitude toward Heir Apparent, 94; take over power for the final time, 176; Wenzong place more confidence in, 95
Noble Monk Jian, 14
Northern Office, 2, 88, 96
Northern Party of Ganling, 28, 29

Onion Ridge, 65
Orchid Gate, 100, 101, 102, 256 n21; Ministries, 151
Terrace (Censorate), 102, 256 n21
original raiment, 202
oriole soaring out from his valley, 153, 261 n11
Ouyang Xiu, Liuyi Shihua, 268 n5

painted hall, 205, 260 n34; tower, 203, 205
pair of carp, 162, 262 n32

Parrot, 190, 265 n 27
pass the country of Wei, 54, 249 n12
Peach Woods, 18
Pearl of Marquis of Sui, 115, 244 n15
Pei Cheng, 178
Pei Du, 135, 243 n58; role in Yuanhe Restroation, 2, 41, 42–3, 246 n34; recommendation of Wen, 42–3, 92; concern about imperial succession, 246 n30
Pei Shen, 183, 184
Pei Tan, 160, 186
Pei Tingyu, 19, 187, 239 n9, 264 n12
Pei Xian, 179, 264 n6
Pei Xiu, 65, 246 n35, 251n46, 264 n4
Pei Yizhi (Drafter 149), 110, 111, 149, 257 n43
Phoenix, Edict, 190, 265 n27; Hall, 113, 257 n47
Pi Rixiu, 221, 268 n5
pig liver, 77, 252 n21
pluck an osmanthus twig, 135
poetic hero, 26
poetry talk (*shihua*), 74, 221
Precious Spouse Huang, 142, 260 n29
Prime Minister Liu, 38
Prime Minister Cui, 109, 152
Prime Minister Duke of Zanhuang, 64. See also Li Deyu
Prince An, 95, 142, 144, 173, 177
Prince Chen, 95, 144, 173, 255 n7
Prince Jingling (Qi Dynasty), 102
Priince Jiu, 34
Prince of Guangling, 143. See also Xianzong
Prince of Huainan, 211. See also Liu An
Prince of Lu, 113
Prince of Zhang Family, 16, 17
Prince of Zhongshan (Han), 243 n55
Prince Ruyi, 241 23n
Prince Sui (Liu Dan), 243 n59
Prince Yuan of Chu, Liu Jiao, 243 n55
Princely Establishment, 5, 239, n11
Princess Anding, 16
Princess Liang'guo, 16
Princess Song'guo, 16, 241 n22
Princess Taiping, 245 n23
pull sleeves, 100, 101
pun (as discussed in this book)
cloud (yun) for cuticle (yun), 164, 167; candle (zhu) for tell (zhu); deeply illuminate it (shen zhu yi), for affectionately exhort him (shen zhu yi), 179; fine drizzle (xiyu) for whisper (xiyu); gentle cold (qinghan) for short letters (qinghan), 188; joint (jie), for moral integrity (jie), 164; lotus (lian) for love (lian), 266 n51; lotus with seeds, for love someone, 266 n39; lotus-silk (ousi) for yearning for lover (ousi); looking for silk for thinking over him, 258 n54; miss the date (weiqi) for (playing) encircling chess (weiqi) 179; needle (zhen) for true, truthful (zhen), 84; red spots carved on bone-made die for bone-penetrating love yearning, 180; seeds (zi) for son (zi), 142; stick or fragrance (xiang) for assist, assistant (xiang), 116; skillful (qiao) for happy coincidence, 259 n10; think (si) for silk (si), 116; willow (liu), for keep from going (liu), 264; worship (si) for Heir (si)
purple-roving-rein, 198, 200, 266 n48
Pusaman, 194, 195, 202, 213; magnum opus, 7; overall explanation of, 202; unique creation of, 195, 196; consummate exemplar, 196; venus without arms, 197; four theories of, 202; two conclusive points of, 202; poetic contents and conclusion of a life time, 213; inspiration from the Book of Changes, 214

Qi (kingdom), 13, 176
Qi, County, 12
Qi, 25 (Dynasty), 26
Qi (Wen's changed name), 162, 166
Qian Prefecture, 63
Qiao (Heir of King Ling of Zhou), 201
Qin Chamber, 124, 136
Qin (district name), 125
Qinhuai River, 252 n11
Qing Dynasty, 26, 126
Qingji, 155, 156

Qingyuan, 12, 71
Qiu Shiliang, 65, 217
Qu Yuan, 202, 257 n34, 264 n16; exiled, 86, 87, 185
Quan Deyu, 248 n10
Que Zi, 261 n19

rattan cane, 51, 248 n6
Raven Robe Alley, 70, 71, 252 n11
Red Bird Ferry, 198, 266 n41
Red Hatchet, 144
red strings, 155, 261 n17
regard with awe, 169, 263 n43
Retainer of Ye, 96, 98
rib of a chicken, 77, 252 n21
River-crossing boat, 71, 252 n12
Rouser Paul, 7, 8
royal cook, 33
Ruan Ji, 86, 250 n28, 251 n42
Ruan Xian, 60, 250 n28
Ruan Xiu, 44, 247 n45
Ruan Yu, 251 n4

Sanggan (River), 55, 249 n16
Sans Soucis, 146, 260 n39. See Gao Wei
Scholar Zhang, 82, 83
scratch head, 158, 262 n24
season the soup, 60, 250 n31
Semi-circular Pool, 50
Sengshilue, 61, 251 n50
Senior Shen, 64
Senior Zhixuan, 66
Seniors of Shang, 96, 97
set a sparrow net by the door, 70, 252 n7
Setting-Sun Pavilion, 56, 249 n19
Seven Masters of the Jian'an Era, 97
Shan Tao (Juyuan), 240 n6, 242 n51, 253 n28; 12, 19, 20–2, 35, 78, 80, alluded to as his father's friend
Shandong, 13
Shang, Mount, 97
Shangguan Yi, 256 n29
Shanglin Garden, 56
Shanglin Park, 124, 133, 249 n18
Shangyang Palace, 55
Shanyang, 21
shaohai, 97, 255 n11
Shaoyang, 204, 267 n58
Shaoyangyuan, 94, 128, 135, 200, 266 n44
Shaoxing, 14
sheep horn, 100, 256 n23
Shen Hui, 73, 75
Shen Yue, 130, 162, 163, 262 n31
Shen Xun, 182, 257 n41
Sheng Hongzhi, 242
Shi Kuang, 33, 260 n1
shi poems in series, 196
Shi Zhecun, 202
Shishi Yaolan, 61
shoot blood, 245 n22
short eaves, 51, 188
shrike, 51, 248 n7
Shu, 57, 58, 60, 70
Shun (sage king), 86
Sichuan, 53, 56, 57, 59, 60. *See also* Shu
silken willows, 210, 267 n66
Sima Qian, 169
Sima usurpers, 22
Sima Xiangru, 131, 249 n24, 257 n34; play role of, 106, 107, 108; Preface to Rhapsody on Changmen Palace, 259 n13; Sir Literary Garden, 124, 134, 259 n20
simurph string, 198, 266 n43
Six Dynastics, 200
six month's ascension, 151, 261 n5
slaying a dragon, 159, 262 n27
Sleeping Dragon, 242 n51
smiling westward,, 55, 249 n17
Song Dynasty, 1, 4, 88, 94, 178
Song, Mount, 128
Song of Protector-General Ding, 54, 249 n13
Song of Heavenly Horse, 259 n19
Song of Reading the Music, 258 n54
Song of Sleeping Dragon, 124, 125, 137
Song of Western-most Heavenly Horse, 259 n19
Song Yu, 106, 107, 257 n34; Rhapsody of Gaotang, 260 n35
Song Yun, 65, 251 n49
Songs of the South, 210, 138; *Lisao*, 138, 248 n6, n7; Summons for A Recluse, 211, 248 n7
Southeastern Peak, 251 n42
Southern airs, 150

Southern Office, 2, 96
Southern Party of Ganling, 28, 29
Southern Qi (Dynasty), 42
Southern Song Dynasty, 14
Southwestern Palace, 199, 266 n44
spirited hawk, 124, 134
Staff of Han, 57, 249 n20
star in Front of the Fire, 96, 97
State Son's University, 12, 218
straight person, 267 n58
straight way, 18, 21
straighten the key link, 151
Su Wu, 146, 249 n19
Sui Dynasty, 12, 15
Suixian County, 85, 184
Sumen, Mount, 251 n42
sun behind clouds, 96, 97
Sun Bin [Shi], 161. *See also* Sun Song
Sun Deng, 251 n42
Sun Jue, 109
Sun Song, 150, 161
Sweet Dew Incident, 193
Sweet Dew Incident, 2, 21, 217; and Li Xun, 65, 67, 96; and Wang Ya, 70, 79; aftermath of, 41, 68, 72, 79, 93
Sword Pass, 57

Taigong, 64
Taihe folksong, 200, 266 n47
Taixuan Scripture, Yang Xiong's, 69, 70
Taiyuan, 12
Tang Dynasty, 76, 79, 86, 117; approaching its end, 14; "former era" of, 79; golden age of Chinese poetry, 1; Wen clan in, 12, 15
Tang Empire, 11, 143, 145, 170; last stability of, 175; Wen's loyalty to, 17, 92
Tao Fan, 245 n21
Tao Hongjing, 42, 246 n38
Thousand-Year Day, 124, 129, 130, 132
three paths 152, 261 n7
thousand taels of gold for the charming smile, 84
Three Gorges, 63
tiger shot by an arrow, 171
Tonglu, 14, 15, 52, 240 n16, 251 n48
Tongxin, 72, 73, 167, 267 n2
Torrent Yanling, 15
Two Wangs and Eight Prefectural Assistants, 22
Tu, 252 n13

Unknown writer, Buganju Shihua, 268 n5
Untitled poem, 125

Venus without arms, 197
vermilion osmanthus, 124
Virtuous Consort Wang, 126, 145; fell prey to Yang's slander, 93, 132, 142; Wen's poem sympathetic to, 108, 131
Viscount Zhi Dao, 33

Wang Ba, 157, 262 n22
Wang Bi, 263 n38
Wang Can, 44, 58, 247 n46
Wang Changling, 258 n59
Wang Dao, 70, 252 n8
Wang Fuzhi, 7
Wang Huzhi (Xiuling), 245 n21
Wang Ji, 60, 249 n27
Wang Jian (Jin), 42, 253 n26
Wang Jian (Tang), 194
Wang Mingsheng, 26
Wang Qi, 97, 105
Wang Qia, 251 n48
Wang Shen, 124, 126, 258 n6
Wang Shuwen, 28
Wang Xizhi, 24, 136
Wang Ya, 3, 79, 193, 251 n6, 253 n25; and Wen's sad Reflection, 69–72; as a good calligrapher, 71, 252 n10; clan extermination of, 69, 71, 72; Viscount of Qingyuan County, 71
Wang Yanshou, 257 n45
Wang Zhan, 249 n27
Wang Zun, 20, 150, 242 n39
wangyou (forgetting-sorrow), 204
Wangyuan (park), 255 n12
Wanyue (Graceful and Restrained)
warming the scroll, 41
Watering My Horse in the Pool of the Great Wall, 262 n32
Weaving Girl, 129
Wei (Defender of Hu County), 5
Wei Dynasty, 21, 22

Wei Palace, 124, 136
Wei River, 55, 136
Wen Daya, 15, 16, 17, 18
Wen Dayou, 15
Wen He, 240 n3
Wen Jie, 16
Wen Jingqian, 16
Wen Junyou, 15
Wen Kerang, 16
Wen Mian, 16
Wen Qi, changed name to, 150; original name was, 72, 159; whipped when young, 72; fled helter-skelter, 181
Wen Ting, 16
Wen Tinghao, 159, 160
Wen Tingyun (works discussed)
 Ancient Idea, 99; Angling by the Pond of the Xue Family, 31; Boshan Censer, 117, 166; Branches of the Willows, 179–80; Casual Encounter, 83 (Carefree Wandering, 9); Epistles Presented to Academician Drafter (first of two), 141;—Bureau Director Han of the Ministry of Personnel, 19, 21, 23, 44, 76–80, 254 n42;—Censor-in-Chief, 50, 181;—Drafter Du, 47, 139–40;—Grand Master Cui, 14, 52;—Minister Feng, 64, 108;—Prime Minister Cui, 153;—Prime-Minister-Duke at the Honor Seat, 17, 54, 60–2;—Prime Minister Linghu, 20, 24;—Prime Minister, 21, 23;—Prime Minister Pei, 13, 18, 32, 36–42, 49, 51, 53, 87, 90, 176;—Vice Minister Jiang (first of two), 12, 138–9, 161;—Vice-Minister Jiang (second), 153;—Vice-Minister, Salt and Iron Commissioner, 82, 176, 251 n46;—Epistles Thanking Minister Duke Hegan, 106–10;—Thanking Minister Li of Xiangzhou, 100–6, 107, 216; Fifty-Rhyme Poem, 12, 20, 35, 44, 45, 46, 99; Heartbroken Lovesickness, 84–5; Hundred-Rhyme Poem (numbers in brackets indicating the order of rhymes in the poem) 5(title), 11(note to 5); 18(6–8); 23(45); 32(52); 33(28); 39(50); 44(82); 44(18); 45(note to 18); 50(47); 54(53–5); 72(56, 57); 81(82, 83); 91(57); 91–2(58–60); 92, 99(11); 112–20(61–74); 125(82); 152(11–13); 154(1, 2); 155(3, 4, 14–16); 17, 18, 156, note to 18; 157(19–22); 158(23–6); 158–9(27–9); 166(52); 169–70(75–81); 170(82–5); 171(86–92); 171–2(93–6); 172–3(97–100); 244 n11(98)
Jiangnan Air, 198–200; Li Yu Recluse Sends me His Newly Brewed Wine, 14; Living in Suburbs of Hu Du, 66; Lodging in Mount Study of a Monk of Qin, 66; Lodging in Yunji Temple, 65; Luoyang, 55–6; Mailed to Assistant Du of He'nan Prefecture, 56; Melody Damozhi, 116, 145–8; My Feelings on Returning to the East, 263 n39; Ode of three Islets, 253 n35; Ode of Brocade City, 58; Old Residence of Recluse Li Yu, 14; On a Casual Topic, 188; On a Spring Day, I Was About to Return, 267 n70; Passing the Residence of the Late Academician Yuan, 26, 71; Presented to Appointed Scholar Zheng, 64; Presented to a Shu General, 57; Presented to Yue Monk Yue Yun, 14, 66; Pusaman, 7, 195–214, 220; Respectfully Mailed to a Few Intimate Friends, 58; Revisiting the Aranya of Chan Master, 65; Sending Off Bureau Director Cui to Military Service, 63; Sent to an Intimate Friend from My Villa of Hu County Suburbs, 23, 66; Sent to Chuwang on Cold Food Festival, 17; Sent to Scholar Lu, 13, 23; Sent to Monk in Pure and Cool Temple, 66; Sent to Someone in the Mountains, 64; Song for the Bingyin Harvest Year, 264 n1; Song of Double Seventh Eve, 259 n17; Song of God of Marquis Jiang, 141–5, 205; Song on a Screen of

[the Heir Apparent's] Birth and Blessing, 205; Song of Spring Field, 253 n35; Song of Zhang Jingwan Gathering Lotus, 140, 141, 266 n50; Temple of Goddess of Mount Wu, 63; Twenty-Two Rhymes on Arched Door, 123–37, 197, 201, 216, 219, 266 n44; Twenty-Two Rhymes on Passing Huaqing Palace, 124; Two Dirges for Late Heir Apparent, Zhuangke, 96–8, 211, 216; Two Elegies for Director of the Secretariat, Lord Pei, 42–3; Two Elegies for Late Minister Liu, Director of the Palace Library, 24–5; Two Poems Written in Courtyard of Monk Taigong, 64; Two Poems Written . . . in Feng'an Alley, 69–71; Visiting Senior Zhixuan, 66; Weaving Brocade, 207; Western Pool of Heir Apparent, 16; Writing my Feelings on My Journey to the West, 55; Written at Wangyuan Post, 267 n66; Yearning for My Old Abode in Tonglu, 14–15

Wen Tingyun, along the River, 53, 62, 63; ambiguity of, 5; ancestral glory of, 15–16; as instructor in State Son's University, 189, 218; as barometer of political situation, 173; ask Han for a minor post, 76–8; at odds with fate, 1–3, 30, 92; attending Heir Apparent, 6, 15, 37, 39, 40, 92, 98, 99, 106; Attending National University of Luoyang, 39, 49–53; autobiographical poem of, 5, 111; belles lettres, 6, 125, 196; biography of, 11, 88, 89, 177–8, 181, 189; birth year of, 35, 36, 40, 46; breeding ground of, 49, 51, 52; change name, 7, 73, 75, 159–68, 191; character of mandarin-ducks, 82, 83; clan marriage with imperial family, 16–17, 30; comprehensive research of, 3, 4, 5; concern with state and people, 218; contrast with Li Shangyin, 220–1; connection with Yongzhen participants, 22, 29; Defender of Fangcheng, 190; demoted to Suixian, 184–7; disparaging tone of historiographers to, 88–9, 178; disciple of the old mountain, 65, 66, 67; early-year economic situation of, 23; Equivalent to Passing, 7, 45, 149–54; family tradition (straight way), 19; friendship with Liu Yuxi, 24–6; genealogical position, 16, 17; helping others in the examination, 177, 181, 182, 184–9, 191; hiding at Drafter Pei's, 150, 258 n43; identification with Dai Yong, 67; influence of Yuan Zhen to, 218; Li Cheng as teacher of, 6, 40, 103–6, 168; likening his late father to Ji Kang, 20–22; love song, 83–6, 253 n35; many years at one or another Marquis, 37, 54; marriage with a singer-prostitute, 6, 44, 81, 86, 87; master of poetry, 1, 127, 196, 221; mischievous sample, 187; native place of, 12–15, 37; nicknamed Zhongkui, 267–8 n2; orphaned in childhood, 20–2; poems nostalgic of Yue region, 240 n11; political allegory for a frustrated, 203; political in the guise of private, 219; profound friendship with Liu Yuxi, 26; reevaluation of, 4, 5, 9; relation with Linghu Tao, 120–1, 193–4; relation with Wang Ya, 69–72; restore family glory, 18, 23, 24; rid influence of Li He, 220; seeking an official position, 177; smiling westward, 55, 56; Sphinx imprisoned, 6; stay at Mount Lu, 64; visit Shu (Sichuan), 52, 53, 56–60; Works related to the Heir Apparent, 240–1; theory of poetic composition, 137–41

Wen Wenggui, 16

Wen Wuyin, 16

Wen Xi, 16, 17

Wen Xu, 240 n3

Wen Xihua, 16, 17, 62

Wen Yanbo, 11, 15, 16, 17, 18

Wen Yang, 16
Wen Zao, 61, 63, 69, 241 n26; a foster father, 16, 17, 53, 55; with Zongmi, 62
Wen Zhang, 16
Wen Zhang, 62
Wen Zhongkui, 267 n2
Wenjun, 59, 249 n24
Wen-Li, 221
Western Garden, 97, 98, 255 n11
Western Mansion, 102
Western Queen Mother, 116
where the jade is buried, 98, 255 n15
White Emperor, 59, 260 n31
White Flower Yang, 199, 266 n46. *See also* Yang Baihua
White Snow, 158, 262 n25
White-Lotus Association, 51, 66
white-robe Prime Minister, 180
whitewashed office, 24, 25, 242 n53
wood slave, 23
Worthy Consort Yang, 93, 95, 96, 126, 142; clan aunt of Yang Sifu, 94; ironic dirge for, 260 n24; killed by Wuzong, 144, 173; unchecked jealousy of, 119, 126, 131, 132, 136
Wu, 171
Wu Ju, 33
Wu, Mount, 63, 66; Goddess of, 144, 145, 260 n35
Wu Yinzhi(Chumo), 245 n21
Wu Yuanji, 41, 42
Wu Yuanji, 42
Wuchang, 63
Wuxing, 73, 76

Xia Chengtao, 35, 161
Xia Dynasty, 260 n26
Xiahou Zhan, 204
Xian, Mount, 42
Xiang River, 86, 87, 185
Xiang Xiu, 21
Xiang Yu, 261 n16
Xiang'gong, 110, 250 n34
Xiangyang, 25, 42, 63
Xiao Tong, 117
Xie An, 25, 27, 70, 243 n58, 250 n27
Xie the Guest, 14, 240 n13
Xie Lingyun, 14, 24, 240 n13, 242 n39
Xie Xuan, 60, 250 n27
Xiezhi, 114
xing, 140,
Xingyang, 77
Xingyuan, 62
Xinjin, 58
Xishii, 70, 200, 202, 260 n24
Xiuling, 37, 245 n21. *See also* Wang Huzhi
Xizhou (Western Prefecture), 26, 27
Xu Ling, 248 n3, 253 n34
Xu Shang, 5, 189, 239 n9, 248 n1, 265 n24, n25
Xu Zhizi, 261 n11
Xun Kai, 247 n42

Yan Yanzhi, 267 n58
Yang Pan'er, 117
Yang Baihua, 266 n46
Yan Guang, 15, 31, 240 n15
Yan Minchu, 15
Yan rat, 155, 261 n19
Yan Terrace, 43, 247 n44. *See also* Gold Terrace
Yan Ying, 161, 246 n25
Yan Youqin, 15
yang, 220, 253 n30
Yang Baihua, 199, 266 n46
Yang Sifu, 15, 94, 95
Yang Tan, 26, 27, 243 n65
Yang Xiong, 70, 251 n3
Yang Zhu, 32, 52, 80, 118, 166, 248 n7
Yangzhou, Xizhou of, 27; Wang Ya's office of, 70; Director Han in, 78, 79; Linghu Tao in, 88, 89, 254 n39; commercial centre, 87, 251 n4, 251 n4, 252 n11
Yangtze Court 78, 79, 87, 89, 90; eunuch-controlled, 88; Salt and Iron Commissioner's Office, 74, 76, 253 n29
Yangtze-Han, 63, 64
Yanling, Mount, 15
Yanran, Mount, 42
Yanying (Palace) Conference, 94, 134, 135
Yao Xu, 75, 76, 78, 79; attitude toward Wen, 73, 74, 87
Yao (sage king), 38, 41

yaoniao, 120
Ye City, 97, 147
Yellow Gate, 70, 80
yellow ribbon, 190, 265 n28
yellow scrolls, 155
Yi River, 156
Yin Dynasty, 260 n26
Yin Hao, 25, 242 n54
Yin You, 103
Yinan (good-for-bearing-sons), 203
Ying River, 252 n9
Yingying, 82, 253 n33
Yingyingzhuan, 82
Yingzhou Prefecture, 110
yongwu, 165
Yongzhen Reform, 2, 22, 25, 28, 29
Yu Liang, 247 n42
Yu Xin, 162, 163; Eulogy to Wudi of Han's Gathering Books, 256 n 27; Lament for the South of the River, 262 n31; Poems Aout the Painted Screen, 102
Yu Yang, 125
Yu, (sage king), 38, 41
Yuan Jiao, 5, 239 n9
Yuan Zhen, 53, 82, 83; and Scholar Zhang, 253 n33; as talented Literatus Yuan, 194
Yuanchu, 172, 263 n47, n50
Yuanhe, Restoration, 2, 41, 143; Style, 53
Yue Stream, 202
Yue Yun, 14
Yue Shifu, 161, 246 n25
Yuezhou, 13, 14, 15, 52, 53

Zaimeng, 162, 163, 164, 165, 166, 167, 216. *See also* Wen Tingyun
Zang, 18
Zang Cang, 32, 37, 76, 80
Zeng Dian, 156, 158
Zhan Antai, 92, 204
Zhang Chang, 117, 259 n8
Zhang Dai, 36, 245 n17
Zhang Fang, 17, 24
Zhang Heng, 263 n45
Zhang Hu, 19, 160, 242 n38
Zhang Hua, 243 n65
Zhang Huiyan (Gaowen), 202, 214
Zhang Ji, 53, 105
Zhang Jie, 268 n7
Zhang Ping, 21, 56 n20, 242 n40
Zhang River, 45, 146, 147, 260 n39
Zhang Sizong, 13
Zhang Tang, 259 n18, 259 n18. *See also* Prince Zhang
Zhang Xing, 100, 256 n20
Zhang Zhongsu, 105
Zhang-Riverbank disease, 45
Zhao Dun, 242 n52
Zhao Jianzi, 115
Zhao Qi (Binqing, Taiqing), 150, 161
Zhao Taiqing, 161
Zhao Zhi, 13
Zhao Zhuan (Madame Wen's husband), 73
Zhaoling, 17
Zhejiang, 12
Zheng Xuan, 107
Zhi Dun, 65, 66, 67, 251 n48
Zhong Hao, 50, 248 n1
Zhong Hui, 242 n50
Zhong Jun, 157, 262 n23
Zhong Kui, 267, 268 n2
Zhong, Mount, 66, 141, 143
Zhong Xuan, 77, 78, 247 n46. *See also* Wang Can
Zhong Yi, 61, 259 n33
Zhongnan, Mount, 66, 136, 251 n47
Zhou Chi, 152
Zhou Chu, 204
Zhou Dehua, 179
Zhou Dynasty, 18
Zhu Bo, 113
Zhu Guangshang, 142
Zhu or Teng, 176, 264 n3
Zhu Yu, 31
Zhuangke, 97. *See also* Heir Apparent
Zhuge Liang, 44, 125, 251 n3, 247 n46; cottage in Nanyang, 70; fearful of marrying a wife, 77, 78; Memorial to the Throne, 249 n1
Ziyun's Terrace, 70
Zong Guai, 102
Zongmi, 62, 65, 67, 251 n50

Praise for
Listen to Your Baby

"In *Listen to Your Baby,* Naomi Aldort offers a way to clear our mind of the external noise from media, experts, people's opinions, and even our own thinking; only then can we hear, understand, and trust our baby. A liberating book that returns us to trust and love."

—**Saffia Farr,** editor, *JUNO* magazine

"Naomi Aldort and I agree that the best expert on a baby's needs is the baby. When we listen to our hearts and to our babies and young children, we can hear what they are asking for, and they only ask for what they need. Thank you, Naomi, for being a voice for babies and young children."

—**Pam Leo,** author, *Connection Parenting*

"As a mother of five and a physician who has spent years guiding women back to their innate wisdom, *Listen to Your Baby* felt like a homecoming. Naomi Aldort gives words to what so many of us know in our hearts—that our babies already know the way. This book is a masterpiece in reminding parents to trust themselves, trust their children, and find joy in simplicity. A must-read for anyone seeking calm, connection, and confidence in motherhood."

—**Dr. Cheryl Kam,** family physician and podcaster

"The title of Naomi Aldort's latest book, *Listen to Your Baby,* tells the whole story. When I read her advice that listening to your baby can awaken your own natural wisdom as a parent, I remember how much the readers of *Mothering* magazine relied on Naomi's advice. They loved her for acknowledging that they could trust themselves. Read this book to reassure yourself that you have the innate wisdom necessary to raise a healthy and emotionally intelligent child."

—**Peggy O'Mara,** former editor and publisher, *Mothering* magazine.

"Naomi Aldort's *Listen to Your Baby* is an essential and much-needed book for all new and soon-to-be parents. I struggled with the same questions when I nursed my three children. I wish I had had Naomi's book then. Even with the advice from the La Leche League, society's dictates to young mothers in the 1990s confused me about how long I 'could and should' breastfeed my children. The struggle for women who wanted to carve out an identity, while also caring for their children, led to a litany of mixed messages. I am sure that had I known the importance of cholesterol to a baby's wellbeing, both physical and mental, I would have breastfed my children for more than 16 months and been better able to listen to my babies. *Listen to Your Baby* fosters a dialogue between mother and child, enabling the mother to better listen to not only her baby but also to herself."

—Dr. Elizabeth Bright, DO, ND